# Macroprudential Policy and Practice

Macroprudential policy is perhaps the most important new development in central bank policymaking circles since the global financial crisis, and reliance on such policies has continued to spread. The crisis, which showed the limits of conventional monetary policy as a tool to deal with financial stability, forced a wide-ranging rethink of economic policies, their interactions and their repercussions. It has led to new forms of intervention, of regulation and of supervisory practice. Macroprudential regulation is now one of the most important topics in modern macroeconomics, because it concerns measures put in place to reduce the risks and costs of the instability caused by financial crises. Written by senior figures from the worlds of academia and banking, this volume combines theoretical approaches with hard evidence of the policy's achievements in many countries. It is the first in-depth analysis of macroprudential instruments for policymakers, banks and economists.

PAUL MIZEN is Professor of Monetary Economics and Director of the Centre for Finance, Credit and Macroeconomics at the University of Nottingham and Chairman of the Money Macroeconomic and Finance Research Group. He previously taught in the Economics Departments of the University of Vienna, the European University Institute, Florence and Princeton University.

MARGARITA RUBIO is an assistant professor at the University of Nottingham. She obtained her PhD in Economics in 2008 at Boston College and holds an MS in Economics with Distinction at the University College London. She has published with the *Journal of Money, Credit and Banking*, *Journal of International Money and Finance*, *Journal of Banking and Finance*, *Journal of Financial Stability* and the *Journal of Macroeconomics*.

PHILIP TURNER is a visiting lecturer at the University of Basel. Until October 2016, he was Deputy Head of the Monetary and Economic Department and a member of the Senior Management of the Bank for International Settlements (BIS) in Switzerland. Between 1976 and 1989, he held several positions at the Organisation for Economic Co-operation and Development (OECD) in Paris. He has also been a visiting scholar at the Bank of Japan in Tokyo. He was a teaching fellow at Harvard University. He read Economics at Churchill College, Cambridge, and has a PhD from Harvard University.

*Macroeconomic Policy Making*

**Series editors:**

Professor JAGJIT S. CHADHA *NIESR*

Professor SEAN HOLLY *University of Cambridge*

The 2007–10 financial crisis has asked some very hard questions of modern macroeconomics. The consensus that grew up during 'the Great Moderation' has proved to be an incomplete explanation of how to conduct monetary policy in the face of financial shocks. This series brings together leading macroeconomic researchers and central bank economists to analyse the tools and methods necessary to meet the challenges of the post-financial crisis world.

**Published titles:**

# Macroprudential Policy and Practice

*Edited by*

**Paul Mizen**
University of Nottingham

**Margarita Rubio**
University of Nottingham

**Philip Turner**
University of Basel

# CAMBRIDGE
UNIVERSITY PRESS

University Printing House, Cambridge CB2 8BS, United Kingdom

One Liberty Plaza, 20th Floor, New York, NY 10006, USA

477 Williamstown Road, Port Melbourne, VIC 3207, Australia

314-321, 3rd Floor, Plot 3, Splendor Forum, Jasola District Centre, New Delhi - 110025, India

79 Anson Road, #06-04/06, Singapore 079906

Cambridge University Press is part of the University of Cambridge.

It furthers the University's mission by disseminating knowledge in the pursuit of education, learning and research at the highest international levels of excellence.

www.cambridge.org
Information on this title: www.cambridge.org/9781108412346
DOI: 10.1017/9781108304429

First published 2018
First paperback edition 2020

*A catalogue record for this publication is available from the British Library*

*Library of Congress Cataloging in Publication data*
Names: Mizen, Paul, editor. | Rubio, Margarita, 1978- editor. |
    Turner, Philip, 1950- editor.
Title: Macroprudential policy and practice / edited by Paul Mizen,
    Professor of Monetary Economics, University of Nottingham,
    Margarita Rubio, Assistant Professor, University of Nottingham,
    Philip Turner, University of Basel.
Description: Cambridge, United Kingdom ; New York : Cambridge
    University Press, 2017. | Series: Macroeconomic policy making |
    Includes index.
Identifiers: LCCN 2017054701| ISBN 9781108419901 (hardback) |
    ISBN 9781108412346 (pbk.)
Subjects: LCSH: Monetary policy. | Banks and banking, Central. |
    Economic policy.
Classification: LCC HG230.3 .M337 2017 | DDC 339.5/3–dc23
LC record available at https://lccn.loc.gov/2017054701

ISBN   978-1-108-41990-1   Hardback
ISBN   978-1-108-41234-6   Paperback

# Contents

# Contributors

RICHARD BARWELL, BNP Paribas Asset Management

JOSÉ A. CARRASCO-GALLEGO, Universidad Rey Juan Carlos

JAGJIT S. CHADHA, National Institute of Economic and Social Research

MATTEO F. GHILARDI, International Monetary Fund

JEAN-PIERRE LANDAU, Sciences Po

MARCIN ŁUPIŃSKI, National Bank of Poland, and Lazarski University

CHRIS MCDONALD, Reserve Bank of New Zealand

PAUL MIZEN, University of Nottingham

STEFANO NERI, Banca d'Italia

MAARTEN R.C. VAN OORDT, Bank of Canada

F. GULCIN OZKAN, University of York

SHANAKA J. PEIRIS, International Monetary Fund

DENNIS REINHARDT, Bank of England

MARGARITA RUBIO, University of Nottingham

RHIANNON SOWERBUTTS, Bank of England

PHILIP TURNER, University of Basel

D. FILIZ UNSAL, International Monetary Fund

CHEN ZHOU, De Nederlandsche Bank, and Erasmus University, Rotterdam

# Introduction

Macroprudential policy is perhaps the most important new development in central bank policymaking circles since the Global Financial Crisis (GFC). This crisis, which showed the limits of conventional monetary policy as a tool to deal with financial stability, forced a wide-ranging rethink of economic policies, their interactions and their repercussions. It has led to new forms of intervention, of regulation and of supervisory practice. As Paul Tucker (2014), Deputy Governor at the Bank of England during the crisis concluded, the central bank – given its pivotal role in the economy's credit system – needs "not merely a monetary constitution, but a money-credit constitution ... with macroprudential policy its instrument of first choice to preserve systemic stability." He also argued that, given greater awareness of risk and new liquidity rules, the demand for central bank money would remain higher than historically, implying unusually large central bank balance sheets. This view has been echoed by, among others, Friedman (2014), Gagnon and Sack (2014) and King (2016).

Monetary policy – guided by inflation targeting and implemented through changes to the very short-term interest rates – had been able to deliver low and stable inflation, and reasonable economic growth throughout the late 1990s and early 2000s. What it could not do was to contain the expansion of credit, the increased risk-taking and sharp rise in asset prices that occurred at the same time. Despite the sizable increase in the Federal funds rate (from 1 percent in mid-2004 to 5.25 percent by mid-2006), credit spreads continued to narrow and market volatility fell further. Higher policy rates thus failed to stop the build-up in risk-taking in global financial markets that ultimately led to the Great Financial Crisis (Figure I.1). Drawing on UK experience in the 1960s and 1970s, Aikman et al. (2016) reach a similar conclusion that interest rate increases were not very effective in curbing credit expansions.

The failure before the GFC to moderate risk-taking in time was primarily microeconomic (Posen, 2009; Turner, 2017). Those responsible for financial sector supervision did not take enough account of how

Composite indicator of risk aversion/volatility renormalised as a credit spread

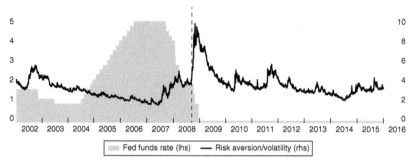

The shaded area represents the target federal funds rate. The vertical dotted line marks 15 September 2008 (the Lehman Brothers bankruptcy).

[1] Simple average of standardized scores of EMBI Global spread, US corporate high-yield spread, implied volatility of US equities (VIX index), implied volatility of US Treasury bonds (MOVE index), implied volatility of G10 exchange rates (JPMorgan GVXF7 index). Calculations cover the period 1 January 2002–31 December 2015.

Sources: Turner (2012), national data and market data.

Figure I.1.  Risk-taking increases despite higher policy rates

externalities, intrinsic to any complex financial system, had become ever more pervasive in the wave of successive financial innovations that took place from the early 1990s (Kenc, 2016). An individual financial firm would typically ignore such externalities, and many took highly leveraged positions that offered opportunities for short-term profits. Normal competitive forces could not be counted upon to produce system-wide risk exposures that were consistent with financial stability (Jeanne and Korinek, 2010b).

The basic features of market failure are well known. Banks made the securitisation of debts ever more complex so that their very opacity would induce buyers to overpay for the resultant products. This proved for a time very profitable. In other words, they deliberately exploited the information asymmetries that lie at the heart of the banking business, not least because other banks were doing exactly the same thing. There was also a classic agency problem: traders took risk positions which earned them handsome bonuses but left banks, and ultimately tax payers, holding large losses. This revealed the underlying moral hazard: because banks were too big to fail, ultimately they had to be bailed out by governments. None of these market failures – information asymmetry, agency problem and moral hazard – is new. Economists have been using these concepts in the study of the banking industry for years. Fixed microprudential ratios (e.g. the higher capital and liquidity requirements on banks under Basel

III) can in effect counter some of these externalities, and in effect limit financial risk-taking (Korinek, 2011).

But simple monetary policy rules and limited macroprudential policies were not enough to counter the expansion of credit and increased risk-taking, which had wider implications due to a number of very strong macroeconomic/financial feedback loops. Consider the following narrative. A rise in aggregate demand encourages firms and households to borrow more. Higher prices for houses and other assets create expectations of further rises (reinforcing the investment boom) and, in addition, give borrowers extra collateral against which to borrow more. Banks, heartened by a cyclical decline in loan defaults, become more willing to lend. When borrowing conditions in capital markets become more favourable, local firms and households find they can borrow more easily. Lower price volatility of financial assets during upswings leads to reduced haircuts on wholesale funding contracts, facilitating increased leverage. And so the financial cycle provides the conducive environment for increasing levels of borrowing, leverage and risk-taking.

When the cycle turns down, however, these favourable macroeconomic/ financial feedback effects reverse. Asset prices begin to falter and then fall, often far more quickly than they rose, making further investment unattractive. When the interest rate cycle turns, borrowers will find themselves exposed to maturity mismatches. During downswings, haircuts rise and investors are forced to scale back their leverage, implying sharp contraction of their positions. Market volatility rises abruptly. The decline in asset prices that results has further feedback effects on the balance sheets of the banks and other investors.

These developments describe a classic boom-bust cycle. Most recently they were exacerbated by low volatility and low interest rates during the Great Moderation. So-called light-touch regulation permitted increases in leverage and risk-taking. Immediately after the financial crisis, central banks were able to cut short-term interest rates, extend liquidity, widen definitions of eligible collateral and purchase assets to lower long-term yields on government securities and to narrow credit or liquidity risk spreads on non-government paper. Monetary policy needs to be forward-looking and central banks need to be ready to take pre-emptive measures to counter excessive credit expansion. But more targeted measures may help for central banks to better address specific externalities.

An important theme of recent literature is that excessive household leverage is associated with aggregate demand externalities (see Farhi and Werning, 2016; Korinek and Simsek, 2016). In the boom period, households behave rationally at the individual level in borrowing more but their leverage is excessive from a social point of view because each household ignores the impact of their decision on aggregate demand. Macroprudential policies offer the best hope of restricting such debt build-ups. According to these (New Keynesian) models, raising interest rates would be an inefficient policy choice because the income of borrowers falls, and their planned borrowing rises. Barring binding financing constraints, this could have the unintended consequence of actually increasing household leverage and thus exacerbating this aggregate demand externality.

One general difficulty is that the use of macroprudential policies to influence credit supply conditions (and perhaps moderate asset price increases) will alter monetary policy transmission. This is especially likely in the case of regulatory ratios that are sensitive to macroeconomic variables. Moderating the amplitude of asset price movements, for example, would reduce the potency of interest rates in managing aggregate demand because asset price movements represent an important transmission channel. Much recent research examines how monetary policy affects the transmission mechanism of macroprudential policy. Gambacorta and Mistrulli (2004), Maddaloni and Peydro (2013), Altunbas et al. (2010), Dell'Ariccia et al. (2013), Jiménez et al. (2014) and Aiyar, Calomiris and Wieladek (2014) show how macroprudential policy affects the monetary policy transmission mechanism. UK Financial Policy Committee member, Don Kohn, has noted that 'monetary policy is a blunt tool for addressing financial stability risks' while 'macroprudential policy may be inefficient' for dealing with cyclical issues (Kohn, 2013). In this context, it is crucial for macroprudential and monetary policies to take coordinated actions (see, for instance, Angelini et al., 2012; Gelain and Ilbas, 2014; Rubio and Carrasco-Gallego, 2014).

Some believe that policy lags are too long for macroprudential policies to be used in a countercyclical way. In reality, of course, macroprudential policy settings are changed through the cycle. The Basel III accord does have a countercyclical capital buffer. Many macroprudential instruments influence the cycle through their effects on financial intermediation: Jean-Pierre Landau argued in his keynote address for greater reliance for countercyclical tools on liquidity/maturity transformation dimensions, and less on capital. It seems a combination of policies is required where monetary policy deals primarily with pressures contributing to inflation, output and credit-related (cyclical) asset bubbles, while macroprudential policies primarily address risk-taking and leverage, and requires a substantial cushion of capital against future shocks (which may vary with the economic cycle).

Macroeconomic/financial feedback loops can take different forms in open economies. A country with an open capital account cannot easily insulate itself from conditions in global financial markets. Many emerging economies which grew more strongly than the advanced economies during the 2010–2014 period found that attempts to maintain tighter monetary policy than in the advanced economies led to strong currency appreciation. Such appreciation often stimulated an expansion of credit as banks come to see households and firms as better credit risks and as a lower country risk premium made it easier for local companies to borrow abroad.

The level of development of local financial markets shapes macroeconomic/financial feedback loops, and so will influence the relative efficiency of alternative macroprudential tools. Where financial markets are illiquid or rudimentary, quantity-based tools will often work better than price-based tools. Low-income and developing economies are in general in a process of financial and institutional development that will have implications both for the nature of financial stability risks and for the conduct of macroprudential policies (see IMF, 2014).

Macroprudential policies have both microeconomic and macroeconomic dimensions. An analysis of market failures should be central to the microeconomic dimension. The focus is on how markets and institutions actually function, and on how regulation can better align private interests with the social interest. Macroprudential policies also need to be explored within a macroeconomic framework. Such a framework could just include the analysis of broad macroeconomic aggregates – aggregate demand, total bank credit, asset prices, capital flows and so on. But because the macroeconomic/financial feedback effects that provide much of the rationale for the macroprudential approach, many researchers have tried to incorporate microeconomic financial behaviour in the macroeconomic models. Using a Dynamic Stochastic General Equilibrium (DSGE) model is one way to do this (for early examples, see Borio and Shim, 2007; N'Diaye, 2009; Antipa et al., 2010).

The main problem confronting any model analysis of macroprudential policy is that the objective 'financial stability' can mean very different things and is not necessarily amenable to computational modelling. For example, it could mean ensuring the resilience of financial firms that are core in the intermediation process. Or it could mean moderating the amplitude of swings in asset prices or credit growth. Another problem is that these policies are new and there is not yet enough evidence to discriminate between different models empirically. Incorporating concepts such as financial stability or systemic risk into models – and testing them – is therefore difficult. (See Galvão and Owyang, 2013 for a discussion on the topic.) Researchers should, however, take heart from progress in developing better, more granular data for financial stability analysis. See Heath and Goksu, 2017 provides an up-to-date review.)

Economists should therefore strive to include those dimensions of macroprudential policy that can be modelled, as illustrated by some of the chapters in this book. Regardless of their limitations, DSGE models bring important advantages for macroprudential analysis. First, they can be compared with a benchmark in which there is only monetary policy. Second, they include many sources of shocks that can be used to check for different economic trajectories. Moreover, they rely on general equilibrium analysis and are suitable for simulations to study the impact of new policy instruments. Furthermore, calibrated parameters can be altered to test for alternative policy scenarios. And finally, because DSGE models are microfounded, they can be suitable for the study of welfare issues. We must be aware of the omissions that such approaches are bound to face, and, while macroprudential policy will increasingly rely on quantified assessment, it will always require an element of judgment.

A specific challenge of analysis in the formulation of macroprudential policies is to better understand and calibrate their effects. This is particularly difficult when policies have not been implemented, as there is little evidence on which to base the analysis. As Charles Goodhart has noted, 'The use of macroprudential instruments is still pretty much in its infancy' (Goodhart 2014). Nevertheless, central banks have considered how policy effectiveness can be assessed ahead of implementation ('ex-ante appraisals'). The BIS recently published a report on the best means to judge the risks and vulnerabilities that need to be addressed, on the appropriate instruments that should be deployed and on the timing of and calibration of the intensity of the instruments for the purpose they were designed (BIS, 2016). The IMF through its Financial Sector Assessment Program and its regular Article IV consultations is building up substantial case study–based knowledge on how these policies have worked (IMF, 2014).

The analysis of macroprudential policy in an open economy (including assessment of any monetary policy alternative) must address several additional questions. A key concern for emerging market central banks is that changes in global financial conditions can lead to large swings in capital flows that almost overwhelm policy-makers in recipient countries. The several case studies in Agénor and Pereira da Silva (2013) illustrate well how monetary policy loses its effectiveness in such circumstances.

A related question is the impact on the exchange rate. This matters because there is increasing evidence of risk-taking channel of currency appreciation, which Philip Turner described in his keynote address (drawing on Hofmann et al., 2016). One implication is that lifting interest rates to limit exuberant domestic credit may aggravate some risk-taking by driving the exchange rate up. This produces an 'easy' reduction in inflation (tradable goods fall in price) but may increase the demand for non-tradables and especially property. Increased borrowing for real estate can itself create risks. Macroprudential policies designed to curb such credit expansion (reducing reliance on interest rate increases) can limit the risks of unwarranted currency appreciation. Bruno et al. (2015) found that twelve Asia-Pacific economies, faced with strong growth and inflation pressures in the mid-2000s, responded by raising interest rates – even in the face of a sharp real exchange rate appreciation. But a renewed rise in their exchange rates as growth strengthened after 2009, led them to rely much more on macroprudential measures. The IMF has carried out a similar major study, but covering more countries. They cover 353 episodes of policy tightening and 125 episodes of policy loosening in forty-six countries: see Zhang and Zoli (2014).

Another question is the nature of the shock macroprudential policies are meant to address, a point that has been emphasised by both the BIS and the International Monetary Fund (IMF) in their discussions about the choice between alternative policy instruments. One important dimension is demand versus supply shocks. Kannan et al. (2012) find that using a macroprudential instrument specifically designed to dampen credit market cycles would also provide stabilization benefits when an economy faces financial sector or housing demand shocks. In this model, the optimal macroprudential rule under productivity shocks is to not intervene. Broader and more aggressive policy regimes can improve stability in the face of financial shocks, and can also help in the face of housing demand shocks, but they raise the possibility of policy mistakes in the face of productivity shocks. Historically, however, productivity shocks have frequently stimulated speculative borrowing in new, uncertain areas. All too often, the extrapolation of a temporary jump in productivity engenders unwarranted optimism about the future. Financial risks would therefore increase, which macroprudential policy might need to counter (Turner, 2012). If the productivity shock at the same time drives down unit costs and prices, monetary policy might need to ease for the central bank to meet its inflation target. In such circumstances, monetary and macroprudential policies might need to move in opposite directions.

Another dimension is external versus internal. Blanchard et al. (2017) and Jeanne and Korinek (2010a) have argued that macroprudential policies are better than capital controls when the problem is that a credit boom has made all borrowing risky: there is no need to discriminate between domestic and foreign lenders. But on other occasions, it is external borrowing that is the source of the distortions (especially bank foreign liabilities) so the authorities should discriminate against resident/ non-resident transactions. A similar argument applies when the problem is one of increased currency mismatches: policies to limit foreign currency debt may be preferred to raising domestic interest rates (which often have the unintended consequence of encouraging firms and households to borrow in low-interest foreign currencies – aggravating financial stability risks).

In some countries these policies have been rapidly applied with only partial analytical support – and just as for a time inflation targeting policies were ahead of theory (King, 2005) – so macroprudential policy has so far been implemented without the theoretical structure that would help central banks understand its full effects. In other countries, the implementation of such policies has been cautious due to the absence of analytical studies to support an over-arching framework. No theoretical modelling approach has emerged as pre-eminent. Perhaps no single theoretical structure will ever emerge, and we will need to use different models to answer different questions. The articles of this book therefore explore various theoretical perspectives with some analytical rigour. This book is the first serious research source book for macroprudential policy-makers, offering an evaluation of alternative policies in a consistent modelling framework.

Some chapters explicitly use *DSGE models* to impose some discipline on our thinking and avoid the kind of ad hoc discussion of systemic risk, the design of instruments and rules for implementation that tends to occur when a new policy regime is in its infancy. Nevertheless, DSGE models still face formidable challenges. Representative agent models built on microeconomic foundations can be misleading when it is heterogeneity which drives financial intermediation. Researchers need to find ways of introducing heterogeneity – different types of forms of household, different lending contracts (e.g. foreign versus domestic currency) and different types of financial intermediation. Another challenge is the need to model defaults.

There is also an important role for *reduced-form macroeconomic models*. This is especially true empirically when, for example, we need to find a variable (with a long run of data) which is closely related to the macroprudential instrument under consideration. Reduced-form macrofinancial models can be useful in working out how the P&L and balance sheets of a large number of banks would respond to macroeconomic or financial market shocks. Such models could help to identify feedback effects coming from common exposures, for instance. One ambitious attempt is the large-scale financial macroeconomic model developed by the Bank of Japan (Ishikawa et al., 2012). This model, which covers more than 350 banks and regional financial co-operatives, relies on estimated behavioural equations for the banks included. Bank supervisors are increasingly conducting stress tests which use such models: see Goldstein (2016) and Kitamura et al. (2014).

Perhaps one of the newest analytical approaches is the use of *network models* to capture contagion risks. One of the lessons from the GFC was that contagion channels could amplify shocks which directly affect only a small sector (e.g. sub-prime mortgages). An early contribution was the analysis by Brunnermeier and Pedersen (2009) of collateralized debt in interbank markets. Gourieroux et al. (2012) developed a network model for the banking system. Gabrieli et al. (2015) use a network model to analyse cross-border contagion risk in the European banking system. Such collateral effects extend far beyond the banking industry. Whenever any debt is collateralised by any marketable asset (including property), fire-sale effects can create powerful feedback loops. Davila and Korinek (2016) review fire-sale externalities. The recent analysis of Korinek and Simsek (2016) show how such feedbacks can exacerbate aggregate demand externalities as asset fire sales reduce aggregate demand by tightening borrowing constraints.

The coverage of the chapters places emphasis on the global perspective, the open economy angles, the actual policies that have been pursued and the question of systemic risk and the practice of policies to date. On an institutional level, the final chapter highlights the importance of the design and governance of macroprudential policy in comparison to the design and governance of monetary policy.

Our contributions are drawn from central bankers, practitioners and academics in many countries ensuring that the insights apply to more than one country or financial system summarising work streams that have been undertaken at the European Central Bank, the Bank of England and the Federal Reserve, as well as the International Monetary Fund and the Bank for International Settlements.

We turn now to a summary of the main contributions. The first chapter, titled 'The Macroeconomics of Macroprudential Policies' (Philip Turner), touches upon a topic that has again become core to central banking. "Again" because the Bank of England became a central bank in the early nineteenth century with what we would now call a macroprudential mandate (Allen, 2014). It was not responsible for price stability – because the restoration of convertibility of Bank of England notes into gold in 1821 after the Napoleonic Wars had taken care of that. The Bank's task was to avoid financial crises and, when crises did threaten, to limit the systemic impact of any bank failure. Many other central banks also saw their job in such terms; for instance, Rotemberg (2014) has pointed out that the goal of Federal Reserve monetary policy from the 1920s was to limit speculative lending. The word "macroprudential" itself seems to have been coined in 1979 by a Bank of England official, the late David Holland. It surfaces in Basel Committee documents at about this time (Green, 2011) and was prominent in policy discussions at the BIS from the early 1980s.

The starting point of his analysis is the Bernanke–Blinder model of the bank lending channel: shifts in the willingness of banks to lend (as 'the perceived riskiness of loans' changes) have an impact on aggregate demand. In this model, the interest rate is not the policy rate but that on domestic bonds, and is therefore endogenous. This model has the advantage of allowing interest rates to react to financial system shocks. Extension in a simple Mundell–Fleming framework then links this interest rate to the exchange rate. Macroprudential prudential policies can be viewed as acting directly on the bank lending channel. Hence he argues that the endogenous responses of the interest rate on domestic bonds and the exchange rate should be taken in to account in any analysis of macroprudential policies.

The chapter titled 'The New Art of Central Banking' (Jagjit S. Chadha) notes that some difficult lessons have been learned over this crisis. First, inflation targeting alone cannot prevent boom and bust and therefore needs to be augmented with more instruments and better judgement. Second, while the financial sector amplifies the impact of economic shocks and properly designed MPIs ought to minimise the effects, through sensible application of liquidity and capital targets via macroprudential policy. But, third, while interactions between fiscal, financial and monetary policy provide support to fragile financial institutions, coordination could be a difficult task and one that needs further research.

The chapter titled 'A Liquidity-Based Approach to Macroprudential Policy' (Jean-Pierre Landau) argues that a cyclical approach to macroprudential policy presents major challenges for central banks and supervisors as it necessitates a comprehensive and operational view of the interactions between the financial system and monetary policy.

This challenge had been neglected in recent decades, when inflation targeting was the dominant monetary policy framework in advanced and emerging economies, New Keynesian models were dominant and monetary policy acted mostly through interest rates with no role for the financial sector. We know that financial institutions play a more important role in the transmission mechanism in a realistic description of the economy. The behaviour of the financial system involves a constant interaction between leverage on the one hand and maturity transformation on the other. Both have an impact on the financial cycle and both contribute to monetary transmission. Financial fragility is the product of such interactions and, logically, macroprudential policy should aim at regulating both leverage and maturity transformation. This chapter argues that current macroprudential policies rely too heavily on the direct control of leverage and too little on liquidity and maturity transformation. If they were to consider liquidity and maturity transformation, they would contribute to greater efficiency and flexibility, making interaction with monetary policy much easier to manage.

Chapter 3, 'Financial Intermediation and Monetary and Macroprudential Policies' (Stefano Neri) begins a new section using New-Keynesian Dynamic Stochastic General Equilibrium (NK-DSGE) models to explore the scope of macro prudential policy. While DSGE models were severely criticised after the outbreak of the global financial crisis in 2008–2009, this paper offers a step forward in incorporating a more realistic modelling of financial intermediation and a role for macroprudential policy. Given the technical and computational difficulties arising from modelling systemic risk, it may take some time before economists come up with new models that allow a comprehensive and integrated approach to the study of the linkages between financial intermediation and the real economy and the role of policies to promote and preserve financial stability. In the meantime, existing models can be used for the analysis of monetary and macroprudential policy and their interaction. This chapter shows that the crisis has to be seen as an opportunity to improve the current framework of policy analysis. Including financial frictions and banking regulation in an otherwise standard model, macroprudential policies can be evaluated in an analogous way as monetary policy. This represents an important contribution to the modelling framework improvement.

A closely related chapter, 'The Macroprudential Countercyclical Capital Buffer in Basel III: Implications for Monetary Policy' (José A. Carrasco-Gallego and Margarita Rubio), argues that Basel III is a comprehensive set of reform measures in banking regulation, supervision and risk management with a strong macroprudential component, which has the aim of preventing future crises by creating a sound financial system. Nevertheless, these changes in financial regulation have to be co-ordinated with monetary policy. They address several key research questions. First, they analyse how the higher capital requirements implied by Basel I, II and III would, for a given monetary policy, affect the welfare of different agents in the economy. Second, they study how these regulations affect the way monetary policy needs to be conducted.

Finally, they propose an automatic rule to implement the macropruden-tial Countercyclical Buffer in Basel III and find the optimal parameters for this rule and for monetary policy. They conclude that a Pareto-superior outcome can be reached using the optimal values, and the macroprudential objective can be achieved.

The open economy dimension to macroprudential policy is first dis-cussed in the chapter 'On the Use of Monetary and Macroprudential Policies for Small Open Economies' (F. Gulcin Ozkan and D. Filiz Unsal). This essay explores optimal monetary and macroprudential policy rules for a small open-economy under a sudden reversal of capital flows. It considers Taylor-type interest rate rules as a function of infla-tion, output and credit growth; and a macroprudential instrument as a function of credit growth. There are two main results. The first is that in the presence of macroprudential measures, there are no significant wel-fare gains from monetary policy also reacting to credit growth above and beyond its response to output gap and inflation. Moreover, monetary responses to financial market developments under both financial and real shocks would actually generate higher welfare losses than macropruden-tial responses. This puts the onus of 'leaning against the wind' squarely on macroprudential policy. The second conclusion is that the source of borrowing is an important determinant of desirability of alternative pol-icies: the larger the scale of foreign currency debt, the greater the effect-iveness of macroprudential instruments. Given the sizable liability dollarisation in emerging economies, this finding provides one explan-ation why macroprudential policies featured so prominently in their response to the 2008–2009 global financial crisis, in contrast to that in advanced economies. This chapter represents an important advance in modelling macroprudential policies, as it gives an international dimen-sion to the problem. Most of the literature has focused so far on advanced and closed economies. The findings of this chapter can be applied to emerging economies, largely dependent on the foreign sector.

Open economy issues are further discussed in the chapter on 'Macroprudential Policy in a Globalised World' (Dennis Reinhardt and Rhiannon Sowerbutts). It acknowledges that while macroprudential instruments have become part of the toolkits of many policymakers, so far the focus of macroprudential policy has been largely domestic. But the interconnectedness of global financial markets and the globalisation of banking pose important challenges to the operation of macropruden-tial policy that cannot be ignored. This chapter considers how capital flows create excessive borrowing, pecuniary externalities and a need for macroprudential regulation. It shows that leakages that make domestic macroprudential policies less effective may result from an uneven application of regulation and macroprudential actions abroad may have spillover effects at home. It outlines arguments for potential international coordination and reciprocity of macroprudential policies to ensure more effective international macroprudential policy. These results are particularly interesting for countries such as the United Kingdom in which a large majority of bank branches are foreign. Domestic macroprudential policies can see their effects reduced or can lead to undesirable outcomes if foreign supervisors do not take the same measures.

A final chapter in this section on 'Capital Flows and Macroprudential Policy: A Framework for Macroprudential Policy in Emerging Asia' (Matteo F. Ghilardi and Shanaka J. Peiris) develops an open-economy DSGE model with an optimizing banking sector to assess the role of capital flows, macro-financial linkages, and macroprudential policies in emerging Asia. The key result is that macroprudential measures can usefully complement monetary policy. Countercyclical macroprudential policies can help reduce macroeconomic volatility and enhance welfare. The results also demonstrate the importance of capital flows and financial stability for business cycle fluctuations as well as the role of supply-side financial accelerator effects in the amplification and propagation of shocks. Asian economies pioneered the introduction of macroprudential policies. This chapter represents a theoretical framework that can serve to test the effectiveness of those policies that have already been put in practice.

Two further sections consider practical matters of macroprudential policy implementation relating to systemic risk and effective use of macroprudential instruments.

The chapter on 'Systemic Risk of European Banks: Regulators and Markets' (Maarten R. C. van Oordt and Bank Chen Zhou) discusses how rules and regulations may have different impacts on risk-taking by individual banks and on banks' systemic risk levels. This makes the implementation of prudential rules and policies more difficult: attention is required to ensure we understand their impact on bank risk and systemic risk. This chapter assesses whether market-based measures of systemic risk and recent regulatory indicators provide similar rankings on the systemic importance of large European banks. They find evidence that regulatory indicators of systemic importance are positively related to systemic risk. In particular, banks with higher scores on regulatory indicators have a stronger link to the system in the event of financial stress, rather than having a higher level of bank risk.

The chapter on 'Macroprudential Tools of Systemic Risk Analysis' (Marcin Łupiński) presents the tools of systemic risk analysis used as a part of stress testing framework and their application to address systemic risk questions facing macroprudential policy decision-makers. It gives special attention to problems present in the Polish banking sector by way of example. The first part of the paper offers alternative definitions of systemic risk, tools of systemic risk measurement and analysis. A reference network model is integrated with the stress-testing framework to empirically evaluate the impact of the systemic risk on the Polish banking sector. Results show that, in general, banks operating in Poland are immune to endogenous and exogenous sources of systemic risk and this type of risk is not a source of instability for the domestic banking sector. However, some shocks emerging from the structure of the Polish banks' capital ownership and characteristics of the mortgage credit portfolio should be carefully monitored in the future.

We then turn to the subject on effective macroprudential instruments. In the chapter 'When Is Macroprudential Policy Effective?' (Chris McDonald), the question is asked whether current macroprudential policy instruments such as limits on loan-to-value (LTV) and debt-to-income (DTI) ratios have similar effects on housing markets through tightening and loosening phases of the policy cycle. This chapter examines whether the relative effectiveness of tightening versus loosening macroprudential measures depends on where in the housing cycle they are implemented. It shows that tightening measures have greater effects when credit is expanding quickly and when house prices are high relative to income. Loosening measures seem to have smaller effects than tightening, but the difference is not that large at weaker parts of the cycle.

The final chapter in this volume 'Macroprudential Policy: Practice Ahead of Theory and a Clear Remit' (Richard Barwell) argues that the scientific approach to economic policy requires clear objectives and a reliable model of the system. In his view, macroprudential policymakers have neither: the rush to define and then use these new instruments has been conducted before a proper theory is in place to understand them. His proposed sequencing is: first, identify market failures and write down a model; second, pin down the objectives of the regime; and third, allocate effective instruments to policy institutions. Six recommendations are made to help deal with the problem of 'learning whilst doing' in the conduct of macroprudential policy: how to achieve the goals of public policy as our understanding of the system we are trying to stabilise evolves.

## Concluding Remarks

The papers in this book demonstrate the many different insights provided by alternative theoretical approaches – DSGE models, reduced-form macroeconomic (and macrofinancial) models and network models. No theoretical paradigm dominates. Because macroprudential policies are comparatively new, empirical assessment of the effectiveness of different instruments is still at an early stage. How the transmission mechanism of such policies works, and how the mutual interactions with monetary policy transmission operate, is a matter of continuing debate.

The lively discussions at our Nottingham conference indicated that there are major disagreements about which macroprudential instruments would work best in practice. The President of the Federal Reserve Bank of New York recently recounted a 'tabletop exercise' of five Federal Reserve Bank presidents (Dudley, 2015). They had debated about the best way of responding to overheating in the commercial real estate market. But they failed to agree on which macroprudential instrument to use. Nor could they agree on the ordering for such tools relative to monetary policy. Empirical work on how actual instruments have worked is still at an early stage. Pragmatic learning-by-doing seems to be the order of the day.

Finally, arrangements giving central banks new macroprudential tools are still new. Many process-related questions remain to be resolved. Should policies be rules-based or discretionary? What targets should central banks follow? How many tools should central banks use? What role should central bank balance sheet policies play? Much remains to be resolved on decision-making processes and on disclosure. Accountability and governance arrangements are likely to be adjusted in the light of experience.

The research agenda facing central banks which now use macroprudential policies is demanding. We hope this book can help such research and so illuminate some of the issues that policymakers face.

## References

Agénor, P. and L. A. Pereira da Silva (2013). *Inflation and Financial Stability*. IDB and CEMLA. Washington, DC.

Aikman, D., O. Bush and A. M. Taylor (2016). 'Monetary versus macroprudential policies: Causal impacts of interest rates and credit controls in the era of the UK Radcliffe Report'. *CEPR Discussion Paper*. June.

Aiyar, S., C. W. Calomiris and T. Wieladek (2014). 'How does credit supply respond to monetary policy and bank minimum requirements?', *Bank of England Working Paper*, no 508.

Allen, W. A. (2014). 'Asset choice in British central banking history, the myth of the safe asset, and bank regulation', *Journal of Banking and Financial Economics*, June, 5–18.

Altunbas, Y., L. Gambacorta and D. Marquez-Ibanez (2010). 'Does monetary policy affect bank risk-taking?', *BIS Working Papers*, no 298.

Angelini, P., S. Neri and F. Panetta (2012). 'Monetary and macroprudential policies', *European Central Bank Working Paper*, no 1,449.

Antipa, P., E. Mengus and B. Mojon (2010). "Would macroprudential policies have prevented the great recession?" Mimeo. Banque de France.

Blanchard, O., J. D. Ostry, A. D. Ghosh and M. Chamon (2017). "Are capital flows expansionary or contractionary? Theory, policy implications and some evidence" *IMF Economic Review, Palgrave Macmillan, IMF* vol 65(3), pp 563–585.

Borio, C. and I. Shim (2007). 'What can (macro-)policy do to support monetary policy?', *BIS Working Papers*, no 242, December.

Bank for International Settlements (2016). 'Report of the Study Group on Experiences with the Ex Ante Appraisal of Macroprudential Policies', *CGFS Papers*, no 56, July.

Brunnermeier, M. and L. Pedersen (2009). Market liquidity and funding liquidity, *The Review of Financial Studies*, vol 22, 2201–2238.

Bruno, V., I. Shim and H. S. Shin (2015). 'Comparative assessment of macroprudential policies', *BIS Working Papers*, no 502, June.

Davila, E. and A. Korinek (2016). 'Fire-sale externalities', *NBER Working Paper*, no 22444, July.

Dell'Ariccia, G., L. Laeven and G. Suarez (2013). 'Bank leverage and monetary policy's risk-taking channel: Evidence from the United States', *IMF Working Paper*, WP/13/143.

Dudley, W. C. (2015). 'Is the active use of macroprudential tools institutionally realistic?', Panel remarks at the Macroprudential Monetary Policy Conference. Boston, October.

Farhi, E. and I. Werning (2016). 'A theory of macroprudential policies in the presence of nominal rigidities', *NBER Working Paper*, no 19313. June.

Friedman, B. M. (2014). 'Has the financial crisis permanently changed the practice of monetary policy? Has it changed the theory of monetary policy?', *NBER Working Paper*, no 20128, May.

Gabrieli, S., D. Salakhova and G. Vuillemey (2015). 'Cross-border interbank contagion in the European banking sector', Banque de France. *Document de travail*, no 545.

Gagnon, J. E. and B. Sack (2014). 'Monetary policy with abundant liquidity: A new operating framework for the Federal Reserve', Policy Brief PB14–4. Peterson Institute for International Economics. January.

Gambacorta, L. and P. Mistrulli (2004). Does bank capital affect lending behavior?, *Journal of Financial Intermediation*, vol 13, no 4, 436–457.

Galvão, A. B. and M. T. Owyang (2013). 'Measuring macro-financial conditions using a factor augmented smooth-transition vector autoregression'. April. Mimeo.

Gelain, P. and P. Ilbas (2014). 'Monetary and macroprudential policies in an estimated model with financial intermediation', *National Bank of Belgium Working Paper*, no 258.

Goldstein, M. (2016). *Banking's Final Exam: Stress Testing and Bank-Capital Reform*. Peterson Institute for International Economics. Washington.

Goodhart, C. (2014). 'The use of macroprudential instruments'. In D. Schoenmaker (Ed.), *Macroprudentialism*. A VoxEU.org eBook edited by D. Schoenmaker. Pp 11–17.

Gourieroux, C., J.-C. Héam and A. Monfort (2012). 'Bilateral exposures and systemic solvency risk', *Banque de France Working Paper*, no 414.

Green, D. (2011). 'The relationship between the objectives and tools of macroprudential and monetary policy', *Financial Markets Group, London School of Economics Special Paper*, no 200, May.

Heath, R. and E. B. Goksu (2017). "Financial stability analysis: What are the data needs?" IMF Working Paper. WP/17/153.

Hofmann, B., I. Shim, and H. S. Shin (2016). 'Sovereign yields and the risk-taking channel of currency appreciation', *BIS Working Papers*, no 538, January.

IMF (2014). 'Staff Guidance Note on Macroprudential Policy-Considerations for Low-Income Countries'.

Ishikawa, A., K. Kamada, Y. Kurachi, K. Nasu and Y. Teranishi (2012). 'Introduction to the financial macro-econometric model', *Bank of Japan Working Paper Series*, no 12-E-1.

Jeanne, O. and A. Korinek (2010a). 'Excessive volatility in capital flows: A Pigouvian taxation approach', *American Economic Review*, vol 100, no 2, 403–407.

(2010b). 'Managing credit booms and busts: A Pigouvian taxation approach', *NBER Working Paper*, no 16377. September.

Jimenez, G., S. Ongena, J.-L. Peydro and J. Saurina (2014). 'Hazardous time for monetary policy: What do twenty-three million bank loans say about the effects of monetary policy on credit risk-taking?', *Econometrica*, vol 82, no 2, 436–505.

Kannan, P., P. Rabanal and A. Scott (2012). 'Monetary and macroprudential policy rules in a model with house price booms, *The B.E. Journal of Macroeconomics*, Contributions, vol 12, no 1.

Kenc, T. (2016). 'Macroprudential regulation: An introduction to history, theory and policy', in "Macroprudential Policy" G20 conference jointly organized by the Central Bank of Turkey, the BIS and the IMF. *BIS Papers*. No 86 pp 1–15.

King, M. (2005). 'Monetary policy: Practice ahead of theory', Mais lecture. 17 May.

(2016). *The End of Alchemy: Money, Banking and the Future of the Global Economy*. W. W. Norton & Company, Ltd.

Kitamura, T., S. Kojima, K. Nakamura, K. Takahashi and I. Takei (2014). *Macro Stress Testing at the Bank of Japan*. Bank of Japan, Reports & Research Papers. Tokyo.

Kohn, D. (2013). *Interactions of Macroprudential Policy and Monetary Policies: A View from the Bank of England's Financial Policy Committee*. Oxford: Oxford Institute for Economic Policy.

Korinek, A. (2011). 'Systemic risk-taking: Amplification effects, externalities and regulatory responses', *ECB Working Paper*, no 1345.

Korinek, A. and A. Simsek (2016). 'Liquidity trap and excessive leverage,' *American Economic Review*, vol 106, no 3, 699–738.

Maddaloni, A. and J.-L. Peydro (2013). 'Monetary policy, macroprudential policy and banking stability: Evidence from the euro area,' *International Journal of Central Banking*, 121–169.

N' Diaye, P. (2009). 'Countercyclical macroprudential policies in a supporting role to monetary policy', *IMF Working Paper*, no WP/09/257. November.

Posen, A. (2009). 'Finding the right tool for dealing with asset price booms', Speech at the MPR Monetary Policy and Economy Conference. London, December.

Rotemberg, J. (2014). 'The Federal Reserve's abandonment of its 1923 principles', *NBER Working Paper*, no 20507, September.

Rubio, M. and J. A. Carrasco-Gallego (2014). 'Macroprudential and monetary policies: Implications for financial stability and welfare'. *Journal of Banking and Finance*, vol 49, 326–336.

Tucker, P. (2014). 'A new constitution for money (*and* credit). Myron Scholes Lecture', *Chicago Booth School of Business*. 22 May.

Turner, P. (2012). 'Macroprudential policies in EMEs: Theory and practice. Financial sector regulation for growth, equity and stability', *BIS Papers*, no 62, 125–139.

(2017). "Did central banks cause the last crisis? Will they cause the next?" London School of Economics. Financial Markets Group. Special Paper 249. November.

Zhang, L. and E. Zoli (2014). 'Leaning against the wind: Macroprudential policy in Asia', *IMF Working Paper*, no 11/22, February.

# 1     The Macroeconomics of Macroprudential Policies

*Philip Turner*[*]

The subject chosen for this conference touches upon a topic that has **again** become core to central banking. 'Again' because the Bank of England became a central bank in the early nineteenth century with what we would now call a macroprudential mandate (Allen, 2015). This mandate was not responsibility for price stability, because the restoration of convertibility of Bank of England notes into gold in 1821 after the Napoleonic Wars had taken care of that. The Bank's task was to avoid financial crises and, when crises did threaten, to limit the systemic impact of any bank failure. Many other central banks also saw their job in such terms. For instance, Rotemberg (2014) has pointed out that the goal of Federal Reserve monetary policy from the 1920s was to limit speculative lending. In a seminal speech at LSE in 1928, Dennis Robertson pointed out the Fed's error in trying to use interest rates to moderate speculative lending. His proposal that monetary policy should be guided by the Principle of Price Stabilisation ("the sole and sufficient objective of [central] banking policy is the stabilisation of the price level") proved to be prescient [Turner 2017]).

The word 'macroprudential' itself seems to have been coined in 1979 by a Bank of England official, the late David Holland. It surfaces in Basel Committee documents at about this time (Green, 2011) and was prominent in policy discussions at the Bank for International Settlements (BIS) from the early 1980s.

[*] I am very grateful for helpful comments and suggestions I received at this conference, at the Central Bank of Argentina's Annual Money and Banking Conference, at a CBRT/BIS/IMF conference in Istanbul and from Ryan Banerjee, Boris Hofmann, Lex Hoogduin, Emanuel Kohlscheen, Anton Korinek, Marco Lombardi, Christopher McDonald, Paul Mizen, Richhild Moessner, Ilhyock Shim, Hyun Shin and Anders Vredin on earlier drafts. Many thanks to Sonja Fritz and Jhuvesh Sobrun for helping me prepare this paper.

## 1.1    Introduction

Many see macroprudential policies as essentially having a **microeconomic** focus, usually to deal with a market failure that an individual bank or other financial firm will not, on its own, address. People often think of such policies as leaving the economy-wide interest rate unchanged. These policies can curb a coordination failure between private firms. They can raise the relative price or availability of credit to those sectors in which the build-up of financial vulnerabilities is most worrisome. By contrast, monetary policy has a **macroeconomic** focus. If financial stability risks are judged to be high, and inflation risks appear because the interest rate is too low, the central bank can curb new borrowing by simply raising rates.

This stylised dichotomy has an important germ of truth. Financial system vulnerabilities are often most acute in certain sectors. For many central bankers, one of the main lessons of the 2007/2008 financial crisis was the need to develop macroprudential policies to address specific aggregate risk exposures – for example, from overvalued asset prices – that even well-managed firms together create (Galati and Moessner, 2014; Hoogduin, 2014; Kohn, 2014; Tucker, 2014a). Echoing Chuck Prince's remark about leaving the dance floor while the music was still playing, Paul Tucker (2014a) observed that macroprudential policies 'can act as a coordinating device for intermediaries to exit the dance floor together, helping to dampen the pro-cyclical dynamic'. Finally, governance and accountability considerations have led many central banks to establish clear and separate primary objectives for monetary policy and macroprudential policies.

But such a dichotomy is of course a simplification. Any plausible assessment of macroprudential policy choices also requires macroeconomic analysis. One obvious reason is that the imposition of any binding regulatory constraint will affect macroeconomic variables. Normally such measures reduce spending and increase saving, with consequences for real income, interest rates and the exchange rate.[1] Economic models seek to work out the macroeconomic reactions induced by a tighter regulatory constraint.

Another reason – which is frequently overlooked – is that domestic macroeconomic policies cannot directly influence all relevant macroeconomic variables. In particular, many macroeconomic variables are mainly determined in world markets and thus largely beyond the reach

---

[1] Portes (2014) develops this argument.

of national policymakers. Prudential regulations (not monetary policy) may need to address what is essentially a macroeconomic problem, and not just a sector-specific problem.[2]

Two examples of such global variables that are of particular relevance to central banks are the interest rate yield curve and the exchange rate. Central banks can set the short-term interest rate in their own currencies, but long-term rates are dominated by developments in global markets. How banks and other financial intermediaries react to this discrepancy – the central bank controlling one end of the yield curve in its own currency with global markets heavily constraining the other end – can have far-reaching implications for financial stability. Movements in the exchange rate can be relevant for financial stability because they have wealth effects and affect risk-taking, both by banks and in capital markets. This risk-taking channel of the exchange rate creates major policy dilemmas for central banks.

I begin my remarks by drawing an analogy with the Bernanke–Blinder (BB) closed economy model of the bank lending channel.[3] This paper replaced the standard goods-market equilibrium IS curve by a CC (that is, commodities and credit) curve. This extension was designed to allow for the impact on aggregate demand of changes in the willingness of banks to lend. In this model, a financial boom caused by the greater willingness of banks to lend – and *not* by monetary policy which is unchanged – drives up the real interest rate on bonds. This model can then be extended to an open-economy world by using the simple Mundell–Fleming relationship between the domestic interest rate and the exchange rate.

Note that, in the IS-LM world of the BB model, the monetary policy assumption is defined in terms of the quantity of money, and the interest rate is endogenous. The attraction of this model is that the interest rate responds to changes in risk-taking by domestic banks. The more 'modern' convention of defining monetary policy in terms of the policy rate implicitly assumes – at least in its basic versions – that there is no direct reaction of interest rates to financial shocks. This is especially so in models which have a macroeconomic Taylor rule and which assume that the long-term rate (a market rate that in reality does react to financial shocks) is just the average expected short-term interest rate. As Boivin et al. (2010) have pointed out, many Dynamic Stochastic General

---

[2] In addition, macroprudential policies have macroeconomic rationales (BIS, 2016). Major recent contributions to the theory of macroprudential policy have stressed (in addition to Pigouvian externalities) aggregate demand externalities (where the aggregate effect of microeconomic choices have macroeconomic effects). An excellent recent summary of this literature is Korinek and Simsek (2016).

[3] This most useful analogy was suggested to me by Paul Mizen.

Equilibrium (DSGE) models have fallen into this trap. Often in such models the path of expected short-term rates depends only on Taylor-rule-type macroeconomic variables (output gap, inflation rate, etc.) – with financial shocks having no direct effect.

A tightening of macroprudential policy can be thought of as reversing the bank lending channel: it curbs bank lending and drives down the interest rate on bonds (Section 1.2). In an open economy, higher market interest rates attract capital inflows and the exchange rate appreciates. Currency appreciation may actually lead to further financial risk taking. A central bank faced with an overvalued exchange rate and excessive or too-unstable capital inflows may therefore prefer to tighten macroprudential policies rather than increase its policy interest rate (Section 1.3). Section 1.4 discusses some recent policy dilemmas in light of exchange rate developments. A particular form of macroprudential policy would be for the central bank to use its own balance sheet to impose *Quantitative Tightening* on banks (Section 1.5). The conclusion is that a flexible exchange rate cannot insulate a country from the 'world' long-term interest rate or from liquidity conditions in global markets. Capital flow or prudential measures may be needed to address the consequences of a macroeconomic variable that is beyond their reach (Section 1.6), and more than just a sectoral problem.

## 1.2    A Regulatory Constraint: Impact on Income and Interest Rates

Can the imposition or tightening of a macroprudential constraint have any sustained impact if the policy interest rate is held constant? The plausible microeconomic logic for saying 'no' is that interest rates determine intertemporal consumption choices. This logic of course ignores liquidity constraints – and macroprudential policies could work by tightening liquidity constraints. Consider the example of restrictions on mortgage lending, a common macroprudential tool in many countries. Faced with the requirement to make a larger down payment, a household will have to save for a bit longer to buy a house. All that the macroprudential constraint will have achieved, this argument runs, is to delay the house purchase.

But such reasoning works only at the level of the individual. It is fallacious at the aggregate level, because it ignores the impact of regulatory intervention on real GDP, on market interest rates and on asset prices. The imposition or tightening of a binding regulatory constraint that actually lowers borrowing is likely to raise domestic saving. Indeed, the logic of most macroprudential measures is exactly this: to get banks to tighten lending standards so that households or firms in effect increase savings. Normally, regulatory tightening will also lower asset prices – for instance, house prices may fall and this would change household balance sheets, with impacts on spending and output. Lower house prices could help financial stability: as house prices fall, new borrowers become 'safer' bets because their equity stake is now a larger proportion of a lower house price – it also reduces what they can borrow on the back of housing collateral.

The shift in aggregate demand induced by a restrictive macroprudential measure will, in simple closed economy models, reduce income and lead to lower interest rates. The credit channel in the BB model provides a simple framework to begin the analysis. Consider a credit expansion that might call for a macroprudential response. Their famous 1988 paper focused on the economy's response to a financial shock. They analysed what would happen if banks became more willing to extend credit (because of 'a decrease in the perceived riskiness of loans', they suggested).[4] In their IS-LM type model, banks choose between loans and bonds (assuming reserves are constant). The beauty of the Bernanke–Blinder model is that it has a market-determined interest rate (the interest rate on bonds) that responds to changes in banks' willingness to alter the composition of their assets between loans and bonds. Macroprudential policies can be seen as acting *directly* on banks' willingness to lend while holding monetary policy unchanged.

Figure 1.1 reproduces their figure. With monetary policy non-accommodating (i.e. a given LM curve corresponding to a fixed money supply), an outward shift in the credit supply function shifts the 'commodities and credit' (CC). Both real GDP ($Y$) and the real interest rate on bonds ($i$) rise – moving along a given LM curve. To repeat a point made earlier: in this framework, the interest rate is not a simple function of a policy rate under the control of the central bank, a point of some importance for the discussion of the term premium in the 'world' long-term interest rate in Section 1.6.

The Bernanke–Blinder model takes both the price level and inflation as given. In practice, however, the response of monetary policy would depend on inflation prospects. If the rise in output takes $Y$ above full employment, the central bank might tighten monetary policy (leftward

---

[4] Stefano Neri's contribution to this volume (Chapter 3) summarises the useful DGSE approach of Angelini et al. (2014), who analyse macroprudential policies working through the impact of regulatory-policy-induced changes in the supply of bank capital on the supply of loans.

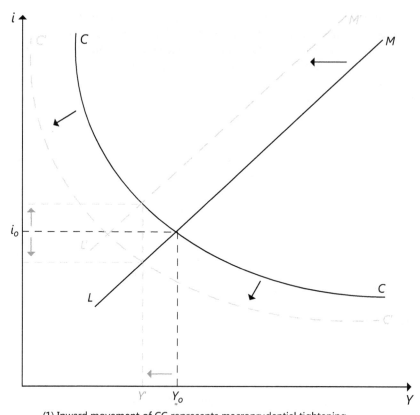

(1) Inward movement of CC represents macroprudential tightening
(2) Leftward movement of LM represents monetary policy tightening

Figure 1.1 Bernanke–Blinder diagram

shift of the LM curve), reinforcing the rise in the interest rate on bonds. Or with high unemployment, it may welcome the more expansionary attitude of banks and loosen monetary policy (rightward shift of the LM curve) to prevent the interest rate on bonds from rising.

Macroprudential policies have the advantage of giving central banks additional instruments to curb bank lending directly. They can change the regulatory risk weights on loans, for instance. The aim would be to affect the behaviour of banks in ways that are akin to changes in the perceived riskiness of loans which Bernanke and Blinder analysed. Hence a tightening of macroprudential policy can be represented as a downward shift in the credit supply function which would shift the CC curve inwards (Figure 1.1). The interest rate on bank loans rises while that on bonds falls.[5] The policy alternative to the macroprudential measure would have been to tighten monetary policy. Figure 1.1 shows a leftward shift in the LM curve that produces exactly the same decline in real GDP from $Y_o$ to $Y'$. But the two policies have the opposite impact on the interest rate on bonds – tightening macroprudential policies lowers this interest rate, while tightening monetary policy increases it.[6]

Such simple macroeconomic models need to be complemented by analyses of balance sheet variables of households. A lower interest rate on bonds in this model, for instance, has a correspondence in a higher market value of bonds. As other asset prices rise, the net worth of borrowers improves and they can borrow more (the balance sheet channel to monetary policy). Changes in the value of marketable collateral held by potential borrowers can have a sizeable effect on their ability to borrow.

Analysing balance sheet effects is not simple. One shortcoming of many financial stability analyses is that the asset side tends to be neglected. Much of the literature has an almost exclusive focus on the liability side of borrowers' balance sheets. 'The balance sheet channel of monetary policy,' wrote Bernanke and Gertler (1995), 'arises because shifts in Fed policy affects ... the financial positions of borrowers, both directly and indirectly.'

The most obvious implication of considering both sides of a balance sheet is that increased financial debts of borrowers are financial assets for the lenders. Changes in stocks of assets – not just debt – can have macroeconomic consequences. Writing about a UK house price boom in the early 2000s, Stephen Nickell, then a member of the Bank of England's Monetary Policy Committee, noted a remarkable correspondence between the substantial accumulation of household financial debts (mostly mortgages) and the accumulation of household financial assets. Developments up to 2007 confirmed his observation (Figure 1.2). There is a 'systemic connection' between debt and assets, Nickell argued, whenever a household takes out a mortgage to buy a house from a seller who has no mortgage and who either inherits a new house or moves into rented property. The seller adds to his stock of financial assets just when

---

[5] It is always dangerous to jump from model to simple fact. Nevertheless, one striking development since the crisis has been the big increase in banks' holdings of government bonds. Part of this is recession-induced. But part has been driven by new regulations, notably liquidity rules (government bonds preferred), and by greater reliance on high-quality collateral against some counterparty exposures.

[6] As Jeanne (2014) has argued, this mechanism means that macroprudential tightening in a large country will push down the global interest rate. Reinhardt and Sowerbutts (Chapter 8) explore cross-border spillovers from macroprudential policies.

As a percentage of gross disposable income

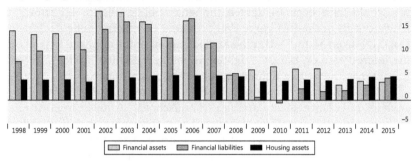

Figure 1.2 The accumulation of household debt and assets in the United Kingdom.
Source: ONS

the borrower adds to his financial liabilities. What is striking about Figure 1.2 is the stability of households' net acquisition of housing assets through all the ups and downs in the property market. Yet large variations in the rate of house price increases seem to generate swings in the acquisition of both financial debts and financial assets that are many times larger than changes in investment in houses. Since the crisis, however, financial debts and assets have been more stable. More work is needed to understand how swings in financial assets could aggravate financial accelerator effects.

## 1.3    A Regulatory Constraint: Impact on the Exchange Rate

The Bernanke–Blinder closed economy model can be extended to an open economy analysed using simple Mundell–Fleming mechanisms linking interest rates and the exchange rate. Consider first the impact of the *domestic shock* that BB considered. A rise in the interest rate on bonds coming from an outward shift of the CC curve – that is, as banks become more willing to lend – will attract foreign as well as domestic buyers of the bonds. One consequence is that the market interest rate rises by less than in a closed economy; and the resultant capital inflows induce a currency appreciation.[7] Currency appreciation may lead to yet further increases in domestic bank lending. The appreciation of their currency

---

[7] At least in the short run. Eventually, a rise in the current account deficit will drive the exchange rate down. Hence the FF curve – representing equilibrium in the foreign exchange market – is shown as backward sloping in Figure 1.3.

makes households (especially those with foreign currency debts, common in emerging market economies [EMEs]) feel better off, and may encourage them to reduce savings.[8]

Such exchange rate impacts add an important dimension to the policy debate on the response to a domestic shock. Regulatory tightening leads to currency depreciation, but monetary tightening leads to currency appreciation. This important difference is not lost on policymakers grappling with what they see as overvalued currencies.

Figure 1.3 illustrates some elements of this issue. It represents an initial situation such that the level of income and the exchange rate generate a trade balance of zero. The consumption and production of tradable goods are exactly equal so that the trade account is in balance. If banks become more adventurous, and lend more, the CC curve shifts outward, the exchange rate rises and the output of tradables falls. The demand for non-tradables is stimulated and a trade deficit emerges.

In practice, of course, the exchange rate can also be driven up by an *external shock*, adding new policy dilemmas. Consider the case of a rise in the world price of the export goods. This is important for developing economies dependent on primary commodities. (A boom in external markets has a similar effect on countries with more diversified export structures.) The trade-related effect of such a shock is an improvement in the terms of trade, which allows the country to balance its currency account with a lower output of tradable goods. The ray B in the figure swivels anti-clockwise. But there may also be a financial aspect that is particularly relevant for capital flows. This is that the higher real value of expected future exports in effect gives the country increased collateral, making foreigners more willing to lend. A decline in the country's risk premium moves the FF schedule leftwards, capital inflows rise and the exchange rate appreciates. This is of course the short-run effect. In the long run, foreign debts gradually increase as the strong exchange rate erodes the country's capacity to produce tradable goods.

Such slow-moving balance sheet effects, not of course included in the Mundell–Fleming framework, can ultimately have major implications for financial stability. Bruno and Shin (2015) have termed this phenomenon

---

[8] More than thirty years ago Obstfeld (1982) highlighted the importance of looking beyond simple income-expenditure models. He argued that balance sheet effects also shape macroeconomic responses to currency appreciation. He showed that a permanent appreciation increases real wealth and so reduces real savings, the reverse of the Laursen–Metzler. A temporary appreciation which raises only current income should increase savings.

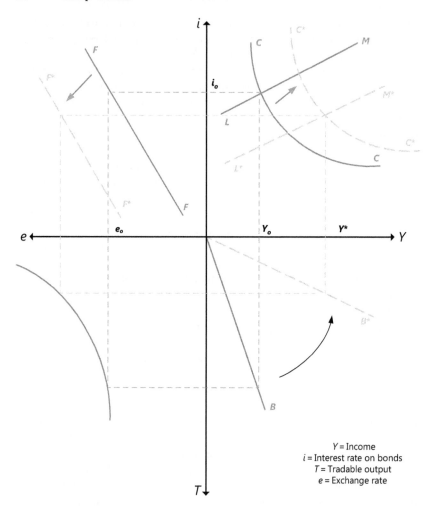

Figure 1.3 Bernanke–Blinder and Mundell–Fleming: The monetary and financial channels of terms-of-trade gains

the risk-taking channel of currency appreciation. Hofmann et al. (2016) have shown how currency appreciation in EMEs is indeed associated with a decline in the country's risk premium (i.e. lower sovereign credit default swap spreads): capital inflows tend to increase and the yields on local currency government bonds fall.

Faced with strong capital inflows, many central banks intervene on a large scale in the foreign exchange market. But buying foreign exchange increases central bank liabilities, usually with the banking system. Bank reserves rise and monetary policy becomes more expansionary (i.e. the LM shifts to the right), tending to drive down the interest rate on bonds. Historically, central banks have found it difficult to fully insulate domestic bank credit from very large and persistent purchases of foreign exchange without resorting to quantitative measures such as reserve requirements. Marcio Garcia (2011) has shown, also using the Bernanke–Blinder model, that selling bonds in order to restore the original interest rate still leaves banks with larger liabilities. Hence banks in this model expand loans in response to sterilised intervention. In any event, even greater holdings of government bonds – not just reserves – make banks' balance sheets more liquid. Gadanecz et al. (2014) find evidence that increased bank holdings of government bonds in EMEs has led to an expansion in bank credit to the private sector. Macroprudential policies with an exchange rate dimension (such as limiting foreign currency borrowing, increasing reserve requirements, capital account management policies, etc.) can support (and perhaps provide reliance on) forex intervention because they limit credit expansion and put downward pressure on the exchange rate (Pereira da Silva and Harris 2012).

There is of course a counterweight that could reverse this conclusion. Real currency appreciation reduces real net exports, driving down income (i.e. moving the CC curve towards the origin). Such competitiveness effects, however, take years to build up and may be weak in countries dependent on commodity exports. The initial impact of real currency appreciation (especially in a commodities boom) is often to increase gross fixed capital formation. This would move the CC curve outwards – and reinforce the impact of credit expansion. For many commodity producers, this effect of increased fixed investment seems to dominate at least for a few years the demand-depressing effect on the output of tradables of lower competitiveness. So capital inflows, the supply of credit, fixed investment and the exchange rate can all rise together when the real terms of trade improve.

A scenario where currency appreciation, forex intervention and domestic credit expansion go hand-in-hand is of more than academic interest. Many financial crises in the past have been preceded by periods when credit expansion and currency appreciation feed on each other. Gourinchas and Obstfeld (2012) report clear evidence that overvalued exchange rates during cyclical booms (with large capital inflows) increase the risk of financial crises. During such periods, policymakers will have to cope with expansionary appreciations. Once there is a 'sudden stop' in capital flows, the currency falls as the country is forced to rapidly correct its trade deficit by reducing income to match the (diminished) level of tradables output. The exchange rate often overshoots hurting these with currency mismatches. The three financial channels go into reverse, and may create what seems like a contractionary devaluation.[9]

A tightening of macroprudential policies during boom periods could counter such a dynamic. It would lower the interest rate on bonds and so drive down the exchange rate ($e$). This in turn increases the output of tradable goods, $T$. A tightening in bank lending standards reduces the demand for non-tradables. The trade deficit is reduced. It is easy to see that tightening monetary policy calibrated in a way to have the same impact on $Y$ as macroprudential tightening would lead to a larger full employment trade deficit because it would drive up the exchange rate and increase capital inflows.

Because a currency appreciation and sizable capital inflows can increase financial risk-taking, monetary tightening may be undesirable: the financial stability consequences of yet-further increases in the exchange rate can be damaging. This story is of course highly stylised – a starting point of analysis, not a final conclusion. The link between interest rates and the exchange rate is not stable or predictable enough to rely on for policy purposes, and in any case relies also on what is happening to 'foreign' short rates. Nothing has been said about the dynamics. The microeconomic impact of a regulatory tightening, which is usually greatest while private sector balance sheets are in the process of adjusting, tends to weaken over time. This may not matter because both financial market conditions and the macroeconomic situation tomorrow will be different from today. A reversal of upward pressure on the currency, for instance, would remove a constraint on raising policy rates so that monetary tightening could then supplement macroprudential tightening.

A deeper analysis would also have to assess the macroeconomic consequences as private agents try to find ways around policy action, be it in monetary policy or in regulatory policy. For instance, if domestic banks are constrained to apply tougher lending standards, borrowers may seek loans from banks abroad, sometimes in foreign currency. This will tend to drive up the exchange rate. This is similar to the consequences of raising the policy rate in local currency, which may induce some to switch to borrowing in foreign currency. Financial stability risks coming from currency mismatches would be aggravated, but – in the short term – borrowing in a depreciating currency will appear to be an attractive trade.

---

[9] See Agénor and Pereira da Silva (2013) for several case studies in emerging economies which illustrate well how monetary policy loses its effectiveness in dealing with the macroeconomic and financial stability risks from external shocks.

In such circumstances, tightening rules on currency mismatches (or on foreign borrowing) might be needed to prevent borrowers from escaping the intent of monetary tightening. Ozkan and Unsal (Chapter 6) argue convincingly that a separate macroprudential instrument is especially needed in economies with sizable foreign borrowing, because domestic monetary policy cannot influence the cost of foreign borrowing.

Several recent papers report simulations with general equilibrium models that tell a similar story as the stylised model. Such models demonstrate that the relative impact on the exchange rate is crucial in deciding between monetary tightening and macroprudential tightening. Using a general-equilibrium model, for instance, Alpanda et al. (2014) find that more targeted tools such as loan-to-value (LTV) regulations are more effective in reducing household debt at a lower cost in terms of GDP than raising the policy rate.[10] The logic is that tightening LTV regulations reduces GDP and inflation. As a central bank following a Taylor rule reduces the policy rate, the real exchange rate falls. This stimulates the demand for tradables. Ozkan and Unsal also use their small open economy general equilibrium model to show that a monetary policy response to a surge in capital outflows (decreasing the policy rate as aggregate demand weakens) can depreciate the currency and motivate more outflows. Mimir et al. (2015) develop a model in which banks have both foreign and domestic sources of funding: they analyse how counter-cyclical reserve requirements can affect real exchange rate developments and the volatility of credit spreads.

## 1.4     The Exchange Rate and Some Recent Policy Dilemmas

The short summary of the discussion in the previous section is that there are three possible financial channels through which currency appreciation or a terms-of-trade gain can lead to an expansion in credit:

- increased bank lending as banks see households and firms (especially those with foreign currency debts, common in EMEs) as better risks
- a lower country risk premium and stronger capital inflows
- monetary expansion in the wake of larger central bank balance sheets

This section considers how relevant such channels may have been in recent policy dilemmas.

---

[10] They report that a 5 percentage point reduction in the LTV lowers household debt by 7.6% at the peak and reduces output by 0.7%. In contrast, a 100 basis point rise in the policy rate would reduce household debt by only 0.5%, at an output cost of 0.4%.

Deflated by the US core CPI; 1990–99 = 100

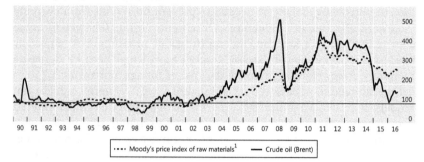

1 Made up of 15 commodities (cocoa, coffee, copper, cotton, hides, hogs, lead, maize, rubber, silk, silver, steel scrap, sugar, wheat and wool) weighted by the level of production or consumption in the United States.

Figure 1.4 Real commodity prices.
Source: Market data

The case of countries dependent on commodities has already been mentioned. Their exchange rate is bound to be driven up by strong rises in the price of their export commodity.[11] This had been a major force up to 2014, as real commodity prices have risen by a factor of three-to-four over their average level in the 1990s (Figure 1.4). Such price increases stimulate investment in commodity-producing and ancillary sectors. Moreover, the country's risk premium typically declines; higher export earnings give the country extra collateral. The consequences are sizable currency appreciation and credit expansion, including those through offshore borrowing. But the subsequent dramatic reversal of commodity prices (especially oil) has put the currencies of several commodity exporters under heavy downward pressure. This serves to illustrate how large changes in relative prices increase the risks of currency overvaluation and subsequent reversal.

In their model of a small open and commodity exporter economy, González et al. (2015) show how, in the commodity boom phase, real currency appreciation and credit growth in effect transfer net worth from the tradable to non-tradable sector. The authors argue that a macroprudential rule aimed at controlling total credit would perversely reinforce the misallocation of credit from the tradable to the non-tradable sector. To avoid this, they formulate a macroprudential forex

[11] For instance, Kohlscheen (2014) finds that a 10% increase in the real price of five commodities exported by Brazil increases the fundamental long-run real exchange rate by almost 5%, a large effect that dominates changes in interest rate differentials.

intervention rule as a function of the deviation of the real exchange rate from its long-run target.

Somewhat comparable forces may operate in non-commodity producing countries. Terms-of-trade gains of whatever source have a mechanical effect of stimulating private consumption in most models. A period of currency appreciation may even persuade households that their permanent income has risen. They feel they can borrow more, and then the banks think that local borrowers have become better risks. Borrowers with foreign currency debts (e.g. in an emerging market) see their balance sheets strengthen when the currency appreciates, and banks are willing to lend them more. Large currency appreciations may lower the 'perceived riskiness of loans', as Bernanke–Blinder put it. Historically, credit expansions and currency appreciation have indeed gone together, suggesting that they actually reinforce each other. The model developed by Bruno and Shin (2014) has currency appreciation making the balance sheets of local borrowers appear even stronger, encouraging banks to lend them even more. The paper by Ozkan and Unsal sheds further light on this issue, by showing that the *source* of borrowing in an economy – whether it is foreign or domestic – matters for any assessment of alternative policy responses to a financial market shock.

The classic response to a terms-of-trade gain and the greater willingness of banks to lend is for households to invest in houses. What if the stimulus to the demand for houses coming from an appreciated exchange rate dominates the restraint coming from higher interest rates? Paradoxically, investment in the non-tradable sector (notably houses) may actually rise following a tightening of monetary policy. If households can borrow in foreign currency while their income is in local currency (e.g. dollar-denominated mortgages in Latin America, Swiss franc mortgages in central Europe, etc.), the stimulus coming from currency appreciation is even stronger.

A central bank cannot be indifferent as to which component of aggregate demand it affects. Stimulating private consumption or house building will not help future growth as much as business fixed investment. Lower investment in tradables but increased investment in non-tradables makes a country more vulnerable to external shocks. Nor can central banks be indifferent about the nature of capital inflows attracted by higher rates. Raising the domestic short-term rates above levels prevailing in the main international markets may attract increased capital inflows into more shorter-term debt paper. Hence the structure of capital inflows becomes more volatile, potentially accentuating financial stability risks. Central banks with financial stability mandates have to worry about such external dimensions.

Assessing the sustainability threshold for the real exchange rate is very difficult. This is particularly true for economies with undiversified export structures (e.g. commodity exporters) because of long swings in relative prices in world markets. An overvalued exchange rate maintained for a prolonged period typically leads to large external debts, which makes the country's external position unsustainable.

The conclusion from this analysis is that the combination of over-valued house prices (requiring a higher policy rate) and an overvalued exchange rate (requiring a lower policy rate) presents the central bank with a dilemma. The Governor of the Reserve Bank of New Zealand recently noted that the IMF considered New Zealand house prices to be overvalued by around 25 per cent – and the real effective exchange rate was about 18 per cent above its fifteen-year average (Wheeler, 2013). The Reserve Bank has noted that it introduced macropruden-tial measures in October 2013 to counter further rapid house price inflation, given that it was not appropriate to raise interest rates because 'annual CPI was running at 0.7%, the exchange rate was strong, and there [was] a negative output gap' (Wheeler, 2014). By reducing housing market pressures, these macroprudential measures allowed the Reserve Bank 'to delay the tightening of interest rates, thereby reducing the incentive for any additional capital inflows into the New Zealand dollar.'

The Bank of England faced a similar dilemma in the first half of the 2000s (Figure 1.5). The United Kingdom began the decade with sterling overvalued and house price inflation very strong. The Bank of England's Monetary Policy Committee in February 2000 agreed that, 'it would be preferable to have a lower exchange rate and higher interest rates from the point of view of economic conditions and balance more generally.' The Committee decided to raise Bank rate by 25 basis points and considered, but rejected, forex intervention. With mounting losses and closures in the tradable sector (especially manufacturing), the central bank came under strong pressure from businesses and unions to cut interest rates and lower the exchange rate (Brittan, 2000).

Given strong domestic demand and continued rises in house prices, however, UK Bank rate did not follow the sharp cuts in the Federal funds rate during 2001. By mid-2001, the United Kingdom had the highest real short-term interest rate in the G7. And UK rates remained 200 basis points or more above US rates until mid-2005. This sustained a substan-tial appreciation of sterling against the dollar, and the real effective exchange rate remained well above historical levels. What prevented the

UK Bank rate and US Federal Funds rate
Per cent

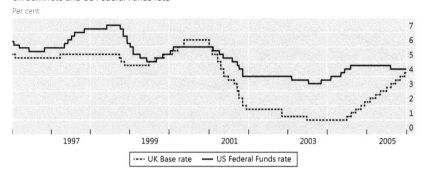

Per GBP                                                    Index

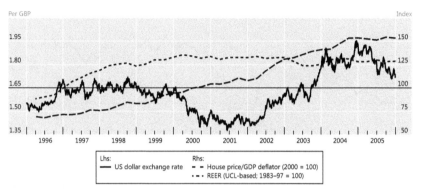

Figure 1.5 Policy rates, UK house prices and the exchange rate.
Source: National data

Bank of England from following US rates was not the risk of failing to meet their inflation target but worries about the apparently inexorable rise in house prices – and the rising household indebtedness associated with it. At that time of course the Bank of England had no macroprudential instrument at its disposal.

A strong real exchange rate has led central banks (or governments) in many emerging markets to put greater emphasis on macroprudential policies, sometimes raising the policy rate less than appears warranted by domestic conditions. Hofmann and Bogdanova (2012) show that the average real policy rate in the EMEs has been somewhat below that implied by a Taylor rule since 2003, and was well below that level in 2010 and 2011. Figure 1.6 from the Bruno et al. (2015) study covering twelve Asia-Pacific economies shows that strong growth and inflation pressure led to rises in policy rates in the mid-2000s. One consequence,

(a)

The policy rate cycle[1]                                                    Per cent

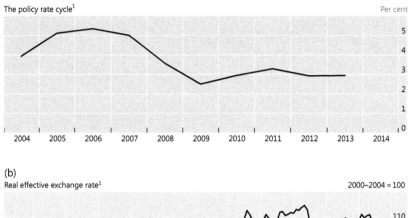

(b)

Real effective exchange rate[1]                                    2000–2004 = 100

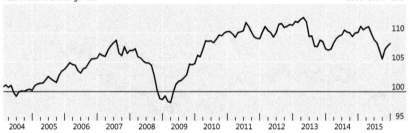

(c)

Macroprudential policy cycles[2]                              Number of measures

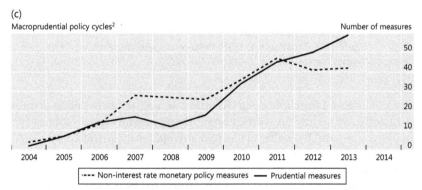

---- Non-interest rate monetary policy measures  ── Prudential measures

[1] Simple average of policy rates for 12 Asia-Pacific economies. [2] Cumulative sum of tightening actions (+1) and loosening actions (-1) taken by 12 Asian-Pacific economies.

Figure 1.6 Monetary policy, macroprudential measures and the real exchange rate in Asia.
Sources: Bruno et al. (2014; panels A and C); national data

however, was a sharp real exchange rate appreciation. As growth strengthened after 2009 and there was a renewed rise in their exchange rates, much greater reliance was therefore placed on macroprudential measures.[12]

## 1.5    Macroprudential Policies and the Central Bank's Balance Sheet

The central bank's balance sheet can be important in influencing bank lending. Central bank liabilities are usually assets for the private sector, normally the banks. When a central bank's balance sheet is very large – whether because of forex intervention or the purchase of domestic assets to counter recession – so too is the balance sheet of the commercial banking system. Even in normal times, the central bank throughout history has been the bank for banks (Billi and Vredin, 2014). Charles Goodhart has argued many times that the central bank could use its own balance sheet to implement macroprudential policy. He argues that the existence of financial frictions, of asymmetric information, of externalities and systemic effects means that the central bank's ability to buy (or sell) claims on the private sector is their 'first macroprudential instrument' (Goodhart, 2011). Such transactions could be used to provide reassurance during panics. Or they could be used to signal disapproval of riskier paper generated during booms: historically, this has been an important function of central bank discounting practices. In a similar vein, Jean-Pierre Landau (Chapter 2) argues that the use of reserves requirements can give macroprudential policy an important systemic liquidity-oriented dimension. Mervyn King (King, 2016) extends these ideas: he proposes that the central bank be the pawn-broker for all seasons, ready to lend to banks against a pre-agreed set of illiquid and risky assets at a pre-agreed haircut.

It is mainly in the emerging markets that macroprudential measures have had close links to the central bank's balance sheet. A particularly important instance is the extensive use of reserve requirements. Heavy and prolonged central bank purchases of foreign exchange had made commercial bank balance sheets in many EMEs too liquid. They therefore raised reserve requirements to counter excess liquidity within the banking system. Differential reserve requirements were also imposed to

---

[12] The IMF has carried out a similar major study, but covering more countries; They cover 353 episodes of policy tightening and 125 episodes of policy loosening in 46 countries (see Zhang and Zoli, 2014).

influence the composition of bank balance sheets (e.g. to combat the dollarisation of local banking systems).

In the advanced economies, by contrast, banks' balance sheets were found, during the financial crisis, to have been too illiquid. Requiring banks to hold a higher proportion of their own balance sheets in liquid assets – as in Basel III – will have implications for the central bank's balance sheet. Because of new regulations requiring financial institutions to have more liquid balance sheets than before the recent financial crisis, the central bank may have to leave more 'liquidity in the financial system on a permanent basis', to use the words of Joe Gagnon and Brian Sack (2014). Jean-Pierre Landau (2015) makes a persuasive case for liquidity regulation as an effective counter-cyclical tool.

Ben Friedman (2014) has argued that the central bank's standard toolkit in normal times is now likely to include its own balance sheet, and not just the policy rate as was the fashion before the crisis.[13] Could the central bank's balance sheet, so useful in correcting dysfunctional markets during slumps, be used to temper over-exuberance during booms? Quantification of the monetary and prudential ramifications of the size and nature of the central bank's balance sheet has been much debated over the years, without any consensus emerging. One lesson of the crisis is that central banks can easily miss latent threats to financial stability if they focus only on short-term interest rates and ignore sizable changes in monetary quantities. A former Deputy Governor of the Bank of England made this crystal clear in a speech before the recent crisis broke (Tucker, 2007). There is also a vigorous debate about how to avoid the trap of a too-active use of central bank balance sheets compromising efficient market functioning.[14]

## 1.6     The Long-Term Interest Rate

The market-determined interest rate on bonds that is linked to the attitude of banks to lending is central to the Bernanke–Blinder analysis. How macroprudential policies could influence market interest rates is a

[13] David Green (2011) argued that policy tools concerned with financial imbalances 'would be entirely familiar to central bankers of earlier decades as part of their monetary policy toolkit ... [including] interest rate ceilings, variable reserve requirements, "window guidance", "corsets", monetary aggregate targeting or capital controls. What central bankers of the past would find much odder was the fact that "monetary policy", at least in some countries, became much more narrowly [focused] than in the past ... purely on price stability, regardless of the condition of the financial system.'

[14] Exit from extraordinarily large central bank balance sheets presents major challenges (Turner, 2015).

very useful question. Economists are often tempted to evade this question by assuming that 'interest rates are determined by monetary policy'. They often fall back on the expectations theory of interest rates, even if this has been falsified by events over the past decade.

We need to think much harder about the determinants of the long-term rate. Many studies have established that, during the past twenty years, long-term interest rates in an increasing number of countries have become more dependent on yields in global bond markets. As capital controls or regulatory limits have been progressively relaxed, international investors now have more influence over the long-term interest rate than the central bank in most economies. Many studies over the years have found that changes in long-term rates of industrial countries are much more correlated across countries than are short-term rates. Obstfeld (2015) finds that a 100 basis point change in the foreign long-term rate leads to a 40 basis point change in the local long-term rate in his sample of emerging markets. A central bank cannot set its own long-term rate even if it has a flexible exchange rate.

Mervyn King and David Low (2014) used advanced economy bond market data to construct an estimate of the 'world' real long-term interest rate, shown in Figure 1.7, panel A. Movements in the yield on ten-year US Treasuries dominate this 'world' interest rate. But it is not true that developments in the United States determine this world rate. US yields themselves respond to global, and not just US, forces. This is because of the extensive use of US dollars in financial contracts between non-US residents that have little or nothing to do with the US economy. US dollar credit to non-bank borrowers outside the United States now exceeds $9 trillion – up from $6 trillion at the start of 2010 (McCauley et al., 2015). In addition, a much larger portion of credit for the US economy comes from abroad than in the past. Mendoza and Quadrini (2010) show that, by the end of 2008, about one-fifth of total net credit liabilities of the US nonfinancial sector was held by agents outside the United States.

The real world long-term interest rate has been falling for more than a decade and is now close to zero. Panel B of the figure, based on calculations from Hördahl et al. (2016), shows that this has been largely driven by a compression of the term premium – the reward for holding long-dated rather than short-dated bonds.[15] In the early 1990s, the term

---

[15] The expectations theory of the interest rate assumes that bonds of different maturities are perfectly substitutable. Arbitrage would ensure that (a) the interest rate on a $n$-period bond equals (b) the (geometric) average of the interest rates on $n$ consecutive one-period bonds. The term premium is the difference between (a) and (b) and rewards the investor for holding longer-dated bonds.

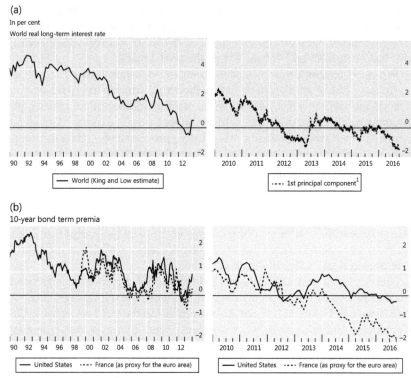

Figure 1.7 The long-term interest rate.
Sources: King and Low (February 2014); national data

premium was around 300 basis points. Then from 1994 to 2003 it was around 150 basis points. Global recession, Quantitative Easing, and a flight to 'safe' assets such as US Treasuries has made it negative in recent years. The euro area's term premium (Panel C, Figure 1.7) has fallen below that on US Treasuries. During much of 2014, lower euro area yields seem to pull down US Treasury yields even as prospects of stronger US growth, higher policy rates and the end of new bond purchases by the Federal Reserve should have pushed yields higher. Even the United States cannot escape the 'world' interest rate.

Understanding the drivers of the term premium and not using the expectations theory of the interest rate to sweep it under the carpet, is a huge present challenge for economists. It is hard to overstate the importance of this because the long-term interest rate is fundamental for financial stability. It provides, first, the discount rate to value the stream of expected earnings of all long-lived assets. Other things equal, a reduction in the long-term rate would tend to raise house prices, equity prices and so on. Hence the level of long-term rates is central to any analysis of asset prices. Second, it provides the risk-free benchmark for financial intermediaries such as pension funds which hold assets in order to meet future long-term liabilities. When long-term rates fall, the steady-state pension from a given stock of assets declines.[16] Funds that cannot cut the pensions they pay may build up losses, and UK corporate pensions have indeed reported mounting funding deficits. And, third, it defines the terms of maturity transformation. Flat near-term yield curves encourage banks and others to extend maturity mismatches in a search for yield.

Collateral practices reinforce the importance of the long-term rate. A rise in bond and other asset prices raises the value of the assets held by borrowers, which can be pledged as collateral. Hence liquidity constraints are eased.

Very low long-term real interest rates at the global level may well be suitable for advanced economies where the scope for productivity growth is limited and with a sizable retired population holding a large stock of financial assets. But developing countries – where real income per head is growing more rapidly and marginal investment returns are higher – would, in a closed economy, have a higher long-term rate. To avoid excessive (and perhaps volatile) debt inflows, the domestic authorities may want to restrict non-resident flows into local debt markets, long as well as short. When global macroeconomic variables are so far away from their long-run equilibrium levels, there may be good second-best arguments for such restrictions.[17]

Several observers (for example, BIS, 2009) have made a lucid case for regarding deliberate capital account management – as opposed to a laissez-faire stance – as an essential element of macroprudential policies in EMEs. How to do this whilst maintaining the benefits of international capital mobility – in disciplining governments as well as private firms – is one challenge. In practice, restrictions often can be evaded by moving

---

[16] When long-term rates fall, pension funds will normally benefit from a one-time rise in the market value of their financial assets. But the present discounted value of their liabilities (which typically have a longer duration) would rise more in most cases.

[17] The general theory of the second best is that the presence of widespread distortions means that removing just one distortion (e.g. a specific restriction on capital movements) does not necessarily enhance overall welfare. This argues against a fully laissez-faire attitude to capital flows: see BIS (2009).

42     Philip Turner

financial transactions offshore, which could make risks worse by obscuring exposures.

### Conclusion

Any analysis of macroprudential policies must take account of the impact on market-determined interest rates, which are not simply determined by monetary policy. The Bernanke–Blinder analysis of the closed economy case is very helpful in showing how macroprudential policies can affect interest rates.

But in an open economy, it is the impact on capital flows and on the exchange rate of alternative policies – in particular, the choice between monetary and macroprudential policy – that will often be decisive. An overvalued exchange rate can increase financial risk-taking through many channels. A central bank contemplating an increase in its policy rate on domestic grounds will have to weigh the financial stability risk of exacerbating exchange rate overvaluation.

Paul Tucker (2014b) has observed, commenting on Jeremy Stein's famous phrase about monetary policy getting into all the cracks, that, in an open economy, 'domestic monetary policy does **not** [his emphasis] penetrate all risk-taking channels and institutions.' Extremely easy global financial conditions – as today – can push the long-term rate in countries with open capital accounts and a flexible exchange rate far below their domestic long-term equilibrium levels. Global liquidity is in many ways the quantity dual of low real interest rates. Landau (2013) has pointed to several channels of transmission of global liquidity to domestic financial markets. As with convergence forces on long-term rates, such channels apply irrespective of the exchange rate regime because international investors move from one market to another when they see risk-adjusted yield differentials emerge. Domestic macroeconomic policies may not be able to do much about such mechanisms of transmission. Macroprudential policies aimed at domestic credit and at foreign borrowing may on occasion be the best option open to the authorities of small countries.

### References

Agénor, P. and L. A. Pereira da Silva (2013). *Inflation targeting and financial stability*, IDB and CEMLA. Washington DC.
Allen, W. A. (2015). 'Asset choice in British central banking history, the myth of the safe asset, and bank regulation', *Journal of Banking and Financial Economics*, vol 2, no 4, 18–31.

Alpanda, S., G. Cateau and C. Meh (2014). 'A policy model to analyze macroprudential regulations and monetary policy', *Bank of Canada Working Paper*, no 2014–6, February.

Angelini, P., S. Neri and F. Panetta (2014). 'The interaction between capital requirements and monetary policy', *Journal of Money, Credit and Banking*, vol 46, no 6, 1073–1112.

Bank for International Settlements (BIS) (2009). *Capital flows to emerging market economies*. (A report of a Working Group chaired by Rakesh Mohan). *CGFS Papers*, no 33. Basel: Bank for International Settlements, January. www.bis.org/publ/cgfs33.htm.

(2014). 'The transmission of unconventional monetary policy to the emerging markets', *BIS Papers*, no 78, August.

(2016). 'Macroprudential policy' *BIS Papers*. No 86. September

Bernanke, B. S. and A. S. Blinder (1988). 'Credit, money and aggregate demand', *American Economic Review*, Paper and proceedings, May, 435–439.

Bernanke, B. S. and M. Gertler (1995). 'Inside the black box: The credit channel of monetary policy transmission', *Journal of Economic Perspectives*, Fall, 27–48.

Billi, R. M. and A. Vredin (2014). 'Monetary policy and financial stability – A simple story', *Sveriges Riksbank Economic Review*, no 2, 7–22.

Boivin, J., M. Kiley and F. Mishkin (2010). 'How has the monetary transmission mechanism evolved over time?' in *Handbook of Monetary Economics*, 1st ed., vol 3, eds. Friedman, B. M. and Woodford, M., 369–422, Elsevier, Amsterdam.

Brittan, S. (2000). 'Beware the politics of sterling', *Financial Times*, 13 April.

Bruno, V., I. Shim and H. S. Shin (2015). 'Comparative assessment of macroprudential policies', *BIS Working Papers*, no 502, June.

Bruno, V. and H. S. Shin (2014). 'Cross-border banking and global liquidity', *BIS Working Papers*, no 458, August.

(2015). 'Capital flows and the risk-taking channel of monetary policy', *Journal of Monetary Economics*, vol 71, 119–132.

Friedman, B. M. (2014). 'Has the financial crisis permanently changed the practice of monetary policy? Has it changed the theory of monetary policy?', *NBER Working Paper*, no 20128, May.

Gadanecz, B., A. Mehrotra and M. S. Mohanty (2014). 'Foreign exchange intervention and the banking system balance sheet in emerging market economies', *BIS Working Papers*, no 415, March.

Gagnon, J. E. and B. Sack (2014). 'Monetary policy with abundant liquidity: A new operating framework for the Federal Reserve', Policy Brief PB14–4. Peterson Institute for International Economics, January.

Galati, G. and R. Moessner (2014). 'What do we know about the effects of macroprudential policy?', *DNB Working Paper*, no 440, September.

Garcia, M. (2011). 'Can sterilized FX purchases under inflation targeting be expansionary?' Pontificia Universidade Catolica do Rio de Janeiro. Department of Economics, no 589.

González, A., F. Hamann and D. Rodríguez (2015). 'Macroprudential policies in a commodity exporting economy', *BIS Working Papers*, no 506, July.

44 Philip Turner

Goodhart, C. (2011). *The macro-prudential authority: Powers, scope and accountability.* LSE Financial Markets Group. Special Paper no 203. October.

Gourinchas, P.-O. and M. Obstfeld (2012). 'Stories of the twentieth century for the twenty-first', *American Economic Journal: Macroeconomics*, vol 4, no 1, 226–265.

Green, D. (2011). 'The relationship between the objectives and tools of macroprudential and monetary policy', Financial Markets Group. London School of Economics. *Special Paper*, no 200, May.

Hofmann, B. and B. Bogdanova (2012): "Taylor rules and monetary policy: A global Great Deviation?" *BIS Quarterly Review*, September, 37–49.

Hofmann, B., I. Shim and H. S. Shin (2016). 'Sovereign yields and the risk-taking channel of currency appreciation', *BIS Working Papers* no 538, January.

Hoogduin, L. (2014). ' How to use the instruments of macroprudential policy.' Duisenberg School of Finance, Policy Brief no 33, July.

Hördahl, P. , J. Sobrun and P. Turner (2016). "Low long-term interest rates as a global phenomenon" *BIS Working Paper* no 574, August.

Jeanne, O. (2014). 'Macroprudential policies in a global perspective', *NBER Working Paper*, no 19967, March.

King, M. (2016). *The end of alchemy: Money, banking and the future of the global economy.* W. W. Norton & Company, Ltd, London.

King, M. and D. Low (2014). 'Measuring the "world" real interest rate', *NBER Working Paper*, no 19887, February.

Kohlscheen, E. (2014). 'Long-run determinants of the Brazilian Real: A closer look at commodities', *International Journal of Finance & Economics*, vol 19, no 4, 239–250.

Kohn, D. (2014). 'Federal Reserve independence in the aftermath of the financial crisis: Should we be worried?', *Hutchins Center on Fiscal and Monetary Policy*. Brookings Institution, Washington, DC.

Korinek, A. and A. Simsek (2016). 'Liquidity trap and excessive leverage', *American Economic Review*, vol 106 no 3, 699–738.

Landau, J.-P. (2013). 'Global liquidity: Public and private', Proceedings. Jackson Hole Economic Policy Symposium. Federal Reserve Bank of Kansas City, 223–259.

McCauley, R. N., P. McGuire and V. Sushko (2015). 'Global dollar credit: Links to US monetary policy and leverage', *BIS Working Papers*, no 483, January.

Mendoza, E. G. and V. Quadrini (2010). 'Financial globalization, financial crises and contagion', *Journal of Monetary Economics*, 24–39.

Mimir, Y. and E. Surel (2015). 'External shocks, banks and monetary policy in an open economy', *BIS Working Papers*, no 528, November.

Nickell, S. (2004). 'Household debt, house prices and consumption growth', speech at Bloomberg, London, 14 September, Bank of England.

Obstfeld, M. (1982). 'Aggregate spending and the terms of trade: Is there a Laursen–Metzler effect?' *Quarterly Journal of Economics*, vol 97, no 2, 251–270.

(2015). 'Trilemmas and tradeoffs: Living with financial globalisation', *BIS Working Papers*, no 480, January.

Pereira da Silva, L. A. and R. Harris (2012). 'Sailing through the global financial storm: Brazil's recent experience with monetary and macroprudential policies', *Central Bank of Brazil Working Paper*, no 290, August.

Portes, R. (2014). 'Macroprudential policy and monetary policy', in *Macroprudentialism*. Ed D. Schoenmaker. Centre for Economic Policy and Research, Washington, DC.

Rotemberg, J. (2014). 'The Federal Reserve's abandonment of its 1923 principles', *NBER Working Paper*, no 20507, September.

Tucker, P. (2007). 'Central banking, and political economy', Speech at Cambridge, 15 June, Bank of England.

(2014a). 'Regulatory reform, stability and central banking'. *Hutchins Center on Fiscal and Monetary Policy*. Brookings Institution, Washington, DC.

(2014b). 'A new constitution for money (*and* credit policy)', Myron Scholes Lecture. Chicago School of Business, 22 May.

Turner, P. (2015). 'The consequences of exit from non-conventional monetary policy', *Journal of Financial Perspectives*, vol 3, no 2, 43–59.

(2016). 'Macroprudential policies, the long-term interest rate and the exchange rate', *BIS Working Papers*, no 588, October.

(2017). "Did central banks cause the last financial crisis? Will they cause the next?" London School of Economics. Financial Markets Group. Special Paper 249.

Wheeler, G. (2013). 'Factors affecting the New Zealand economy and policy challenges around the exchange rate and the housing market', speech to the Institute of Directors, Auckland, 30 May, Reserve Bank of New Zealand.

(2014). 'Cross-border financial linkages – Challenges for monetary policy and financial stability', BIS/RBNZ Conference on Cross Border Financial Linkages, Wellington, 23 October.

Zhang, L. and E. Zoli (2014). 'Leaning against the wind: Macroprudential policy in Asia', *IMF Working Paper*, no 11/22, February.

# 2    A Liquidity-Based Approach to Macroprudential Policy[*]

*Jean-Pierre Landau*

## Introduction

Macroprudential policy has two purposes: (1) increase the resilience of the financial system as a whole – as opposed to individual institutions; and (2) regulate the financial cycle. Significant progress has been made on the first part. The set of reforms imbedded in Basel III have created a more robust financial environment. The second objective is very much a work in progress. Thousands of pages have been written on counter-cyclical macroprudential tools. Very few measures have actually been taken, most of them with very traditional tools, such as loan-to-value ratios and margin requirements.

A cyclical approach to macroprudential policy presents major challenges for central banks and supervisors as it necessitates a comprehensive and operational view of the interactions between the financial system and monetary policy.

This challenge had been neglected in recent decades, when inflation targeting was the dominant monetary policy framework in advanced and emerging economies. Inflation targeting is associated with a neo-Keynesian model where monetary policy acts only – and directly – through interest rates. There is no role for the financial sector. Changes in (nominal and real) interest rates are transmitted to the economy through a simple, inter-temporal substitution effect whereby they induce expenditures shifting across time. Money and financial institutions play no role in that mechanism, and credit is implicitly supposed to respond only to interest rate movements.

Obviously, ignoring the financial sector does not provide a realistic description of the economy. The paradox is that inflation targeting has been extremely successful. That success may be partially attributed to the

[*] I am deeply indebted to Philip Turner for numerous suggestions, advice and guidance in preparing this paper. He suggested many new ideas and improvements. All errors are mine only.

absence of significant economic volatility during the 'Great Moderation'. Moving policy rates may suffice to stabilize the economy when small shocks move it not far away from equilibrium; they may prove inadequate to face the big non-linear discontinuities that have characterised the Great Recession.

Financial frictions matter both for financial stability and for the transmission of monetary policy. However there is a difficulty. From a monetary policy point of view, the objective is to eliminate frictions that impair the transmission mechanism. From a financial stability point of view, however, the very purpose of a cyclical macroprudential policy is to introduce frictions in order to prevent the build-up of imbalances. Reconciling those two objectives requires a management of the financial system that makes policy makers uncomfortable and may prove extremely difficult to achieve. Trade-offs are not easy to define, even theoretically.

The behaviour of the financial system involves a constant interaction between leverage on the one hand and maturity transformation on the other. Both have an impact on the financial cycle and both contribute to monetary transmission. Financial fragility is the product of such interactions. And, logically, macroprudential policy should aim at regulating both leverage and maturity transformation.

This is what Basel III aims to achieve by strengthening both capital and liquidity requirements. But there is an asymmetry. Whereas capital requirements have a cyclical objective (through the countercyclical buffer), this is not the case for liquidity ratios. This paper argues that this is the reason why little progress has been made in regulating the credit and financial cycle. Current macroprudential policies rely too exclusively on the direct control of leverage. That may be appropriate if the objective is to increase the resilience of the financial system to systemic shocks. But it is not very efficient if the aim is to moderate the financial cycle. By contrast, measures that act on liquidity and maturity transformation directly would contribute to greater efficiency and flexibility. It would also make interaction with monetary policy much easier to manage. Both the framework and the tools for cyclically regulating liquidity inside the financial system are currently available. They may prove especially useful and efficient over the next period when 'the balance sheets of central banks are expected to stay large in proportion of domestic GDP in advanced and emerging economies'.

## Leverage Regulation: An Imperfect Cyclical Tool

Can a macroprudential approach to leverage help in controlling the overall credit cycle? If yes, the benefits would be obvious. As noted by

Turner in Chapter 1, independently acting on the credit channel would give monetary policy an additional degree of freedom – and efficiency. It would enable authorities to more directly target domestic demand, and avoid unwanted side-effects that monetary policy triggers through exchange rate appreciation (depreciation).

The cyclical component in the behaviour of leverage over time is well documented. It is associated with the measure and perception of risk (Adrian and Shin, 2009). It seems therefore natural to counteract this natural procyclicality by moving capital requirements over time. This is the rationale for the countercyclical capital buffer created by Basel III.

Practically, however, there are reasons to doubt whether an aggregate leverage control can be efficiently used to smooth out the credit cycle. There may be three difficulties.

First, co-ordination problems will arise. Under some circumstances it has been shown (Cecchetti and Kohler, 2012) that capital requirements and interest rates are perfect substitutes as monetary tools. There is a distinct possibility that monetary and macroprudential policies pull in opposite directions, thereby nullifying each other and creating unwanted side effects in the financial system.

Second, there is considerable uncertainty about leads and lags. Under Basel III, the implementation lag could be quite long: banks will have up to twelve months to comply with a countercyclical buffer. How much longer will it take to effectively act on credit distribution? We don't really know. There is not enough experience to assess the elasticity of credit aggregates to changing capital requirements. Recent attempts to act more directly on the marginal capital ratio through 'funding for lending' schemes (that carried zero capital requirements for new credits) have not been considered as fully successful.

Finally, there is a calibration issue. One characteristic of capital ratios as cyclical tools is that the denominator is composed of long-term (slow rotation) assets. Cyclical changes in the overall capital ratios will generally take place after credit decisions have been taken. They will therefore only affect the marginal (not average) profitability of leverage. While this increases efficiency, the impact can be quite brutal and this may inhibit authorities in taking the necessary measures.

Countercyclical capital requirements will be rule-based. In theory, banks can anticipate their evolution and adjust ex ante their credit behaviour. However, because rules will necessarily refer to aggregate (credit) quantities, banks would have to assess the behaviour of all other intermediaries, which – in a competitive environment – opens the way for many possibilities of strategic interactions and multiple equilibria.

Taking into account those practical difficulties, it may be more efficient to regulate the cyclical component of leverage may be at the sector and instrument levels (through haircuts, loan to value [LTV] ratios and minimum margins). Geneakoplos (2010) lists several advantages of such an approach. Different securities include different amounts of 'embedded leverage'. The leverage of an investor is often a meaningless number, for instance when losses reduce equity and arithmetically increase leverage (additional prudential action may, in this case, aggravate the situation). A focus on securities leverage would lead to better control of derivatives. More generally, it is harder to hide securities leverage than investor leverage.

Overall, aggregate capital ratios should best be left to fulfil their essential function, as buffers against unexpected losses. And cyclical regulation of credit may be best achieved by other tools.

The next section makes the case that liquidity – and maturity transformation – dynamics are an important – maybe dominant – driver of the credit cycle. Therefore, if authorities were able to cyclically 'regulate' liquidity they may have a powerful tool to prevent the build-up of financial imbalances.

## Liquidity and Maturity Transformation Drive Leverage[1]

When discussing liquidity, an important distinction is traditionally be made between inside liquidity – created between private economic agents – and outside liquidity, provided by the official sector. In this paper, a more restrictive definition of inside liquidity is given and the term refers to liquidity created inside the financial sector (excluding non-financial firms). That definition broadly overlaps Shin's concept of 'non-core' liabilities (Hamh et al., 2012).

To identify channels for macroprudential action, it is useful to have a (very) stylized vision on the inner workings of the financial system. The following description draws heavily on recent literature and proceeds in three steps.

First, there are obvious and close links between maturity transformation, funding liquidity and leverage. Maturity transformation makes leverage profitable: there are no benefits in borrowing and lending with the same maturity (i.e. at the same interest rate). Liquidity makes

---

[1] Here, the words 'maturity transformation' are used in a very loose sense to designate three possible transformations: from short-term to long-term; from safe to risky; and from liquid to illiquid assets.

leverage possible, as asset growth is naturally constrained by the amount of liquidity that intermediaries can access.

Second, recent research and literature has shown how liquidity itself is endogenously created inside the financial system. Banks create private (inside) money by issuing short-term instruments that are accepted by other financial intermediaries. The process is commonly known as 'funding'. In economies where 'shadow banks' and securitization play an important role, financial intermediaries permanently both issue and trade very short-term debt instruments especially through repo markets operations. Intermediation is organized through a 'long chain' of financial institutions, with new liquidity created at each and every step, together with progressive maturity transformation. That mechanism allows maturity transformation and, at the same time, fuels leverage. As a result, 'an important fraction of private money creation now takes place entirely outside of the formal banking sector, via the large volumes of short-term collateralised claims created in the "shadow banking" sector' (Gorton and Metrick 2010).

This process ensures the smooth functioning of credit markets, but also creates potential fragility (maturity mismatch) and drives the endogenous expansion of balance sheets. If funding is easy, maturity transformation is inexpensive and can seem riskless. As a consequence, leverage grows. It is therefore no exaggeration to say that liquidity drives leverage[2].

The next step is to understand that liquidity moves endogenously with risk appetite. Again, this well documented in recent research. To quote Brunnermeier (2014): 'funding is not an input'. It is the result of a dynamic process depending on the (time-varying) propensity of intermediaries to take counterparty risk on each other. When inside liquidity dried up during the crisis, credit stopped. Because it depends on risk perception and appetite, there is also a strong 'cyclical' component in inside liquidity and this cyclical component is subsequently reflected in the evolution of leverage.

Overall, a stylized description of cyclicality would go as follows. Depending on the policy rate and their risk appetite, financial intermediaries engage into reciprocal transactions, some of them very short-term through which they issue and accumulate claims on each other. Those transactions may be secured or unsecured. In the process, they simultaneously create (destroy) 'inside' liquidity and expand (contract) their balance sheets.

---

[2] One would conjecture further that *expectations* on the availability of future funding liquidity drive decisions on leverage.

As a result, the consolidated balance sheet of the financial sector can expand or contract for a given level of the interest rate. In turn, it can be shown the size of the financial system's balance sheet determines credit, risk premia, asset prices and overall financial conditions (Adrian and Shin, 2010).

From a monetary policy point of view, money (and credit) multipliers may be highly unstable as leveraging and de-leveraging takes place independently of policy rates. 'In this richer environment, monetary policy as it is conventionally practised is generally not sufficient to rein in excessive money creation' (Stein, 2011). From a macroprudential perspective, the main takeaway is that the dynamics of inside liquidity and maturity transformation ultimately drive leverage and the financial cycle. It is therefore natural to look at the possibility and modalities of regulating liquidity and maturity transformation in a countercyclical fashion.

### Maturity Transformation, the Financial Cycle and Macroprudential Policy

Maturity transformation is a permanent fixture of our financial systems. Without maturity transformation, it would be impossible to reconcile the preferences of savers and investors. Capital allocation in the economy would be extremely inefficient. Maturity transformation also carries specific risks and is the source of major fragilities and negative externalities (runs on short-term liabilities possibly leading to fire sales of illiquid assets). Whatever their underlying causes, all crises develop start and amplify through a breakdown in intermediation and maturity transformation. The last one was no exception.

There are good reasons to try to limit the extent of maturity transformation through appropriate regulation. Basel III has marked major steps forward with the creation of the LCR and NSFR. Both ratios, in effect, put quantitative limits on maturity transformation performed by a specific bank. They do not, however, allow for cyclically adjusted constraints or requirements. While they permanently strengthen the resilience to idiosyncratic liquidity shocks, it is not their objective, nor their effect, to prevent the build-up of excessive maturity transformation across the system; nor do they provide an effective protection against aggregate liquidity shocks.

We can think of maturity transformation as a service provided by the financial sector, for which there is a demand, a supply and a price. Repressing demand may lead to massive unintended consequences. It may migrate in other, less secure, parts of the financial system. Or equilibrium could be reached at the wrong price. Because that price can be measured as the spread between safe/liquid and risky/illiquid assets, mispricing appears under different guises. For instance, safe assets can be overpriced and returns abnormally low. Alternatively, the implicit spread required to perform maturity and risk transformation may be very high, so that only those physical investments with very high expected returns would be undertaken. These are all symptoms currently observed in advanced economies where corporates are simultaneously piling up debt and cash reserves while investment rates are well below historical norms. One possible interpretation of this so-called disconnect between economic and financial risk taking, could be an insufficient supply of maturity (and risk) transformation. Reaching a proper equilibrium, therefore, is a matter of great importance for policy makers aiming at the best possible trade-off between efficiency and stability in the financial system.

A comprehensive analysis of the demand for – and supply of – maturity transformation is beyond the scope of this paper.[3] Some insights may help to grasp implications for macroprudential and monetary policies.

The demand for maturity transformation depends on a host of factors. There is, obviously, a strong structural component. How financial intermediation is organised defines the nature of our financial systems and how they perform maturity transformation: modalities are very different according to the length of the intermediation chain and to whether banks or capital markets are dominant.

Maturity transformation is also subject to discontinuous and sudden shocks. This is well known and extensively analysed in the literature. Tools exist to deal with those shocks. In policy terms, this is the 'raison d'être' of the lender of last resort.

Less deeply analysed are the cyclical variations in maturity transformation that may fuel the dynamics of leverage and, more generally, the financial cycles. The economic cycle, the slope of the yield curve and the risk appetite are potential causes for increased or decreased demand for maturity transformation. Economic uncertainty increases the demand for safe (liquid) assets, hence the demand for maturity transformation for given levels of credit and investment.

How should authorities react to those cyclical fluctuations? Borrowing from monetary theory literature, it may be said that the supply of maturity transformation must be elastic enough, but not too much. It has to be

---

[3] In particular, the determinants of supply will not be discussed, except to mention that it may be constrained by impaired bank balance sheets (insufficient capital) and/or by regulatory requirements.

elastic because the demand itself is time-varying. But excesses should be avoided, because they can lead to dangerous financial fragility.

Providing an elastic supply of maturity transformation would perform a double function. One is monetary. Maturity transformation, when done by banks, frequently involves money creation. Too low maturity transformation may therefore lead to insufficient supply of money and deflation (Brunnermeier and Sannikov, 2014).[4] The other is financial stability. An excess supply of maturity transformation may create financial fragility.

In theory, there should be, at any point in time, an optimal level of maturity transformation that would balance the benefits in efficiency against the costs in terms of financial fragility. In practice, the optimum has to be found by trial and error. For that reason, it is important for the authorities to have the tools to regulate permanently the amount of maturity transformation in the economy.

The two sets of such tools that are potentially available are discussed in the following sections.

First, central banks can step in and 'put their balance sheet at work' in undertaking maturity transformation on their own. They have done so extensively during the crisis. An important question is whether, with very large balance sheets, this may become a more permanent feature for managing the interactions between price and financial stability.

Second, central banks may influence the price of maturity transformation by creating a 'tax' through an appropriate system of reserve requirements and liquidity provision.

### The Central Bank's Balance Sheet as a Financial Stability Tool

By their nature, all central banks are engaged in maturity transformation. This role has traditionally been marginal, as their balance sheets – and the volume of reserves kept by banks – were small in proportion of the overall size of the financial sector in most countries. In addition, in many countries, the access of financial intermediaries to the central bank balance sheet is restricted. Assets acquired through open market operations have generally been very short-term.

Following the crisis, those balance sheets have considerably expanded and are now commensurate with the size of annual GDP. In addition to traditional refinancing operations through repos, central banks have

[4] Well-capitalized banks are therefore a necessary – maybe not sufficient – condition for an elastic supply of maturity transformation.

purchased long-term (and sometimes risky) assets in implementing unconventional monetary policies. Through various new facilities, they gained direct access to (until then) remote parts of the financial system. In that new environment, the role of central banks in financial intermediation and maturity transformation can hardly be ignored.

From a monetary policy perspective, the consequences are numerous. Through the asset side of their balance sheets, central banks have triggered portfolio rebalancing in the private sector and exerted significant influence on term premia, long-term rates and overall financial conditions. Although the precise quantitative impact remains a matter for discussion and debate, the existence and direction of such effects are widely recognized.

The financial stability impact is as important, if less advertised. Central banks are the ultimate issuers of redeemable liabilities. For many decades, before the crisis, this liquidity provision function had been 'passive' as central banks accommodated the demand for reserves at the policy interest rate. But, during and post-crisis period, the central banks' balance sheets have taken up an active role and carried out an intermediation function that the private sector was (temporarily) no longer capable of providing (Papadia, 2014). By actively providing outside liquidity, central banks have reduced the risk of market disruption, eliminated any uncertainty on funding and, ultimately, encouraged maturity transformation and risk-taking by all financial intermediaries (both banks and non banks).

Can those monetary and financial stability effects be independently managed in the future, when balance sheets will stay large?

In theory, the answer is positive. Central banks implement monetary policy through changes in policy interest rates (a 'price' effect). They also can influence financial stability through the amount of central bank money (reserves) dispensed to financial institutions (a 'quantity' effect). Although, in principle, one cannot control both prices and quantities, there are practical ways to make those instruments independent of each other. Paying interest on reserves or, more generally, implementing a 'corridor' or a 'floor' approach, enable central banks to dissociate the amount of liquidity they provide from the price attached to this liquidity provision (Goodhart, 2009). Thus, money can be 'divorced' from monetary policy, giving authorities an additional degree of freedom to pursue both price and financial stability objectives (Keister et al., 2008). The so-called 'separation principle' (between liquidity provision and monetary policy) should hold. Operational frameworks will be reinforced by the introduction of new instruments, such as overnight (and term) reverse repos that will allow more fine-tuning of liquidity in an environment of abundant excess reserves.

That approach has worked well until and during the crisis. Will it continue to do so when the times come to exit unconventional policies? Exit can be done in a number of different sequences, starting either by raising policy interest rates or reducing the size of central banks' balance sheets, or both. But exit to where? As noted by Turner (2015), there is no consensus on the 'new normal' for the balance sheets of central banks. Broadly speaking, there are two sets of (intertwined) arguments. One is on the size of balance sheets: should central banks try to come back to pre-crisis levels? Or will they accept as permanent the situation created by the legacy of the crisis and expanded assets and liabilities. The other argument is about instruments: will, in the future, central banks keep a diverse set of (conventional and unconventional) tools, therefore acting on different parts of the financial system (including long-term bonds rates)? Or will they rely only on the short-term policy rate, coming back to the 'benign neglect of the long-term rate' (Turner 2013) that has prevailed until the crisis?

Those fundamental policy choices matter enormously, of course, for the implementation of monetary policy. They are also matter for financial stability. The idea of using the central bank's balance sheet as a financial stability tool is increasingly accepted. Many analysts, however, still consider central banks' expanded role in financial intermediation as a necessary, but temporary evil. They long for a situation where interbank markets would return to their pre-crisis level of activity and functions. Other policy makers see merits for central banks in keeping expanded balance sheets for some time. An ample balance sheet is one way for the central bank to provide an elastic supply of safe asset (Bernanke, 2015) or, equivalently, an elastic supply of maturity transformation.

In all cases, there is near certainty that central banks' balance sheets will remain very large for a significant number of years. Such an unprecedented environment offers both new opportunities and new challenges in managing the interaction between monetary and financial stability policies. Shrinking balance sheets will have complex effects on the economy and the financial system. Term premia and long-term rates will be affected as well as the volume of central bank money and liquidity. It may be more difficult to disentangle monetary and financial stability policies.[5] Using all available tools will certainly help in managing the complex trade offs involved.

---

[5] One example of complexity is provided by the discussion of overnight reverse repo (see Frost et al. 2015). On the one hand, ONRP is very useful to withdraw excess reserves and keep fed fund rate close to the policy rates. On the other, concerns have been expressed that it would provide easy way to "flight to quality" and create or aggravate potential disturbances in the money markets.

## Reserve Requirements and Liquidity Regulation

As underlined in the previous section, what is needed is a regime of liquidity regulation that allows for cyclical action on inside liquidity and maturity transformation. It turns out that basis for such a regime exists in the literature and that instruments are potentially available. It rests upon three pillars: (1) the ability to impose reserve requirements on a broad range of short-term liabilities; (2) the use of interest on reserves as a separate and independent tool; and (3) the ability of the central bank to set the monetary policy rate separately from the remuneration of reserves.[6] The analytical foundations have been extensively developed in Stein (2012) and Kashyap and Stein (2012).

Reserve requirements (RR) introduce a wedge between market rates and funding costs. An intermediary that issues a short-term liability subject to RR would, in effect, pay an additional charge (a 'tax'). The weight would depend on the reserve coefficient and the interest rate paid on reserves (that has to be lower than the policy rate). In effect, the central bank would have three instruments available to pursue price and financial stability; two interest rates (the policy rate and the interest on reserves) and one coefficient (on reserve requirement). Depending on the structure of the financial system, for a given (monetary) policy rate, the authorities could choose to move one or the other two instruments to counter unwanted cyclical movements in maturity transformation. By doing so, the central bank can make maturity transformation more or less expensive, with very quick effect as, by assumption, those liabilities are very short-term and would have to be rolled over at high frequency.

Kashyap and Stein (2012) show how authorities can independently control the quantity of base money on the one hand and interest rates, on the other by decomposing the policy rate into the sum of two components: (1) the remuneration of compulsory reserves, and (2) an add-on representing the 'scarcity value' of reserves, borne out of their convenience yield. That second component can be controlled by adjusting the supply of reserves so that the overnight interbank market settles on the policy rate.

Kashyap and Stein (2012) note that the demand for maturity transformation depends on information that is not spontaneously available to supervisors (notably the return on long-term illiquid assets). One advantage of their system is that it would reveal the 'price' attached by financial

---

[6] Most EMEs actually operate under such a kind of framework except for, in most cases, paying interest on reserves.

intermediaries to maturity transformation and the availability of short-term liquidity. Supposing that supervisors are able to determine (or approximate) the optimal social cost of maturity transformation at any single point in time, they can react by adjusting (or not) the gap between the interest on reserves and the policy rate without changing the latter (i.e. by keeping the monetary stance as defined by the policy rate constant). In real life, the optimum may be unknown, but supervisors have the benefit of a long series of data and instant information on many market parameters (both prices and quantities). And what is required of them is to make sensible adjustments that would steer the financial system in the right direction, not to reach a perfectly determined optimal value.

## Further Considerations on Reserve Requirements

Prior to the crisis, compulsory reserve requirements had basically been abandoned by central banks in most advanced economies. They continued to exist at low rates in some jurisdictions – in the euro area, in particular – as an accessory tool of short-term liquidity management, helping the central bank to create a permanent excess demand for reserves.

The demise of compulsory reserves can be attributed to several causes. They are seen as a distortionary tax on bank intermediation, thus pushing maturity transformation into other, less secure, parts of the financial system. They seemed to relate to an outdated intellectual framework: the simplistic 'money multiplier approach' through which controlling banks' reserves would also ensure control of the money supply and (with constant velocity) help achieve price stability. Finally, of course, in an era of (very ample) excess reserves, compulsory requirements may seem redundant and superfluous.

The approach developed here takes a totally different tack. First compulsory reserves are used as a financial stability – not a monetary policy – tool. Second, there is no presumption of any stability of the money multiplier. On the contrary, as mentioned previously, endogenous fluctuations in the multiplier are taken as a defining feature of contemporary financial systems. Influencing those fluctuations is therefore a major intermediary objective for macroprudential policy. Finally, interest is paid on reserves, but the rate of interest may differ from the policy rate that the central bank wants to target for monetary policy purposes.

Obviously there would be numerous technical, practical and legal difficulties in implementing such a system, especially in deciding on the perimeter of liabilities subject to reserve requirements.[7] Basically, regulators would give themselves the right to influence the relative costs of different sources of funding. Yet, this is exactly what they have been doing recently with the creation of the LCR and the NSFR. These new ratios have the same 'taxing' and distortionary effect with less transparency. And they will probably lead to a lasting increase the demand for reserves as Gagnon and Sack (2014) have argued. But how far the demand for reserves will rise when these new instruments come into force is unknown. This instrument uncertainty itself creates a case for considering more direct measures such as varying required reserves. As compared to quantitative ratios, reserve requirements can be introduced and changed flexibly. They can be made to vary according to risk (for instance with higher coefficients for short-term or foreign currency deposits). Maturity transformation is now severely constrained by 'quantitative' tools. Using compulsory reserves in a flexible way would introduce a 'price' component in liquidity regulation that would increase the overall efficiency of macroprudential policy.

## Conclusion

Since the global financial crisis, considerable progress has been made in strengthening the resilience of financial systems. New regulations have created or increased capital and liquidity buffers, in effect quantitatively constraining leverage and maturity transformation especially in 'systemic' institutions.

This paper argues that those efforts could usefully be complemented by an additional 'pillar' for macroprudential policy, with the objective of regulating the financial cycle, preventing the build-up of imbalances and reducing the risk of financial fragility. The best approach is to cyclically regulate liquidity creation and maturity transformation inside the financial system as, ultimately, they drive the dynamics of leverage and credit supply. Central banks have the necessary tools. They can use their expanded balance sheets to bring some elasticity in the supply of maturity transformation in the economy. They can also put a price on maturity transformation by financial intermediaries through a flexible use of reserve requirements and interest paid on reserves.

---

[7] Maturity transformation may migrate outside the perimeter of reserves implementation. This is already happening as an increased share of maturity transformation is directly taking place on securities markets where there are doubts concerning market liquidity. This new kind of maturity transformation, however, is dissociated from leverage and raises different issues that relate to the overall fragility of the financial system rather than to its cyclical behaviour.

## References

Adrian, T. and H. S. Shin (2009). 'Prices and quantities in the monetary transmission mechanism', *Federal Reserve Bank of New York Staff Report*, no 396.
    (2010). 'Financial intermediaries and monetary economics', *Federal Reserve Bank of New York Staff Report*, no 398.
Bernanke, B. (2015). 'Monetary policy in the future', Remarks at the IMF Conference on 'Rethinking Macro', Washington, April 15, 2015.
Bernanke, B. and A. Blinder (1988). 'Credit, money and aggregate demand', *NBER Working Paper*, no 2534.
Brunnermeier, M. and Y. Sannikov (2014). 'Monetary analysis: Price and financial stability', *ECB Forum on Central Banking*, May.
Brunnermeier, M., T. M. Eisenbach and Y. Sannikov (2012). 'Macroeconomics with financial frictions: A survey', March.
Cecchetti, S. and A. Kohler (2012). 'When capital adequacy and interest rate policy are substitutes (and when they are not)', *BIS Working Paper*, no 379, May.
Dudley, W. C. (2015). Remarks at the 2015 US monetary policy forum, Federal Reserve Bank of New York, 27 February.
Frost, J., L. Logan, A. Martin, P. McCabe, F. Natalucci and J. Remache 'Overnight RPP operations as a monetary policy tool; Some design considerations', *Federal Reserve Board, Finance and Economic Discussion Series*, 2015–10.
Gagnon, J. E. and B. Sack (2014), 'Monetary policy with abundant liquidity: A new operating framework for the Federal Reserve', *Policy Brief PB14–4*. Peterson Institute for International Economics, January.
Goodhart, C. (2011). *The macro-prudential authority: Powers, scope and accountability*. LSE Financial Markets Group. *Special Paper*, no 203. October.
    (2009). 'Liquidity management', Proceedings of the Economic Policy Symposium at Jackson Hole. Federal Reserve Bank of Kansas City, 157–168.
Geanakoplos, J. (2010). 'Solving the present crisis and managing the leverage Cycle', *Federal Reserve Bank of New York Economic Policy Review*, August.
Gorton, G. and A. Metrick (2010). 'Securitized banking and the run on repo'.
Hahm, J. H., H. S. Shin and K. Shin (2012). 'Non-core bank liabilities and financial vulnerability', *NBER Working Paper*, no 18428, September.
Kasyap, A. and J. Stein (2012). 'The optimal conduct of monetary policy with interest on reserves', *American Economic Journal: Macroeconomics* 1, 266–282.
Keister, T., A. Martin and J. McAndrews (2008). 'Divorcing money from monetary policy', *Federal Reserve Bank of New York Economic Policy Review*, September.
McCauley, R. N., P. McGuire and V. Sushko (2015). 'Global dollar credit: Links to US monetary policy and leverage,' *BIS Working Papers*, no 483, January.
McCauley, R. and P. McGuire (2014). 'Non-US bank claims on the Federal Reserve', *BIS Quarterly Review*, March.

Papadia, F. (2014). 'Lender of last resort ? A European Perspective'. *BIS Papers*, no 79.

Repullo, R. and J. Saurina (2011). 'The countercyclical capital buffer of Basel III: A critical assessment', *CEMFI Working Paper*, no 1102, June.

Rochet, J.-C. (2008). 'Liquidity regulation and the lender of last resort', *Banque de France Financial Stability Review*, no 11, February.

Stein, J. (2012). 'Monetary policy as financial – Stability regulation', *Quarterly Journal of Economics* 127(1): 57–95

Tucker, P. (2007). 'Money and credit: Banking and the macro economy', *Speech at the Monetary and the Markets Conference*, December.

Turner, P. (2015). The Macroeconomics of Macroprudential Policies (this volume)

(2015). 'The consequences of exit from non-conventional monetary policy' *Journal of Financial Perspectives*, vol 3, no 2, 43–59.

Turner, P. (2014). 'The exit from non-conventional monetary policy: What challenges?', *BIS Working Paper*, no 448, May.

(2013). 'The benign neglect of the long-term interest rate,' *BIS Working Papers*, no 403, February.

(2011). 'Macroprudential policies in EMEs: Theory and practice', *BIS Papers*, no 62.

# 3 Financial Intermediation and Monetary and Macroprudential Policies

*Stefano Neri**

Banca d'Italia

*New-Keynesian Dynamic Stochastic General Equilibrium (NK-DSGE) models have been severely criticised after the outbreak of the global financial crisis in 2008. Intensive research is underway in both academia and central banks to incorporate a more realistic modelling of financial intermediation and a role for macroprudential policy. Given the technical and computational difficulties arising from modelling systemic risk, it may take some time before economists develop new models that allow a comprehensive and integrated approach to the study of the linkages between financial intermediation and the real economy and the role of policies to promote and preserve financial stability. In the meantime, existing models can be used for the analysis of monetary and macroprudential policy and their interaction.*

## Introduction[1]

*When a theorist builds a model, it is an attempt to highlight the features of the world the theorist believes are the most important for the question at hand*          (R. E. Lucas, The Economist, 6 August 2009).

Dynamic Stochastic General Equilibrium (DSGE) models were initially designed to study business cycle fluctuations (Kydland and Prescott, 1982) and then evolved into the so-called New-Keynesian framework

---

* Banca d'Italia, Economic Outlook and Monetary Policy Directorate. Email: stefano.neri@bancaditalia.it.

The views expressed in the paper do not necessarily reflect those of the Banca d'Italia or the Eurosystem.

[1] A short version of this chapter was presented at the SUERF/Deutsche Bundesbank/IMFS conference 'The ESRB at 1', Berlin, 8–9 November 2011 and was published in the conference volume with the title 'Financial intermediation and the real economy: implications for monetary and macroprudential policies'. The chapter is based on my works with Paolo Angelini, Andrea Gerali, Fabio Panetta, Luca Sessa and Federico Signoretti. The author thanks Alessandro Notarpietro, Mario Pietrunti, Tiziano Ropele and Federico Signoretti for their comments, and Valentina Schirosi and Ivano Galli for their editorial assistance in preparing this chapter.

(Rotemberg, 1982). They are now part of the toolkit of central banks for the formulation of monetary policy.

These models have undergone severe criticisms since the start of the 2008–2009 global financial crisis. While there is wide agreement on many of these criticisms and on the need to improve macroeconomic models, researchers must bear in mind that: (1) models are tools that allow understanding the working of an economy; (2) models are inevitably based on assumptions; and (3) models can answer questions for which they have been designed. The quotation at the start of this section clearly underlines the importance of developing theoretical models for answering specific questions.

Despite intensive criticism, research is going on in both academia and central banks to incorporate financial intermediation and macroprudential policy into DSGE models. It will probably take some time before the profession eventually comes up with a new framework that allows a comprehensive and integrated approach to the study of the linkages between financial intermediation and the real economy and the role of macroprudential policies in preserving financial stability.[2]

Policy-makers, however, cannot wait for a new generation of models to answer important questions. For example, the assessment of the long-term economic impact of the Basel Committee's proposed capital and liquidity reforms was carried with a set of models that were available at that time (Basel Committee on Banking Supervision, 2010). DSGE models with a role for bank capital and liquidity were also used.

Meanwhile, there is no alternative but to implement some adjustments – the most important of which is to include a more realistic modelling of financial intermediation – to the New-Keynesian framework. This chapter first discusses the advances in the theoretical literature after the global financial crisis and then offers three examples of how a NK-DSGE model with financial intermediation can be used to study monetary and macroprudential policies. The chapter also refers to recent measures adopted by macroprudential authorities, the effectiveness of which could be studied within this model.

The remainder of the chapter is organised as follows: the following section briefly describes the New-Keynesian framework and the key features of the global financial crisis. The third section discusses the main critiques to NK-DSGE models and briefly describes some recent contributions. The fourth section presents three applications of a model

---

[2] Gersbach (2011) outlines a policy framework for addressing the issue of how monetary policy, macroprudential policy and microprudential regulation of banks should be organised and conducted.

with financial intermediation on monetary and macroprudential policies. The final section provides a conclusion.

## The New-Keynesian Paradigm and the 2008–2009 Global Financial Crisis

*The Benchmark New-Keynesian Model*

The New-Keynesian framework, as described in detail in Woodford (2003) and Galí (2008), represents the core of almost all NK-DSGE models developed in the literature. In its simplest version it describes a cashless economy with a representative household and a representative firm. Prices and wages are sticky, credit markets are complete and, hence, financial intermediation plays no role.[3] Medium-scale versions of such models (Christiano et al., 2005; Smets and Wouters, 2003) – featuring several real and nominal frictions – are used in many central banks (e.g. RAMSES, the model used at the Sveriges Riksbank, NEMO at the Norges Bank or the New Area Wide model at the European Central Bank, to mention some leading examples).[4] Smets and Wouters (2003, 2007) have shown that a medium-scale model can fit post-war US and the euro area data as good as Bayesian Vector AutoRegressive (BVAR) models. This model can provide a structural interpretation to the evolution of macroeconomic time series.

New-Keynesian DSGE models were developed in a period in which inflation was low and stable and economic activity was significantly less volatile than in previous decades (Figure 3.1), and in which financial shocks did not play a major role in shaping macroeconomic dynamics. The volatility of real GDP growth increased sharply after the outbreak of the global financial crisis after having declined for more than two decades.

*The 2008–2009 Global Financial Crisis*

The global financial crisis showed that many of the assumptions that characterized the New-Keynesian framework were wrong and that

---

[3] These models are described as having better micro-foundations than the large-scale models of the seventies and are robust to the Lucas' critique.

[4] See https://www.riksbank.se/en-gb/press-and-published/publications/regular-publications/working-paper-series/occasional-paper-series/occasional-paper-series-no.-12-ramses-ii–model-description/ for RAMSES II and for NEMO http://www.norges-bank.no/en/Monetarypolicy/Models-for-monetary-policy-analysis-and-forecasting/NEMO/.

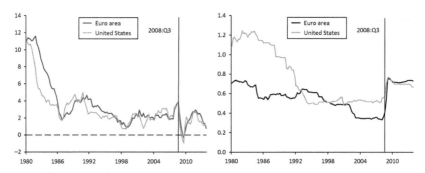

Figure 3.1 Inflation (annual percentage changes; left panel) and
volatility of quarterly real GDP growth (right panel).
*Note*: HICP data for the euro area, PCE deflator for the US 10-year (uncentred)
moving average of the standard deviation of real GDP growth.
Source: Eurostat and Bureau of Economic Analysis

financial markets, far from being complete, mattered in originating as
well as in propagating shocks.

Modern macroeconomic models, however, were designed to explain
'normal' times, periods in which economies fluctuate around a smooth
balanced growth path (King et al., 1988). Jordi Galí in an interview with
Andrew Scott (former Scientific Chair of the Euro Area Business Cycle
Network, EABCN) made this point very clearly: 'The paradigm that has
emerged as the workhorse paradigm is one that is clearly applicable to
normal times, I would even say normal times in developed, stable economies. You can see that just looking at some of the underlying assumptions, the kinds of imperfections that the paradigms focus on and so on'.[5]
The nature of DSGE models prevents their use in 'exceptional' times
such as financial crises; it also makes it very difficult to incorporate
structural changes in the real economy and in financial markets.

The global financial crisis showed how markets can become severely
dysfunctional and impair the monetary policy transmission mechanism.
In August 2007 tensions emerged in money markets. Risk premia –
measured by the difference between interest rates on unsecured and
secured interbank loans – soared and market activity declined sharply
as the result of lack of confidence among market participants and increasing uncertainty on their financial soundness. Figure 3.2 shows that the
Coincident Indicator of Systemic Stress (CISS) for the euro area
increased significantly, reaching levels never seen prior to the beginning

---

[5] The transcripts are available at http://www.eabcn.org/podcast/andrew-scott-interviews-
jordi-gali-upf.

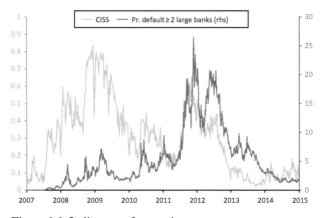

Figure 3.2 Indicators of systemic stress.
Source: European Central Bank

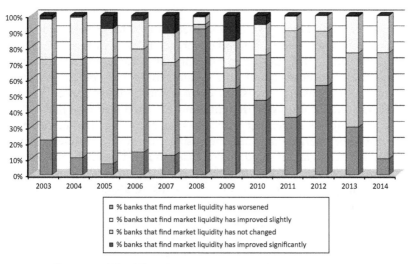

Figure 3.3 Liquidity of the money market in the euro area.
Source: Money market survey of the European Central Bank
See https://www.ecb.europa.eu/stats/money/mmss/html/index.en.html

of the global financial crisis. The probability of default of two or more large banks in Europe also increased at the end of 2008. Both indicators reached very high values in late 2011, at the peak of the tensions in sovereign debt markets in the euro area. Figure 3.3 shows that, according to market participants' assessment, liquidity in the money market worsened substantially after 2008.

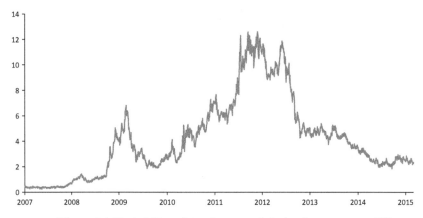

Figure 3.4  Probability of simultaneous default of two or more EU
sovereign.
Source: European Central Bank

In early 2010, however, tensions emerged in some government bond
markets of the euro area. Sovereign spreads relative to German Bunds
increased and CDS-implied probability of default soared reflecting
increasing concerns about the sustainability of public finances
(Figure 3.4). Tensions intensified in the summer of 2011 when spreads
on Italian and Spanish government bonds reached historical highs.

As a result of increasing difficulties in accessing market funding,
balance sheet constraints and increasing borrowers' riskiness, banks
further tightened credit standards on loans to non-financial corporations
and households in the third quarter of 2011 (Figure 3.5). This, in turn,
had significant effects on real variables, causing a sharp contraction of
investment.

After the European Systemic Risk Board (ESRB) General Board
meeting of 21 September 2011, the press release stated that 'risks to
the stability of the EU financial system have increased considerably...
Over the last months, sovereign stress has moved from smaller economies to some of the larger EU countries... The situation has been
aggravated by the progressive drying-up of bank term funding markets.'
In late 2011 the ECB introduced the three-year refinancing operations to
provide relief to banks' funding. In the spring of 2012 sovereign yields of
the countries under financial stress increased sharply, also reflecting fears
of a euro-area break-up.

The consequences of the global financial and sovereign debt crises on
banks funding and credit supply and on the market assessment of the
ability of governments to fulfil their obligations reminded us of the

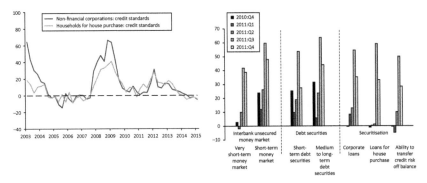

Figure 3.5 Results from the Bank Lending Survey of the Eurosystem.
*Note*: The left panel shows net percentages of banks tightening credit standards on loans to non-financial corporations or households; right panel shows net percentages of banks reporting deteriorated market access over the past three months.
Source: Eurosystem

importance of the links between financial markets and the real economy. They also showed the severe limitations of pre-crisis generation of NK-DSGE models which did not include a meaningful role for financial intermediation and risk.

There are two related possibilities to explain why researchers did not pay attention to these features until the global financial crisis: (1) post–World War II recessions in advanced economies were not caused by shocks originating within financial markets; and (2) there had been not many episodes of financial stress (Figure 3.6).

### A Critical View on Dynamic Stochastic General Equilibrium Models

Since early 2009, a few months after the bankruptcy of Lehman Brothers, some economists (e.g. Buiter, Goodhart, Cecchetti, Spaventa and De Grauwe) expressed their criticism of DSGE models.[6] Their main shortcomings include the impossibility of the model to answer questions about insolvency, default and illiquidity, to study the consequences of changes in regulation of intermediaries and markets, and to provide suggestions on how to prevent booms and busts in asset markets.

---

[6] See Goodhart and Tsomocos (2011), 'The unfortunate uselessness of most "state of the art" academic monetary economics' by W. Buiter published on http://www.voxeu.org/article/macroeconomics-crisis-irrelevance on 6 March 2009; Cecchetti, Disyatat and Kohler (2009) and Spaventa (2009).

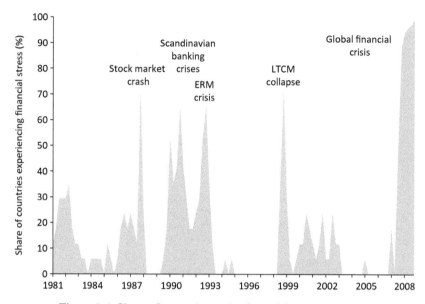

Figure 3.6 Share of countries under financial stress.
Source: World Economic Outlook, October 2008. International Monetary Fund

Buiter (2009) argued that standard macroeconomic theory not only did not allow the key questions about insolvency and illiquidity to be answered but also did not allow such questions to be asked. De Grauwe (2010) criticized the assumption of rational expectations arguing that 'other branches of economics, like game theory and experimental economics have increasingly recognized the need to incorporate the limitations agents face in understanding the world.' De Grauwe also criticized the dependence of DSGE models on exogenous shocks to generate economic fluctuations arguing that models should be able to endogenously create financial stress that can build up and lead to a crisis.

However, many of the criticisms to DSGE models that have been put forward are not rooted in the nature of these models but rather in specific assumptions. Assumptions, however, are necessary to build models and models are needed to provide answers to questions. In response to an article by The Economist (16 July 2009), Robert Lucas (The Economist, 6 August 2009) argued that 'we cannot fully understand how the economy works without employing models of some sort, and we cannot build coherent models without using analytic tools such as mathematics. Some of these tools are very complex, but there is nothing wrong with sophistication so long as sophistication itself does not become the main goal, and sophistication is not used as a barrier to entry into the theorist's club rather than an analytical device to understand the world'. In his discussion Lucas underlines that models are built to answer specific questions.

Not only academics but also politicians became interested in understanding the reasons for the failure of DSGE models in predicting the global financial crisis and accounting for the macroeconomic consequences. In July 2010 the Subcommittee on Investigations and Oversight of the Congress of the United States held a hearing to examine the promise and limits of modern macroeconomic theory in the light of the economic crisis that followed the outbreak of the global financial crisis. Among the witnesses there were Solow (Massachusetts Institute of Technology) and Chari (University of Minnesota). In his testimony, Solow blasted the use of DSGE models arguing that 'I do not think that the currently popular DSGE models pass the smell test. They take it for granted that the whole economy can be thought about as if it were a single, consistent person or dynasty carrying out a rationally designed, long-term plan, occasionally disturbed by unexpected shocks, but adapting to them in a rational, consistent way... The protagonists of this idea make a claim to respectability by asserting that it is founded on what we know about microeconomic behavior, but I think that this claim is generally phony. The advocates no doubt believe what they say, but they seem to have stopped sniffing or to have lost their sense of smell altogether.'

In his testimony, Chari offered a more optimistic reading of the debate, pointing out that 'Now, macroeconomic research has changed a lot in the last 25 years, and I want to emphasize the nature of that change and I believe that much of that change constitutes progress. The state-of-the-art DSGE model in, say, 1982 had a representative agent, no unemployment, no financial factors, no sticky prices and wages, no crises, no role for government. What do the state-of-the-art DSGE models of today look like? They have heterogeneity, all kinds of heterogeneity arising from income fluctuations, unemployment and the like. They have unemployment. They do have financial factors. They have sticky prices and wages. They have crises. And they have a role for government... DSGE models ... is one ingredient, and a very useful ingredient, in policy making.'[7]

---

[7] Kocherlakota (2010) acknowledges that DSGE models were not very useful for analysing the financial crisis of 2007–2010. Nonetheless, he argues that the applicability of these models is improving, and that there is growing consensus among macroeconomists that DSGE models need to incorporate both price stickiness and financial market frictions.

*Crises as Opportunities*

Between the publication of Bernanke et al. (1999; BGG henceforth) and the outbreak of the global financial crisis in 2008 there have been few attempts to model financial intermediation in a general equilibrium framework. The financial accelerator mechanism of BGG has only recently been reconsidered in standard medium-scale DSGE models (Christiano et al., 2014; Gilchrist et al., 2009). The BGG model was developed to quantify the contribution of credit factors to cyclical fluctuations and to the transmission of monetary policy. Even though credit factors were among the main suspects behind financial crises in many advanced and developing countries (the Great Depression, the 1990s Japanese crisis, the many Latin American and the 1997 Asian crises, among others) they have not become part of the New-Keynesian framework.

The word 'crisis' in ancient Greek (κρίσις) refers also to a decisive point or situation, a turning point. In Hippocratic medicine a crisis is a point in the progression of a disease at which either the patient would succumb to death or the natural processes would make the patient recover.[8] In a sense, the global financial crisis represents an opportunity to modify the current macroeconomic framework just as the Great Inflation of the 1970s highlighted the importance of agents' expectations and the credibility of monetary policy. Indeed, the models of the 1970s ignored the role that expectations play in influencing economic decisions.

Gertler and Kiyotaki (2010) express their hopes for a change in their chapter on 'Financial Intermediation and Credit Policy in Business Cycle Analysis of the *Handbook of Monetary Economics*: 'If nothing else, we hope that our Handbook chapter helps dispel the notion that macroeconomists have not paid attention to the financial sector'. Woodford (2010) also acknowledges referring to the need for 'a framework for macroeconomic analysis in which intermediation plays a crucial role' that 'the development of a new generation of macroeconomic models with these features is now well underway'.

*Some Recent Contributions and Their Limitations*

In the past six years, a series of important contributions to the introduction of financial intermediation in DSGE models has appeared in the literature (see, among others, Angeloni and Faia, 2009; Meh and Moran,

---

[8] The word *krisis* origins from the verb *krino* (κρίνω) which means also to separate. See also '*The writings of Hippocrates and Galen*, epitomized from the original Latin translation by J. R. Coxe, M.D., Philadelphia, Lindsay and Blakiston, 1846, available at http://oll.libertyfund.org/titles/1988.

2010; Cúrdia and Woodford, 2010; Gertler and Kiyotaki, 2010; Gertler and Karadi, 2011; Gerali et al., (2010)). A survey of all the recent contributions is beyond the scope of this chapter.[9]

Angeloni and Faia (2009) introduce banks, modelled following Diamond and Rajan (2000, 2001) in DSGE model and study the interaction between monetary policy and bank capital regulation. Risk-based capital requirements (as in the Basel II regulation) amplify the cycle and are welfare detrimental. Meh and Moran (2010) develop a model in which bank capital mitigates an agency problem between banks and depositors. Bank capital helps intermediaries attracting deposits which are used to provide loans to firms. Cúrdia and Woodford (2010) introduce a very simplified financial sector in the basic three equations smallscale new-Keynesian model and analyse the macroeconomic effects of including a reaction to interest-rate spreads or to credit in the monetary policy rule. Gertler and Kiyotaki (2010) endogenize financial frictions by introducing an agency problem between borrowers and lenders which gives rise to a spread between the cost of external finance and the opportunity cost of internal finance as in the BGG financial accelerator. Gertler and Karadi (2011) develop a DSGE model with financial intermediaries that face endogenous balance sheet constraints, which is used to assess the effectiveness of unconventional monetary policy to offset the consequences of a financial crisis. In their model the central bank is less efficient at providing credit, but can do so by issuing riskless government debt and without being constrained. The benefits of the central bank credit intermediation role are substantial when the zero lower bound constraint on the nominal interest rate is binding. Clerc et al. (2015) develop a DSGE model with default and use it to study bank capital regulation. The model, however, does not feature a role for monetary policy.

Gerali et al. (2010) set up a model that includes several real and nominal rigidities, financial frictions à la Kiyotaki and Moore (1997), monopolistic competitive banks and a role for bank capital.[10] The model, which has been estimated using data for the euro area over the period of 1998–2009, has been used to study: (1) the role of financial frictions and

---

[9] A brief survey is also available in Angelini, Nicoletti-Altimari and Visco (2012). Galati and Moessner (2013) offer a review of the existing literature and identify key future research questions that need to be addressed in order to aid in the implementation of macroprudential policy instruments.

[10] The project started in September 2007, a month after the outbreak of the tensions in interbank markets, and aimed at developing a model that could be used in the Economic Outlook and Monetary Policy Directorate of Banca d'Italia to study issues related to monetary policy and to understand the impact of shocks hitting banks in the euro area.

banks in the transmission of shocks (Gerali et al., 2010); (2) the macro-economic effects of a credit crunch (Gerali et al., 2010); (3) the procy-clicality of Basel II regulation (Angelini et al., 2011); (4) the interaction between monetary and macroprudential policies (Angelini et al., 2014); (5) the macroeconomic impact of Basel III regulation (Angelini and Gerali, 2012); and (6) the ability of monetary policy to lean against asset prices (Gambacorta and Signoretti, 2014). The model has many limita-tions, some of which are common to other models; for example, there is no risk and there are no interbank markets and banks do not perform any maturity transformation.

The models just described, despite their differences, are all linearized around their steady state (i.e. local approximation). A different line of research, which relies on more complex solution methods (i.e. global approximation), has emerged in parallel to the one just described. Bianchi and Mendoza (2010), Mendoza (2010), Jeanne and Korinek (2010) and Bianchi (2011), modifying the framework of Kiyotaki and Moore (1997), show that when access to credit is subject to an occasionally binding collateral constraint, an externality arises, driving a wedge between the competitive and the planner equilibria. This externality induces house-holds to over-borrow, as they fail to internalize the effect of their own actions on the price of the collateral. Depending on certain features and parameterizations, such models can display either over-borrowing or under-borrowing (Benigno et al., 2010). Brunnermeier and Sannikov (2014) develop a model of an economy which in normal times is in a steady state with low volatility and only occasionally moves to a regime with high volatility as the result of strong negative feedback from the financial sector to the real economy. This feature arises because individually market par-ticipants take prices as given, but collectively they affect them.

A common problem with these models is that, in order to overcome technical and computational complexities, they are extremely simplified and have an insufficient level of detail in modelling the financial sector or monetary policy. Buiter (2009) writes that 'if one were to hold one's nose and agree to play with the New Classical or New Keynesian complete markets toolkit, it would soon become clear that any potentially policy-relevant model would be highly non-linear, and that the interaction of these non-linearities and uncertainty makes for deep conceptual and technical problems.'

*Systemic Risk*

The most relevant limitation of the models described earlier is that they all fall short of modelling systemic risk. Almost all economists agree that more research is needed in modelling and measuring systemic risk. However, a meaningful measurement requires a clear definition of systemic risk and thoughtful modelling; and modelling is still at an early stage. According to Brunnermeier et al. (2011) systemic risk presents an attractive and intellectually stimulating area of research: 'dynamic stochastic equilibrium models ... have gained considerable prominence in research departments of central banks and have improved our understanding of price stability... There is a sharp contrast between our understanding of price stability and our understanding of financial stability and systemic risk, where the gaps in our knowledge are much more pronounced.'[11]

Hansen (2012) explores some conceptual challenges related to modelling and measuring systemic risk. Interestingly, he argues that 'producing better models to support policy discussion and analysis is a worthy ambition... Without such modelling pursuits, we are left with a heavy reliance on discretion in governmental course of action. Perhaps discretion is the best we can do in some extreme circumstances, but formal analysis should provide coherency and transparency to economic policy.'

### Models for Assessing the Role of Monetary and Macroprudential Policies

In the past couple of years some papers have studied the role of monetary and macroprudential policies in the context of NK-DSGE models featuring financial frictions.

Beau et al. (2011) suggest that the combination of an independent macroprudential policy leaning against 'excessive' credit growth and a monetary policy focusing on inflation is the best response to financial shocks in order to preserve price stability. Moreover, a central bank that takes into account the macroeconomic effects resulting from macroprudential policies will maximise agents' welfare. Bean et al. (2010) use a modified version of Gertler and Karadi (2011).

Gelain and Ilbas (2014) estimate the Smets and Wouters (2007) model augmented with the Gertler and Karadi (2011) financial intermediation sector using US data on real and financial variables. The estimated model is used to assess if and how macroprudential policy, which sets tax/subsidy on bank capital stabilize nominal credit growth

---

[11] See Schultze and Newlon (2011), *'Ten Years and Beyond: Economists Answer NSF's Call for Long-Term Research Agendas'* (Compendium), Charles L. Schultze and Daniel H. Newlon, eds., American Economic Association, available at SSRN: http://ssrn.com/abstract=1886598.

and the output gap, could complement monetary policy in pursuing macroeconomic and financial stability. The authors find that monetary policy gains from co-ordination with the macroprudential regulator when the weight assigned to output fluctuations in the macroprudential mandate is large.

Quint and Rabanal (2014) study the optimal mix of monetary and macroprudential policies in an estimated two-country model of the euro area which features nominal and real rigidities and financial frictions à la BGG in the housing market. The introduction of a macroprudential rule helps reducing macroeconomic volatility, improves welfare, and partially substitutes for the lack of national monetary policies.

Rubio and Carrasco-Gallego (2014) analyse the implications of macroprudential and monetary policies for business cycles, welfare and financial stability in a DSGE model with housing and collateral constraints. Macroprudential policy sets the loan-to-value ratio according to credit growth while monetary policy follows a standard Taylor rule in setting the policy rate. The two policies together improve the stability of the economy.

### Monetary and Macroprudential Policies in a Model with Financial Intermediation

Setting up a new framework that takes into account to the largest possible extent the criticism that have been raised since the onset of the financial crisis will probably require some time. Unfortunately, policy makers are confronted with questions that require timely answers, such as the one discussed in the Introduction on the macroeconomic effects of higher capital requirements. Researchers in both the academia and in central banks can fruitfully cooperate to develop new models, tools and methods. Meanwhile, one possibility that I explore in this section is to adapt the current generation of NK-DSGE models with a role for financial intermediation.

This section discusses three applications of the model in Gerali et al. (2010), with a focus on the implications for monetary and macroprudential policies. The first application quantifies the contribution of shocks originating in the banking sector to the 2009 downturn in the euro area and the role of the ECB monetary policy. The second application focuses on the interaction between monetary and macroprudential policies. The final application studies the role of macroprudential policy in leaning against financial cycles. For the last two exercises the model is modified to include Basel II regulation and countercyclical capital requirements

(Angelini et al., 2014). Time-varying risk weights (which characterise Basel II regulation) for loans in the capital asset ratio are defined as:

$$w^i_t = (1 - \rho_i)\overline{w}^i + (1 - \rho_i)\chi_i(Y_t - Y_{t-4}) + \rho_i w^i_{t-1} \tag{1}$$

where $w^i_t$ are the weights ($i=F,H$, $F$ for firms and $H$ for households), $Y_t$ is output, $\chi_i$ measures the sensitivity of risk weights to output growth, $\rho$ their persistence and $\overline{w}$ their steady state level. As the model does not feature risk, eq. (1) allows for the cyclical patterns of risk by linking them directly to output. As for the second modification, it is assumed that macroprudential policy sets capital requirements as to stabilise the loans-to-output ratio according to the rule:

$$v_t = (1 - \rho_v)\overline{v} + (1 - \rho_v)\chi_v\left(\frac{L_t}{Y_t} - \frac{\overline{L}}{\overline{Y}}\right) + \rho_v v_{t-1} \tag{2}$$

where $L$ are loans to households and firms, $v$ banks' capital requirement and $\chi_v$ measures the response of capital requirements to the loan-to-output ratio. The monetary policy rule is:

$$R_t = (1 - \rho_R)\overline{R} + (1 - \rho_R)[\chi_\pi(\pi_t - \overline{\pi}) + \chi_y(Y_t - Y_{t-1})] + \rho_R R_{t-1} \tag{3}$$

where $R_t$ is the policy rate, $\pi_t$ is inflation and $Y_t$ is output.

### The Effects of Financial Shocks and the Role of Monetary Policy

In this section, I use the model in Gerali et al. (2010) to quantify the contribution of shocks originating in the banking sector (shocks that either pushed up the cost of loans or reduced the amount of credit available to the economy) to the contraction of euro-area economic activity in 2009 and 2010. The sample has been extended up to the fourth quarter of 2010. Christiano et al. (2014) also provide an assessment of the role of financial shocks in the 2009 recession in the euro area. Figure 3.7 reports the results.

The shocks in the model are grouped into three categories: a 'macro-economic' group, which pools shocks to neutral technology, to preferences, to housing demand, to the investment-specific technology, and to price and wage mark-ups; the 'monetary policy' group isolates the contribution of the non-systematic monetary policy; the 'banking' group consists of shocks to the LTV ratios on loans, shocks to the mark-up on bank interest rates and a shock to banks' balance sheet.

The sharp contraction started in 2008 was almost entirely caused by adverse shocks to the banking sector and, to a smaller extent, by the simultaneous retreat of the positive stimulus coming from

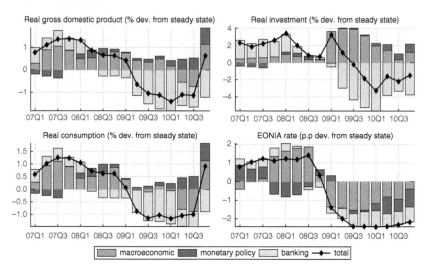

Figure 3.7  Contribution of selected shocks to the euro-area economy:
2007–2010
*Note*: The estimation sample covers the period of1998:Q1–2010:Q4. The
historical decomposition is computed using the median of the posterior
distribution of the parameters.

macroeconomic shocks.[12] The upturn in output at the end of 2010 is the
result of positive macroeconomic shocks and expansionary monetary
shocks that more than offset the still large effect of shocks originating in
the banking sector.

The sharp reduction of key policy rates in 2008 and 2009 contributed to
attenuating the strong and negative effect of the financial crisis on the
euro-area economy. In addition, the endogenous response of the ECB to
the shocks to the banking sector has been substantial as it can be gauged
from the relative large contribution of these shocks to the EONIA rate
since the end of 2008. The model does not make it possible to quantify the
effects of the so-called enhanced credit support implemented by the ECB.
For a tentative assessment, see Fahr et al. (2011) and Cahn et al. (2014).

### Monetary and Macroprudential Policies

This section presents the key results in Angelini et al. (2014), who focus
on the interaction between monetary and macroprudential policies.

---

[12] Because the model describes a closed-economy, it does not capture the effects of the
contraction in global demand.

A priori, the two policies should influence each other through their effects on asset prices and credit aggregates.

Angelini et al. (2014) propose a framework to organize the discussion on the effectiveness of macroprudential policy and the interaction with monetary policy. The authors adopt a positive approach and take the presence of macroprudential regulation for granted. To model the operational objective and tools of the macroprudential authority, the authors draw on true policymakers' stated goals. As to the objective, they assume that macroprudential policy aims at stabilising the loans-to-output ratio.

The interaction between monetary and macroprudential policies is modelled in two ways: (1) a cooperative case in which the two policies are set by a single policymaker that controls the two instruments (the monetary policy rate and capital requirements) and minimizes a joint loss function; and (2) a non-cooperative case in which each authority sets optimally her policy instrument, as to minimize her loss function, taking as given the policy of the other authority.[13]

The analysis shows that in 'normal' times – when the business cycle is driven by supply shocks – macroprudential policy yields negligible additional benefits over the case in which there is only monetary policy, even if the two authorities cooperate (Figure 3.8; left column). If the two authorities do not cooperate, the policy tools become extremely volatile. This is because macroprudential policy and monetary policy act on closely related variables in the model (interest rates, credit and asset prices) but have different objectives, so that at times they may push in different directions (Bean et al., 2010 define this result as 'push me-pull you'). The benefits of introducing macroprudential policy become sizeable when economic fluctuations are driven by financial shocks, which affect the supply of loans through a fall in bank capital, regardless of the type of interaction between the two authorities (Figure 3.8; right column).

The responses are also compared with those derived under the assumption that monetary policy is left alone in stabilizing the economy. In this case the impact of the shock is even larger, reflecting the sharper rise in the lending rate and the larger contraction in lending.

---

[13] The loss function of the central bank is a function of the volatility of inflation, output and the change in the policy rate, that of the macroprudential authority of the volatility of the loans-to-output ratio, output and the change in capital requirements.

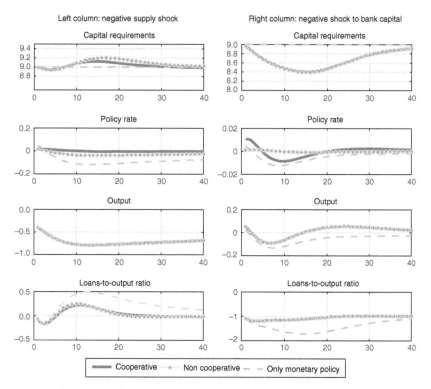

Figure 3.8 Impulse responses to a negative supply and bank capital shock

*Note*: capital requirements: percentage points; output: percentage deviations from steady state; loans-to-output ratio: percentage points in deviation from steady state; policy rate: deviations from steady state.

## Leaning against the Financial Cycle: Implications for Macroprudential Policy

Several years after the outbreak of the global financial crisis, economists agree that it was the result of the bursting of an unprecedented housing bubble that originated in the United States. Many factors behind the boom in the housing market have been identified, including innovations in the financial industry, overly optimistic expectations about future housing demand and housing prices and extremely low risk premia.

Expectations of low risk premia could give rise to a broad rise in asset prices and start a credit boom through their effect on Value at Risk (VaR) measures which are essential to determining the size and leverage of banks' balance sheets (Adrian and Shin, 2010). Indeed, an expected reduction in aggregate risk (a key element of the VaR methodology) provides an incentive to banks to expand their balance sheets and increase leverage. There are various reasons behind a permanent reduction in aggregate volatility and investors' perception of risk (Panetta et al., 2006): (1) improved market liquidity; (2) greater role of institutional investors; (3) the rapid growth of the market for risk transfer instruments; and (4) important changes and improvements in the conduct of monetary policy including increased gradualism, greater transparency and improved communication.

The model by Angelini et al. (2014) can help quantifying the preventing the build-up of financial imbalances. Suppose agents expect to hold, *ceteris paribus*, less capital in one year's time, for example because of improved macroeconomic conditions. Suppose also that banks have a target for their leverage. For a given target for the leverage ratio, banks have incentives to expand their balance sheets and increase lending. In the model this mechanism can be captured by including a shock $\varepsilon_t$ to bank capital:

$$K_{b,t} = (1 - \delta_b) K_{b,t-1}\varepsilon_t + \Pi_{b,t-1} \tag{4}$$

where $\varepsilon_t$ follows an autoregressive process of the form:

$$\varepsilon_t = (1 - \rho) + \rho\varepsilon_{t-1} + \mu_t + \mu_{t-4} \tag{5}$$

and $\mu_t$ is an *i.i.d.* zero mean process. At time $t$, agents receive a signal about future macroeconomic conditions at time $t+4$, that is $E_t\,\varepsilon_{t+4} = \mu_t$. This specification of the shock has been used in Schmitt-Grohé and Uribe (2008). It is assumed that when the time comes for the shock to materialise, agents realise that bank capital will not increase at all (that is $\mu_t = -\mu_{t-4}$). A similar exercise is carried out in Lambertini et al. (2013) who use the model developed in Iacoviello and Neri (2010) to study which shocks can generate booms and busts in the housing market. Figure 3.9 reports the results of the simulation.

Following the positive news on bank capital, intermediaries immediately increase the supply of credit to households and firms and reduce bank rates. Output starts increasing and reaches the peak four quarters after the shock. In response to the boom in economic activity, macroprudential policy tightens capital requirements while the central bank marginally reduces the policy rate in response to falling inflation. The loans to output ratio displays a similar dynamic response to output. After a year, agents realise that the positive shock has not occurred and banks immediately reduce lending forcing output to return to its steady state level. Macroprudential policy slowly brings back the capital requirement to its steady state level (9 per cent).

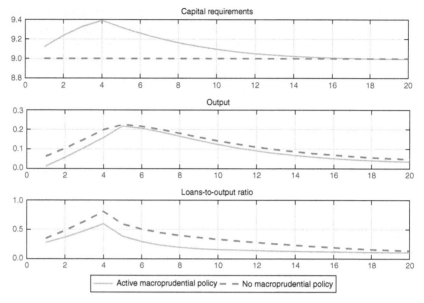

Figure 3.9 Impulse responses to a positive news shock about future bank capital

*Note*: capital requirements: percentage points; output: percentage deviations from steady state; loans-to-output ratio: percentage points in deviation from steady state.

A very different picture emerges when capital requirements are not actively used to lean against the upswing in the credit cycle. In this case, the fall in bank rates is larger and this determines an increase in output and the loans-to-output ratio which is larger than in the case in which macroprudential policy tightens capital requirements.

### Implications for Monetary and Macroprudential Policies: A Summary

To sum up, the following implications for monetary and macroprudential policies can be drawn from the exercises discussed in this chapter. First, an aggressive easing of monetary policy can mitigate the negative impact of shocks to the real economy originating in the banking system. Second, monetary and macroprudential policies should closely co-operate to avoid excessive volatility of the policy instruments and *push me-pull you* situations. Third, an active management of countercyclical capital requirements by the macroprudential authority can yield significant benefits when the economy is hit by financial shocks that by reducing bank capital limit the supply of credit to the private sector. Finally, macroprudential policy can be effective in leaning against the financial cycle by varying capital requirements.

The model developed in Angelini et al. (2014) can be adapted to study the effectiveness of macroprudential measures aiming at stabilizing the housing market, such as those adopted in the last couple of years some in European countries. In Belgium the central bank introduced in November 2013 a flat-rate five-percentage point add-on risk-weights on mortgages for those institutions calculating their minimum regulatory capital requirements for Belgian mortgage loans according to internal ratings-based (IRB) methods. In Sweden, the Financial Supervisory Authority (Finansinspektion) also raised the risk weight floor to 25 per cent (from 15 per cent which was set in May 2013) in November 2014 in order to reduce risks related to households' indebtedness. In the Netherlands loan-to-value (LTV) ratios are being gradually reduced and should reach 100 per cent in 2018, from 105 in 2013.

## Concluding Remarks

Macroeconomic models belonging to the New-Keynesian framework have undergone severe criticisms since the start of the 2008–2009 global financial crisis. There is no doubt that the current macroeconomic framework must be modified.[14] The directions that have been put forward by economists are many and all equally important. Among them, particular attention should be paid to default and systemic risk. Modelling asset price bubbles in macroeconomic models is also an important and necessary avenue for future research. Intensive research in both the academia and in central banks is currently under way and aiming, in particular, at incorporating financial intermediation into medium-scale NK-DSGE models.

It is important to take into account the computational costs that are likely to be faced were many of the desirable features discussed in this chapter to be included in a benchmark model. For example, models such as those by Kiyotaki and Moore (1997) are usually solved under the

---

[14] Some scepticism is expressed by Jordi Galí in the interview with Andrew Scott: 'It's not obvious to me that we should engage in large modifications of the standard model to accommodate some phenomena that we may not see again or we may not see again in the specific form that it has taken this time around. So, I'm a bit of a skeptic, though I understand and I sympathize with some of the current efforts to introduce, say, financial imperfections in the standard DSGE model and so on. I'm a bit skeptical about its usefulness when things go back to normal, and I have to say I'm also skeptical or very pessimistic, if you want, about the possibility of using such augmented DSGE model to explain the crisis itself endogenously.'

assumption that borrowing constraints are always binding; this choice allows standard methods to be used and delivers a linear system. Moving to occasionally binding constraints would allow precautionary savings to emerge but this would require abandoning standard (linear) solution techniques and substantially larger computation costs and time. Models with non-linear effects tend to be rather simplified in modelling the financial sector. They are also likely to have a hard time in accounting for the main features of the data, which is something to be valued as essential if the ultimate objective is for economists to provide a quantitative assessment of the effects of a policy intervention. An interesting approach can be found in Iacoviello and Guerrieri (2015), who have developed a toolkit for studying relatively large models with occasionally binding constraints without relying on global solution methods.

The profession will inevitably face trade-off between theoretical foundations and empirical relevance. It will probably require some time before researchers come up with modifications to the current framework that will allow a comprehensive and integrated approach to the study of the linkages between financial markets and the real economy and the role of policies to promote financial stability. But the prize is worth the effort, as Hansen (2012) has recently argued ('producing better models to support policy discussion and analysis is a worthy ambition'.)

Policy-makers, however, cannot wait for this next generation of models. 'Economic policy management cannot very long do without reliable quantitative information, especially in troubled and uncertain times; such information can only be obtained using models that have been adjusted on the basis of past experience' (Visco, 2009). Researchers in policy institutions and in academia need to cooperate closely in developing new ways of incorporating financial intermediation in a meaningful way in the current framework for policy analysis. Meanwhile, one possibility is to adapt the current generation of DSGE models featuring a role for financial intermediation and use them to address policy issues such as the role of macroprudential policies and the interaction with monetary policy. The analyses described in the preceding section are examples of how these models can be used despite their well-known limitations.

### References

Adrian, T. and H. S. Shin (2010). 'Liquidity and Leverage', *Journal of Financial Intermediation*, vol 19, no 3, 418–437.

Angelini, P., A. Enria, S. Neri, F. Panetta and M. Quagliariello (2011). 'Pro-cyclicality of capital requirements: Is it a problem? How to fix it?', in Adam Posen, Jean Pisani-Ferry, Fabrizio Saccomanni, eds. '*An ocean apart? Comparing Transatlantic Responses to the Financial Crisis*', Brussels, Bruegel Institute, 263–311.

Angelini, P. and A. Gerali (2012). 'Banks' Reactions to Basel-III', *Banca d'Italia Discussion papers*, no 876.

Angelini, P., S. Neri and F. Panetta (2014). 'The interaction between capital requirements and monetary policy', *Journal of Money, Credit and Banking*, vol 46, no 6, 1073–1112.

Angelini, P., S. Nicoletti-Altimari and I. Visco (2012). 'Macroprudential, microprudential and monetary policies: Conflicts, complementarities and trade-offs', *Banca d'Italia, Occasional papers*, no 140.

Angeloni, I. and E. Faia (2009). 'A tale of two policies: Prudential regulation and monetary policy with fragile banks', *Working Paper*, no 1569, Kiel Institute for the World Economy.

Basel Committee on Banking Supervision (2010). 'An assessment of the long-term economic impact of stronger capital and liquidity requirements', *Bank for International Settlements*.

Bean, C., M. Paustian, A. Penalver and T. Taylor (2010). 'Monetary policy after the fall', Paper presented at the Federal Reserve Bank of Kansas City Annual Conference, Jackson Hole, Wyoming.

Beau, D., L. Clerc and B. Mojon (2011). 'Macro-Prudential Policy and the Conduct of Monetary Policy', *Banque de France, Document de travail*, no 390.

Benigno, G., H. Chen, C. Otrok, A. Rebucci and E. Young (2010). 'Revisiting overborrowing and its policy implications', *CEPR Discussion Paper*, no 7872.

Bernanke, B. S., M. Gertler and S. Gilchrist (1999). 'The financial accelerator in a quantitative business cycle framework', in J. B. Taylor and M. Woodford, eds., *Handbook of Macroeconomics*, Vol 1C. Amsterdam: Elsevier Science, North–Holland, 1341–1393.

Bianchi, J. (2011). 'Overborrowing and systemic externalities in the business cycle', *American Economic Review*, vol 101, no 7, 3400–3426.

Bianchi, J. and E. G. Mendoza (2011). 'Overborrowing, financial crises and macroprudential policy', *International Monetary Fund, Working Paper*, no 24.

Brunnermeier, M., L. P. Hansen, A. Kashyap, A. Krishnamurthy and A. W. Lo (2011). 'Modeling and measuring systemic risk', in *Ten Years and Beyond: Economists Answer NSF's Call for Long-Term Research Agendas*, C. L. Schultze and D. H. Newlon, eds., American Economic Association. Available at SSRN: http://ssrn.com/abstract=1886598.

Brunnermeier, M. and Y. Sannikov (2014). 'A macroeconomic model with a financial sector', *American Economic Review*, vol 104, no 2, 379–421.

Buiter, W. (2009). 'The unfortunate uselessness of most "state of the art" academic monetary economics' available at http://www.voxeu.org.

Cahn, C., J. Matheron and J.-G. Sahuc (2014). 'Assessing the macroeconomic effects of LTROS', *Banque de France working papers*, no 528.

Cecchetti, S. G., P. Disyatat and M. Kohler (2009). 'Integrating financial stability: New models for a new challenge', prepared for the joint BIS-ECB

Workshop on 'Monetary policy and financial stability', Basel, Switzerland, 10–11 September 2009.

Christiano, L., M. Eichenbaum and C. Evans (2005). 'Nominal rigidities and the dynamic effects of a shock to monetary policy', *Journal of Political Economy*, vol 113, no 1, 1–46.

Christiano, L., M. Rostagno and M. Motto (2014). 'Risk shocks', *American Economic Review*, vol 104, no 1, 27–65.

Clerc, L., A. Derviz, C. Mendicino, S. Moyen, K. Nikolov, L. Stracca, J. Suarez and A. P. Vardoulakis (2015). 'Capital regulation in a macroeconomic model with three layers of default', *International Journal of Central Banking*, vol 11, no 3.

Cúrdia, V. and M. Woodford (2010). 'Credit spreads and monetary policy', *Journal of Money Credit and Banking*, vol 42, no S1, p. 3–35.

De Grauwe, P. (2010). 'The scientific foundation of dynamic stochastic general equilibrium (DSGE) models', *Public Choice*, vol 144, no 3–4, 413–443.

Diamond, D. W. and R. G. Rajan (2000). 'A theory of bank capital', *Journal of Finance*, vol LV no 6, 2431–2465.

(2001). 'Liquidity risk, liquidity creation and financial fragility: A theory of banking', *Journal of Political Economy*, vol 109, no 2, 287–327.

Fahr, S., R. Motto, M. Rostagno, F. Smets and O. Tristani (2011). 'A monetary policy strategy in good and bad times: Lessons from the recent past', *European Central Bank, Working Paper*, no 1336.

Fernández-Villaverde, J. and J. F. Rubio-Ramírez (2005). 'Estimating dynamic equilibrium economies: Linear versus nonlinear likelihood', *Journal of Applied Econometrics*, vol 20, 891–910.

Galati, G. and R. Moessner (2013). 'Macroprudential policy – A literature review', *Journal of Economic Surveys*, vol 27, no 5, 846–878.

Galí, J. (2008). *Monetary Policy, Inflation and the Business Cycle: An Introduction to the New Keynesian Framework*, Princeton: Princeton University Press.

Galí, J. (2009). 'Interview with Andrew Scott' (former Scientific Chair of the EABCN)' at https://eabcn.org/podcast/andrew-scott-interviews-jordi-gali-upf

Gambacorta, L. and F. M. Signoretti (2014). 'Should monetary policy lean against the wind?', *Journal of Economic Dynamics and Control*, vol 43, 146–174.

Gelain, P. and P. Ilbas (2014). 'Monetary and macroprudential policies in an estimated model with financial intermediation', *National Bank of Belgium, Working Paper*, no 258.

Gerali, A., S. Neri, L. Sessa and F. M. Signoretti (2010). 'Credit and banking in a DSGE model of the euro area', *Journal of Money, Credit and Banking*, vol 42, no S1, 107–141.

Gersbach, H. (2011). 'A framework for two macro policy instruments: Money and banking combined', *CEPR Policy Insight*, no 58.

Gertler, M. and P. Karadi (2011). 'A model of unconventional monetary policy', *Journal of Monetary Economics*, vol 58, 17–34.

Gertler, M. and N. Kiyotaki (2010). 'Financial intermediation and credit policy in business cycle analysis' in B. M. Friedman and M. Woodford, eds.,

*Handbook of Monetary Economics*, vol 3A, 547–599, Amsterdam: Elsevier Press.

Gilchrist, S., A. Ortiz and E. Zakrajsek (2009). 'Credit risk and the macroeconomy: Evidence from an estimated DSGE model', mimeo, Boston University and Board of Governors of the Federal Reserve System.

Goodhart, C. and D. P. Tsomocos (2011). 'The role of default in macroeconomics,' *IMES Discussion Paper Series*, 2011-E-23.

Guerrieri, L. and M. Iacoviello (2015). 'Occbin: A toolkit to solve models with occasionally binding constraints easily', *Journal of Monetary Economics*, vol 70, 22–38.

Hansen, L. P. (2012). 'Challenges in identifying and measuring systemic risk', *NBER Working Paper*, no 18505.

Holló, D., M. Kremer and M. Lo Duca (2012). 'CISS: A composite indicator of systemic stress in the financial system', *European Central Bank, Working Paper*, no 1426.

Hubrich, K. and R. J. Tetlow (2015). 'Financial stress and economic dynamics: The transmission of crises', *Journal of Monetary Economics*, vol 70, 100–115.

Iacoviello, M. and S. Neri. (2010). 'Housing market spillovers: Evidence from an estimated DSGE model', *American Economic Journal: Macroeconomics*, vol 2, 125–164.

Jeanne, O. and A. Korinek (2010). 'Managing credit booms and busts: A pigouvian taxation approach', *CEPR Discussion Paper*, vol 8015.

Kydland, F. E. and E. C. Prescott (1982). 'Time to build and aggregate fluctuations', *Econometrica*, vol 50, no 6, 1345–1370.

King, R. G., C. I. Plosser and S. T. Rebelo (1988). 'Production, growth and business cycles: I. The basic neoclassical model', *Journal of Monetary Economics*, vol 21, no 2–3, 195–232.

Kiyotaki, N. and J. Moore (1997). 'Credit cycles', *Journal of Political Economy*, vol 105, no 2, 211–248.

Kocherlakota, N. (2010). 'Modern macroeconomic models as tools for economic policy', *2009 Annual Report Essay*, Federal Reserve Bank of Minneapolis.

Lambertini, L., C. Mendicino and M. T. Punzi (2013). 'Leaning against boom–Bust cycles in credit and housing prices', *Journal of Economic Dynamics and Control*, vol 37, no 8, 1500–1522.

Lucas, R. E. (2009). 'In defense of the dismal science', *The Economist*, 6 August.

Meh, C. A. and K. Moran (2010). 'The role of bank capital in the propagation of shocks', *Journal of Economic Dynamics and Control*, vol 34, no 3, 555–576.

Mendoza, E. G. (2010). 'Sudden stops, financial crises and leverage', *American Economic Review*, vol 100, no 5, 1941–1966.

Panetta, F., P. Angelini, G. Grande, A. Levy, R. Perli, P. Yesin, S. Gerlach, S. Ramaswamy and M. Scatigna (2006). 'The recent behaviour of financial market volatility', *BIS Papers*, no 29.

Quint, D. and P. Rabanal (2014). 'Monetary and macroprudential policy in an estimated DSGE model of the euro area', *International Journal of Central Banking*, vol 10, no 2, 170–236.

Rotemberg, J. J. (1982). 'Sticky prices in the United States', *Journal of Political Economy*, vol 90, no 6, 1187–1211.

Rubio, M. and J. A. Carrasco-Gallego (2014). 'Macroprudential and monetary policies: Implications for financial stability and welfare', *Journal of Banking and Finance*, vol 49, 326–336.

Schmitt-Grohé, S. and M. Uribe (2008). 'What's news in business cycles', *NBER Working Paper*, no 14215.

Schultze, C. L. and D. H. Newlon (2011). 'Ten years and beyond: Economists answer NSF's call for long-term research agendas (Compendium)', available at SSRN: http://ssrn.com/abstract=1886598.

Smets, F. and R. Wouters (2003). 'An estimated dynamic stochastic general equilibrium model of the euro area', *Journal of the European Economic Association*, vol 97, no 3, 1123–1175.

(2007). 'Shocks and frictions in US business cycles: A Bayesian DSGE approach', *American Economic Review*, vol 97, no 3, 586–606.

Spaventa, L. (2009). 'Economists and economics: What does the crisis tell us?', *CEPR Policy Insight*, no 38, available at http://www.cepr.org/pubs/policyinsights

The Economist (2009). '*What went wrong with economics*', 16 July.

Visco, I. (2009). 'The financial crisis and economists' forecasts', *BIS Review*, vol 49, 26–47.

Woodford, M. (2003). *Interest and Prices: Foundations of a Theory of Monetary Policy*, Princeton: Princeton University Press.

(2010). 'Financial intermediation and macroeconomic analysis', *Journal of Economic Perspectives*, vol 24, no 4, 21–44.

# 4   The New Art of Central Banking

*Jagjit S. Chadha*[*]

[T]he result has been not merely that the world has been insufficiently prepared to deal with the new problems of Central Banking which have arisen in the years since the War, but that it has failed even to attain the standard of wisdom and foresight that prevailed in the nineteenth century.

Moreover, they should endeavour to adapt their measures of credit regulation, as far as their domestic position permits, to any tendency towards an undue change in the state of general business activity. An expansion of general business activity of a kind which clearly cannot be permanently maintained should lead Central Banks to introduce a bias towards credit restriction into the credit policy which they think fit to adopt, having regard to internal conditions in their own countries. On the other hand, an undue decline in general business activity in the world at large should lead them to introduce a bias towards relaxation. In pursuing such a policy the Central Banks will have done what is in their power to reduce fluctuations in business activity.
                                                     R. G. Hawtrey (1932).

The received wisdom is that risk increases in recessions and falls in booms. In contrast, it may be more helpful to think of risk as increasing during upswings, as financial imbalances build up, and materialising in recessions.
                                                     A. D. Crockett (2000).

## Introduction

Without doubt, money and monetary policy making has evolved significantly. The original function of money was to allow trade with a standardised unit of account. Earliest monetary policy would originally have implied simply some arrangement of institutional practice so that the

[*] Professor of Economics, University of Kent, Visiting Professor at the University of Cambridge and Mercer's Memorial Professor of Commerce at Gresham College. I am grateful for comments from participants at the conference at the University of Nottingham in 2014. Richard Barwell, Francis Breedon, Germana Corrado, Luisa Corrado, Alex Waters and particularly the editors Paul Mizen and Philip Tuner were a source of helpful conversations and comments.

right amount of commodity-based money could be used to facilitate the level of trade. It is probably the case, as is still the case in many parts of the world, that large amounts of trade stood outside the monetary system and relied on barter or non-pecuniary grace and favours. Even standard-isation was no easy matter as it is no simple task to set the correct relative prices between various types of monies and goods to ensure the absence of counterfeiting or clipping, and to decide on how to get the right amount of money into circulation.

The experiences of the late eighteenth and nineteenth centuries involved both a recognition that the monetary rate of exchange might be changed in the event of crises but also that the banking and financial system required regular bouts of support. The guiding principles were framed by Walter Bagehot, and the evolution of monetary orthodoxy, or sound money, was evident. This orthodoxy suggested some adherence to low levels of public debt in peacetime, a gold standard and circumspect choices in the policy rate. The suspension of the Gold Standard associ-ated with World War I, the interwar boom and bust and the Great Depression provided an incentive and a 'Keynes-inspired' blueprint for the operation of countercyclical monetary and fiscal policy. Whilst it is not clear whether these policies were responsible for the economic recov-ery prior to World War II, it is clear that there had been a profound change in the responsibilities of government. From then forward, the rate of inflation and economic growth would continue to be the government's problem and an important backdrop to the assessment of the perform-ance of political leadership, which at some level is rather odd given that the dominant models of economic fluctuations do not predict a perman-ent impact on output from monetary policy.

Accordingly, in the post-war period, there was an incredible intellec-tual effort to understand not only the mechanical interplay between monetary policy and the real economy but also how monetary policy effectiveness was a function of its interplay with private agents' plans and expectations. The elegant models that were developed allowed the study of optimal monetary policy and the development of strategies to minim-ise inefficient fluctuations in output, particularly in the aftermath of the end of Bretton Woods and the subsequent costly periods of inflation and disinflation. The great mirage of the Long Expansion (1992–2007) was that, whilst it appeared that business cycle risks had been eliminated, they were – in fact – increasing rapidly. Once the risks became apparent (2007–2008), the economy quickly jumped to a world of profound financial constraints which acted to bear down on activity in a persistent manner. Nominal interest rates hit the lower zero bound and public debt got stoked up to precarious peace-time levels.

Practically speaking, two issues were then exposed, which have occupied much of the debate on the setting of monetary policy since the start of the global financial crisis. How should policy makers deal with a response to large, negative economic shocks that seem to threaten to exhaust policy ammunition? What kind of defences should be put up so that such shocks could not build up in the same way, or that stocks of policy ammunition would still be available? The former problem led to the re-discovery of open market operations as a way of influencing long-term interest rates. And the latter problem led to a search for new tools that constrain financial intermediation. But there is another issue that has become more relevant. As well as thinking in terms of normal times – with small changes from the steady-state – and abnormal times as the world we are now in, with low growth and extraordinary policies, it is becoming increasingly clear that there is a transitional state to work through. Debt does not disappear, default notwithstanding, overnight and so balance sheet repair is a tricky and time-consuming business.[1] Public debt will take time to get back to pre-crisis levels and financial intermediaries may eventually start to allocate capital to the most productive firms but at the same time, policy has to deal with nursing a sick economy rather than licking a healthy one into shape.

In this chapter, I examine the implications for policy from unbundling the consumption problem into lenders and borrowers. In the next section, I consider the main policy lever used in the financial crisis, quantitative easing. I then examine the case for macro-prudential instruments in the following section. The case for considering the policy nexus as some point in monetary-financial-fiscal space is still being explored, but in this triplet lies a generalised way of thinking about policy and its transmission. The final section offers some brief conclusions.

## Incorporating Risky Borrowing and Lending

In this section, I examine the optimality conditions for a saver household and a borrower household and consider the implications arising from a restriction of loanable funds.[2] I examine the equilibrium from an unconstrained, and supply constrained perspective and ultimately consider the case for macroprudential instruments (MPIs) as a Pigovian tax that may be imposed because the social costs of intermediation are under-priced. In this model, policy may operate either through the standard short rate

[1] See chapter 3 of the 2013/4 BIS Annual Report for an overview of recovery from a balance sheet recession.
[2] This section is a simplified version of Chadha, Corrado and Corrado (2013).

set by the central bank or through operations in the bond market. Let us consider the standard consumer problem utility maximisation, for a saver, in a real, endowment economy, which we modify with a preference for holding bonds:

$$\max C = E_0 \sum_{t=0}^{\infty} \beta^t (\log C_t + \chi_t \log B_t), \tag{1}$$

where $C$ is consumption of the saver household, $E_0$, are expectations formed at time 0, $\beta$ is the discount factor for saver households and utility increases in consumption and the stock of bonds held, $B_t$, for which there is a stochastic level of preferences, $\chi_t$. The saver households maximise consumption subject to their flow budget constraint:

$$C_t + D_t + B_t = Y_t + R_{t-1}^D D_{t-1} + R_{t-1}^B B_{t-1}, \tag{2}$$

where $D_t$ are deposits with a commercial bank, $R_t^D$ is the rate of interest on deposits, $R_t^D$ is the rate of interest on one-period bonds and $Y_t$ is the income endowment. The left-hand side of (2) represents current period consumption and savings and the right-hand side, represents disposable income. The standard optimality conditions for this problem include:

$$R_t^D = \beta^{-1} \frac{C_{t+1}}{C_t}, \tag{3}$$

$$\frac{\chi_t}{B_t} = \left(\frac{1}{C_t}\right) - \frac{\beta R_t^B}{C_{t+1}}. \tag{4}$$

Savers have two assets in which to save: deposits and government bonds. Deposits with the commercial bank yield the deposit rate, $R_t^D$, which we can also think of as the policy rate set by the central bank as it reflects the costs of funding. The government bond yield has a wedge over the policy rate in the terms of the marginal utility from holding government debt $\frac{\chi_t}{B_t}$. Note that if this marginal utility is driven to zero, the $R_t^B$ converges to the deposit rate, $R_t^D$. In both cases, we can note that the current level of consumption by savers is a negative function of both $R_t^D$ and $R_t^B$, and so the pool of savings is increasing in these interest rates.

We now consider the same problem from the perspective of a borrower rather than a saver, where $C^b$ is the consumption borrower households:

$$\max C^b = E_0 \sum_{t=0}^{\infty} \beta^t (\log C_t^b), \tag{5}$$

subject to a resource constraint:

$$C_t^b + R_{t-1}^D L_{t-1} = Y_t^b + L_t, \tag{6}$$

where the borrowers can borrow at the deposit rate and receive their own income endowment per period. We can add a further constraint reflecting some limit to the borrowing, for which the Lagrange multiplier is $v_t$, that takes the form:

$$L_t < \frac{k_t q_t W_t}{R_t^D}, \tag{7}$$

where lending cannot be greater than the one period discounted present value of collateralisable wealth, $k_t q_t W_t$, where $k_t$ is the loan to value ratio, $q_t$ is the asset price and $W_t$ is wealth, which normally comprises net equity in housing for consumers. The optimality conditions in this case include:

$$v_t = \left(\frac{1}{C_t^b}\right) - \frac{\beta R_t^D}{C_{t+1}^b} \tag{8}$$

which we can see will equate to the deposit rate, (3), if the constraint on borrowing does not apply i.e. $v_t = 0$. But the log linear approximation of this expression gives us the external finance premium, as $v_t$:

$$R_t^D + v_t \approx c_{t+1}^b - c_t^b \approx \dot{y}_{t+1}^b + n\dot{l}_{t+1}.$$

This expression explains how today's consumption by borrowers is deferred if the loan rate, $R_t^D + v_t$, increases. We can then re-write this expression in terms of the resource constraint, (6), and write net lending as $L_t - R_{t-1}^D L_{t-1} = nl_t$ and if we substitute the lending constraint we can see that:

$$nl_t = \frac{k_t q_t W_t}{R_t^D} - k_{t-1} q_{t-1} W_{t-1}. \qquad \text{(demand for loans)}$$

Net lending is constrained by the growth of the present value of collateralisable wealth. So that any policy that acts on the borrowing constraint directly will act to reduce net lending. We shall return to this point. The supply of lending is provided by a financial intermediary:

$$max_\Pi f(L_t) - \left(R_t^D\right)D_t,$$

assuming, for the moment, that $L_t = D_t$ and taking optimality conditions, with no risk premium then the marginal return from lending equals the costs of funding:

$$f'(L) = \left(R_t^D\right),$$

but with a financial premium that results from the borrowing constraint then this condition is modified to:

$$f'\left(\frac{k_t q_t W_t}{R_t^D}\right) = R_t^D + v_t. \qquad \text{(supply of loans)}$$

As loans increase, the external finance premium, $v_t$, falls for standard marginal conditions. An increase in the policy rate will also reduce the finance premium. But if the supply through financial intermediation or demand does not price social welfare, we may have more lending than is socially optimal. There are three possible reasons why intermediation may not price social welfare accurately:

- Risk shifting by the borrower – the borrower may walk away from the debt and not pay the principal back;
- Risk shifting by the lender – the financial intermediary may fail to make provisions for losses if the state (via taxes on savers) will pay;
- Consumption may move sectorally or in aggregate strongly with asset prices and become too procyclical.

It follows that we can then make the following statements:

1. Consumption of savers and of borrowers will be negatively correlated and this will act reduce overall business cycle variance of aggregate consumption.
2. The unconstrained equilibrium will clear the savings market, but in the presence of an external finance premium aggregate demand will be attenuated.
3. The market determined external finance premium may not accurately reflect the social costs of financial intermediation, which may also vary over the business cycle. And so MPIs, as a Pigovian tax on intermediation, may eliminate the social costs arising from excessive (inefficient) financial intermediation.

Figure 4.1 illustrates the basic case for MPIs that flows from our analysis. The supply of savings increase in the average real interest rate, $R_t$, which we can think of as some combination of the deposit rate and the bond rate. The level of aggregate consumption is set by $R_t$, which determines the level of consumption by savers and borrowers. At the unconstrained equilibrium, the external finance premium, $v_t$, is driven to zero and consumption is maximised at $C^*$ for both savers and borrowers. When we add in a positive external finance premium, the level of consumption for borrowers is lower and higher for savers. Indeed to the left of $C^*$, consumption of borrowers and savers at time $t$ move in opposite directions. Total demand in this economy is determined by the average real interest rate, $R_t$, and the sensitivity of borrower household

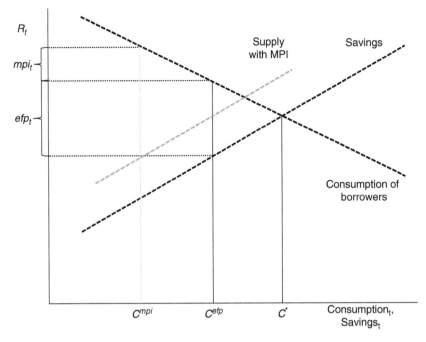

Figure 4.1 Saving and borrowing with a Pigovian tax

consumption to resultant changes in the external finance premium. I show there is a possible equilibrium $C^{efp}$ and note that the external finance premium falls when real rates rise and increases when it falls.[3]

But if the supply of savings, which is intermediated through the bank, does not price social costs of lending, then it may be appropriate to place a tax on supply and this will tend to reduce further the consumption of borrowers. The lower level of consumption here by borrowers may act to reduce the build-up in risks over the business cycle. Figure 4.1 shows the a restricted supply of savings, which maintains the same level of $efp_t$ but for which there is an additional cost of intermediation, $mpi$, which means that consumption by borrowers is even lower at $C^{mpi}$. Typically we move towards $C^*$ as the economy expands and rates tend to their natural level but at the same time the *EFP* will tend to fall and this will encourage borrowing. If there are social costs associated with intermediation, time-variation in the incidence of MPIs may act to constrain the build-

---

[3] Note also that changes in the lending constraint will change the size of the external finance premium.

up of risks over the business cycle. More generally, any policies that allow the central bank to act on the constellation of interests encompassed by the idea of the external finance premia may be of some help in containing risks or helping with macroeconomic stabilisation.

## Quantitative Easing

Following the financial crisis of 2008, Quantitative Easing (QE) – which I define as large scale purchases of financial assets in return for central bank reserves – became a key element of monetary policy for a number of major central banks whose nominal short-term policy rates were at, or close to, the zero lower bound. But despite its widespread use, the question of the effectiveness of QE remains highly controversial. Given that consumption is tilted by any variation in the policy rate or the bond rate, then such policies may be able to offset constraints on policy rates.

### Effectiveness

Early work on the impact of large-scale asset purchases as a tool of monetary policy began following Operation Twist in the United States in 1961. Although not the same as full Quantitative Easing in the sense of being financed by base money creation, this operation involved Federal Reserve purchases of long-term bonds (financed by sales of short-term treasury bills) as well as a change in treasury issuance with the aim of lowering long-term interest rates to 'twist' the yield curve. Modigliani and Sutch (1966) found that this operation had no significant effect on bond yields, though more recent work by Swanson (2011) has found that this operation had a significant impact on yields. In one of those interesting bits of interpretation the studies separated by more than forty years agreed on the basic impact in terms of basis points on yields but not on interpretation of their importance.

More recently, the QE programme implemented by the Bank of Japan from 2001 to 2006 generated new interest in unconventional monetary policy implemented through large scale asset purchases. In a survey of empirical evidence in the Japanese case, Ugai (2007) found mixed evidence. He concluded that QE had some signalling impact on market expectations of short rates by confirming that interest rates would remain low for some time, but the evidence of whether QE operations had any direct effect on bond yields or risk premia was mixed. However, when Bernanke et al. (2004) examined the Japanese experience with QE, they found little by way of announcement effects but some evidence of movement in the yield curve to suggest that Japanese yields were roughly 50bp lower than expected during QE. Unsurprisingly perhaps, the QE programmes implemented by the United States and the United Kingdom in the aftermath of the 2008 financial crisis have led to a dramatic increase on research in this topic. Most notably, the Federal Reserve's QE programme has spawned a large and rapidly growing literature; drawing on a wide range of methodological approaches, there is near-unanimous agreement that the US programme had significant effects on longer-term bond yields, though estimates of the scale of the effect vary considerably. For example Gagnon et al. (2010) find that the $300bn of US bond purchases, which amount to approximately 2 per cent of GDP, resulted in drops of some 90bp in US 10-year treasuries, while Krisnamurthy and Vissing-Jorgensen (2011) find that a reduction in public debt outstanding of around 20 per cent of GDP would reduce yields by between 61 and 115 basis points. The UK's QE programme has attracted some interest. Empirical estimates of the impact of the initial £125bn of QE and then the full £200bn (14 per cent of GDP) on UK gilt yields by Meier (2009) and then Joyce et al. (2010) suggest that yields are some 40–100bp lower than they would have been in the absence of QE. Caglar et al. (2011), however, suggest that the event study methodology may have overestimated the effects because of the dominant, possibly exaggerated, impact of the first rather than the subsequent announcements.

### QE as an Open Market Operation

Generally speaking, QE is really just an extended open market operation involving the unsterilised swap of central bank money for privately held assets. The key difference is that the duration of the swap is both intended to be long-term and of uncertain length. An open market operation, if unsterilised, leads to an increase in the quantity of base or outside money. This money represents claims on the public sector and will not be neutral with respect to any given expenditure plans if there is a real balance effect that induces a fall in interest rates. This is because the increase in money changes the price of claims on the public sector. If, however, the private sector fully discounts the present value of taxes that will need to be paid to meet these obligations, then these bonds will not represent net wealth and the operation will be neutral. The debate on the efficacy of such operations hinged on the question of whether the supply of outside money changed the wealth position of the private sector (see Gale, 1982).

But the analysis of such operations lies outside the remit of the work-horse New Keynesian (NK) model in which the evolution of monetary aggregates (simply a veil by which real planned transactions were effected) provides no additional feedback to the state of the economy. These models are highly tractable and are used to develop simple, precise policy prescriptions, even when interest rates hit the lower zero bound. For example, it was possible to conceive of statements about the path of interest rates that would influence expectations about the duration of interest rates at the lower zero bound so that an exchange rate depreciation or positive inflation shocks might be induced. In these models, open market operations are neutral because at the lower zero bound money and bonds become perfect substitutes and any swap of one for the other does not change the wealth position of the private sector. In fact, in these models, QE-type policies are simply forms of commitment strategies that provide signals about the long-term intentions of the central bank to hit a given inflation target.

The NK argument that monetary policy can only work through the management of expectations is not a universal result as it relies on particular assumptions. In these models, financial markets are assumed to be complete, and so where a representative agent can spring into life and who allocates financial wealth over an infinite life. Idiosyncratic risk in these economies can be perfectly hedged and asset prices depend on state-contingent payoffs. In this case, the prices of financial assets are not influenced by changes in their net supply, as demand is perfectly elastic. It seems quite possible, however, that demand curves for assets, particularly which are issued in large quantities, may become downward sloping, in which case changes in net supply can affect their relative prices. This possibility then means that the relative supply of money or credit can influence market interest rates and so impact directly on expenditure paths without having to rely on pure signalling effects. It is this possibility which gives quantitative easing its influence.

## Macroprudential Instruments

There is no workhorse model (yet) for understanding financial frictions, but Hall (2009) provides a useful taxonomy. He reminds us that an increase in any financial friction will tend to increase the interest rate wedge between those who provide capital and the cost of capital paid by firms; such a wedge will tend to depress output and employment. The story is similar to the Diamond-Mirrlees analysis of the inefficiency of taxation of intermediate products, with capital playing the role of an intermediate product. The legs of the argument are that an increase in financial frictions acts to increase the price of capital and so reduce its demand and because of the economy-wide resource constraint this will increase both the output-capital ratio and the consumption-capital ratio accordingly. Through the Cobb-Douglas production function, the labour-capital ratio rises along with the output-capital ratio. And the lower level of capital induces a fall in output. The argument goes through in the opposite direction with a fall in the size of financial frictions. Indeed, under this kind of analysis financial frictions are embedded in the supply side of the economy and may be particularly hard to understand in a NK model, which concentrates on demand and cost-push shocks in the production of goods.

### Monetary and Financial Stability

It is possible to take the view that financial and monetary policy should simply run in tandem. So that managing the latter well also requires attention to be paid and information to be exchanged in the pursuit of the two objectives jointly. Indeed the historical record suggests a similar juxtaposition – that the nature and scope of the regulation of financial intermediation was closely linked to the monetary policy regime. And so the immediate post-war period with the Bretton Woods system of fixed-but-adjustable exchange rates was associated with both extensive regulation of the financial system and also the virtual elimination of banking crises, apart from in Brazil in 1962.[4]

But the cost of such extensive supervision was such that it is probably the case that the financial system did not allocate investment particularly efficiently over this period and momentum for deregulation built up to a considerable degree. In principle, therefore, there is a trade-off between designing instruments to stabilise the financial system and prevent excessively volatile financial outcomes and ensuring that the financial sector retains the correct incentives to locate investment opportunities and allocate funds accordingly. It is not initially clear that employment of MPIs in single currency area can work independently of further controls on the movement of capital across currency regions, particularly when financial intermediaries have interests overseas. And so what we are looking for are instruments that will work, given some form of monetary policy regime that closely resembles what we currently have in place.

From the perspective of monetary policy makers, the initial debate was whether inflation targeting could be modified to include an additional instrument that could be used to stabilise financial imbalances or directly control the extent of financial intermediation. The answer that emerged,

---

[4] See Allen and Gale 2007, chapter 1 on this observation.

prior to the full force of the financial crisis being experienced, was that scope was limited. Bean (2004) argues that it is optimal under discretion to ignore any asset price boom and only mitigate any fallout on collapse and under commitment it turns out there is even less incentive to stabilise output when the economy is overheating. Svensson (2009) considers that 'flexible inflation targeting' that stabilises output and inflation may have an occasionally binding constraint to ensure financial stability and booms (busts) can justify an inflation undershoot (overshoot), as well as an extended period of adjustment back to target. Even if a limited number of modifications to monetary policy operating procedures are sufficient to stabilise macroeconomic outcomes, they may not be enough to realise financial stability for which appropriate supervision and regulation are unlikely to be replaced simply by new instruments.

Another instrument was developed but this was quantitative easing and was designed to deal directly with the lower zero-bound constraint.[5] There seems to be little attempt to consider whether using the stock of bonds, or indeed other assets held, may help regulate the financial system on an ongoing basis. Because under risk aversion financial intermediaries cannot create sufficient liquidity, in principle the central bank can regulate the flow of liquidity over the business cycle in order to prevent excessive amplification of the business cycle by financial intermediaries.[6]

In fact, a number of unconventional monetary policy tools have been developed here and overseas that might have implications for both monetary and financial stability. In recent work, Caglar et al. (2011) found that each of a number of unconventional tools augmented the stabilising properties of the interest rate rule from each of the asset (via reserves) and liability (via bank capital) sides of a bank's balance sheet as well as preferences of household to hold short run bonds and also implied less financial volatility. Overall, unconventional tools would seem to have some financial stability considerations. There is (i) guidance or signalling, which includes the recent fashion for central bank forecasts of policy rates for extended periods, which fits in with both the New Keynesian orthodoxy, in which monetary operations do not impact on net wealth

[5] The purchase of gilts under QE1 seems to have driven medium term yields down by the extent to which they might have been expected to fall had short term interest rates been lowered by some 2–4%. The swap of reserves for bonds has not palpably augmented bank lending but the counterfactual - with a changing regulatory framework for liquidity in prospect and a large shortfall in output below its pre-2007 trend - is rather hard to evaluate.

[6] See Gale (2011) on this point, who also argues that when risk appetite is high, too much liquidity can be created.

and therefore do not affect consumption but might impact on the expected path of interest rates[7]; (ii) there have been temporary liquidity injections of reserve money, or extended OMOs, which are essentially QE; and (iii) the direct purchase of distressed assets. And on the fiscal side, there is bank recapitalisation and credit easing and although in the latter case, this has come to mean in the US context the composition of the central bank's balance sheet rather than direct lending directly to the private sector. Therefore, I think we have (i) signalling; (ii) liquidity; (iii) asset support; and (iv) quasi-fiscal policy. Clearly, there are elements of each in the others, and any operation is surely tantamount to a signal of some sort, as well as providing some fiscal support by reducing the cost of debt service; and although they have been described as monetary policy tools, each of these can be viewed through some lens as a form of macroprudential instrument as they have some influence on financial intermediaries' balance sheets but they are not specifically designed to target any particular aspect of the asset or tliability structure of their balance sheets.

*Loss Function*

Macroprudential instruments involve the setting of explicit targets for any or all of capital, margin, liquidity and equity-loan ratios. There is a danger that, given the recent experience of an overextended financial system, the mind-set with which MPIs are being pursued implies an asymmetric concern with the stability of the financial system, rather like that with the foundations of a building or the construction of a dam, so that we are generally concerned with reining in excessive intermediation rather than too little. Put rather bluntly: who on a committee setting MPIs would lose their job if the financial system were considered to be excessively safe compared to the converse?

But an asymmetric loss function does not necessarily have to be pursued asymmetrically. The policy maker simply has to pursue a slightly different target. This is because the minimum loss of an asymmetric loss function, such as that presented in Figure 4.2, is not at the minimum but at some point in the opposite direction of the steeper asymmetric loss. As drawn, the minimum would lie to the left of the 0. In fact it would be given by a term in governing the asymmetry of the function and the likely size of any shocks. So the target will be driven further to the left for larger shocks and greater asymmetry in the loss function. Once this principle

---

[7] There is an older tradition involving the 'governor's eyebrows'.

## LINEX and Quadratic Losses Compared

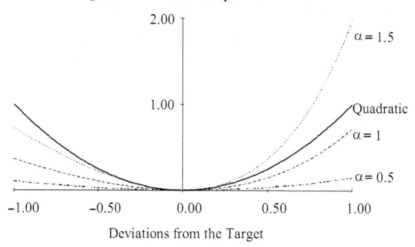

Figure 4.2 Asymmetric losses

has been established, it makes sense to develop steady state targets that build in a precautionary target for more liquidity, capital and equity to loan ratios than a strict minimum might imply. So if we want capital or liquidity buffers to be changed over the business cycle in a symmetric manner, but we are basically worried about the failure of the system from insufficient capital or liquidity, then the targets themselves need to be higher than any strict minimum in a term reflecting the size of shocks and the extent to which we are averse to financial shocks.

### Target and Instruments

As is rather well known, we want to count the number of independent instruments and objectives. In the current arrangement, the central bank will continue to set short rates so as to pursue the inflation target and it will be the financial policy unit that will have, or develop, instruments at its disposal to pursue financial stability. To the extent that we cannot be sure about the impact of any instrument, the Brainard uncertainty intro-duces a trade-off between the achievement of the target and the mini-misation of uncertainty induced by the use of an instrument. There are two further problems here in the case of MPIs: (i) there is likely to be considerably more uncertainty with a set of untried instruments that may also be correlated; because (ii) they may alter the behaviour of the financial system and may interact with the impact of monetary policy.

On the first point, it might be that we can treat the new MPIs as a portfolio of instruments that jointly will reduce the idiosyncratic risk of using any one new instrument. But without specification, calibration or testing of the impact of any one instrument in combination with the others, we cannot probably be very sure at all whether such a portfolio of instruments will be available. We need to give more thought to how instruments may be used together that does not induce greater uncertainty into the operation of monetary policy.

To the extent that changing the constraints faced by financial intermediaries will alter the financial conditions, as the choice made on the quantity and price of intermediation will be affected, there may not only be an impact on the appropriate stance of monetary policy but also an impact on the appropriate MPIs conditioned on the monetary policy stance. Consider a world in which the monetary policy maker wishes to smooth the response of consumption to a large negative shock to aggregate demand and reduces interest rates faced by collateral-constrained consumers. Simultaneously, financial stability may be considered to be threatened and various MPIs may be tightened, which would act against the interest rate changes made by the monetary policy maker and may need further or extended lower rates of interest. If on the other hand, sufficient precautionary moves had been made by the financial policy committee in advance there may be no immediate conflict. So co-ordination is clearly required to ensure that MPIs work with monetary policy.

### Operating MPIs

MPIs may be used to help stabilise the financial system over the business cycle. There are quite separate issues to consider when designing MPIs to help stabilise a reasonably well functioning financial system, which might be thought of as 'leaning against the wind', and in considering the correct responses for a highly vulnerable and undercapitalised financial system. The former implies the use of cyclical instruments to prevent a problematic build-up of risk, and the latter suggests some attention to the superstructure of the financial system with individual firms and the sector as a whole not only able to withstand shocks but be sufficiently robust as not to amplify them.

And yet the financial system is already undergoing a considerable deleveraging that has involved a build-up in core capital, increased holdings of liquid assets and greater margin requirements. In a sense, the financial system is moving from a loose regime to another tighter one, but if the transition is too sudden, it may have unwanted macroeconomic consequences. The extent to which difficulties in obtaining finance may

constrain the investment or consumption plans of some firms and households may imply that although what may be optimal are tougher long-run
regulatory targets there may be some sense in thinking about how to
allow the divergence from these targets for extended periods. Rather. a
credible fiscal regime that ensures sustainable public finances is more
likely to allow the full force of automatic stabilisers to operate. In this
sense, if banks are forced to observe a target at all times, this may be
counterproductive for the system as a whole. It is an example of Goodhart's (2008) taxi: where a taxi at a railway station at night could not
accept a fare because of a regulation that at least one taxi had to be at the
railway station all the time.

One of the results to emerge from the analysis of monetary policy is
that the control of a forward-looking system is best achieved by setting
predictable policy that allows forward-looking agents to plan conditionally on the likely policy response. There has been considerable work to
suggest that the impact of monetary policy is a function of both the level
and the path of interest rates, which is likely to be closely related to
predictability. Policy makers will have to pay careful attention to how
expectations of changes in MPIs are formed and whether partial adjustment towards some intermediate or cyclical target for a given level of
capital, liquidity or loan-to-value will be adopted. Otherwise new
requirements may induce large adjustment costs for the financial sector
and the use of considerable resources to predict future movements in
requirements. The private sector may bring forward or delay financial
transactions depending on the expectations of collateral requirements. In
a slightly different context, the pre-announced abolition of double rates
of mortgage interest relief at source (MIRAS) may have played a role in
stoking some aspects of the house price boom of the late 1980s.[8] Under
some circumstances, such a response reflecting strong intertemporal
switching may be entirely what a policymaker may wish to bring about
but, more generally, when agents are well informed and forward-looking
some thought has to be given to developing a framework for understanding agents' responses to any expected or pre-announced changes in the
rules governing financial intermediation.

### Monetary Policy and Liquidity

Following the financial crisis and the need to undo the Separation
Principle for monetary and financial stability, we can agree that there

---

[8] See Lawson (1992) on this point.

are missing instruments and there is a hunt to locate ones that can be employed, or suggested for us, by policymakers. The use of MPIs as additional instrument of policy flows from the following observation, that the central bank can supply (remove) liquidity to a financial market that is otherwise short (long) of liquidity and hence allows other financial spreads to move less violently over the cycle to compensate. But it is a concern as to how long-run targets for capital, liquidity and asset-mix and lending criteria will be set and whether a bias to over-regulation may be set in tandem. It is not at all clear how many new cyclical MPIs will interact with each other and impact on the setting of monetary policy. A reverse causation is also possible, whereby the stance of monetary policy may have implications for the correct setting of MPIs. The management of expectations over any announcements of changing MPIs will be a crucial area in a modern financial system – it was probably significantly easier in a world of extensive capital and exchange controls that characterised the immediate post-war period. All that said, early results from a new generation of micro-founded macro models do suggest that there may be significant gains from getting the calibration of these new instruments right but much work remains to be done.

### The Interaction of Government Debt, Monetary Policy and Financial Policy

In some senses, the classical monetary model places a lot of the action off stage and so brings into focus the heroic role of the monetary policy maker. Actually, there at least two key interactions that both limit and channel the actions of the monetary policy maker: fiscal policy and the operations of the financial sector. MPIs clearly are designed to ensure that financial policy complements the stabilisation effort. A further interaction concerns that between the financial sector and the fiscal policy maker, as we consider the role that public sector purchases of financial institutions played in stabilising the financial sector and also the extent to which financial sectors liabilities are hedged with government IOUs of one sort or another. Ultimately, we must have a happy triumvirate.

The fiscal policy maker is typically charged with respecting the government's present value budget constraint, which means establishing plans for expenditure and taxes that mean the level of debt is expected to be (low and) stable under likely states of nature. The financial sector operates to translate savings into stable returns by intermediating between current investors and consumers and future investors and consumers, otherwise known as savers. The stable income streams offered by the government sector may be of value to the private sector as it seeks nominal or real payments that are stable in the face of business cycle shocks. And may provide a benchmark for the construction of other market interest rates. The monetary policy maker sets the costs of funding for the financial sector and also has a huge influence on the costs of funding government debt. The level of economic activity depends to a large degree on the financial and fiscal sector so it is an outcome of the central bank's responses to the behaviour of these two sectors.

And I am not necessarily arguing that there is a need for explicit co-ordination. But the Nordhaus (1994) example of monetary-fiscal inter-actions may be instructive if not completely comparable to that of the financial sector and our triumvirate. Consider a *y*-axis representing economic activity and the *x*-axis interest rates, *R*. Also accept that a conservative bank chooses a preferred level of interest rates for every level of activity on a path that will tend to drive the economy to its preferred point. The financial sector (let us put the fiscal sector aside for the moment), may be stabilising and act to drive up activity when it is below the socially preferred point and help bear down on it when activity is above the socially preferred point. This is because asset prices and market interest rates may act to generate levels of activity that act as a conduit from monetary policy to the overall level of activity back to some notion of long-run equilibrium (Figure 4.3).

So in normal times, the central bank relies on the financial sector to be stabilising and carry out a large part of the stabilising response. But in times of boom and bust it may stoke up excessive fluctuations in activity, which begs the question of why any financial agent pursues plans that differ from those the central bank might choose? There are three reasons: (1) because it has different preferences; (2) because it has different information; and (3) because it will not bear the consequences of its choices. As a result without any co-ordination, the Nash equilibrium may

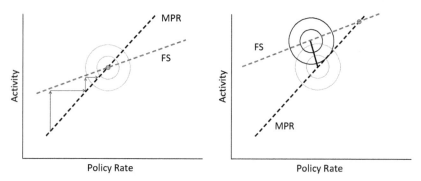

Figure 4.3 Monetary-financial co-operation monetary-financial tension

imply high interest rates. But the respective bliss points for the monetary policy maker, the MPC, and the financial sector policy maker, FS, imply a contract curve along which losses for each policy maker will be less than under the Nash equilibrium, which means that some form of co-operation is to be preferred. Whether that co-operation can be constructed in a manner that brings us firmly back to our preferred equilibrium is the key question for the economic settlement after the crisis.

### Concluding Remarks

I am not sure that wisdom and foresight has necessarily been lost in the search for a simple, credible monetary policy. The ultimate decisions of any policy rely on judgement and that can, unfortunately remain faulty even in the presence of wisdom and foresight. Both judgement and intuition are often formed with reference to the experience of working with models. But because no model can provide a perfect guide to the menu of choices, we must learn not only to choose which ones are useful for policy makers but also to think through the implications of our models being wrong. The robustification of policy may mean working through the implications, however unpalatable, of the unlikely as well as the preferred circumstances. To some extent this observation explains the need for MPIs.

Some difficult lessons have been learnt over this crisis that bear repeating. First, and rather obviously, inflation targeting alone cannot prevent boom and bust and needs to be augmented with more instruments and better judgement. The operations of the financial sector through the creation of various elements of broad money and also at the zero lower bound, as it changes its demand for central bank money, complicates choices about the path and long run level of policy rates. The act of financial intermediation has the propensity to amplify the impact of economic shocks and properly designed MPIs ought to minimise inefficient amplification.

Not only do financial frictions complicate the choices of policy makers because changes in the financial settlement may make the transmission of policy hard to gauge, but they also act through the traditional supply and demand side. This means that they make capacity judgements very hard and it is probably the case, the key monetary policy judgement involves working out the current and likely future levels of spare capacity in the economy. The sensible application of liquidity and capital targets via macroprudential policy may seem likely to reduce business cycle variance albeit at some cost of permanent output and so transitional judgements will have to be even more careful than usual not to treat the permanent as the temporary and vice versa.

The interactions between fiscal, financial and monetary policy have become clear. And we also now accept that fiscal policy, as well as underpinning aggregate demand, can also provide support to fragile financial institutions, if and only if the private sector wishes to hold government IOUs. This further contingent role for government debt makes the case for slightly more conservative fiscal policy than aggregate demand considerations would themselves imply. During the long and lonely march back to normality, public debt will take ten to fifteen years to get back to 'normal', and as long as demand remains inelastic, positive or negative changes in net supply will impact on price and complicate monetary and financial choices. And so it would seem that plotting the policy path will be considerably more complicated during recovery. Indeed with some rates going negative, the financial sector may have even more need to robustify itself against unanticipated economic outcomes.

## References

Allen, F. and D. Gale (2007). *Understanding Financial Crises, Clarendon Lectures in Finance,* Oxford University Press: Oxford.

Bank for International Settlements (2013/4), Annual Report.

Bean, C. R. (2004) 'Asset prices, financial instability, and monetary policy,' *American Economic Review, Paper and Proceedings,* vol 94, no 2, 4–18.

Barwell, R. and J. S. Chadha (2013). 'Complete forward guidance', in den Haan, W. (Ed.) *Forward Guidance,* Chapter 10, VoxEU.

Bernanke, B., V. Reinhart and B. Sack (2004). 'Monetary policy alternatives at the zero bound: An empirical assessment'. *Brookings Papers on Economic Activity,* vol 35, no 2, 1–100.

Blinder, A. (1998), *Central Banking in Theory and Practice,* Cambridge, MA: MIT Press.

Breedon, F., J. S. Chadha and A. Waters (2012). 'The financial market impact of UK quantitative easing,' *Oxford Review of Economic Policy,* vol 28, no 4, 702–728.

Caglar, E., J. S. Chadha, J. Meaning, J. Warren and A. Waters (2011). 'Central bank balance sheet policies: Three views from the DSGE literature', in *Interest Rates, Prices and Liquidity.* In Chadha and Holly (2011). Cambridge University Press, 240–273.

Chadha, J. S., G. Corrado and L. Corrado (2013). 'Stabilisation policy in a model of consumption, housing collateral and bank lending', in *Studies in Economics 1316,* University of Kent Discussion Paper.

Chadha, J. S. and S. Holly (Eds.) (2011). *Interest Rates, Prices and Liquidity,* Cambridge University Press: Cambridge.

Chadha, J. S. and P. Schellekens (1999). 'Monetary policy loss functions: Two cheers for the quadratic,' *Bank of England working paper,* no 101.

Gagnon, J., M. Raskin, J. Remache and B. Sack (2010). 'Large-scale asset purchases by the Federal Reserve: Did they work?', *Economic Policy Review*, May, 41–59.

Gale, D. (1982). *Money in Equilibrium*, Cambridge: Cambridge University Press. (2011). 'Liquidity and monetary policy,' in Chadha and Holly (Eds.), *op cit.*

Goodhart, C. A. E. (2008). 'The future of finance - And the theory that underpins it,' Chapter 5 in Adair Turner and others (2010), The Future of Finance: The LSE Report. London School of Economics.

Hall, R. (2009). 'The high sensitivity of economic activity to financial frictions', *NBER mimeo*.

Hawtrey, R. G. (1932). *The Art of Central Banking*, Longmans, Green and Company.

Joyce, M., A. Lasaosa, I. Stevens and M. Tong (2010). 'The financial market impact of Quantitative Easing'. *Bank of England Working Paper*, no 393, 1–44.

Krishnamurthy, A. and A. Vissing-Jorgensen (2011). 'The effects of Quantitative Easing on long-term interest rate'. *Northwestern University Working Paper*, 1–47.

Lawson, N. (1992). *The View from No.11: Memoirs of a Tory Radical*, Bantam Press: London.

Meier, A. (2009). 'Panacea, curse, or nonevent: Unconventional monetary policy in the United Kingdom'. *IMF Working Paper*, no 09/163, 1–48.

Modigliani, F. and R. Sutch (1966). 'Innovations in interest rate policy'. *American Economic Review*, vol 52, 178–197.

Nordhaus, W. D. (1994). 'Marching to different drummers: Coordination and independence in monetary and fiscal policies', *Cowles Foundation* Discussion Papers, no 1067.

Svensson, L. E. O. (2009). 'Flexible inflation targeting - Lessons from the financial crisis,' comments at Netherlands Bank, Amsterdam 21st September 2009.

Swanson, E. (2011). 'Let's twist again: A high-frequency event-study analysis of operation twist and its implications for QE2', *Brookings Papers on Economic Activity Spring*, pp 151–207.

Ugai, H. (2007). 'Effects of the Quantitative Easing policy: A survey of empirical analyses', *Monetary and Economic Studies, Institute for Monetary and Economic Studies, Bank of Japan*, vol 25, no 1, 1–48.

# 5 The Macroprudential Countercyclical Capital Buffer in Basel III

## Implications for Monetary Policy

*José A. Carrasco-Gallego*[*] *and Margarita Rubio*[†]

Basel III is a comprehensive set of reform measures in banking regulation, supervision and risk management with a strong macroprudential component, which has the aim of preventing future crises by creating a sound financial system. Nevertheless, these changes on financial regulation have to co-ordinate with monetary policy. We address several key research questions. First, we analyse how the higher capital requirements implied by Basel I, II and III affect welfare for a given monetary policy of different agents in the economy. Second, we study how these regulations affect the way monetary policy needs to be conducted. Finally, we propose an automatic rule to implement the macro-prudential countercyclical buffer in Basel III and find the optimal parameters for this rule and for monetary policy. We conclude that a Pareto-superior outcome can be reached using the optimal values, and the macroprudential objective can be achieved.

*The question now is whether Basel III, ratified at the G20 meeting in Seoul (November 2010), can meet the challenge of global stability by incorporating macroprudential innovation, which has previously fallen between the gaps in the regulatory system, and the extent to which this regulatory standard will be implemented by local regulators around the world.* (European Commission, 2013)

## Introduction

The Basel III agreement is a broad set of reform measures in banking regulation, supervision and risk management developed by the Basel

[*] Universidad Rey Juan Carlos. P. de los Artilleros s/n. 28032. Madrid, email: jose.carrasco@urjc.es
[†] University of Nottingham, University Park, Sir Clive Granger Building, Nottingham,. email: margarita.rubio@nottingham.ac.uk.

Committee on Banking Supervision (BCBS) at the Bank for International Settlements (BIS), to strengthen the banking sector and achieve financial stability. Furthermore, this set of measures is aimed at preventing future crises, creating a sound financial system in which financial problems are not spread to the real economy.

The implementation of this new regulatory framework is already here. On April 16, 2013, the European Parliament approved the legislation known as CRD IV, which largely implements Basel III banking reforms. This package replaced the Capital Requirements Directives (2006/48 and 2006/49) with a new directive and a regulation: The Capital Requirements Directive (2013/36/EU) (CRD), which must be implemented through national law; and the Capital Requirements Regulation (575/2013), which is directly applicable to firms across the European Union (EU).

CRD IV applies the Basel III agreement in the EU. This legislation comprises improved requirements for the quality and quantity of capital; a basis for new liquidity and leverage requirements; new rules for counterparty risk; and new macroprudential standards, including a Countercyclical Capital Buffer and capital buffers for systemically important institutions. The greater part of the rules contained in the new legislation are applicable from 1 January 2014. All this regulatory reform is a major step towards creating a sounder and safer financial system. These norms affect more than 8,000 banks operating within the EU, regardless of whether they operate in the Eurozone or not.

However, these changes to financial regulation have to coexist with monetary policy; therefore, the interaction of the policies conducted by central banks with the set of new regulations is an essential topic of study for central banks that have to implement both. In particular, the transmission and the optimal monetary policy may change depending on the regulations that are in place.

Therefore, there is an urgent need to provide research on the effects of these new regulations in order to contribute as much as possible to understanding how well they function. This new framework will affect all citizens, financial institutions, governments and firms within the whole EU. And, because its effects are long-lasting, they will prevail in the economy for decades. A mistake in the implementation of this policy could be a burden to be carried for years, making research on the topic is absolutely essential. Following this inspiration, this chapter[1] is devoted to show, in a non-technical way, the effects of the Capital Requirement Ratio (CRR) and the Countercyclical Capital Buffer (CCB) of Basel III,

---

[1] This chapter is partially based on Rubio and Carrasco-Gallego (2016).

on the main economic aggregates and society's welfare, and to propose a way to implement the regulation which brings the maximum welfare and stability to the EU economy.

The rest of the chapter continues as follows. The next section explains the main macroprudential features of the Basel III accord. The following section makes a review of the literature. The fourth section presents the modelling framework. The fifth section analyses the welfare effects of different CRR for a given monetary policy. The sixth section finds the optimal values for the monetary policy given several values of the CRR and for different agents. The penultimate section shows the optimal values for the implementation of the macroprudential CCB of Basel III and for monetary policy. The final section concludes.

## The Macroprudential Element of Basel III

The BCBS aims to provide some guidance for banking regulators on what is the best practice for banks. Its standards are accepted worldwide and are generally incorporated in national banking rules. The first set of international banking regulations put forth by the BCBS was the agreement signed in 1988 and known as Basel I. Afterwards, Basel II, was published in 2004; and Basel III, agreed in 2010.

These subsequent Basel regulations have introduced, among other elements, higher compulsory CRR for banks. Basel I and II required a minimum total CRR of 8 per cent. Nevertheless, Pillar I of Basel II significantly increased the risk sensitivity of the capital rule, with respect to Basel I, and considered different approaches to compute the minimum CRR. However, for the goal of this chapter, we only take into account the quantitative level of the CRR, not the qualitative implications; therefore, we will analyse Basel I and Basel II together because they require the same quantitative level of CRR.

The Basel III reform package is a major overhaul of Basel I and II. Basel III includes a comprehensive set of rules encompassing tighter definitions of capital, a framework for capital conservation and Countercyclical Buffers, improved risk capture, a non-risk-based leverage ratio, and a novel regime for liquidity risk. The objective of these new rules is to promote a more resilient banking sector in order to improve its ability to absorb shocks arising from financial and economic stress, thus reducing the risk of spillover from the financial sector to the real economy.[2] In this chapter, we are interested in the Capital Requirement Ratio and the Countercyclical Buffer as a macroprudential tool. Specifically, Basel III

---

[2] See Basel Committee on Banking Supervision (2010a).

introduced a mandatory capital conservation buffer of 2.5 per cent designed to enforce corrective action when a bank's capital ratio deteriorates. Therefore, although the minimum total capital requirement remains at the current 8 per cent level, yet the required total capital increases to 10.5 per cent when combined with the conservation buffer.

Furthermore, Basel III adds a dynamic macroprudential element in the form of a discretionary countercyclical seasonal buffer up to another 2.5 per cent of capital, which entails banks to hold more capital in good times to prepare for downturns in the economy. The BCBS states the objectives of this additional CCB: 'The primary aim of the Countercyclical Capital Buffer regime is to use a buffer of capital to achieve the broader macroprudential goal of protecting the banking sector from periods of excess aggregate credit growth that have often been associated with the build-up of system-wide risk' (Basel Committee on Banking Supervision, 2010b).

Consequently, the macroprudential approach of Basel III has two components: on the one hand, it increases the static CRR permanently, on the other hand, it adds a dynamic macroprudential buffer which will depend on economic conditions. Nevertheless, it leaves the implementation of the CCB as a relatively open question, encouraging national authorities to apply judgment in the setting of the buffer using the best information available.

The BCBS also claims that the CCB is not meant to be used as an instrument to manage economic cycles or asset prices; these are issues that should be addressed by other policies such as monetary policy. Then, the interaction of the Basel regulation with monetary policy is of extreme relevance. Therefore, it is very timely to do research on this topic to provide some general guidance to correctly implement this regulation, together with monetary policy.

Thus, the aim of this chapter is to show the welfare effects of the Basel I, II and III regulations on CRR as well as its interactions with monetary policy. In order to do that, we calculate the best policy mix, macroprudential and monetary policies, to maximize total welfare of society. Once we know the optimal policy mix, we can disentangle the effects of these policies on the three different agents of the model: savers, borrowers and bankers. Therefore, we provide some general lines to correctly implement this new macroprudential regulation, together with monetary policy, and we specify its effects for the agents of the model.

### Literature Review

The interest in macroprudential policies and regulations that deliver a more stable financial system is a recent topic that is in the limelight after the crisis. Furthermore, the experience with this kind of policies is still scarce. Policy makers and economic researchers coincide on the need to re-orient the regulatory framework towards this perspective. For example, the European Systemic Risk Board, hosted and supported by the European Central Bank (ECB), specifies that the ultimate objective of macroprudential policy is to contribute to the safeguard of the stability of the financial system as a whole (Official Journal of the European Union, 14–02–2012) and has recently included capital requirements as one of the main instruments of macroprudential policies (Official Journal of the European Union, 15–06–2013). Basel III is one example of this type of policies.

However, although there is consensus about the need for these policies, the effects of them are still unclear, particularly on monetary policy and also the real economy. Thus, given the novelty of this perspective and the uncertainty about its effects, the literature on the topic, although flourishing, is also quite recent and full of gaps that need to be filled.

Borio (2003) was one of the pioneers on the topic. He distinguished between microprudential regulation, which seeks to enhance the safety and soundness of individual financial institutions, as opposed to the macroprudential view which focuses on welfare of the financial system as a whole. Following this work, Acharya (2009) points out the necessity of regulatory mechanisms that mitigate aggregate risk, in order to avoid future crises. Brunnermeier has done extensive work on the topic. For instance, Brunnermeier et al. (2009) suggests that all systemic institutions should be subject both to micro-prudential regulation, examining their individual risk characteristics, and to macroprudential regulation, related to their contribution to systemic risk.

The literature has proposed several instruments to be implemented as macroprudential tools. A complete description of them appears in Bank of England (2009) and (2011), or Longworth (2011); however, only some of them have been analysed in depth. Among the most popular proposed instruments we can find limits on the loan-to-value ratio (LTV). The LTV reflects the value of a loan relative to its underlying collateral (e.g. residential property). Kannan, Rabanal and Scott (2012) examine the interaction between monetary and a macroprudential instrument based on the LTV. Rubio and Carrasco-Gallego (2013) evaluate the performance of a rule on the LTV interacting with the traditional monetary policy conducted by central banks and they find that introducing the macroprudential rule mitigates the effects of booms on the economy by restricting credit. Also, they show that the combination of monetary policy and the macroprudential rule is unambiguously welfare enhancing. Rubio and Carrasco-Gallego (2014) study a macroprudential policy based on the LTV and finds that by using this policy, together with the monetary policy, a more stable financial system can be achieved.

Basel III regulation is based on limits on capital requirements. Borio (2011) states that several aspects of Basel III reflect a macroprudential approach to financial regulation. However, there is some controversy around this regulation that has been pointed out by the literature. In particular, some concerns have been raised about the impact of Basel III reforms on the dynamism of financial markets and, in turn, on investment and economic growth. The reasoning is that Basel III regulation could produce a decline in the amount of credit and impact negatively in the whole economy. Critics of Basel III consider that there is a real danger that reform will limit the availability of credit and reduce economic activity. Repullo and Saurina (2012) show that a mechanical application of Basel III regulation would tend to reduce capital requirements when GDP growth is high and increase them when GDP growth is low. Then, if banks increase capital requirements during crises, credit will be reduced and the economic growth will be even lower; with a lower growth, the welfare would decrease. This is the so-called risk of procyclicality; that is, Basel III could cause a deeper recession in bad times and a higher boom in good ones. Furthermore, it could have an adverse impact on growth plans of the industry, as pointed out by Kant andJain (2013). If capital requirements ratios increase, households and industries could not borrow as much, and their plans for recovery would be affected, affecting the whole economy. Some authors have attempted to evaluate the effects of capital ratios, such as Angeloni and Faia (2013) and Repullo and Suárez (2013). They compare the procyclicality of Basel I and Basel II, the previous frameworks. They find that Basel II is more procyclical than Basel I. That means that probably the newer regulation of Basel III, with even higher capital requirements ratios, would boost the recession in the case that the economy is in a crisis. In our analysis, we explicitly introduce a countercyclical rule so that we avoid this effect.

Our model dynamics show that after an expansionary shock, when GDP is going up, the regulator increases capital requirements. Our results are related to Drehmann and Gambacorta (2011) which shows a simulation that indicates that the CCB scheme might reduce credit growth during credit booms and decrease the credit contraction once the buffer is released. This would help to achieve higher banking sector resilience to shocks. Nevertheless, this procedure is subject to the Lucas critique: had the scheme been in place, banks' lending decisions would probably have been different. Our approach is robust to this critique because is based on a Dynamic Stockastic General Equilibrium (DSGE) model. A number of other studies have also found that increasing capital requirements may reduce credit supply (Kishan and Opiela, 2000; Gambacorta and Mistrulli, 2004). In the same line, Akram (2014) finds that the proposed increases in capital requirements under Basel III are found to have significant effects especially on house prices and credit.

This chapter also contributes to this line of research analysing distributional welfare effects among agents, derived from the Basel regulation. As Van den Heuvel (2008) and Kant and Jain (2013) find in earlier work, we find that capital requirements have a large welfare cost for banks. We also find that, even the regulation by itself is not welfare enhancing for savers, it can be welfare enhancing when the macroprudential and monetary policies optimally interact.

In a similar way, Angeloni and Faia (2013) consider that the best combination of policy rules for welfare includes mildly countercyclical capital ratios (as in Basel III) and a response of monetary policy to asset prices or bank leverage. We find the optimal parameters of both policies acting together with a typical Taylor rule for monetary policy and the macroprudential CCB based on credit deviation from its steady state.

Our research is connected to the literature that uses a DSGE model to study the effects of a macroprudential rule acting together with the monetary policy. Among them, for instance, Borio and Shim (2007) emphasize the complementary role of macroprudential policy to monetary policy and its supportive role as a built-in stabilizer. Also, N'Diaye (2009) shows that monetary policy can be supported by countercyclical prudential regulation and that it can help the monetary authorities to achieve their output and inflation targets with smaller changes in interest rates. In addition, Antipa et al. (2010) use a DSGE model to show that macroprudential policies would have been effective in smoothing the past credit cycle and in reducing the intensity of the recession. Angelini et al. (2014) also find, by using a DSGE model featuring bank capital, that a prudential rule that increases the capital requirement when the credit/output ratio rises is capable of reducing output variance relative to the baseline (where no CCB is in place). In our study, we also use a DSGE framework to find an optimal parameterization of the macroprudential CCB and the monetary policy to maximize welfare.

Additionally, our model is part of a new generation of models that attempt to incorporate banks in the analysis. The arrival of the financial crisis led to realize that the mainstream dynamic model, even Bernanke, Gertler, and Gilchrist (1999), does not include specific banks and no specific role for bank capital. New models including Gertler and Karadi (2011), Meh and Moran (2010), Gertler and Kiyotaki (2010) or Iacoviello (2015) now ensure financial intermediaries are included in the model structure. Their strategy, and ours, can be summarized as consistent with adding a second layer of financially constrained agents, which are the banks. Similarly to our case, Angelini et al. (2014) use a DSGE model with a banking sector following Gerali et al. (2010). They show interactions between the Capital Requirement Ratio that responds to output growth (while we model Countercyclical Capital Buffers in line with the current regulatory framework responding to credit), and monetary policy. They find that no regime, co-operative or non-cooperative between macroprudential and monetary authorities, makes all agents, borrowers or savers, better off. Our results show that this is the case for banks. However, we could find a system of transfers à la Kaldor-Hicks that generates a Pareto-superior outcome.

## The Model

The modelling framework that has been used to assess the effects of a higher CRR and the CCB of Basel III is a DSGE model with a housing market, following Iacoviello (2015). In this model, the economy features patient and impatient households, banks and a final goods firm. Households work and consume both consumption goods and housing. Patient and impatient households are savers and borrowers, respectively. Impatient households have a lower discount factor than patient households and a borrowing constraint that limits their borrowing to the present discounted value of their housing holdings; that is, they use housing as collateral.

Savers, the first type of agents, maximize their utility function by choosing consumption, housing and labor hours:

$$\max E_0 \sum_{t=0}^{\infty} \beta_s^t \left[ \log C_{s,t} + j \log H_{s,t} - \frac{(N_{s,t})^{\eta}}{\eta} \right],$$

where $\beta_s \in (0, 1)$ is the patient discount factor, $E_0$ is the expectation operator and $C_{s,t}$, $H_{s,t}$ and $N_{s,t}$ represent consumption at time $t$, the housing stock and working hours, respectively. $1/(\eta - 1)$ is the labor supply elasticity, $\eta > 0$. $j > 0$ constitutes the relative weight of housing in the utility function. Subject to the budget constraint:

$$C_{s,t} + d_t + q_t(H_{s,t} - H_{s,t-1}) = \frac{R_{s,t-1}d_{t-1}}{\pi_t} + w_{s,t}N_{s,t} + \frac{X_t - 1}{X_t} Y_t,$$

$$(1)$$

where $d_t$ denotes bank deposits, $R_{s,t}$ is the gross return from deposits, $q_t$ is the price of housing in units of consumption, and $w_{s,t}$ is the real wage rate. The last term refers to firms profits, which are rebated back to the saver, being $X_t$ the firm's markup and $Y_t$ the output. The first order conditions for this optimization problem are as follows:

$$\frac{1}{C_{s,t}} = \beta_s E_t \left( \frac{R_{s,t}}{\pi_{t+1} C_{s,t+1}} \right),$$
(2)

$$\frac{q_t}{C_{s,t}} = \frac{j}{H_{s,t}} + \beta_s E_t \left( \frac{q_{t+1}}{C_{s,t+1}} \right),$$
(3)

$$w_{s,t} = (N_{s,t})^{\eta-1} C_{s,t}.$$
(4)

Equation (2) is the Euler equation, the intertemporal condition for consumption. Equation (3) represents the intertemporal condition for housing, in which, at the margin, benefits for consuming housing equate costs in terms of consumption. Equation (4) is the labor-supply condition.

Borrowers, the second type of agents, solve:

$$\max E_0 \sum_{t=0}^{\infty} \beta_b^t \left[ \log C_{b,t} + j \log H_{b,t} - \frac{(N_{b,t})^{\eta}}{\eta} \right],$$

where $\beta_b \in (0, 1)$ is impatient discount factor, subject to the budget constraint and the collateral constraint:

$$C_{b,t} + \frac{R_{b,t} b_{t-1}}{\pi_{t+1}} + q_t (H_{b,t} - H_{b,t-1}) = b_t + w_{b,t} N_{b,t},$$
(5)

$$b_t \leq E_t \left( \frac{1}{R_{b,t+1}} k q_{t+1} H_{b,t} \pi_{t+1} \right),$$
(6)

where $b_t$ denotes bank loans and $R_{b,t}$ is the gross interest rate. $k$ can be interpreted as a loan-to-value ratio. The borrowing constraint limits borrowing to the present discounted value of their housing holdings. The first order conditions are as follows:

$$\frac{1}{C_{b,t}} = \beta_b E_t \left( \frac{1}{\pi_{t+1} C_{b,t+1}} R_{b,t+1} \right) + \lambda_{b,t},$$
(7)

$$\frac{j}{H_{b,t}} = E_t \left( \frac{1}{C_{b,t}} q_t - \beta_b E_t \left( \frac{q_{t+1}}{C_{b,t+1}} \right) \right) - \lambda_{b,t} E_t \left( \frac{1}{R_{b,t+1}} k q_{t+1} \pi_{t+1} \right),$$
(8)

$$w_{b,t} = (N_{b,t})^{\eta-1} C_{b,t},$$
(9)

where $\lambda_{b,t}$ denotes the multiplier on the borrowing constraint.[3] These first order conditions can be interpreted analogously to the ones of savers.

Financial intermediaries, the third type of agents, solve the following problem:

$$\max E_0 \sum_{t=0}^{\infty} \beta_f^t \left[ \log \text{div}_{f,t} \right],$$

where $\beta_f \in (0,1)$ is the financial intermediary discount factor, subject to the budget constraint and the collateral constraint and $\text{div}_{f,t}$ are dividends, which we assume are fully consumed by bankers every period, so that $\text{div}_{f,t} = C_{f,t}$:

$$\text{div}_{f,t} + \frac{R_{s,t-1} d_{t-1}}{\pi_t} + b_t = d_t + \frac{R_{b,t} b_{t-1}}{\pi_t}, \tag{10}$$

where the right-hand side measures the sources of funds for the financial intermediary, household deposits and repayments from borrowers on previous loans. These funds can be used to pay back depositors and to extend new loans, or can be used for their own consumption. As in Iacoviello (2015), we assume that the bank, by regulation, is constrained by the amount of assets minus liabilities. That is, there is a capital requirement ratio. We define capital as assets minus liabilities:

$$Cap_t = b_t - d_t. \tag{11}$$

Thus, the fraction of capital with respect to assets has to be larger than a certain ratio:

$$\frac{b_t - d_t}{b_t} \geq CRR. \tag{12}$$

Simple algebra shows that this relationship can be rewritten as:

$$d_t \leq (1 - CRR) b_t. \tag{13}$$

If we define $\gamma = (1 - CRR)$, we can reinterpret the capital requirement ratio condition as a standard collateral constraint, so that banks liabilities cannot exceed a fraction of its assets, which can be used as collateral:[4]

---

[3] Through simple algebra it can be shown that the Lagrange multiplier is positive in the steady state and thus the collateral constraint holds with equality.

[4] Clerc et al. (2014) find, using a DSGE model, that the probability of default for banks is negligible for capital requirement ratios higher than 10%. Basel III imposes a capital requirement ratio of 10.5%, therefore, we assume that, taking into account the goal of the paper, in our model we do not have to include default risk for banks.

$$d_t \leq \gamma b_t, \tag{14}$$

where $\gamma < 1$. The first order conditions for deposits and loans are as follows:

$$\frac{1}{div_{f,t}} = \beta_f E_t \left( \frac{1}{div_{f,t+1}\pi_{t+1}} R_{s,t} \right) + \lambda_{f,t}, \tag{15}$$

$$\frac{1}{div_{f,t}} = \beta_f E_t \left( \frac{1}{div_{f,t+1}\pi_{t+1}} R_{b,t+1} \right) + \gamma\lambda_{f,t}, \tag{16}$$

where $\lambda_{f,t}$ denotes the multiplier on the financial intermediary's borrowing constraint.[5]

There is a continuum of identical final goods producers that operate under perfect competition and flexible prices. They aggregate intermediate goods according to the production function

$$Y_t = \left[ \int_0^1 Y_t(z)^{\frac{\varepsilon-1}{\varepsilon}} dz \right]^{\frac{\varepsilon}{\varepsilon-1}}, \tag{17}$$

where $\varepsilon > 1$ is the elasticity of substitution between intermediate goods. The final good firm chooses $Y_t(z)$ to minimize its costs, resulting in demand of intermediate good $z$:

$$Y_t(z) = \left( \frac{P_t(z)}{P_t} \right)^{-\varepsilon} Y_t. \tag{18}$$

The price index is then given by:

$$P_t = \left[ \int_0^1 P_t(z)^{1-\varepsilon} dz \right]^{\frac{1}{\varepsilon-1}}. \tag{19}$$

The intermediate goods market is monopolistically competitive. Following Iacoviello (2005), intermediate goods are produced according to the production function:

$$Y_t(z) = A_t N_{s,t}(z)^\alpha N_{b,t}(z)^{(1-\alpha)}, \tag{20}$$

where $\alpha \in [0, 1]$ measures the relative size of each group in terms of labor.[6] This Cobb-Douglas production function implies that labor efforts of

---

[5] Financial intermediaries have a discount factor $\beta_f < \beta_s$. This condition ensures that the collateral constraint of the intermediary holds with equality in the steady state, since $\lambda_f = \frac{\beta_s - \beta_f}{\beta_s} > 0$

[6] Notice that the absolute size of each group is one.

constrained and unconstrained consumers are not perfect substitutes. This specification is analytically tractable and allows for closed form solutions for the steady state of the model. This assumption can be economically justified by the fact that savers are the managers of the firms and their wage is higher than the one of the borrowers.[7]

$A_t$ represents technology and it follows the following autoregressive process:

$$\log (A_t) = \rho_A \log (A_{t-1}) + u_{At}, \tag{21}$$

where $\rho_A$ is the autoregressive coefficient and $u_{At}$ is a normally distributed shock to technology. We normalize the steady-state value of technology to 1.

Labor demand is determined by:

$$w_{s,t} = \frac{1}{X_t} \alpha \frac{Y_t}{N_{s,t}}, \tag{22}$$

$$w_{b,t} = \frac{1}{X_t} (1 - \alpha) \frac{Y_t}{N_{b,t}}, \tag{23}$$

where $X_t$ is the markup, or the inverse of marginal cost.[8]

The price-setting problem for the intermediate good producers is a standard Calvo-Yun setting. An intermediate good producer sells its good at price $P_t(z)$, and $1 - \theta, \in [0, 1]$, is the probability of being able to change the sale price in every period. The optimal reset price $P_t^*(z)$ solves:

$$\sum_{k=0}^{\infty} (\theta\beta)^k E_t \left\{ \Lambda_{t,k} \left[ \frac{P_t^*(z)}{P_{t+k}} - \frac{\varepsilon/(\varepsilon-1)}{X_{t+k}} \right] Y_{t+k}^*(z) \right\} = 0. \tag{24}$$

where $\varepsilon/(\varepsilon - 1)$ is the steady-state markup.

The aggregate price level is then given by:

$$P_t = \left[ \theta P_{t-1}^{1-\varepsilon} + (1 - \theta) (P_t^*)^{1-\varepsilon} \right]^{1/(1-\varepsilon)}. \tag{25}$$

Using (24) and (25), and log-linearizing, we can obtain a standard forward-looking New Keynesian Phillips curve $\hat{\pi}_t = \beta E_t \hat{\pi}_{t+1} - \psi \hat{x}_t + u_{\pi t}$, that relates inflation positively to future inflation and negatively to the markup ( $\psi \equiv (1 - \theta)(1 - \beta\theta)/\theta$ ). $u_{\pi t}$ is a normally distributed cost-push shock.[9]

---

[7] It could also be interpreted as the savers being older than the borrowers, therefore more experienced.
[8] Symmetry across firms allows us to write the demands without the index $z$.
[9] Variables with a hat denote percent deviations from the steady state.

The total supply of housing is fixed and it is normalized to unity, therefore house prices will be determined by demand. The market clearing conditions are as follows:

$$Y_t = C_{s,t} + C_{b,t} + C_{f,t},\qquad(26)$$

$$H_{s,t} + H_{b,t} = 1.\qquad(27)$$

Labor supply (Equations 4 and 9) and labor demand (Equations 22 and 23) are equal to each other, so that labor markets also clear. Equilibrium in financial markets is dictated by the regulatory constraint for banks, that is, $D_t = (1 - CRR)b_t$.

## Monetary Policy

In this model, we consider that the central bank follows a Taylor rule for the setting of interest rates which responds to inflation and output growth:

$$R_{s,t} = (R_{s,t-1})^\rho \left( (\pi_t)^{\left(1+\phi_\pi^R\right)} (Y_t/Y_{t-1})^{\phi_y^R} (1/\beta_s) \right)^{1-\rho} \varepsilon_{Rt},\qquad(28)$$

where $0 \le \rho \le 1$ is the parameter associated with interest-rate inertia, $\phi_\pi^R \ge 0$ and $\phi_y^R \ge 0$ measure the response of interest rates to current inflation and output growth, respectively. $\varepsilon_{Rt}$ is a white noise shock with zero mean and variance $\sigma_\varepsilon^2$.

In the standard New Keynesian model, the central bank aims at minimizing the variability of output and inflation to reduce the distortion introduced by nominal rigidities and monopolistic competition. We consider a benchmark case in which the coefficient for interest-rate smoothing is 0.8, which represents an empirically plausible value on quarterly data; and the reaction parameters for inflation and output are 0.5, as in the original paper by Taylor.

However, in models with collateral constraints, welfare analysis and the design of optimal policies involve a number of issues not considered in standard sticky-price models. In models with constrained individuals, there are three types of distortions: price rigidities, credit frictions and loan frictions. These distortions create conflicts and trade-offs between borrowers, savers and banks. Savers may prefer policies that reduce the price stickiness distortion. However, borrowers may prefer a scenario in which the pervasive effect of the collateral constraint is softened. Borrowers operate in a second-best situation. They consume according to the borrowing constraint as opposed to savers that follow an Euler equation for consumption. Borrowers cannot smooth consumption by themselves, but a more stable financial system would provide them a setting in which their consumption pattern is smoother. In turn, banks may prefer policies that ease their capital constraint, since Capital Requirement Ratios distort their ability to leverage and increase their dividends.

In the standard sticky-price model, the Taylor rule of the central bank is consistent with a loss function that includes the variability of inflation and output. In order to rationalize the objectives of the countercyclical buffer in Basel III, we follow Angelini et al. (2014) in which they assume that the loss function in the economy also contains financial variables, namely borrowing variability, as a proxy for financial stability. Then, there would be a loss function for the economy that would include not only the variability of output and inflation but also the variability of borrowing: $L = \sigma_\pi^2 + \lambda_y \sigma_y^2 + \sigma_b^2$ where $\sigma_\pi^2$, $\sigma_y^2$ and $\sigma_b^2$ are the variances of inflation, output and borrowing. $\lambda_y \geq 0$, represents the relative weight of the central bank to the stabilization of output.[10] The last term would represent the objective of the countercyclical capital buffer in Basel III regulation (Basel III $^{CB}$).

## Welfare Evaluation of the CRR

In this section we analyse welfare for different Capital Requirement Ratios, including those stated in Basel I, II and III. Throughout the section, we keep monetary policy fixed.

The two approaches that have recently been used for welfare analysis in DSGE models, as discussed in Benigno and Woodford (2012), include either characterizing the optimal Ramsey policy, or solving the model using a second-order approximation to the structural equations for given policy and then evaluating welfare using this solution. As in Rubio (2011), we take this latter approach to be able to evaluate the welfare effects of the CRR and the CCB of Basel III on the three types of agents (savers, borrowers and banks) separately. As in Mendicino and Pescatori (2007), we take this latter approach to be able to evaluate the effects for the three types of agents separately.[11] The individual welfare

---

[10] This loss function would be consistent with the studies that make a second-order approximation of the utility of individuals and find that it differs from the standard case by including financial variables.

[11] We used the software Dynare to obtain a solution for the equilibrium implied by a given policy by solving a second-order approximation to the constraints, as in Schmitt-Grohe and Uribe (2004). See Monacelli (2006) for an example of the Ramsey approach in a model with heterogeneous consumers.

for savers, borrowers, and the financial intermediary, respectively, is as follows:

$$W_{s,t} \equiv E_t \sum_{m=0}^{\infty} \beta_s^m \left[ \log C_{s,t+m} + j \log H_{s,t+m} - \frac{(N_{s,t+m})^{\eta}}{\eta} \right], \quad (29)$$

$$W_{b,t} \equiv E_t \sum_{m=0}^{\infty} \beta_b^m \left[ \log C_{b,t+m} + j \log H_{b,t+m} - \frac{(N_{b,t+m})^{\eta}}{\eta} \right], \quad (30)$$

$$W_{f,t} \equiv E_t \sum_{m=0}^{\infty} \beta_f^m \left[ \log C_{f,t+m} \right]. \quad (31)$$

### Parameter Values

The discount factor for savers, $\beta_s$, is set to 0.99 so that the annual interest rate is 4 per cent in steady state.[12] The discount factor for the borrowers is set to 0.98.[13] We set the discount factors for the bankers at 0.965 which, for a bank leverage parameter of 10 per cent, implies a spread of about 1 percent (on an annualized basis) between lending and deposit rates.[14] The steady-state weight of housing in the utility function, $j$, is set to 0.1 in order for the ratio of housing wealth to GDP to be approximately 1.40 in the steady state, consistent with the US data.[15] We set $\eta = 2$, implying a value of the labor supply elasticity of 1.[16] For the parameters controlling leverage, we set $k$, in line with the US data.[17]

---

[12] Since the seminal paper by Kydland and Prescott (1982), the literature on DSGE models considers a calibrated value of the discount factor of 0.99, to pick up the value of the interest rate in the steady state. It is considered that a reasonable value is 1% in a quarterly model (4% annualized).

[13] Lawrance (1991) estimated discount factors for poor consumers at between 0.95 and 0.98 at quarterly frequency. We take the most conservative value.

[14] For discount factors, it is only needed for the solution of the model that both borrowers and banks are more impatient than savers. Lowering discount factors for any agent would make them more impatient and therefore their marginal propensity to consume would increase. Sensitivity of their consumption with respect to shocks would be higher. However, changes in the discount factors within a realistic range represent negligible difference.

[15] Increasing the weight of housing in the utility function would in turn make this variable more sensitive to shocks. However, it is realistically calibrated in line with Iacoviello (2005) and Iacoviello and Neri (2010). Unless it is unrealistically increased, differences are negligible.

[16] Lowering $\eta$ and make it approach to 1, would make the utility function become linear in leisure, which is arguable. The value we have used make it closer to realistic values widely used in macro models with collateral constraints, closer to the value estimated by Iacoviello and Neri (2010). In fact, microeconomic estimates usually suggest values in the range of 0 and 0.5 (for males). Domeij and Flodén (2006) show that in the presence of borrowing constraints this estimates could have a downward bias of 50%.

[17] See Iacoviello (2015).

$\gamma$ is the parameter governing the CRR, which will set according to the Basel regulation that we are considering (CRR of 8 per cent for Basel I, II and 10.5 per cent for Basel III). The labor income share for savers is set to 0.64, following the estimate in Iacoviello (2005).

We assume that technology, $A_t$, follows an autoregressive process with 0.9 persistence and a normally distributed shock.[18] Table 5.1 presents a summary of the parameter values used:

Table 5.1 *Parameter values*

| | | |
|---|---|---|
| $\beta_s$ | .99 | Discount Factor for Savers |
| $\beta_b$ | .98 | Discount Factor for Borrowers |
| $\beta_f$ | .965 | Discount Factor for Banks |
| $j$ | .1 | Weight of Housing in Utility Function |
| $\eta$ | 2 | Parameter Associated with Labor Elasticity |
| $k$ | .90 | Loan-to-Value Ratio |
| $\alpha$ | .64 | Labor Income Share for Savers |
| $\rho_A$ | .9 | Technology Persistence |
| BI,II $CRR$ | .08 | CRR for Basel I, II |
| BIII $CRR$ | .105 | CRR for Basel III |
| BIII $CRR_{SS}$ | .105 | Steady State CRR for Basel III $^{CCB}$ |

*Welfare Analysis of the CRR for Given Monetary Policy*

In this section, we analyse welfare for different capital requirement ratios, including the ones stated in Basel I, II and III. Throughout this section, we keep monetary policy fixed. Even though the paper takes a positive approach, this evaluation permits us understand how macroeconomic and financial stability operate through the different channels in the model.

Figure 5.1 presents each welfare agent for different values of the CRR, given monetary policy.[19] This figure displays how welfare is affected by this parameter for each agent of the economy separately, and for the household aggregate.[20] The blue circle represents the values corresponding to the Basel I and II CRR, whereas the red triangle corresponds to the Basel III CRR. Notice that results are presented in

---

[18] The persistence of the shocks is consistent with the estimates in Iacoviello and Neri (2010).

[19] We consider a benchmark case in which the coefficient for interest-rate smoothing is 0.8, which represents an empirically plausible value, and the reaction parameters for inflation and output are 0.5, as in the original paper by Taylor.

[20] Following Mendicino and Pescatori (2007), Rubio (2011), and Brzoza-Brzezina et al. (2013), we aggregate taking into consideration the discount factor of each individual.

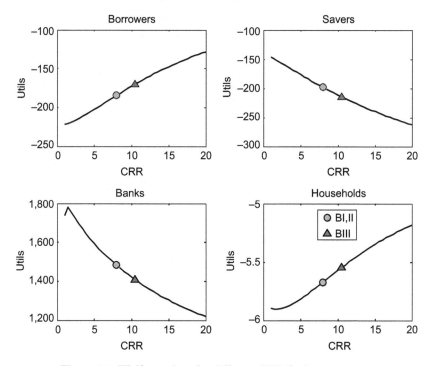

Figure 5.1 Welfare values for different CRR for borrowers, savers, banks and households (given baseline monetary policy).

welfare units, as the purpose of this figure is to illustrate the issue from an ordinal point of view.[21]

In this model, the welfare of the three agents is driven by different forces. This creates conflicts and trade-offs between them. Because savers, who own the firms, care about the sticky-price distortion, inflation affects them negatively. Furthermore, inflation makes their savings less valuable. Borrowers are collateral constrained in the amount they can borrow. Because their collateral constraint is binding, they always borrow the maximum amount they can, making it difficult for them to smooth consumption. Therefore, even though higher capital requirements pro-duce a negative level effect in their borrowing, situations that reduce the

---

[21] In this section and the next one, we do not consider welfare in consumption equivalent units since it is not clear what the benchmark situation would be. However, in the last section, when we make the comparison between Basel I and II with Basel III, we take the first case as a benchmark and present welfare gains from the new regulation in consumption equivalents.

collateral distortion and help them smooth consumption are beneficial for them. More financially stable scenarios would do it, creating a second order positive effect. Moreover, inflation is beneficial for them, because their debt repayments are lower in real terms. In turn, banks are constrained in the amount they can lend because they are required to hold a certain amount of capital by regulation. This capital requirement distorts its intertemporal consumption decision (see Equation 16). Therefore, easing their constraint reduces this distortion for banks.

The top two panels of Figure 5.1 show the trade-off that appears between borrowers and savers. A higher CRR implies a more stable financial system, because banks are constrained in the amount they can lend. Borrowers do not follow an Euler equation for consumption, like savers do; they are not able to follow a smooth path of consumption. Their consumption is, however, determined by the amount they can borrow, which in turn depends on the amount banks can lend. Therefore, even though as a level effect they can borrow less, increasing the capital requirement ratio is welfare enhancing for borrowers. This happens at the expense of savers, who are not financially constrained.

Furthermore, higher CRR makes monetary policy less effective to stabilize inflation, because the money multiplier (financial accelerator in this case) is weaker. This means that the higher the CRR, the less stabilizing monetary policy and the higher the inflation volatility. Savers suffer from the sticky-price distortion and their savings are worth less. Borrowers see their debt repayments decreasing in real terms.

If we look at the bottom right panel, we can see the evolution of the aggregate welfare. There we observe a benefit from the increase in the CRR. Thus, the transition from Basel I and II to Basel III is beneficial in aggregate terms.

Nevertheless, in the model, we have a third agent, the financial intermediary. The left bottom panel shows how banks lose in terms of welfare with the increase in the CRR, because this tightens their constraint and affects negatively their intertemporal consumption decisions.

This welfare analysis shows that the effects of the Basel regulation are not evenly distributed. A stricter regulation makes borrowers the winners, at the expense of bankers and savers, who are the losers. However, in the next sections we will show how monetary policy can help savers not to lose with the regulation.

*Welfare Analysis of Optimal Monetary Policy for Different CRR*

In the previous section, we were considering that monetary policy was taken as given, that is, that a different CRR did not affect the behaviour of

Table 5.2 *Optimal monetary policy and variabilities under different CRR*

| CRR | $1 + \phi_\pi^{R*}$ | $\phi_y^{R*}$ | $\sigma_\pi^2$ | $\sigma_y^2$ | $\sigma_b^2$ |
|---|---|---|---|---|---|
| 1% | 10.7 | 3.1 | 0.14 | 1.97 | 2.70 |
| 2% | 11 | 3.6 | 0.16 | 1.95 | 2.43 |
| 5% | 10.9 | 3.6 | 0.16 | 1.95 | 2.26 |
| **8% (BI, II)** | **17.6** | **5.8** | 0.16 | 1.95 | 2.00 |
| 10% | 20.7 | 6.6 | 0.16 | 1.96 | 1.91 |
| **10.5% (BIII)** | **20.7** | **6.6** | 0.16 | 1.96 | 1.89 |
| 15% | 20.5 | 6.6 | 0.16 | 1.96 | 1.74 |
| 20% | 20.7 | 6.6 | 0.16 | 1.96 | 1.61 |

the central bank. Although, this hypothesis does not need to be the case. It seems plausible that the optimal conduct of monetary policy changes when the CRR increases. Now, we analyse how the optimized parameters of the Taylor rule for monetary policy change for different values of the CRR. We define the optimized reaction parameters as those that maximize households (savers and borrowers) welfare. It seems plausible that the optimal conduct of monetary policy changes when the CRR increases. Then, in this subsection, we analyse how the optimized parameters of the Taylor rule for monetary policy change for different values of the CRR. We define the optimized reaction parameters as those that as those that maximize household welfare.[22] The table shows the specific values corresponding to Basel I, II and III, so that we can compare between these two regimes.[23]

Table 5.2 displays optimal monetary policy under different values of the CRR. We have presented CRR values for Basel I, II and III, on bold, and six other CRR, only for informational purposes. Results show that now monetary policy can optimally react and stabilize inflation. As we pointed out, when the CRR increases, the money multiplier (or in turn the financial accelerator) is smaller. Therefore, in order to obtain the same impact on macroeconomic volatilities, monetary policy needs to

[22] Beck et al. (2014) estimate that, on average, the financial industry accounts for about 5% of a country's GDP, based on a sample of 77 countries for the period 1980–2007. Several other authors have recently used similar measures of value added of the financial sector, including Philippon (2008), Philippon and Reshef (2013), and Cecchetti and Kharroubi (2012). Therefore, for simplicity, we consider that the regulator only considers household welfare.

[23] We have not reported results for more extreme values of the CRR because the model does not converge for CRR higher than 39%.

be more aggressive. We find that especially for the inflation reaction parameter, this is the case. If we look at the macroeconomic and financial volatilities (Columns 4–6 of Table 5.2), we observe that the macroeconomic volatility is very similar for the different values of the CRR but the financial volatility decreases, meaning that a higher CRR enhances financial stability and can thus be interpreted as a macroprudential policy.[24]

### Optimal Implementation of the Countercyclical Buffer

So far, we have only considered the compulsory capital requirements of Basel I, II and III. However, Basel III has a dynamic macroprudential component, a Countercyclical Capital Buffer that should also be taken into account. In this section, we make this Countercyclical Capital Buffer interact with monetary policy and we analyse the optimal implementation of both policies together.

### *A Rule for the Countercyclical Capital Buffer*

Following the Basel III guidelines, for the countercyclical buffer, we propose a Taylor-type rule that includes deviations of credit from its steady state, in order to explicitly promote stability and reduce systemic risk. This rule is analogous to the rule for monetary policy, but using the CRR as an instrument. It implies that the capital requirement ratio fluctuates around a steady state value, corresponding to the Basel III requirement for capital (10.5 per cent), and it increases when credit grows above its steady state. The implementation of this rule would include the Countercyclical Capital Buffer stated in Basel III $^{CCB}$. Then, the optimal implementation of Basel III $^{CCB}$ would be the value of the reaction parameter that maximize welfare:

$$CRR_t = (CRR_{SS}) \left(\frac{b_t}{b}\right)^{\phi_b} \tag{32}$$

This rule states that, whenever regulators observe that the credit deviate is above its steady-state value, they automatically increase the capital requirement ratio to avoid an excess in credit.

[24] The measure that we take as a proxy for financial stability is the variability of credit. The collateral constraint is introducing a distortion in the economy that motivates the presence of macroprudential policies. Macroprudential policies make the variability of credit decrease and therefore help palliate the second-order perverse effects of the collateral constraint, by creating a more stable financial system. The measure chosen is in line with the discussion provided by Angelini et al. (2014).

*Optimal Policy Parameters*

Table 5.3 presents results on the optimal implementation of Basel III $^{CCB}$ when it is interacting with monetary policy. We find the optimized values of both rules, monetary policy and Basel III $^{CCB}$ that maximize welfare.[25] Notice that, in this section, welfare results are presented in consumption equivalent units; that is, how much each agent would be willing to pay, in terms of consumption, in order to be in a more preferable situation.

First, we see that the transition from Basel I and II to Basel III, without its dynamic macroprudential component (the CCB) is Pareto improving for households. The appropriate re-optimization of monetary policy can make savers and borrowers better off. This is due to the fact that optimal policies aid to reach a more stable financial system, which helps borrowers to smooth consumption, and a lower inflation, which benefits savers. However, banks are always worse off because a higher CRR reduces their leverage and their capacity to make dividends.

Second, results are even better for households if we move from Basel III to Basel III plus the optimal values for the CCB and monetary policy. Furthermore, in terms of volatilities, we observe that monetary policy increases its aggressiveness when moving to Basel III and Basel III plus CCB. That means savers do not experience welfare loss with the regulation because macroeconomic stability is not in danger. We also see that introducing the Countercyclical Capital Buffer increases financial stability even more and it also helps to reduce inflation volatility.[26]

Then, implementing Basel III plus the CCB is only Pareto improving for households. If we include banks, there are winners and losers. However, if the welfare gain of winning agents were large enough, there could be room for Pareto-superior outcomes. In order to do that, we apply the concept of the Kaldor-Hicks efficiency, also known as the Kaldor-Hicks criterion.[27] Under this criterion, an outcome is considered more efficient if a Pareto-superior outcome can be reached by arranging sufficient compensation from those that are made better-off to those that are made worse-off so that all would end up no worse-off than before. The Kaldor-Hicks criterion does not require the compensation actually being paid,

---

[25] We have considered both the cases in which monetary policy and the authority taking care of implementing Basel III $^{CCB}$, act both in a coordinated and in a non-coordinated way. We have found that results do not differ for both cases. Therefore, we have reported them as a single case.

[26] We have performed a robustness check exercise including the credit to GDP with respect to their steady states in the countercyclical buffer rule. With this new specification, we have obtained very similar values, namely 2.3 for $\phi_b^*$, 45 for $1 + \phi_\pi^{R*}$ and 7.8 for $\phi_y^{R*}$.

[27] See Scitovsky (1941).

Table 5.3 *Optimal monetary policy and CB, consumption equivalent changes and variabilities*

|  | Basel I, II | Basel III | Basel III $^{CCB}$ |
|---|---|---|---|
| $\phi_b^*$ | - | - | 2.4 |
| $1 + \phi_\pi^{R*}$ | 17.6 | 20.7 | 49 |
| $\phi_y^{R*}$ | 5.8 | 6.6 | 7.4 |
| Consumption Equivalents (CE) | - | 0.045 | 0.057 |
| Borrowers CE | - | 0.012 | 2.385 |
| Savers CE | - | 0.033 | 0.077 |
| Banks CE | - | −0.669 | −0.999 |
| $\sigma_\pi^2$ | 0.16 | 0.16 | 0.08 |
| $\sigma_y^2$ | 1.95 | 1.96 | 2.1 |
| $\sigma_b^2$ | 2.00 | 1.89 | 0.82 |

merely that the possibility for compensation exists, and thus need not leave each at least as well off.

In Table 5.3, we see that this is the case. Introducing the Basel III CCB is not beneficial for banks. Albeit, a system of transfers in which borrowers and savers would compensate the banks with at least the amount they are losing; so that they are at least indifferent between having the new regulation or not. Then, the new outcome would be desirable for the society and there would be no agent that would lose with the introduction of the new policy.

### Dynamic

Impulse responses help illustrate the dynamic of the results. Figure 5.2 presents impulse responses for an expansionary monetary policy shock for the optimized values found in Table 5.3. Impulses responses show the three cases analysed: Basel I, II, Basel III and Basel III $^{CCB}$.

We perceive that, even if the shock is expansionary, the strong inflation coefficients in the Taylor rule make the nominal policy rate actually increase so that inflation is contained. However, the real rate is still negative and output is increasing. As far as real interest rate is negative, the expansion makes borrowing increase. Nevertheless, it increases by more in the case of Basel I and II because the Capital Requirement Ratio is not as high as under Basel III and Basel III with the CCB. Then, increasing the Capital Requirement Ratio reduces borrowing. In terms of the response of house prices, we see that they decrease, following the increase in the nominal interest rate. House prices are an asset price and they move inversely with the nominal interest rate. However, borrowing still increases due to the

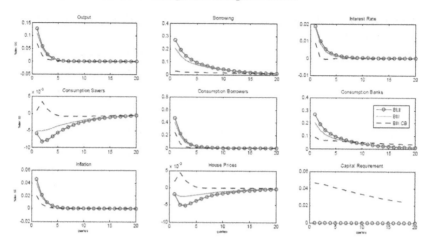

Figure 5.2 Impulse responses to a positive monetary shock. BI, II versus BIII and BIII $^{CCB}$. Optimized monetary and CB parameters.

decrease in real rates. The behavior of house prices is mainly coming from the strong response of monetary policy to inflation.

When we allow for the Countercyclical Buffer to operate, borrowing increases only slightly. The regulator, which observes that borrowing is increasing with respect to its steady state, uses its instrument to avoid this situation. Then, the Capital Requirement Ratio increases above its steady state and helps containing credit.

Therefore, increasing the static Capital Requirement Ratio, that is, going from an 8 per cent in Basel I, II to a 10.5 per cent in Basel III dampens the effects of expansionary monetary policy shocks. And introducing the Countercyclical Capital Buffer mitigates them even more. The channel comes mainly through borrowing; higher capital requirements reduce the capacity of consumers to borrow.

## Concluding Remarks

In this chapter, we apply a DSGE model with housing to compute the welfare effects of Basel I, II and III regulations and its interactions with monetary policy. The model features three types of agents: savers, borrowers and banks. The two latter are financially constrained. Banks are constrained by Basel minimum requirements ratios because they are required to hold a certain amount of capital in order to extend loans. Borrowers are constrained because they require collateral to obtain credit. There are two policy authorities: the central bank, in charge of monetary policy, and the macroprudential authority, taking care of macroprudential policies. The objective of the first one is to achieve macroeconomic stability (inflation an output), through the interest rate. The goal of the second one is to attain financial stability, using the Capital Requirement Ratio of Basel regulations.

We study the effects on welfare of increasing the Capital Requirement Ratio in the spirit of the Basel regulations for a given monetary policy. Results shows that welfare effects of Basel regulations are not evenly distributed. We find that while borrowers benefit from this measure, because it increases financial stability, savers and banks are worse off.

Then, we analyse the interaction of the higher capital requirements in Basel I, II and III regulations with monetary policy. We show that the optimal monetary policy becomes more aggressive the higher the capital requirement is, in order to compensate for a lower money multiplier. We find that a higher capital requirement increases financial stability and households' welfare.

Finally, we study the Countercyclical Capital Buffer proposed by Basel III, interacting with monetary policy. We approximate this regulation by a rule in which the capital requirement responds to deviations of credit from its steady state. We show that the transition from Basel I and II to Basel III, without its dynamic macroprudential component is Pareto improving for households and it increases financial stability. Adding the capital buffer raises even more the welfare gains for savers and borrowers, improves the financial stability by more, and it helps to reduce inflation volatility. Furthermore, even though bankers are worse off, they can be compensated by households à la Kaldor-Hicks, so that it represents a Pareto-superior outcome.

When we analyse the dynamics of the model under the optimized values, we find that higher CRR and the CCB dampen the effects of expansionary shocks through a credit restraint; therefore, achieving a macroprudential objective.

We can conclude that there exists a way to implement the Basel III regulation in order to achieve a welfare enhancing situation in a more stable financial scenario. More research and efforts should be making in order to guarantee that these reforms succeed, because that would increase the likelihood of stability, growth, innovation and investment, in which deep crises are avoided.

### References

Acharya, V. V. (2009). 'A theory of systemic risk and design of prudential bank regulation', *Journal of Financial Stability*, vol 5, no 3, 224–255.

Akram, Q. F. (2014). 'Macro effects of capital requirements and macroprudential policy', *Economic Modelling*, vol 2, 77–93.

Angelini, P., S. Neri and F. Panetta (2014). 'The interaction between Countercyclical Capital Requirements and monetary policy', *Journal of Money, Credit and Banking*, vol 46, no 6, 1073–1112.

Angeloni, I. and E. Faia (2013). 'Capital regulation and monetary policy with fragile banks', *Journal of Monetary Economics*, vol 60, no 3, 311–324.

Antipa, P., E. Mengus and B. Mojon (2010). 'Would macroprudential policy have prevented the Great Recession?' Mimeo, Banque de France.

Cecchetti, S. G. and E. Kharroubi (2012). Reassessing the impact of finance on growth, *BIS Working Paper Series*, no 381.

Bank of England (2009), 'The role of macroprudential policy', A Discussion Paper. (2011), 'Instruments of macroprudential policy', A Discussion Paper.

Basel Committee on Banking Supervision (2010a). Basel III: A global regulatory framework for more resilient banks and banking systems, *BIS document*. (2010b). Guidance for national authorities operating the Countercyclical Capital Buffer, *BIS document*.

Beck, T., H. Degryse and C. Kneer (2014). 'Is more finance better? Disentangling intermediation and size effects of financial systems', *Journal of Financial Stability*, vol 10, 50–64.

Benigno, P. and M. Woodford (2012). 'Linear-quadratic approximation of optimal policy problems,' *Journal of Economic Theory*, vol 147, no 1, 1–42.

Bernanke, B. S., M. Gertler and S. Gilchrist (1999). The financial accelerator in a quantitative business cycle framework. In: Handbook of Macroeconomics, ed. by J. B. Taylor and M. Woodford, vol 1, chap. 21, pp. 1341–1393, Elsevier.

Borio, C. (2003). Towards a macroprudential framework for financial supervision and regulation? *BIS Working Papers*, no 128. (2011). Rediscovering the macroeconomic roots of financial stability policy: Journey, challenges and a way forward. *BIS Working Papers*, no 354.

Borio, C. and I. Shim (2007). What can (macro-)policy do to support monetary policy?, *BIS Working Paper*, no 242.

Brunnermeier, M., A. Crockett, C. Goodhart, A. Persaud and H. Shin (2009). 'The fundamental principles of financial regulation', *Geneva Report on the World Economy 11*, ICCBM, Geneva and CEPR, London.

Brzoza-Brzezina, M., Kolasa, M., Makarski, K., 2013. Macroprudential policy andimbalances in the euro area, NBP Working Paper, 138.

Clerc, L., L. Derviz, C. Mendicino, S. Moyen, K. Nikolov, L. Stracca, J. Suarez and A. Vardulakis (2014). 'The 3D model: A framework to assess capital regulation,' *Economic Bulletin and Financial Stability Report Articles*, Banco de Portugal, Economics and Research Department.

Drehmann, M. and L. Gambacorta (2011). 'The effects of Countercyclical Capital Buffers on bank lending', *Applied Economics Letters*, vol 19, no 7, 603–608.

Domeij, D. and Flodén, M. (2006). The labor-supply elasticity and borrowing constraints: why estimates are biased. *Review of Economic Dynamics*, 9, 242–262.

European Commission (2013). *Scientific evidence for policy-making*. Research insights from Socio-economic Sciences and Humanities.

Gambacorta, L. and P. E. Mistrulli (2004). 'Does bank capital affect lending behavior?', *Journal of Financial Intermediation*, vol 13, 436–457.

Gerali, A., S. Neri, S. Sessa and F. Signoretti (2010). Credit and banking in a DSGE model of the euro area. *Bank of Italy Economic Working Papers*, no 740.

Gertler, M. and P. Karadi (2011). 'A model of unconventional monetary policy,' *Journal of Monetary Economics, Elsevier*, vol 58, no 1, 17–34.

Gertler, M. and N. Kiyotaki (2010). 'Financial intermediation and credit policy in business cycle analysis', in B. Friedman and M. Woodford (Eds.), *Handbook of Monetary Economics*. Pp. 547–599. Elsevier, Amsterdam, Netherlands.

Iacoviello, M. (2005). 'House prices, borrowing constraints and monetary policy in the business cycle', *American Economic Review*, vol 95, no 3, 739–764.

(2015). 'Financial business cycles', *Review of Economic Dynamics*, vol 18, no 1, 140–164.

Iacoviello, M. and Neri, S. (2010). Housing market spillovers: Evidence from an estimated DSGE model. *American Economic Journal: Macroeconomics*, vol 2, 125–164.

Kannan, P., P. Rabanal and A. Scott (2012). 'Monetary and macroprudential policy rules in a model with house price booms', *The B.E. Journal of Macroeconomics, Contributions*, vol 12, no 1, 1–44.

Kant, R. and S. Jain (2013). 'Critical assessment of capital buffers under Basel III', *Indian Journal of Finance*, vol 7, no 4, 6–12.

Kydland, F. and Prescott, E. (1982). Time to build and aggregate fluctuations. *Econometrica*, vol 50, no 6, 1345–1370.

Kishan, R. P. and T. P. Opiela (2000). 'Bank size, bank capital and the bank lending channel', *Journal of Money, Credit and Banking*, vol 32, 121–141.

Lawrance, E. (1991). 'Poverty and the rate of time preference: Evidence from paneldata.' *Journal of Political Economy*, vol 99, no 1, 54–77.

Longworth, D. (2011). A Survey of Macro- prudential Policy Issues. Mimeo, Carleton University.

Meh, C. A. and K. Moran (2010). 'The role of bank capital in the propagation of shocks', *Journal of Economic Dynamics and Control*, vol 34, no 3, 555–576.

Mendicino, C. and Pescatori, A. (2007). Credit frictions, housing prices and optimalmonetary policy rules. Mimeo.

Monacelli, T. (2006). Optimal monetary policy with collateralized household debtand borrowing constraint. In: Conference Proceedings "Monetary Policy and Asset Prices" edited by J. Campbell.

N'Diaye, P. (2009). Countercyclical macro prudential policies in a supporting role to monetary policy. *IMF Working Paper*, November.

Official Journal of the European Union (14–02–2012). Recommendation of the European Systemic Risk Board of 22 December 2011 on the macroprudential mandate of national authorities.

(15–06–2013). Recommendation of the European Systemic Risk Board of 4 April 2013 on intermediate objectives and instruments of macroprudential policy.

Philippon, T. (2008). Why has the US financial sector grown so much? The role of corporate finance, *NBER Working Paper Series*, no 13405.

Philippon, T. and A. Reshef (2013). 'An international look at the growth of modern finance: Income and human capital costs,' *Journal of Economic Perspectives*, vol 27, no 2, spring, 73–96.

Repullo, R. and J. Saurina (2012). 'The Countercyclical Capital Buffer of Basel III: A Critical Assessment'. In *The Crisis Aftermath: New Regulatory Paradigms*. M. Dewatripont and X. Freixas (Eds.). Centre for Economic Policy Research (CEPR), London.

(2013). 'The procyclical effects of bank capital regulation', *Review of Financial Studies*, vol 26, no 2, 452–490.

Rubio, M. (2011). 'Fixed- and variable-rate mortgages, business cycles, and monetary policy'. *Journal of Money, Credit and Banking*, vol 43, no 4, 657–688.

Rubio, M. and J. Carrasco-Gallego (2013). 'Macroprudential measures, housing markets, and monetary policy', *Moneda y Crédito*, no 235, 29–59.

(2014). 'Macroprudential and monetary policies: Implications for financial stability and welfare', *Journal of Banking & Finance*, vol 49, 326–336.

(2016). 'The new financial regulation in Basel III and monetary policy: A macroprudential approach', *Journal of Financial Stability*, vol 26, 294–305.

Schmitt-Grohe, S. and Uribe, M. (2004). 'Solving dynamic general equilibrium modelsusing a second-order approximation to the policy function', *Journal of Economic and Dynamic Control*, vol 28, 755–775.

Scitovszky, T. (1941). 'A note on welfare propositions in economics', *The Review of Economic Studies*, vol 9, no 1, 77–88.

Van den Heuvel, S. J. (2008). 'The welfare cost of bank capital requirements', *Journal of Monetary Economics*, vol 55, no 2, 298–320.

# 6     On the Use of Monetary and Macroprudential Policies for Small Open Economies

*F. Gulcin Ozkan* [*] *and D. Filiz Unsal* [†]

This paper explores optimal monetary and macroprudential policy rules for a small open economy under a sudden reversal of capital flows.[1] We consider Taylor-type interest rate rules as a function of inflation, output, and credit growth; and a macroprudential instrument as a function of credit growth. We have two key results. First, in the presence of macroprudential measures, there are no significant welfare gains from monetary policy also reacting to credit growth above and beyond its response to the output gap and inflation. Moreover, monetary responses to financial market developments under both financial and real shocks generate higher welfare losses than macroprudential responses; pointing to the desirability of delegating "leaning against the wind" squarely to macroprudential policy. Second, we find that the source of borrowing is an important determinant of the desirability of alternative policies: the larger the scale of foreign currency debt, the greater the effectiveness of macroprudential instruments. Given the sizable liability dollarization in emerging economies, this finding provides one explanation why macroprudential policies featured so prominently in their response to the 2008–2009 global financial crisis, in contrast to that in advanced economies.

[*] Department of Economics and Related Studies (DERS), University of York, Heslington, York, YO10 5DD, UK; Tel: 01904-434673; E-mail:gulcin.ozkan@york.ac.uk.
[†] Research Department, International Monetary Fund, 700 19th Street, N.W. Washington, D.C. 20431, USA; Tel: 202-6234352; E-mail:dunsal@imf.org.

[1] We would like to thank Chris Adams, Yunus Aksoy, Parantap Basu, David Cobham, Martin Ellison, Lynne Evans, Refet Gurkaynak, Marcus Miller, Patrick Minford, Peter Sinclair, Joe Pearlman, Rafael Portillo, Damiano Sandri, Mike Wickens, Stephen Wright, Tony Yates and seminar participants at the MMF Annual Conference, Dublin, 6–8 September 2012; at the 'Macroprudential Regulation' conference at Loughborough University, 18–19 September 2012; at seminar at Heriot-Watt University 16 January 2013 and at seminar at the Bank of England, 17 July 2013 for comments and suggestions. The views expressed in this paper are those of the authors and should not be attributed to the IMF, its Executive Board, or its Management.

## Introduction

The recent global financial crisis, widely viewed as the worst since the Great Depression of the 1930s, has forced a serious rethink of how monetary policy should be conducted. A key feature of the 2008–2009 crisis is that it was preceded by a build-up of financial vulnerabilities, particularly in housing and credit markets, in many economies against the backdrop of low inflation and robust economic activity. The role of monetary policy in contributing to the build-up of the asset price bubble and its limited ability to effectively respond to the bubble's collapse have come under close scrutiny since the onset of the crisis in 2008 (see, for example, Cecchetti, 2008 and Taylor, 2008).

Whether monetary policy should respond to the build up of asset price bubbles or to their collapse is not a new phenomenon. There had been an active debate on this issue long before the global financial crisis. Notwithstanding some prominent counter-arguments, this so called "lean versus clean" debate had led to a general agreement that monetary policy should react to asset market developments only insofar as they provide useful information for forecasting the variables in the objective function of the central bank. Central to this policy prescription was the understanding that potential costs of cleaning up after a bubble bursts are not large, a notion seriously undermined by the experiences of crisis-inflicted countries since 2008.

It is now widely recognized that price stability, the primary focus of monetary policy in the pre-crisis period, is not sufficient for financial stability. A clear consensus has emerged on the need for policy to react to asset market misalignments as a way of preventing financial instability and adverse macroeconomic outcomes. There is, however, an ongoing debate on the choice of policy instruments to be used for that purpose. The limits of using the policy rate to trade-off multiple goals – macroeconomic and financial stability – are well-known. Hence, incorporating financial stability into macroeconomic policy objectives may require looking beyond the traditional policy instruments of central banks to adopt other tools such as macroprudential measures.

Underlying the prescription of such policy measures is the notion that financial markets are inherently procyclical. That is, during boom times, perceived risk declines; asset prices increase; and lending and leverage become mutually reinforcing. Firms increase new borrowing, and the rise in domestic inflation reduces the real debt burden for leveraged households, leading to an increase in output and inflation. The opposite happens during a bust phase: a vicious cycle can arise between delever-aging, asset sales, and the real economy. In principle, macroprudential measures could address procyclicality of financial markets and reduce the amplitude of the boom-bust cycles by design.

But how is responding to financial developments through the policy rate different from responding through a macroprudential instrument? Although both instruments affect aggregate demand and supply as well as financial conditions in similar ways, they are not perfect substitutes. First, the policy rate may be "too blunt" an instrument, as it impacts all lending activities regardless of whether they represent a risk to the stability of the economy. In contrast, macroprudential regulations can be aimed specifically at markets in which the risk of financial stability is believed to be excessive. Second, in economies with open financial accounts, an increase in the interest rate is likely to have only a limited impact on credit expansion if firms can borrow at a lower rate abroad. Moreover, long-term rates are largely driven by global developments rather than a policy rate, limiting the role for monetary policy in promoting financial stability (Turner, Chapter 1 in this volume). Third, interest rate movements aiming to ensure financial stability could be inconsistent with those required to achieve macroeconomic stability, and that discrepancy could destabilize inflation and even risk de-anchoring inflation expectations.

The literature on the use of macroprudential instruments has been expanding on two fronts. The first line of research has focused on the impact of macroprudential measures in managing negative externalities that arise out of agents not internalizing the effect of their individual decisions on financial instability. For example, Jeanne and Korinek (2010) and Bianchi (2011) focus on overborrowing and consequent externalities. In these papers, regulations induce agents to internalize the consequences of their actions and thereby increase macroeconomic stability. However, overborrowing is a model-specific feature. For example, Benigno et al. (2013) find that in normal times, underborrowing is much more likely to emerge rather than overborrowing. Our paper fits into a second strand of research which analyzes the potential role of macroprudential regulations in equilibrium models where monetary policy has a non-trivial role in stabilizing the economy after a shock (see, for example, Kannan et al., 2012; Unsal, 2013; Quint and Rabanal, 2014; Angeloni et al., 2015).

We utilize an open economy New Keynesian dynamic stochastic general equilibrium (DSGE) model featuring financial frictions. The model draws on elements of the models by Bernanke et al. (1999), Gertler et al. (2007), Kannan et al. (2012), and particularly Ozkan and Unsal (2012) and Unsal (2013). In our framework, a preemptive response through monetary policy (Taylor rule) entails a reaction to a financial market variable (nominal credit growth). Macroprudential policy, on the other hand, gives rise to higher costs for financial intermediaries that are passed on to borrowers in the form of higher lending rates – what we call a "regulation premium." The regulation premium is defined as a rule which responds to nominal credit growth. This setup captures the notion that such measures make it harder for firms to borrow during boom times, and hence make the subsequent bust less dramatic, dampening the scale of fluctuations.

Our main findings are as follows. Responding to credit growth through the monetary instrument improves macroeconomic stability and hence welfare following a (negative) financial shock. However, in the presence of macroprudential measures, there are no significant welfare gains from monetary policy also reacting to credit growth above and beyond its response to output gap and inflation. In addition, welfare costs of responding to credit growth in the aftermath of a productivity shock are much higher if the response is through the policy rate than through the macroprudential instrument, pointing to the desirability of a policy mix that delegates leaning against the wind squarely to macroprudential policy. We also show that the scale of external borrowing plays a key role in the relative effectiveness of one set of policies against the other in promoting financial and macroeconomic stability. Hence, we argue that emerging market economies where foreign borrowing is sizeable are likely to find macroprudential policies particularly effective as the monetary policy responses required to stabilize financial markets in this case are unduly large.

The remainder of the chapter is organized as follows. The next section summarizes the structure of our model while leaving the details of household, firm and entrepreneurial behavior to Appendix A. The following section presents an analysis of macroeconomic outcomes under monetary and macroprudential policy regimes in the face of financial and real shocks. The fourth section conducts a quantitative welfare analysis of monetary and macroprudential policies and computes welfare maximizing responses through monetary and macroprudential policies. The final section provides the concluding remarks.

## The Model

### Basic Model Structure

Our framework is a DSGE model of an emerging economy that features the financial accelerator a lá Bernanke et al. (1999). Following Gali and Monacelli (2005) and De Paoli (2009), among many others, we derive the dynamics of small open economy (SOE) as a limiting case of a two country model where the size of the SOE is negligible relative to the size of the rest of the world (ROW). The economy is populated by households, firms, entrepreneurs, financial intermediaries and a monetary authority.

*Households* Households receive utility from consumption and provide labor to the production firms. They participate in domestic and (incomplete) international financial markets. The households own the firms in the economy and therefore receive profits from these firms.

*Firms* There are three types of firms in the model. Production firms produce a differentiated final consumption good using both capital and labor as inputs. These firms engage in local currency pricing and face price adjustment costs. As a result, final goods prices are sticky in terms of the local currency of the markets in which they are sold. Importing firms also have some market power and face adjustment costs in changing prices. Price stickiness in export and import prices causes the law of one price to fail such that exchange rate pass through is incomplete in the short run. Finally, there are competitive firms that combine investment with rented capital to produce unfinished capital goods that are then sold to entrepreneurs.

*Entrepreneurs* As is the case in this class of models, entrepreneurs are key players. They transform unfinished capital goods that are then rented to the production firms. Each entrepreneur has access to a stochastic technology in transforming unfinished capital into finished capital goods.

Entrepreneurs finance their investment by external borrowing channeled through perfectly competitive financial intermediaries. The existing literature on financial crises in emerging market economies focuses exclusively on either foreign or domestic borrowing as a source of these funds. In this paper, we consider three alternative assumptions regarding the source of borrowing: (1) only foreign borrowing, (2) only domestic borrowing, and (3) both foreign and domestic borrowing. Such a set up enables us to explore whether the composition of outstanding obligations impacts how best to respond to financial market developments.

As a benchmark scenario, we start off with the case where entrepreneurs can only borrow from foreign lenders and in foreign currency – a feature particularly relevant for emerging market countries.[2] Productivity

---

[2] See, Lane and Milesi-Ferretti (2003) for international evidence on the scale of external borrowing.

is observed by the entrepreneur, but lenders can only observe it at a monitoring cost which is assumed to be a certain fraction of the return (costly state verification). As is shown by Carlstrom and Fuerst (1997) and Bernanke et al. (1999), the optimal contract between the enterpreneurs and the lenders ensures that the entrepreneur maximizes their expected return subject to the participation constraints of the lender, leading to the following conditions

$$E_t[R_{t+1}] = E_t[(1 + i_t^*)(1 + \Phi_{t+1})],$$    (1)

where $R_{t+1}$ is the cost of borrowing to the enterpreneur, $i_t^*$ is foreign interest rate, $(1 + \Phi_{t+1})$ is the external finance premium, and $E_t$ is the expectation operatior. Clearly, the greater the perceived risk of default, the greater the external finance premium the enterpreneur needs to pay to secure funding. A greater use of external financing generates an incentive for entrepreneurs to take on more risky projects, which raises the probability of default. This, in turn, will increase the external finance premium, $\Phi$. Similarly, a fall in the entrepreneurs' net worth increases their leverage, leading to an upward adjustment in $\Phi$.

### Financial Intermediaries and Macroprudential Policy

There exists a continuum of perfectly competitive financial intermediaries who channel funds from lenders to entrepreneurs. In the baseline case with only foreign borrowing, the zero profit condition implies that the lending rates are equal to $E_t[(1 + i_t^*)(1 + \Phi_{t+1})]$ in the absence of macroprudential measures.

How does macroprudential policy influence the lending rate? The policy debate has already established a list of instruments that could be used to preserve the stability of the financial system. This includes countercyclical capital requirements, time-varying margins on certain financial transactions, limits on interbank exposures, size dependent leverage limits and caps on loan-to-value ratios, among others (see, for example, IMF, 2011). It is widely understood that, irrespective of its specific form, macroprudential policy would create higher costs for financial intermediaries (see, Angeloni et al., 2015).

We therefore base our formulation of macroprudential policy on this notion rather than deriving the impact of a particular type of macroprudential measure on the borrowing cost. We follow Kannan et al. (2012), Unsal (2013) and Quint and Rabanal (2014) to focus on a generic case where macroprudential measures raise the cost of financial intermediation. These costs are then passed on to borrowers in the form of higher interest rates.[3] We refer to the increase in lending rates brought by macroprudential measures as the "regulation premium" and maintain that it is linked – positively – to nominal credit growth. Macroprudential policy is therefore countercyclical by design: countervailing to the natural decline in perceived risk in good times and the subsequent rise in the perceived risk in bad times.

In the presence of macroprudential regulations, the spread between the lending rate and the policy rate is affected by both the external finance and the regulation premium. Hence, the lending cost for foreign borrowing, $E_t[R_{t+1}]$, becomes:

$$E_t[R_{t+1}] = E_t\left[(1 + i_t^*)(1 + \Phi_{t+1})(1 + RP_t)\right], \tag{2}$$

where $RP_t$ is the regulation premium, which is defined as a function of the credit growth in the economy. In the baseline case, it is given by:

$$RP_t = \Psi\left(\frac{S_t D_t}{S_{t-1} D_{t-1}} - 1\right) \tag{3}$$

where $S_t$ denotes the nominal exchange rate in period $t$, defined as the price of foreign currency in terms of domestic currency and $D_t$ denotes the level of external borrowing in foreign currency terms. In this definition of macroprudential policy, it is implicit that the policy objective is defined in terms of aggregate credit activity. Reasons for the choice of credit growth as our preferred financial market indicator are two-fold. First, restrictions on credit or credit growth have been among the most widely used macroprudential measures since 2008 (see, for example, Lim et al., 2011). Second, the structure of our basic model with explicit financial frictions provides a natural setting to explore the impact of policy responses to the changes in credit growth in a tractable manner.

### Monetary Policy

As is standard in the literature, we model monetary policy in terms of simple implementable rules in which the central bank sets the policy rate in response to some observable variables:

$$1 + i_t = \left[(1 + i)(\pi_t)^{\varepsilon_\pi}(Y_t/Y)^{\varepsilon_Y}(\text{credit growth})^{\varepsilon_D}\right]^\varpi[1 + i_{t-1}]^{1-\varpi}, \tag{4}$$

---

[3] By adopting a more elaborate banking sector, Angeloni et al. (2015) show that macroprudential measures indeed lead to a rise in the cost of borrowing.

where $i_t$ denotes policy rate, $\pi_t$ is CPI inflation, $Y_t$ is aggregate output, *credit growth* denotes nominal credit growth in the economy in domestic currency terms and $\varpi$ is the interest rate smoothing parameter. In (4), $i$ and $Y$ denote the steady-state levels of nominal interest rate and output. We start with an initial set of values for $\varepsilon_\pi, \varepsilon_Y, \varepsilon_D$, and $\varpi$ in the calibration. We then derive $\{\varepsilon_\pi, \varepsilon_Y, \varepsilon_D\}$ as well as $\Psi$ (the coefficient of nominal credit growth in the macroprudential tool) optimally by computing the values that maximize the total welfare of economic agents.

We solve the model numerically up to a second-order approximation around the non-stochastic steady state. We calibrate the model for a generic emerging market economy, using established values in the literature. Table 6.B1 in Appendix B summarizes the parametrization of the model for consumption, production, entrepreneurial sector and monetary policy.

## Model Dynamics

### *Monetary and Macroprudential Policy*

In this section, we explore the interaction between the financial sector and the real economy and the role of monetary and macroprudential policies in mitigating the impact of financial and productivity shocks.

We first consider an unanticipated financial shock – leading to a 1 percent rise in the perceived risk – which results in a reversal of capital of about 2.5 percent of output under the baseline scenario. We characterize this scenario as an unfavorable perception shock regarding the credit worthiness of the domestic borrowers, reflecting the commonly observed phenomenon of widespread pessimism in financial markets during financial crisis episodes. When the investors' perception about the distribution of the entrepreneurs' productivity changes, lending to domestic entrepreneurs becomes more risky, leading to a rise in the external finance premium on impact. As the cost of borrowing rises, entrepreneurs reduce their use of external financing by undertaking fewer projects. This decline in leverage causes a downward adjustment in the risk premium, mitigating the initial impact of the financial shock. Lower borrowing, however, decreases the future supply of capital and hence brings about a decrease in investment in the economy. The fall in the inflow of capital also lowers the demand for domestic currency, leading to its depreciation. Because the entrepreneurs' borrowing is denominated in foreign currency, this unanticipated change in the exchange rate also creates balance sheet effects through a rise in the real debt burden.

We then turn to the case of a negative productivity shock of 1 percent in magnitude, leading to a fall in consumption, investment and output, but a rise in inflation. A key difference between the financial and the productivity shock is that there is a tension between macroeconomic and financial stability objectives as inflation and credit growth move in opposite directions in the latter as opposed to the former case. An unfavorable productivity shock brings about a fall in real variables such as consumption, investment and output as well as in credit growth, asset prices and capital flows, similar to the case of a financial shock. However, in contrast to falling inflation under the financial shock, inflation rises following the productivity shock, leading to a rise in the policy rate and the following fall in the real exchange rate. The fact that credit growth and inflation move in opposite directions presents a trade-off between macroeconomic and financial stability objectives, with implications for the welfare ranking of alternative policy regimes.

### Should Monetary Policy Lean against the Wind?

Figures 6.1 and 6.2 present the impact of the two shocks under three policy options: (1) a standard Taylor rule; (2) a macroprudential instrument accompanying the Taylor rule; and (3) Taylor rule that responds to nominal credit growth.

In the first scenario with the financial shock (Figure 6.1), policy rates are lowered in response to a negative output gap and lower inflation (see Table 6.1 for the parameters of the policy rules, exogenously given at this stage). The lower policy rate partially offsets the impact of the higher risk premium on lending rates, stabilizing output as consumption becomes less costly. The stabilization of demand also helps to raise inflation.

Figure 6.1 compares impulse responses under the standard Taylor rule with the Taylor rule combined with a macroprudential instrument that directly counteracts the tightening of lending conditions and thus the financial accelerator effect. As is seen from Figure 6.1, macroprudential policy dampens the responses of all (plotted) real and financial variables. The reason for this is that, given the countercyclical nature of macroprudential policy, the regulation premium falls following the unfavorable financial shock, reducing the lending rate, which helps contain the fluctuations in the economy. Therefore, the consequences for output and inflation are also more muted.

In Figure 6.1, we also present the case where policymakers react to nominal credit growth in the Taylor rule, above and beyond its effect on output gap and inflation, referred to as the Taylor rule with credit growth. The policy rate is lowered more significantly under this regime,

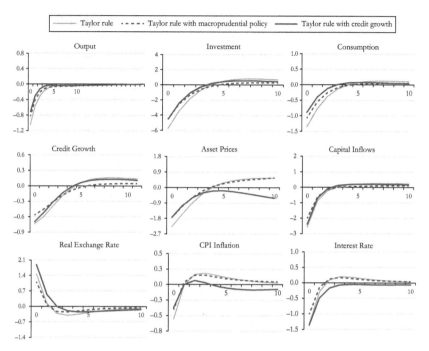

Figure 6.1. A negative financial shock: Taylor rule and
macroprudential policy[†] (percent deviations from the steady state)
[†] The figures show the impact of a 1% negative shock to the perception of
investors regarding the productivity of domestic entrepreneurs. The variables are
presented as log-deviations from the steady state (except for interest rate),
multiplied by 100 to have an interpretation of percentage deviations.

relative to the first scenario, which helps mitigate the impact of the shock
on lending rates. Indeed, the decreases in consumption, investment and
output, as well as in asset prices and credit growth are all lower under this
regime. Lower interest rates lead the exchange rate to depreciate  further.[4] Despite this, a lower decline in investment and consumption lead
to a smaller fall in output and inflation, as compared with the one under
the standard Taylor rule.

So far, the responses to macroeconomic and financial variables
through monetary policy and macroprudential measures are aligned –
both are expansionary. How do the responses change with a reaction

[4] Using a stylized open economy model, Turner (Chapter 1) emphasizes that monetary
policy and macroprudential responses to financial market developments differ mainly in
their impact on the exchange rate.

Table 6.1 *Parameters of the policy rules and the macroprudential instrument*

|  | Monetary policy | | | Macroprudential policy |
|---|---|---|---|---|
|  | Inflation | Output gap+ | Credit gr. | Credit gr. |
| Taylor rule | 1.5 | 0.5 | 0 | 0 |
| Taylor rule with credit gr. | 1.5 | 0.5 | 0.75 | 0 |
| Taylor rule + macroprud. | 1.5 | 0.5 | 0 | 0.75 |

+ Output gap is calculated as a deviation of output from its steady state.

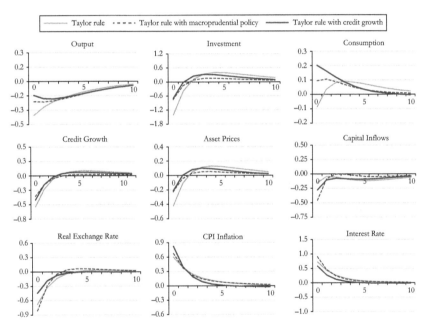

Figure 6.2. A negative productivity shock: Taylor rule with credit growth and macroprudential policy[†] (percent deviations from the steady state)
[†] The figures show the impact of a 1% negative productivity shock. The variables are presented as log-deviations from the steady state (except for interest rate), multiplied by 100 to have an interpretation of percentage deviations.

to financial market developments when there is a trade-off between macroeconomic and financial stability objectives? The responses of the economy to a productivity shock under the three policy regimes are presented in Figure 6.2. The falls in investment, output, credit growth and asset prices are smaller in the presence of macroprudential policy (Figure 6.2). However, expansionary macroprudential policy under that scenario results in higher inflation, by undoing some of the tightening brought about by the rise in the policy rate. Figure 6.2 also illustrates that when there is a response to credit growth in the Taylor rule, the impact of the productivity shock on output and credit are mitigated when compared with the standard Taylor rule. Similar to the case with macroprudential policy, however, inflation rises by about 50 percent more compared to the baseline case. It therefore appears that under the productivity shock, responding to financial market developments improves financial stability, but not necessarily macroeconomic stability.

Overall, our results suggest that leaning against the wind in the face of the financial shock through either the policy rate or the macroprudential instrument helps improve macroeconomic and financial stability. However, stabilization benefits of responding to financial market developments decline under a productivity shock.

As stated earlier, our analysis in this section is based on exogenously given parameters in both the monetary and the macroprudential rule. Next section reexamines the question of how best to respond to financial instability when policy rules are set in an optimal way.

## Optimal Policy Rules and Welfare Evaluations

We now consider the welfare gains from responding to financial market developments – proxied by nominal credit growth in our experiments – through monetary and macroprudential policy instruments.

Following Faia and Monacelli (2007) and Gertler and Karadi (2010), we start with expressing the household utility function recursively:

$$V_t = U(C_t, H_t) + \beta E_t V_{t+1}^{HH} \tag{5}$$

where $V_t$ denotes the utility function of households. We then take a second order approximation of $V_t$ around the deterministic steady state. Using the second order solution of the model, we calculate $V_t$ in each of the separate cases of monetary and macroprudential policies. We present a comparative analysis of alternative policies in terms of a consumption equivalent, $Y$, given by the fraction of consumption required to equate

Table 6.2 *Welfare results for alternative policies in response to a financial shock*

|  | Welfare loss ($\Upsilon$) |
|---|---|
| Taylor rule (TR) | 0.2106 |
| TR with credit growth (CG) | 0.1593 |
| TR + macroprudential policy (MP) | 0.1140 |
| Optimized Taylor rule (OTR) | - |
| OTR with CG | −0.0324 |
| OTR + optimized MP (OMP) | −0.1098 |
| OTR with CG+ OMP | −0.1178 |

$\lambda$ Welfare loss ($\Upsilon$) is expressed in units of steady state consumption. It represents the fraction of consumption (in %) required to equate welfare under any given policy rule to the one under the optimal simple rule, in the face of a 1% financial shock. Welfare is calculated as conditional to the initial deterministic steady state in each case.

Table 6.3 *The optimized coefficients of monetary and macroprudential policy rules in response to a financial shock*[*]

|  | Monetary policy | | Macroprudential policy | |
|---|---|---|---|---|
|  | Inflation | Output gap+ | Credit gr. | Credit gr. |
| Opt.Taylor rule (OTR) | 1.1 | 0 | - | - |
| OTR with CG | 1.1 | - | 0.6 | - |
| OTR + OMP | 2.4 | - | - | 1.1 |
| OTR with CG+OMP | 1.7 | - | 0.1 | 0.9 |

+ Output gap is calculated as a deviation of output from its steady state.
[*] We calculate the optimized parameters by searching numerically in the grid of parameters $\{\varepsilon_\pi, \varepsilon_y, \varepsilon_D, \Psi\}$ that optimize welfare $V_t$ in response to the 1% financial shock. Welfare is calculated as conditional to the initial deterministic steady state in each case.

welfare under any given monetary and macroprudential policies, to the one under the optimal Taylor rule.

As presented in Tables 6.2 and 6.4, $\Upsilon$ is a measure of welfare loss in units of steady state consumption – a higher value implies a higher welfare loss, and hence indicates that the policy is less desirable from a welfare point of view. To find the optimal simple monetary and macroprudential policy rules, we then search numerically in the grid of parameters $\{\varepsilon_\pi, \varepsilon_y, \varepsilon_D, \Psi\}$ that optimize $V_t$ in response to the financial

Table 6.4 *Welfare results for alternative policies in response to a productivity shock*

|  | Welfare loss $(\Upsilon)^{\wedge}$ |
| --- | --- |
| Taylor rule (TR) | 0.2163 |
| TR with credit growth (CG) | 0.3302 |
| TR + macroprud. policy (MP) | 0.2411 |
| Optimized Taylor rule (OTR) | - |
| OTR with CG | - |
| OTR + optimized MP (OMP) | - |
| OTR with CG+ OMP | - |

$\wedge$ Welfare loss $(\Upsilon)$ is expressed in units of steady state consumption. It represents the fraction of consumption (in %) required to equate welfare under any given policy rule to the one under the optimal simple rule, in the face of a 1% productivity shock. Welfare is calculated as conditional to the initial deterministic steady state in each case.

Table 6.5 *The optimized coefficients of monetary and macroprudential policy rules in response to a productivity shock*[*]

|  | Monetary policy | | | Macroprudential policy |
| --- | --- | --- | --- | --- |
|  | Inflation | Output gap+ | Credit gr. | Credit gr. |
| Opt.Taylor rule (OTR) | 1.1 | 0 | - | - |
| OTR with CG | 1.1 | - | 0 | - |
| OTR + OMP | 1.1 | - | - | 0 |
| OTR with CG+OMP | 1.1 | - | 0 | 0 |

+ Output gap is calculated as a deviation of output from its steady state.
* We calculate the optimized parameters by searching numerically in the grid of parameters $\{\varepsilon_\pi, \varepsilon_y, \varepsilon_D, \Psi\}$ that optimize welfare $V_t$ in response to the 1% productivity shock. Welfare is calculated as conditional to the initial deterministic steady state in each case.

and productivity shocks. Tables 6.3 and 6.5 show the optimized monetary and macroprudential policy parameters.

### Optimal Monetary versus Macroprudential Policy Rules

Under both financial and the productivity shocks, we find that the optimal response to inflation is close to unity, and response to output gap is zero in line with Schmitt-Grohe and Uribe (2007) and Faia and Monacelli (2007). Hence, in what follows we set $\varepsilon_Y$ to zero, and focus on the parameters of inflation and nominal credit growth in the monetary policy rule, and nominal credit growth in the macroprudential policy rule.[5]

Clearly, responding to credit market developments following a financial shock is welfare improving. The welfare loss decreases by about 0.05 and 0.1 percent of steady state consumption under the Taylor rule with a credit growth response and the macroprudential policy rule, respectively (Table 6.2). More interestingly, even when the coefficients of the Taylor rule are optimized to minimize the welfare losses in response to the shock, the optimized coefficient for credit growth in the macroprudential instrument is not zero (1.1) (Table 6.3). The presence of the macroprudential instrument, however, calls for a more aggressive monetary policy response to inflation (2.4 as opposed to 1.1). This is because a strong expansionary macroprudential response could outweigh the negative impact of the shock on credit conditions, and result in increases in demand and inflation, which calls for a more aggressive anti-inflationary stance. Nonetheless, the improvement in welfare from using the macroprudential instrument is significant (0.1 percent of steady state consumption) compared to even the optimal Taylor rule. The optimized coefficient for the credit growth in the Taylor rule is not zero either (0.6), but the welfare gains relative to the optimal Taylor rule are rather small (0.03).

In the face of a financial shock, there is little role for financial market developments in the monetary policy rule when the macroprudential instrument is in place. As shown in Table 6.2, the welfare effects of incorporating nominal credit growth in the policy rule (last row) is negligible. Consistently, the optimized coefficient is also close to zero (Table 6.3).

Tables 6.4 and 6.5 present the welfare losses and the optimized coefficients of alternative policies following the productivity shock. The welfare loss increases by about 0.12 percent of steady state consumption when the policy rate responds to credit growth. Not surprisingly, the coefficient of the nominal credit growth in the Taylor rule turns out to be zero (Table 6.5). Under a productivity shock, macroprudential measures also decrease welfare, but welfare costs are one-fifth of the costs under the policy where the Taylor rule responds to credit growth.

---

[5] We only report the results for interest rate inertia coefficient $\varpi = 0.5$. The optimized coefficients and welfare evaluations slightly change for varying values of $\varpi$, but the results remain valid.

*The Role of the Source of Borrowing*

The source of borrowing (foreign versus domestic) plays an important role in the desirability of alternative policies in responding the financial market developments. There are two reasons for this. First, with foreign borrowing (denominated in foreign currency), the depreciation of the exchange rate reduces entrepreneurial net worth and amplifies the financial accelerator mechanism, thereby leading to a more severe impact on the financial sector. As a result, promoting financial stability through monetary policy would require a more aggressive response, jeopardizing macroeconomic stability. Second, when the only source of credit for entrepreneurs is external, the borrowing cost is a function of the foreign interest rate, external finance premium, and the regulation premium. Hence, in contrast to the macroprudential policy, the policy rate does not directly influence the cost of credit, and consequently responding to financial market developments through the monetary policy instrument is less effective. In contrast, when borrowing is of domestic origin only, the policy rate directly influences the cost of credit. In this case, the benefits of using two separate instruments relative to responding to financial markets through the policy rate tend to be negligible.

We now turn to welfare results and optimized coefficients under the three different borrowing assumptions, as presented in Table 6.6. Welfare outcomes reveal that, under foreign borrowing, responding to

Table 6.6 *The optimized responses to credit markets under a financial shock: Sources of borrowing*

| Sources of Borrowing | Welfare loss ($\Upsilon$) | | Opt. coefficient of credit Gr.* | |
|---|---|---|---|---|
| | Opt. Taylor Rule | Opt. MP Rule | Taylor Rule | MP Rule |
| Foreign | −0.0321 | −0.1098 | 0.63 | 1.14 |
| Domestic | −0.0205 | −0.0310 | 0.47 | 0.65 |
| Domestic and Foreign | −0.0262 | −0.0447 | 0.51 | 0.82 |

$\wedge$ Welfare loss ($\Upsilon$) is expressed in units of steady state consumption. It represents the fraction of consumption (in %) required to equate welfare under any given policy rule to the one under the optimal simple rule in the face of a 1% financial shock. Welfare is calculated as conditional to the initial deterministic steady state in each case.

* We calculate the optimized responses by searching numerically in the grid of parameters $\{\varepsilon_\pi, \varepsilon_y, \varepsilon_D, \Psi\}$ that optimize welfare $V_t$ in response to the 1% financial shock. Welfare is calculated as conditional to the initial deterministic steady state in each case.

financial market developments using the monetary instrument following a financial shock is greatly inferior – about 7 percent of steady state consumption – to using the macroprudential instrument. Indeed, the optimized coefficient for credit growth in the macroprudential rule (1.14) is higher than the optimized coefficient of credit growth in the monetary policy rule (0.63). The difference in welfare gains (optimized coefficients) between using the two policies narrows down to about 2 percent when the model allows for both foreign and domestic borrowing. When borrowing is only of a domestic type, responding through the policy rate or the macroprudential instrument becomes indifferentiable from a welfare point of view, and the optimized coefficients for the nominal credit growth in both instrument are close. Note that the welfare gains from both policies are smaller under domestic borrowing as compared with the other two cases, as the impact of the shock on the financial sector and the overall economy is smaller in this case, as mentioned previously.

The finding that the source of borrowing matters for the choice of policy instrument in responding to credit market developments has practical policy implications. For emerging market economies where the size of foreign borrowing is typically large, using monetary policy in promoting financial stability is likely to generate more macro-financial instability than using macroprudential measures. Indeed, countries with significant external obligation have employed a number of macroprudential tools after the global financial crisis (Lim et al., 2011).

### Conclusions

A key lesson from the recent financial crisis experience is that the objective of financial stability should be made a central part of macroeconomic management. Motivated by this issue, we explore how best to design monetary and macroprudential policies in an open economy New Keynesian general equilibrium model, incorporating the complementarities between the two sets of policies.

In our set-up, a response to credit market developments through monetary policy entails a reaction to a financial market variable in the policy rule while macroprudential policy imposes costs on financial intermediaries that are then passed on to borrowers. We have modelled the initial shock as an increase in investors' perception of risk, which leads to a sudden reversal of capital inflows and hence tightening in credit conditions. Given the explicit consideration of financial frictions, both monetary and macroprudential policies have a non-trivial role in mitigating the impact of this shock.

Our results can be summarized as follows. Following a financial shock, leaning against the wind either through the policy rate or through macroprudential measures helps towards macroeconomic and financial stability, although macroprudential policy does a better job quantitatively. However, when macroprudential measures are in place, welfare gains from responding to credit growth through traditional monetary policy tools is negligible. Moreover, under a productivity shock, it is more costly from a welfare point of view to respond to financial market developments through monetary policy than through macroprudential policies. We also find that in economies with sizable foreign borrowing, using a separate macroprudential instrument is even more desirable. The reason for this is that, as opposed to the macroprudential tool, monetary policy cannot directly influence the cost of foreign borrowing, and hence promoting financial stability would require large policy rate changes which could exacerbate macroeconomic and financial volatility.

In this paper, among other simplifying assumptions, we maintain that exchange rate is fully flexible. We have thus excluded exchange rate interventions from the policy toolkit, and only focus on monetary and macroprudential policy rules. However, many emerging markets have intervened in foreign exchange markets during and after the global financial crisis to dampen movements in exchange rates and smooth the impact of volatile capital flows. We believe that examination of this issue together with monetary and macroprudential policies can make important contributions to our understanding of how best to preserve the stability of financial systems following a shock to capital inflows and intend to take up these issues in future research.

## References

Angeloni, I., E. Faia and M. Lo Duca (2015). "Monetary policy and risk taking," *Journal of Economic Dynamics and Control*, vol 52, 285–307.

Benigno, G., C. Huigang, O. Christopher, R. Alessandro and E. Young (2013). "Financial crisis and macroprudential policies," *Journal of International Economics*, vol 89, no 2, 453–470.

Bernanke, B. S., M. Gertler and S. Gilchrist (1999). "The financial accelerator in a quantitative business cycle framework." In J. B. Taylor and M. Woodford (Eds.), *Handbook of Macroeconomics*, Vol 1C, Amsterdam: North-Holland, 1341–1393.

Bianchi, J. (2011). "Overborrowing and systemic externalities in the business cycle," *American Economic Review*, vol 101, no 7, December, 3400–3426.

Carlstrom, C. and T. Fuerst (1997). "Agency costs, net worth, and business fluctuations: A computable general equilibrium analysis." *American Economic Review*, vol 87, no 5, 893–910.

Cecchetti, S. G. (2008). "Measuring the macroeconomic risks posed by asset price booms." In J. Y. Cambell (Ed.), *Asset Prices and Monetary Policy*. Chicago: University of Chicago Press, 9–34.

Curdia, V. (2007). *Monetary policy under sudden stops. Federal Reserve Bank of New York*, Staff Report No. 278.

    (2008). *Optimal monetary policy under sudden stops. Federal Reserve Bank of New York*, Staff Report no. 323.

De Paoli, B. (2009). "Monetary policy and welfare in a small open economy," *Journal of International Economics*, vol 77, no 1, 11–22.

Devereux, M. B., P. R. Lane and J. Xu (2006). "Exchange rates and monetary policy in emerging market economies," *The Economic Journal*, vol 116, 478–506.

Faia, E. and T. Monacelli (2007). "Optimal interest rate rules, asset prices and credit frictions," *Journal of Economic Dynamics & Control*, vol 31, 3228–3254.

Galí, J. and T. Monacelli (2005). "Monetary policy and exchange rate volatility in a small open economy," *Review of Economic Studies*, vol 72, no 3, 707–734.

Gertler, M. and P. Karadi (2011). "A model of unconventional monetary policy," *Journal of Monetary Economics*, vol 58, 17–34.

Gertler, M., S. Gilchrist and F. Natalucci (2007). "External constraints on monetary policy and the financial accelerator," *Journal of Money, Credit and Banking*, vol 39, 295–330.

International Monetary Fund (2011). *World Economic Outlook: Tensions from the Two-Speed Recovery: Unemployment, Commodities, and Capital Flows*. Washington, April.

Jeanne, O. and A. Korinek (2010). Managing credit booms and busts: A Pigouvian taxation perspective. *NBER Working Paper*, no 16377.

Kannan, P., P. Rabanal and A. Scott (2012). "Monetary and macroprudential policy rules in a model with house price booms," *B.E. Journal of Macroeconomics, Contributions*, vol 12, no 1, Article 16.

Lane, P. and G. Milesi-Ferretti (2003). "International financial integration," *IMF Staff Papers*, vol 50, 82–113.

Lim, C., F. Columba, A. Costa, P. Kongsamut, A. Otani, M. Saiyid, T. Wezel and X. Wu (2011). Macroprudential policy: What instruments and how to use them? *IMF Working Paper*, no.11/238.

Ozkan, G. and D. F. Unsal (2012). *Global financial crisis, financial contagion, and emerging markets. IMF Working Paper*, no. 12/293.

Quint, D. and P. Rabanal (2014). "Monetary and macroprudential policy in an estimated DSGE model of the Euro Area," *International Journal of Central Banking*, vol 10, no 2.

Rotemberg, J. (1982). "Sticky prices in the United States," *Journal of Political Economy*, vol 90, 1187–1211.

Schmitt-Grohe, S. and M. Uribe (2007). "Optimal simple and implementable monetary and fiscal rules," *Journal of Monetary Economics*, vol 54, no 6, 1702–1725.

Taylor, J., 2008. The financial crisis and the policy responses: An empirical analysis of what went wrong, *Keynote Lecture at the Bank of Canada, Ottawa*, November.

Unsal, D. F. (2013). "Capital flows and financial stability: Monetary policy and macroprudential responses," *International Journal of Central Banking*, vol 9, no 1, 233–285.

# Appendix

## A    Model Equations: Domestic Economy

The model for the domestic small open economy is presented in this section. Although asymmetric in size, the domestic and foreign countries share the same preferences, technology and market structure for consumption and capital goods.[6] In what follows, variables without superscripts refer to the domestic economy variables, while variables with a star indicate variables from the foreign economy or ROW, unless indicated otherwise.

### A.1    Households

An infinitely lived representative household seeks to maximize $E_0 \sum_{t=0}^{\infty} \left( \beta^t \frac{1}{1-\sigma} \left( C_t - \frac{H_t^{1+\varphi}}{1+\varphi} \right)^{1-\sigma} \right.$, where $C_t$ is a composite consumption index, $H_t$ is hours of work, where $0 < \beta < 1$, $\sigma > 0$, and $\varphi > 0$.
$C_t = \left[ (1-\alpha)^{\frac{1}{\gamma}} C_{H,t}^{(\gamma-1)/\gamma} + (\alpha)^{\frac{1}{\gamma}} C_{M,t}^{(\gamma-1)/\gamma} \right]^{\gamma/(\gamma-1)}$ is the composite consumption index, where $\gamma > 0$. Demand functions for home $(C_{H,t})$ and imported goods $(C_{M,t})$ are:

$$C_{H,t} = (1-\alpha) \left( \frac{P_{H,t}}{P_t} \right)^{-\gamma} C_t, \tag{A.1}$$

$$C_{M,t} = \alpha \left( \frac{P_{M,t}}{P_t} \right)^{-\gamma} C_t, \tag{A.2}$$

and the corresponding price index is given by:

$$P_t = \left[ (1-\alpha) P_{H,t}^{1-\gamma} + \alpha P_{M,t}^{1-\gamma} \right]^{1/(1-\gamma)}, \tag{A.3}$$

---

[6] We use a similar version of the model for the foreign economy with the exception that entrepreneurs in the domestic country borrow in foreign currency while entrepreneurs in the foreign country borrow in their own currency.

where $P_{H,t}$ and $P_{M,t}$ represent the prices for domestic and imported goods and $P_t$ denotes the consumer price index.

Households have access to two types of non-contingent, one-period debt; one denominated in domestic currency, $B_t$, and the other in foreign currency, $D_t^H$. Households need to pay a premium $\Psi_{D,t} = \frac{\Psi_D}{2}\left[\exp\left(\frac{S_t D_{t+1}^H}{P_t GDP_t} - \frac{SD^H}{PGDP}\right) - 1\right]^2$, where $S_t$ is the nominal exchange rate when borrowing from the ROW.

The first order conditions for representative household are given by:

$$\chi H_t^\varphi = W_t, \tag{A.4}$$

$$\left(C_t - \frac{\chi}{1+\varphi}H_t^{1+\varphi}\right)^{-\sigma}$$
$$= \beta(1+i_t)E_t\left[\left(C_{t+1} - \frac{\chi}{1+\varphi}H_{t+1}^{1+\varphi}\right)^{-\sigma}\frac{P_t}{P_{t+1}}\right], \tag{A.5}$$

$$\left(C_t - \frac{\chi}{1+\varphi}H_t^{1+\varphi}\right)^{-\sigma}$$
$$= \beta(1+i_t^*)\Psi_{D,t}E_t\left[\left(C_{t+1} - \frac{\chi}{1+\varphi}H_{t+1}^{1+\varphi}\right)^{-\sigma}\frac{P_t}{P_{t+1}}\frac{S_{t+1}}{S_t}\right]. \tag{A.6}$$

### A.2     Production Firms

Each production firm produces a differentiated good indexed by $j \in 0,1]$ using the production function $Y_t(j) = A_t N_t(j)^{1-\eta}K_t(j)^\eta$, where $A_t$ denotes labor productivity, and $N_t(j) = H_t(j)^{1-\Omega}H_t^E(j)^\Omega$ is the labor input which is a composite of household, $H_t(j)$, and entrepreneurial labor, $H_t^E(j)$. $K_t(j)$ denotes capital provided by the entrepreneur.

Firms segment domestic and foreign markets with local currency pricing, where $P_{H,t}(j)$ and $P_{X,t}(j)$ denote the price in the domestic market and price in the foreign market. Firms also face quadratic menu costs in changing prices given by $\frac{\Psi_i}{2}\left(\frac{P_{i,t}(j)}{P_{i,t-1}(j)} - 1\right)^2$ for $i = H, X$.[7]

Domestic and foreign demand for the domestically produced good $j$ are given by $Y_{H,t}(j)$ and $Y_{X,t}(j)$. We assume that different varieties have the same elasticities in both markets, so that the demand for good $j$ can

---

[7] The existence of menu costs generates a gradual adjustment in the prices of goods in both markets, as suggested by Rotemberg (1982).

be written as $Y_{i,t}(j) = \left(\frac{P_{i,t}(j)}{P_{i,t}}\right)^{-\lambda} Y_{i,t}$, for $i = H, X$; where $P_{H,t}$ is the aggregate price index for goods sold in the domestic market and $P_{X,t}$ is the export price index. $Y_{X,t}$ denotes the foreign aggregate export demand for domestic goods and determined in the ROW block of the model.

Cost minimizing behavior implies the following first order conditions:

$$W_t = \frac{(1-\eta)(1-\Omega)Y_t MC_t}{N_t}, \tag{A.7}$$

$$W_t^E = (1-\eta)\Omega Y_t MC_t, \tag{A.8}$$

$$R_t = \frac{\eta Y_t MC_t}{K_t}, \tag{A.9}$$

where $W_t^E$ is the entrepreneurial wage rate, $R_t$ is the rental rate of capital and $MC_t$ is the marginal cost.

Since the profit maximization condition is symmetric among firms, the optimal price setting equations can be written in aggregate terms:

$$P_{H,t} = \frac{\lambda}{\lambda-1}MC_t - \frac{\Psi_H}{\lambda-1}\frac{P_t}{Y_{H,t}}\frac{P_{H,t}}{P_{H,t-1}}\left(\frac{P_{H,t}}{P_{H,t-1}}-1\right)$$
$$+ \frac{\Psi_H}{\lambda-1}E_t\left[\Theta_t\frac{P_{t+1}}{Y_{H,t}}\frac{P_{H,t+1}}{P_{H,t}}\left(\frac{P_{H,t+1}}{P_{H,t}}-1\right)\right], \tag{A.10}$$

$$S_t P_{X,t} = \frac{\lambda}{\lambda-1}MC_t - \frac{\Psi_X}{\lambda-1}\frac{P_t}{Y_{X,t}}\frac{P_{X,t}}{P_{X,t-1}}\left(\frac{P_{X,t}}{P_{X,t-1}}-1\right)$$
$$+ \frac{\Psi_X}{\lambda-1}E_t\left[\Theta_t\frac{P_{t+1}}{Y_{X,t}}\frac{P_{X,t+1}}{P_{X,t}}\left(\frac{P_{X,t+1}}{P_{X,t}}-1\right)\right], \tag{A.11}$$

where $\Theta_t = \beta\frac{\left(C_{t+1} - \frac{\chi}{1+\varphi}H_{t+1}^{1+\varphi}\right)^{-\sigma}}{\left(C_t - \frac{\chi}{1+\varphi}H_t^{1+\varphi}\right)^{-\sigma}}\frac{P_t}{P_{t+1}}$.

### A.3   Importing Firms

Let $Y_{M,t}$ denote the aggregate import demand of the domestic economy. The price index for the imported goods is:

$$P_{M,t} = \frac{\lambda}{\lambda-1}S_t P_t^* - \frac{\Psi_M}{\lambda-1}\frac{P_t}{Y_{M,t}}\frac{P_{M,t}}{P_{M,t-1}}\left(\frac{P_{M,t}}{P_{M,t-1}}-1\right)$$
$$+ \frac{\Psi_M}{\lambda-1}E_t\left[\Theta_t\frac{P_{t+1}}{Y_{M,t}}\frac{P_{M,t+1}}{P_{M,t}}\left(\frac{P_{M,t+1}}{P_{M,t}}-1\right)\right], \tag{A.12}$$

## A.4    Unfinished Capital Producing Firms

Aggregate investment in period $t$, denoted by $I_t$, $= [\alpha^{\frac{1}{\gamma}} I_{H,t}^{(\gamma-1)/\gamma} + (1-\alpha)^{\frac{1}{\gamma}}$
$I_{M,t}^{(\gamma-1)/\gamma}]^{\gamma/(\gamma-1)}$ is composed of domestic and imported investment goods,
which are priced the same as their consumption goods' counterparts,
$P_{H,t}$ and $P_{M,t}$.

Competitive firms use investment as an input, $I_t$ and combine it with
rented capital $K_t$ to produce unfinished capital goods. We allow for
adjustment costs, $\frac{\psi_I}{2}\left(\frac{I_t}{K_t} - \delta\right)^2$ where $\delta$ is the depreciation rate.

The optimality condition for the unfinished capital producing firms
with respect to the choice of $I_t$ gives the nominal price of a unit of capital
$Q_t$. The cost minimization problem of the unfinished capital producer
firms yields:

$$I_{H,t} = (1-\alpha)\left(\frac{P_{H,t}}{P_t}\right)^{-\gamma} I_t \tag{A.13}$$

and

$$I_{M,t} = \alpha\left(\frac{P_{M,t}}{P_t}\right)^{-\gamma} I_t. \tag{A.14}$$

## A.5    Entrepreneurs

There is a continuum of entrepreneurs indexed by $k$ in the interval $[0,1]$.
Each entrepreneur has access to a stochastic technology in transforming
$K_{t+1}(k)$ units of unfinished capital into $\omega_{t+1}(k)K_{t+1}(k)$ units of finished
capital goods. The idiosyncratic productivity $\omega_t(k)$ is assumed to be i.i.d.,
drawn from a distribution $F(.)$, with p.d.f of $f(.)$ and $E(.) = 1$.[8]

We describe here the baseline scenario where entrepreneurs can only
borrow from foreign lenders in foreign currency. At the end of period $t$,
the budget constraint of the entrepreneur is $P_t NW_t(k) = Q_t K_{t+1}(k) - S_t D_{t+1}^F(k)$, where $NW_t(k)$ is the net worth and $D_{t+1}^F$ denotes foreign
currency denominated debt.

Productivity is observed by the entrepreneur, but not by the lenders.
Following Curdia (2007, 2008) we specify the lenders' perception of
$\omega_{t+1}(k)$ as given by $\omega_{t+1}^*(k) = \omega_{t+1}(k)\varrho_t$ where $\ln(\varrho_t) = \rho_\varrho \ln(\varrho_{t-1}) + \varepsilon_\varrho$
is the misperception factor over a given interval $[0,1]$. We take the origin

[8] Following Bernanke et al. (1999) and Gertler et al. (2007), among others, we assume
$\log(\omega_t(k)) \sim N\left(\frac{-1}{2}\sigma_\omega^2, \sigma_\omega^2\right)$.

of the financial shock as a change in lenders' perception regarding idiosyncratic productivity ($\varepsilon_\varrho$).

Entrepreneurs observe $\omega_{t+1}(k)$ ex post, but the lenders can only observe it at a monitoring cost which is a certain fraction ($\mu$) of the return. The contracting problem identifies the capital demand of entrepreneurs $K_{t+1}(k)$ and a cut off value, $\overline{\omega}_{t+1}(k)$, below which the borrowers default.

One can write the expected return to entrepreneurs and lenders, respectively as follows:

$$E_t\left[R^K_{t+1}Q_tK_{t+1}\left(\int_{\overline{\omega}_{t+1}}^{\infty}\omega f(\omega)d\omega - \overline{\omega}_{t+1}\int_{\overline{\omega}_{t+1}}^{\infty} f(\omega)d\omega\right)\right]$$
$$= E_t\left[R^K_{t+1}Q_tK_{t+1}z(\overline{\omega}_{t+1})\right], \qquad (A.15)$$

$$E_t\left[R^K_{t+1}Q_tK_{t+1}\left(\overline{\omega}^*_{t+1}\int_{\overline{\omega}_{t+1}}^{\infty} f(\omega^*)d\omega^* + (1-\mu)\int_0^{\omega_{t+1}} \omega^*_{t+1}f(\omega^*)d\omega^*\right)\right]$$
$$= E_t\left[R^K_{t+1}Q_tK_{t+1}g(\overline{\omega}_{t+1};\varrho_t)\right], \qquad (A.16)$$

where $R^K_t$ denotes the *ex-post* realization of return to capital, $z(\overline{\omega})$ is the borrowers' share of the total return, and $g(\overline{\omega};\varrho)$ represents the lenders' share of the total return, itself a function of both the idiosyncratic shock and the perception factor.

For lenders, the participation condition is given by:

$$E_t\left[\frac{R^K_{t+1}Q_tK_{t+1}}{S_{t+1}}g(\overline{\omega}_{t+1};\varrho_t)\right] = (1+i^*_t)D_{t+1}, \qquad (A.17)$$

Given that $z(\overline{\omega}_t)+g(\overline{\omega}_t,\varrho_t) = 1 - v_t$ (where $v_t$ is the cost of monitoring), we can rewrite entrepreneurs' net worth as:

$$P_tNW_t = \vartheta R^K_t Q_{t-1}K_t(1-v_t) - (1+i^*_{t-1})S_tD_t] + W^E_t, \qquad (A.18)$$

The entrepreneurs leaving the scene at time $t$ consume their return on capital. The consumption of the exiting entrepreneurs, $C^E_t$, is given by:

$$P_tC^E_t = (1-\vartheta)[R^K_t Q_{t-1}K_t(1-v_t) - (1+i^*_{t-1})S_tD_t]. \qquad (A.19)$$

Entrepreneurs' demand functions for domestic and imported consumption goods are:

$$C_{H,t}^E = (1 - \alpha) \left( \frac{P_{H,t}}{P_t} \right)^{-\gamma} C_t^E, \tag{A.20}$$

$$C_{M,t}^E = \alpha \left( \frac{P_{M,t}}{P_t} \right)^{-\gamma} C_t^E. \tag{A.21}$$

### A.6    Financial Intermediaries and Macroprudential Policy

See the second section in the text.

### A.7    Monetary Policy

See the fourth section in the text.

### A.8    General Equilibrium

$$Y_t = Y_{H,t} + Y_{X,t}^*, \tag{A.22}$$

where

$$Y_{H,t} = C_{H,t} + C_{H,t}^E + I_{H,t} + (1 - \alpha) \left( \frac{P_{H,t}}{P_t} \right)^{-\gamma}$$
$$\left[ \sum_{i=H,X} \frac{\Psi_i}{2} \left( \frac{P_{i,t}}{P_{i,t-1}} - 1 \right)^2 + \frac{\Psi_M}{2} \left( \frac{P_{M,t}}{P_{M,t-1}} - 1 \right)^2 + \nu_t \frac{R_t^K}{P_t} Q_{t-1} K_t \right], \tag{A.23}$$

$$Y_{X,t}^* = C_{M,t} + C_{M,t}^E + I_{M,t} + \alpha \left( \frac{P_{M,t}}{P_t} \right)^{-\gamma}$$
$$\left[ \sum_{i=H,X} \frac{\Psi_i}{2} \left( \frac{P_{i,t}}{P_{i,t-1}} - 1 \right)^2 + \frac{\Psi_M}{2} \left( \frac{P_{M,t}}{P_{M,t-1}} - 1 \right)^2 + \nu_t \frac{R_t^K}{P_t} Q_{t-1} K_t \right]. \tag{A.24}$$

## B    Calibration

We calibrate the model for a generic emerging market economy, using established values in the literature. Table 6.B1 summarizes the parametrization of the model for consumption, production, entrepreneurial sector and monetary policy. The discount factor, $\beta$ is set at 0.99, implying a riskless annual return of approximately 4 percent in the steady state

Table 6.B1 *Parameter values for consumption, and production sectors*

| | |
|---|---|
| $\beta = 0.99$ | Discount factor |
| $\sigma = 2$ | Inverse of the intertemporal elasticity of substitution |
| $\gamma = 1$ | Elasticity of substitution between domestic and foreign goods |
| $\varphi = 2$ | Frisch elasticity of labor supply |
| $(1 - \alpha) = 0.35$ | Degree of openness |
| $\eta = 0.35$ | Share of capital in production |
| $\lambda = 11$ | Elasticity of substitution between domestic goods |
| $\delta = 0.025$ | Quarterly rate of depreciation |
| $\Omega = 0.01$ | Share of entrepreneurial labor |
| $\psi_I = 12$ | Investment adjustment cost |
| $\psi_D = 0.0075$ | Responsiveness of household risk premium to debt/GDP |
| $\psi_i; \psi_M = 120$ | Price adjustment costs for i = H;X |
| $\varpi = 0.5$ | Inertia in the policy rule |
| $\rho_Q = 0.5$ | Persistence of the domestic perception shock |
| $\phi_t = 0.02$ | External risk premium |
| $\mu = 0.2$ | Monitoring cost |
| $\vartheta = 0.9933$ | Survival rate |

(time is measured in quarters). We set the inverse of the elasticity of intertemporal substitution, $\sigma$, at 1, in line with much of the literature. The inverse of the elasticity of labour supply $\varphi$ is set at 2. The degree of openness, $(1 - \alpha)$, and the share of capital in production, $\eta$, are set at 0.35, consistent with Gertler et al. (2007). Following Devereux et al. (2006), the elasticity of substitution between differentiated goods of the same origin, $\lambda$, is taken to be 11, implying a flexible price equilibrium mark-up of 1.1, and price adjustment cost is assumed to be 120 for all sectors. The quarterly depreciation rate $\delta$ is taken to be 0.025, a conventional value used in the literature. The share of entrepreneurs' labour, $\Omega$, is set at 0.01, implying that 1 percent of the total wage bill goes to the entrepreneurs. With respect to monetary policy, we use the original Taylor estimates and set $\varepsilon_\pi = 1.5$ and $\varepsilon_Y = 0.5$ in the baseline calibration. The degree of interest rate smoothing parameter ($\varpi$) is chosen as 0.5. Similarly, $\rho_\rho$ is taken to be 0.5, so that it takes 9 quarters for the shock to die away. The steady state leverage ratio and the value of quarterly external risk premium in the domestic economy are set at 0.3 and 200 basis points. We set the monitoring cost parameter, $\mu$, at 0.2 as in Devereux et al. (2006). These parameter values imply a survival rate, $\vartheta$, of approximately 99.33 percent.

# 7 Capital Flows and Macroprudential Policy
## A Framework for Emerging Asia

*Matteo F. Ghilardi[\*] and Shanaka J. Peiris[†]*

International Monetary Fund, 700 19th Street NW, Washington, DC 20431. Email: mghilardi@imf.org

### Introduction: Asia's Experience with Macroprudential Policy[1]

Emerging Asia is at the forefront of development of macroprudential measures. From a sample of thirteen Asian economies and thirty-three economies from other regions since 2000, it emerges that Asia has made extensive use of housing-related macroprudential measures – especially loan-to-value (LTV) caps – and more than other regions (Zhang and Zoli, 2014). Changes in reserve requirements on local currency deposits have also been quite common, both in Asia and elsewhere, probably reflecting their use as a monetary policy tool.[2] However, other liquidity tools, credit limits, dynamic provisioning,[3] restrictions on consumer loans, and capital measures have been rarely utilized in Asia. Measures to discourage transactions in foreign currency have been deployed less frequently in the region than in Central and Eastern Europe/ Commonwealth of Independent States (CEE/CIS) – where forex-denominated or indexed loans were widespread – and Latin America. Residency-based capital flow management measures have been employed only to a small extent in Asia.

There is significant cross-country heterogeneity in the tools that have been used in Asia since early 2000, as Asian economies had to confront different potential threats to financial stability. New Zealand introduced

---

[\*] International Monetary Fund, 700 19th Street NW, Washington, DC 20431. Email: mghilardi@imf.org
[†] International Monetary Fund, 700 19th Street NW, Washington, DC 20431. Email: speiris@imf.org
[1] This chapter is based on the IMF working paper version of the work of Ghilardi and Peiris "Capital Flows, Financial Intermediation and Macroprudential Policies" (IMF, 2014). We would like to thank the organizer and the participants of the CFMC conference on "Effective Macro-Prudential Instruments" held at the University of Nottingham.
[2] Reserve requirements are categorized as macroprudential policies in several studies (e.g. IMF, 2013b).
[3] Dynamic provisioning requires building a cushion of reserves during the upswing phase of the business cycle that can be released when the cycle turns.

162

a minimum requirement on core funding and, recently, has revised its macroprudential framework to introduce countercyclical capital buffers, overlays to sectoral capital requirements, and loan-to-value restrictions. Hong Kong SAR and Singapore have predominantly relied on housing-related tools. Korea, in addition to housing measures, imposed a levy on bank non-deposit foreign currency liabilities and a ceiling on bank foreign-exchange derivative positions. China and India have been heavy users of reserve requirements (as a monetary policy tool). Among ASEAN economies, domestic prudential tools and reserve requirements on foreign exchange deposits have been used. Capital flow measures have been adopted in Indonesia and Thailand, including minimum holding periods for central bank bills in the former, and withholding taxes for non-resident investors in the latter.

To get a sense of how macroprudential and capital flow management policies evolved and built up over time in Asia and other regions, two aggregate indices were constructed – one for macroprudential policies and one for capital flow measures.[4] Based on these indices, there appears to have been a structural tightening of the macroprudential policy stance over time that is particularly pronounced in Asia (Figure 7.1). Macro-prudential policies were most heavily used in the pre-crisis boom period during 2006–2007, and then again after the crisis, as capital flowed back into the region and asset prices inflated. By contrast, Asian economies have tightened residency-based capital flow measures or instruments to discourage transactions in foreign currency less than other regions.

An empirical investigation of the effectiveness of macroprudential and capital flow management measures in Asia over 2000Q1–2013Q1 suggests that housing-related macroprudential instruments contributed to the reduction in credit growth, house price inflation, and bank leverage in the region (Zhang and Zoli, 2014).[5] The housing-related instruments that have been particularly effective include LTV ratio caps and housing tax measures. On average, a tightening in housing-related tools is esti-mated to have reduced credit growth in Asia by 0.7 percentage point after

---

[4] This categorization between MPP and CFM involves some degree of judgment, given the overlap between certain macroprudential and capital flow management measures. Nevertheless, it tries to reflect as closely as possible the broad definitions of macroprudential and capital flow measures discussed in IMF (2012, 2013b).

[5] A number of empirical studies have tried to assess the effectiveness of macroprudential policies on a sample of countries from different regions, and typically found that some individual macroprudential instruments, such as LTV caps, debt-to-income ratios and reserve requirements, have been effective in curbing excessive credit and asset price growth (Lim et al., 2011; Arregui et al., 2013). Other studies have provided illustrative evidence that macroprudential policy can contain credit booms (Dell'Ariccia et al., 2012).

**Macroprudential Policies: Cumulative Actions by Region**
*(Average per country in each region; 2000:Q1-2013:Q1)[1]*

[1] Index summing up housing-related measures, credit measures, reserve requirements, dynamic provisioning and core funding ratio. Simple average across countries within country groups.
[2] Central and Eastern Europe and Commonwealth of Independent States.

**Capital Flow Management Measures: Cumulative Actions**
*(Average per country in each region; 2000-2013Q1)[1]*

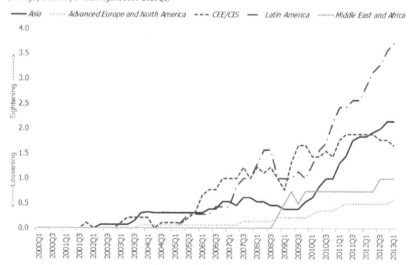

[1] Index summing up foreign currency and residency-based measures. Average across countries within country groups.

Figure 7.1  Use of macroprudential policies and capital flows management

a quarter and by 1.5 percentage points after a year. The impact of these instruments on housing price inflation has been larger: a tightening in housing-related measures is estimated to have lowered house price growth by 2 percentage points after one quarter.

Other non-housing-related domestic macroprudential tools, measures to discourage transactions in foreign currency, and residency-based capital flow management measures have not had a significant impact on lending, leverage, housing price growth, or portfolio inflows in Asia. Nevertheless, these policies may have affected the distribution of risks in the financial system and the resilience of the system against systemic pressures. For example, foreign-exchange-related macroprudential policy can contain currency, maturity and liquidity mismatches within the banking system without having a strong impact on loan growth and asset prices. On the other hand, it has to be recognized that macroprudential policy also entails costs, mainly arising from higher intermediation charges and their effect on long-term output (Arregui et al., 2013).

As macroprudential policies appear to have helped mitigate the build-up of financial risks in Asia, going forward they can play an important role in managing systemic risks from capital flow volatility in the region. But how can the region's existing macroeconomic policy framework be enhanced further? One relevant issue is how macroprudential policy could be used in the event of asset price declines, slowing credit growth, and/or capital flow reversals. Although macroprudential policies have sometimes been loosened in a countercyclical fashion, most notably in 2008–2009 as the global financial crisis unfolded, more experience needs to be gained on whether and how these instruments should be recalibrated when the financial cycle turns. Nevertheless, theory suggests that loosening macroprudential policies should be considered to prevent excessive deleveraging in the downward phase of the financial cycle.[6]

Against this background, consideration could be given to the adoption of countercyclical capital requirements (CCR) and dynamic provisioning.[7] These could be helpful instruments in a context of high volatility, as they are specifically designed to build buffers during the upswing phase of the cycle that can be used during a downswing. Even though there is little empirical evidence about their effectiveness, these instruments seem

---

[6] On theoretical grounds, the use of macroprudential policy as a countercyclical tool can be justified in a context where financial frictions create procyclicality in the financial system, exacerbating business cycle fluctuations (see, e.g. Angeloni and Faia, 2013).

[7] China introduced the CCR in 2010 and New Zealand introduced the CCR framework in 2013.

useful particularly in increasing resilience, as well as the predictability of regulatory changes through the cycle. The focus of this chapter is to assess the potential effectiveness of CCRs in the context of capital flows and strong macro-financial linkages in Asia.[8]

## Literature Review

The importance of financial shocks in terms of how they affect the real economy has long been realized, but until the 2007 financial crisis most of the general equilibrium models developed to study macro-financial linkages have focused only on the demand side of credit markets. In particular, Kiyotaki and Moore (1997), Bernanke, Gertler and Gilchrist (1999), Iacoviello (2005) and Gertler, Gilchrist, and Natalucci (2007) have introduced credit and collateral requirements to analyze the transmission and amplification of financial shocks. These models have abstracted from modeling the banking sector explicitly, and assume that credit transactions take place through the market (thereby not assigning any role to financial intermediaries such as banks). The credit spread that arises in equilibrium (the external finance premium) is a function of the riskiness of the entrepreneurs' investment projects and/or his/her net wealth. Banks, operating under perfect competition, simply accommodate the changing conditions from the demand side. The growing importance of banks in the modern financial system and the global crisis has demonstrated that the role of financial intermediation cannot be overlooked, and we need to model the supply of credit to understand business cycle fluctuations better. Also, modeling credit supply is essential to study the transmission of shocks originating in the credit markets or financial stability risks. To this extent, after the 2007 financial crisis several models have been developed to study the impact and the transmission of financial shocks and how real shocks are amplified through banking frictions. Gertler and Karadi (2011) and Gertler and Kiyotaki (2010) introduce a financial accelerator on the supply side of credit. In their framework, banks are subject to an incentive constraint that limits the amount of funds that can be raised from depositors. Curdia and - Woodford (2010, 2011) use a heterogeneous agent framework to study how monetary policy (both conventional and unconventional) should respond to a variety of real and financial disturbances. Gerali, Neri, Sessa and Signoretti (2010) study the importance of credit supply factors and monetary policy in a framework in which banks issue a collateralized

---

[8] Apart from theoretical exercises and assessments that are numerically simulated, empirical studies of how the CCR mechanism actually works are absent.

loans with loans margins depend on the bank's capital-to-asset ratio and on the degree of price stickiness.

Alongside the role of credit supply frictions and shocks, the macro-financial literature considers the benefits of introducing financial and macroprudential regulation. Two main strands of literature can be identified. The first one considers how excessive borrowing can distort agents' decisions. In this case, negative externalities arise because the outcome of individual decisions is not internalized by agents and regulation can force agents to internalize the negative externalities associated with their decisions. Some examples on how over-borrowing can create negative externalities and how financial regulation can mitigate them can be found in Bianchi and Mendoza (2011), Jeanne and Korinek (2010) and Bianchi (2011). The second strand focuses on how macroprudential policy can mitigate the impact of shocks and the interactions with monetary policy. Some examples of this literature are: Angeloni and Faia (2009); Kannan, Rabanal, and Scott (2009); N'Diaye (2009); and Unsal (2013). These papers find an important role for macroprudential policies and non-trivial interactions between financial regulation and monetary policy. However, these papers have a demand-side "financial accelerator" framework but lack a full-specific banking sector to gauge financial stability and credit supply shocks.

This paper develops a model with a micro-founded banking sector and following this second strand of the literature, takes banking capital requirements as the choice of macroprudential instrument for two main reasons. First, based on past experience, systemic crises inevitably affect bank capital and the supply of credit, either directly or indirectly. And, not surprisingly, bank capital has taken centre stage in the ongoing debate on regulatory reform. The countercyclical capital rule can be viewed as an example of the countercyclical capital buffer introduced by Basel III. Second, countercyclical risk weights and provisioning rates have been used frequently in Asia as a tool of macroprudential policy, which also predominantly works through a bank capital channel.

## The Model

In this section we provide a broad review of the model, for a complete description of the model we refer the reader to Ghilardi and Peiris (2014). The core framework is an open economy model along the lines of Obstfeld and Rogoff (1995), Galì and Monacelli (2005) and Gertler et al. (2007). The key modification is the inclusion of a micro-founded banking sector as developed by Gertler and Karadi (2011) and Gertler and Kiyotaki (2010). The financial accelerator mechanism in the banking sector links the demand for loans (and therefore for capital) to the balance sheet of banks. As a consequence, a shock in the economy is amplified via the balance sheet of the bank. In what follows, we first describe the players of the model and then we discuss how we model macroprudential policy.

### The Economic Agents

**Households**. Households are divided into bankers and workers. They consume, work and have access to financial markets in the form of bank deposits and domestic and foreign bonds. Consumption consists of home produced and foreign goods. To motivate the purchase of foreign bonds, we assume that foreign borrowing is subject to a risk premium.

**Banks**. In the model, banks borrow from other banks and make loans to firms. Financial frictions affect real activity via the impact of funds available to bank. As in Gertler and Karadi (2011) and Gertler and Kiyotaki (2010) we assume that there are financial frictions between households and banks and there are no frictions in transferring funds between banks and non-financial firms. Given a certain level of deposits, banks can lend frictionlessly to non-financial firms against their future profits. In this regard, firms can offer a perfect state contingent security. In order to introduce the endogenous constraint we introduce the following agency problem. We assume that after the bank obtains funds from depositors, the bank's manager can transfer a fraction of assets to his/her family. In the recognition of this possibility, households limit the amount of funds they lend.

**Firms**. In the model, there are three types of firms: capital producers, goods producers and a retail sector. The capital producers simply produce new capital that is sold at the goods producers. The peculiarity is that gross investment consists of domestic and foreign final goods. The goods producers produce output according to a Cobb-Douglas production function with capital and labor as inputs. The retail sector uses a homogeneous wholesale good to produce a basket of differentiated goods for consumption. In the model they provide the source of nominal price stickiness.

**Central Bank**. The central bank conducts monetary policy by adjusting the policy rate according to a Taylor rule. In our analysis we consider two rules. The first rule, used in the baseline scenario, uses a standard Taylor rule with the lagged interest rate, expected inflation and output gap. The second rule adopts a leaning-against-the-wind type of rule and, in addition, it reacts to credit growth.

*Macroprudential Policy*

As we want to study the impact of capital regulation, in our model macroprudential policy affects the capital of banks and more precisely the net worth of existing bankers. To this extend we assume that banks have to pay a penalty when their leverage ratio deviates from a regulatory given target. In the model, net worth of bankers evolves according to:

$$NW_t = \left( (\theta + \xi)(Z_t + (1 - \delta)Q_t)S_t - R_t D_{t-1} - pen^* f\left(\frac{NW_t}{Q_t S_t} - MP_t\right) \right) BC_t$$

where $NW_t$ indicates the net worth of the banker, $S_t$ are the loans and $Q_t$ their respective price, $D_{t-1}$ represents deposits and $R_t$ the interest rate paid on them. The parameter $\theta$ indicates the survival probability of the banker to be in business in the next period, $\xi$ the transfer that the banker receives when he/she starts his/her business activity and $\delta$ is the depreciation rate.

The term $pen^* f\left(\frac{NW_t}{Q_t S_t} - MP_t\right)$ represent the penalty of deviating from a given macroprudential target. This represents the capital requirements that the banks face in a form of macroprudential policy. We express $MP_t$ as:

$$MP_t = (1 - \rho_{MP})MP + (1 - \rho_{MP})(X_t - X) + \rho_{MP}MP_t$$

we set the steady state level of MP equal to the steady state level of the leverage ratio and the variable $X_t$ equal to the growth rate of output. In this case a positive value of $X_t$ corresponds to a countercyclical policy: capital requirements increase in good times (banks must hold more capital for a given amount of loans) and decrease in recessions. This is in line with the proposed regulatory reform of Basel III. Finally, $BC_t$ represents a bank capital shock.

## How Can Macroprudential Policy Reduce Procyclicality?

In order to illustrate the role of macroprudential policy in reducing procyclicality we compare the effects of several financial and non-financial shocks of an economy without macroprudential policy with an economy that has a set of active policies to reduce procyclicality. We consider three types of shocks: (1) foreign borrowing shock, (2) bank capital shock, and (3) asset price shock.

The main result we obtain is that macroprudential policy in the form of countercyclical capital regulation is a powerful tool in increasing the resilience of the financial system and the economy as a whole. In all the

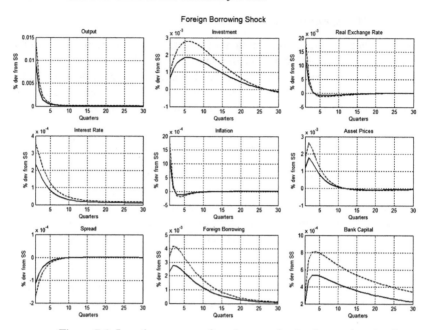

Figure 7.2 Impulse response function to a foreign borrowing shock. The dashed line represents the model without capital regulation and the solid line the model with capital regulation

shocks considered, we register a decrease in the volatility of the banks' capital and therefore in the leverage ratio. This affects the real economy through the amount of lending and consequently the amount of investment. As a consequence, this reduces the volatility in the real economy and it may help to prevent the classic boom and bust cycle.

Figure 7.2 shows the effects of a shock on foreign borrowing. As expected, higher foreign borrowing increases the future supply of capital though the investment channel, which in turn responds to an anticipated future rise in profits relative to the cost of funds. The outcome is a higher demand and inflationary pressures, together with a boom in credit growth in the economy following the capital inflow surge. As a consequence, interest rates rise and the real exchange rates appreciate. In the model, this mechanism is further amplified because, as banks are allowed to borrow from abroad, there is a financial accelerator mechanism at play. The effects of countercyclical capital regulation are shown in the comparison between the dashed and the solid line. The mechanism at play is straightforward: an increase in foreign borrowing expands the balance sheet of the banking sector and with a consequent increase of

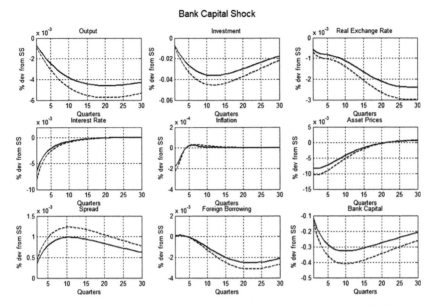

Figure 7.3 Impulse response function to a bank capital shock. The dashed line represents the model without capital regulation and the solid line the model with capital regulation

the net worth. Because the capital regulation is modeled after a penalty on the excessive leverage it works to counteract the build-up of the intermediary net worth thus reducing the amount of lending and therefore the amount of investment.

The response to a bank capital shock is shown in Figure 7.3. As before, it clearly demonstrates the importance of financial stability to business cycle fluctuations as well as the need to account for supply side financial accelerator effects in the amplification and propagation of shocks. The initiating disturbance is an exogenous decline in capital quality or bank capital shock. What we are trying to capture in a simple way is an exogenous force that triggers a decline in the value of intermediary assets such a large non-performing asset. Within the model economy, the initial exogenous decline is then magnified in two ways. First, because banks are leveraged, the effect of a decline in assets values on bank net worth is enhanced by a factor equal to the leverage ratio. Second, the drop in net worth tightens the banks' borrowing constraint inducing effectively a fire sale of assets that further depresses asset values. The crisis then feeds into real activity as the decline in asset values leads to a fall in investment and output. The transmission mechanism at work during a financial crisis is

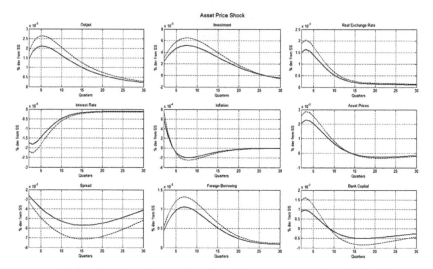

Figure 7.4 Impulse response function to an asset price shock. The dashed line represents the model without capital regulation and the solid line the model with capital regulation

reflected in the behavior of the spread between the expected return to capital and the riskless interest rate. With financial frictions, the spread rises on impact as a product of the decline in bank net worth. The increase in the cost of capital is responsible for the magnified drop in investment and output. Financial factors also contribute to the slow recovery back to trend. To reduce the spread between the expected return to capital and the riskless rate, bank net worth must increase. So long as the spread is above trend, financial factors are a drag on the real economy. Note that throughout this convergence process, banks are effectively deleveraging because they are building up equity relative to debt. In this way, the model captures how the deleveraging process can slow down a recovery.

Finally, Figure 7.4 shows the effects of a positive asset price shock. An increase in asset prices relaxes the financial constraint and creates incentives for greater banking lending which increases investment and output. This results in an accumulation of bank's capital and creates the conditions for further lending. Moreover, it leads to a short-term exchange rate appreciation and a surge in capital inflows and classic symptoms of macroeconomic overheating. Furthermore, inflation increases in the absence of technology gains necessitating interest rate hikes. Also in this case, the macroprudential policy is an effective tool in reducing the volatility of the economy.

## Macroprudential Policy Interactions with Monetary Policy and Leaning-Against-the-Wind Policy

The interaction of monetary policy with macroprudential policies suggests scope to minimize macro-financial instability by combining a modified Taylor rule with a macroprudential overlay. In this section, we study how macroprudential policy in the form of countercyclical capital regulation interacts with monetary policy.

In order to assess the importance of such interactions, we consider four scenarios. In the first scenario, we employ a standard Taylor rule with weights on lagged interest rate, expected inflation and output gap. In the second scenario, we modify the Taylor-rule to incorporate a weight on credit growth. In this scenario we want to analyze whether a modified Taylor rule can reduce the welfare loss and hence stabilize the economy. The third scenario aims at showing the importance of macroprudential policy and, to this extent, we introduce the macroprudential framework in the analysis and we use the standard Taylor rule. In the fourth and final scenario, we employ the augmented Taylor rule in the macroprudential policy framework. We consider this last case as the reference scenario.

Table 7.1 shows the computed welfare losses. To compute the welfare loss in terms of consumption equivalence we employ the methodology as in Schmitt-Grohè and Uribe (2007) and we calculate the welfare loss

Table 7.1 *Welfare loss*

|  | Welfare Loss |
| --- | --- |
| **Foreign Borrowing Shock** | |
| Taylor rule | 0.352 |
| Taylor rule with credit growth | 0.268 |
| Taylor rule and macroprudential policy | 0.082 |
| Taylor rule with credit growth and macroprudential policy | – |
| **Bank Capital Shock** | |
| Taylor rule | 0.434 |
| Taylor rule with credit growth | 0.310 |
| Taylor rule and macroprudential policy | 0.104 |
| Taylor rule with credit growth and macroprudential policy | – |
| **Asset Price Shock** | |
| Taylor rule | 0.396 |
| Taylor rule with credit growth | 0.274 |
| Taylor rule and macroprudential policy | 0.094 |
| Taylor rule with credit growth and macroprudential policy | – |

using a second order approximation of the utility function. This represents the fraction of consumption (in percentage terms) that is required to equate welfare under a given policy rule to the one given by the reference scenario in the face of a one percent given shock.

The first result that Table 7.1 highlights is that the augmented Taylor rule in the macroprudential policy framework is the more effective as the welfare loss is positive in all the cases.

A second important result is that the welfare loss is higher when financial shocks hit the economy. In particular, the bank capital shock produces the highest welfare loss followed by the asset price shock. In turns, macroprudential policy and, more in general, a stabilizing policy produces the best results for these shocks. For the bank capital shock the difference between the standard Taylor rule scenario and the scenario with an augmented Taylor rule in the macroprudential policy framework is 0.434. Similarly, for the asset price shock, the difference is 0.396. The difference is quite relevant for the foreign borrowing but it is not so marked.

Finally, the results suggest that macroprudential policy is more effective than the standard Taylor rule and the Taylor rule augmented with credit growth. This can be seen in the welfare loss difference when macroprudential policy is introduced in the model. As an example we consider the foreign borrowing shock. In terms of welfare the difference between the standard Taylor rule and the augmented Taylor rule is 0.84 (difference between the first and the second line). However, when macroprudential policy is considered, the difference becomes 0.270 (difference between the first and the third line). The relatively small role of Taylor rules augmented with credit growth is recorded also when this policy option is included in a framework in which macroprudential policy is present. In this case the welfare loss difference is 0.082. This result applies to all the shocks considered. This implies that, if a central bank wants to mitigate the impact of negative financial shocks, macroprudential policy is more effective than targeting financial variables in the Taylor rule.

Overall, the results suggest that financial stabilization and in particular, macroprudential measures in the form of capital requirement, play a crucial role in the stabilization policy and especially in the stabilization of financial shocks.

## Conclusions

This chapter assesses the role of capital flows, macro-financial linkages, and macroprudential policies in Emerging Asia. Using a DSGE model, we show that macroprudential measures can usefully complement monetary policy in response to most types of exogenous shocks. Countercyclical macroprudential polices can help reduce macroeconomic volatility and enhance welfare in combination with a modified Taylor rule that also places a weight on credit developments. The results also demonstrate the importance of capital flows and financial stability for business cycle fluctuations as well as supply side financial accelerator effects in the amplification and propagation of shocks in an emerging Asian economy.

Asset prices and banking lending are the key channels of transmission of capital flows in emerging Asia. The large capital inflows received by emerging Asian countries can result in macroeconomic overheating pressures such as higher inflation and real exchange rate appreciation as well as financial stability risks as capital inflows fuel rapid asset price inflation and credit growth. Our analysis suggests that the best response to financial and foreign shocks would be to implement countercyclical macroprudential polices as they help reducing macroeconomic volatility and procyclicality of the financial system in combination with a modified Taylor rule that places some weight on credit growth. Indeed, as the welfare analysis showed, among the policy options considered the welfare loss in minimized when countercyclical regulation is taken into account together with an augmented Taylor rule. This seems a more attractive option than contemplating direct measures to control capital inflows and large-scale foreign exchange interventions that have been shown to be suboptimal even in models without optimizing banking sectors.

Financial instability or shocks to bank capital triggered by a large non-performing loan, for example, has a pervasive and significant impact on the real economy through macro-financial linkages. The model sheds light on the key transmission mechanism of a financial crisis by showing how bank leverage amplifies the initial shock to capital and tightens the banks' borrowing constraint inducing effectively a fire sale of assets. The crisis then feeds into real activity as the decline in asset values is responsible for the magnified drop in investment and output. In this way the model captures how the deleveraging process can slow down a recovery as observed in the global financial crisis and Asian financial crisis. This transmission mechanism also highlights the importance of maintaining an adequate bank capital buffer, avoiding a rapid growth in credit that often leads to rash of non-performing loans, and role of asset prices in amplifying business cycles. Here again, macroprudential policies could help minimize macro-financial instability by combining a modified Taylor rule with a countercyclical capital requirement.

## References

Angeloni I. and E. Faia (2009). "A tale of two policies: Prudential regulation and monetary policy with fragile banks," *Kiel Working Papers*, no 1569, Kiel Institute for the World Economy.

Angeloni I., and Ester F. (2013). "Capital regulation and monetary policy with fragile banks," *Journal of Monetary Economics*, vol 60, no 3, 311–324.

Arregui, N., J. Benes, I. Krznar, S. Mitra and A. Oliveira Santos (2013). "Evaluating the net benefits of macroprudential policy: A cookbook," *IMF Working Paper*, no 13/167 (Washington: International Monetary Fund).

Bernanke, B., M. Gertler and S. Gilchrist (1999). "The financial accelerator in a quantitative business cycle framework." In J. B. Taylor and M. Woodford (Eds.) *Handbook of Macroeconomics*, vol 1, 1341–1393. Amsterdam: North-Holland.

Bianchi, J. (2011). "Overborrowing and systemic externalities in the business cycle," *American Economic Review, American Economic Association*, vol 101, no 7, 3400–3426.

Bianchi J. and E. G., Mendoza (2011). "Overborrowing, financial crises and macro-prudential policy," *IMF Working Papers*, no 11/24, International Monetary Fund.

Curdia V. and M. Woodford (2010). "Credit spreads and monetary policy," *Journal of Money, Credit and Banking, Blackwell Publishing*, vol 42, no s1, 3–35.

(2011). "The central-bank balance sheet as an instrument of monetary policy," *Journal of Monetary Economics*, Elsevier, vol 58, no 1, 54–79.

Dell'Ariccia Giovanni, G., D. Igan, L. Laeven, H. Tong, B. B. Bakker and J. Vandenbussche, 2012, "Policies for macrofinancial stability: How to deal with credit booms," *IMF Staff Discussion Note*, no 12/06 (Washington: International Monetary Fund).

Galí J. and T. Monacelli, 2005. "Monetary policy and exchange rate volatility in a small open economy," *Review of Economic Studies, Wiley Blackwell*, vol 72, no 3, 707–734.

Gerali A., S. Neri, L. Sessa, F. M. Signoretti (2010). "Credit and banking in a DSGE model of the euro area," *Journal of Money, Credit and Banking, Blackwell Publishing*, vol 42, no s1, 107–141.

Gertler M., S. Gilchrist and F. Natalucci (2007). "External constraints on monetary policy and the financial Accelerator," *Journal of Money, Credit and Banking*, vol 39, 295–330.

Gertler, M. and P. Karadi (2011). "A model of unconventional monetary policy," *Journal of Monetary Economics, Elsevier*, vol 58 no 1, 17–34.

Gertler, M. and N. Kiyotaki (2010). "Financial intermediation and credit policy in business cycle analysis." In B. M. Friedman and M. Woodford (Eds.). *Handbook of Monetary Economics*, Vol 3, 547–599. Philadelphia: Elsevier.

Ghilardi M. F. and S. J. Peiris (2014). "Capital flows, financial intermediation and macroprudential policies," *IMF Working Papers*, no 14/157, International Monetary Fund.

Iacoviello M. (2005). "House prices, borrowing constraints, and monetary policy in the business cycle," *American Economic Review, American Economic Association*, vol 95, no 3, 739–764.

International Monetary Fund, 2008, "Exchange rate assessments: CGER methodologies," *Occasional Paper*, no 261 (Washington).

2012, "The liberalization and management of capital flows – An institutional view" (Washington: International Monetary Fund).

2013a, "The interaction of monetary and macroprudential policies – Background paper" (Washington).

2013b, "Key aspects of macroprudential policy" (Washington).

2014c, "Regional economic outlook: Asia and Pacific," April (Washington).

Jeanne, O. and A. Korinek (2010). "Managing credit booms and busts: A Pigouvian taxation approach," *NBER Working Papers*, no 16377, National Bureau of Economic Research, Inc.

Kannan P., P. Rabanal and A. Scott (2009)."Monetary and macroprudential policy rules in a model with house price booms," *IMF Working Papers*, no 09/251, International Monetary Fund.

Kiyotaki, N. and J. Moore (1997). "Credit cycles," *Journal of Political Economy, University of Chicago Press*, vol 105, no 2, 211–248, April.

Lim, C., F. Columba, A. Costa, P. Kongsamut, A. Otani, M. Saiyid, T. Wezel and X. Wu (2011). "Macroprudential policy: What instruments and how to use them? Lessons from country experiences," *IMF Working Paper*, no 11/238 (Washington: International Monetary Fund).

N'Diaye, P., 2009, "Countercyclical macroprudential policies in a supporting role to monetary policy," *IMF Working Paper*, no WP/09/257.

Obstfeld M. and K. Rogoff (1995). "Exchange rate dynamics redux," *Journal of Political Economy*, vol 103, no 3, 624–660, June.

Schmitt-Grohe, M. and M. Uribe (2007). "Optimal simple and implementable monetary and fiscal rules," *Journal of Monetary Economics*, vol 54, no 6, 1702–1725.

Unsal D. F. (2013). "Capital flows and financial stability: Monetary policy and macroprudential responses," *International Journal of Central Banking, International Journal of Central Banking*, vol 9, no 1, 233–285, March.

Zhang, L. and E. Zoli (2014). "Leaning against the wind: Macroprudential policy in Asia," *IMF Working Paper*, no 14/22 (Washington: International Monetary Fund).

# 8    Macroprudential Policy in a Globalised World

*Dennis Reinhardt and Rhiannon Sowerbutts*[*]

## Introduction: Macroprudential Policy and the Globalisation in Banking

Following the global financial crisis, there has been considerable and wide-reaching change in regulation and macroprudential policies have become part of many central banks' toolkits. The tools are being used actively: a recent IMF survey revealed that more than forty countries had already used some kind of macroprudential instrument as of 2013.[1] The ESRB's website – which collects data for EU countries – lists more than fifty policy measures taken in 2014 and more than ninety in 2015. The Czech Republic, Hong Kong, Sweden and Norway have set positive rates for their countercyclical capital buffers, and in the United Kingdom the Financial Policy committee has announced that it expects to set a countercyclical capital buffer in the region of 1 per cent when risks are 'neither subdued nor elevated'. Macroprudential policies are not just of academic and policy maker interest: indeed as Figure 8.1 taken from Google Trends shows, interest in macroprudential policy has exploded since the onset of the crisis.

So far the focus of policymakers has largely been on the domestic effects: we have examined the notifications and press reports that countries have made about macroprudential measures and found that cross-border effects on other countries barely get a mention. Often analysis of such policies is limited to the observation that because the measure will benefit the stability of the national financial system, it will – indirectly – also contribute to the stability of the financial system of other countries.

[*] Dennis Reinhardt is a senior economist in the International Directorate of the Bank of England and Rhiannon Sowerbutts is a senior economist in the Financial Stability Strategy and Risk Directorate of the Bank of England. We would like to thank Philip Turner for valuable comments and suggestions. The views expressed in this paper are those of the authors, and not necessarily those of the Bank of England or the Monetary Policy Committee, Financial Policy Committee or PRA Board.
[1] See Cerutti, Claessens and Laeven (2015) for a description of the IMF Survey on Global Macroprudential Policy Instruments (GMPI).

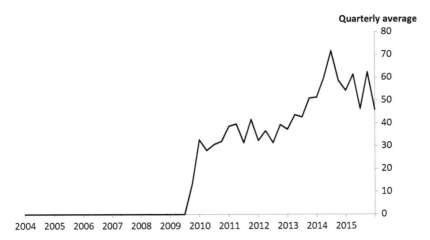

Figure 8.1 Interest in macroprudential policy after the crisis.
Source: Google Trends. The numbers on the graph reflect how many searches
have been done for a particular term, relative to the total number of searches
done on Google over time. They don't represent absolute search volume
numbers, because the data is normalized and presented on a scale from 0 to 100.
When we don't have enough data, 0 is shown

Financial systems are, however, not closed national systems, but have
important global links. This can be illustrated by using a simple proxy for
cross-border financial integration taken from Lane and Milesi-Ferretti
(2007, updated to 2011) the sum of foreign (i.e. held externally) assets
and foreign liabilities of advanced economies (AEs) (expressed as a
percentage of GDP). Figure 8.2 plots the rapid expansion in this measure
of globalisation from the late 1990s, showing that it hit a peak of almost
600 per cent of GDP for AEs as a whole. Within this period, there were
two acceleration phases, with a steep increase in the growth of cross-
border positions in the mid-1990s and a further intensification during
2004–2007. While this measure contracted substantially in 2008, it
subsequently recovered and remains high. The rise of banking external
assets and liabilities has been equally steep. After the crisis they have
retrenched somewhat but remain large relative to GDP.

Financial globalisation is particularly important in Europe, partly
reflecting monetary union and integrated regulation. Figure 8.3 shows
the gross borrowing of non-banks[2] around the world from foreign banks.
It is notable that the relevance of such borrowing is higher in most

---

[2] Non-banks includes non-bank financial institutions as well as firms and households.

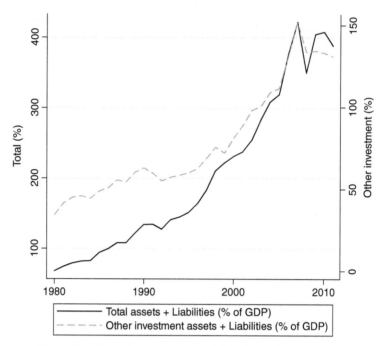

Figure 8.2 Cross-border assets and liabilities of advanced economies (% of GDP).
Source: IMF WEO and Lane and Milesi-Ferretti (2007)

European countries compared to other advanced economies such as the United States or Japan, in particular in the United Kingdom.

Foreign banks play a particularly large role in the UK banking system as shown in Figure 8.4. In 2013, there were 150 deposit-taking foreign branches and 98 foreign subsidiaries in the United Kingdom from 56 different countries. Those foreign banks constitute around half of UK banking sector assets on a residency basis, with the combined assets of the largest ten foreign subsidiaries in the United Kingdom (including their non-deposit-taking entities) totalling approximately £2.75 trillion. Foreign branches account for approximately 30 per cent of total UK-resident banking assets and around a third of UK interbank lending (Bush, Knott and Peacock, 2014; Hoggarth, Hooley and Korniyenko, 2013). Nearly one-fifth of global banking activity is booked in the United Kingdom, and UK-resident banks' foreign assets and liabilities account for over 350 per cent of UK GDP, more than four times the median figure for Organisation for Economic Co-operation and Development (OECD) countries.

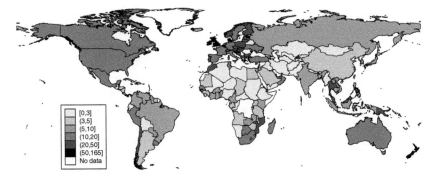

Figure 8.3  Gross external liabilities of non-banks (% of GDP, 2013Q4)
Note: The chart displays liabilities of domestic non-banks to BIS reporting banks
cross-border or locally from their affiliates as of 2013 Q4. The data are taken
from the BIS Consolidated Banking Statistics.

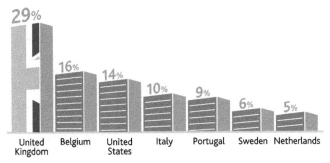

Figure 8.4  The UK banking system

This globalisation of banking poses a number of challenges and opportunities for macroprudential regulation which will be discussed in this chapter: capital flows can create excessive borrowing, pecuniary externalities and therefore a role for macroprudential regulation; the limited scope of national regulators mean that regulation may be unevenly applied potentially changing the effectiveness of macroprudential regulation; and macroprudential actions at home may have spillover effects abroad. This chapter also discusses the potential case for reciprocation and coordination of macroprudential policy at an international level.

The conventional (pre-Global Financial Crisis) policy prescription was that financial globalisation was unambigiously positive and that the benefits of capital flows would be reaped by removing the impediments to unfettered capital movements. However recent experience, such as the sharp capital flow reversals in Europe, has shown that even advanced economies may be vulnerable to unintended consequences of capital account liberalization; particularly when the procyclicality inherent in capital flows is not adequately addressed.

Brunnermeier and Sannikov (2015), Korinek (2011) and Bianchi (2011) all illustrate this phenomenon, and demonstrates a role for macroprudential policy in open economy models. As with the plethora of closed-economy models which motivate macroprudential policies, each of these papers includes an externality that means that firms overborrow as they do not take into account the negative externality on others when they are forced to sell assets in a down-turn while open capital markets allow countries to borrow using debt financed from abroad.

The open economy aspect of these papers provides additional challenges and exacerbates this penuniary externality and can cause reversals in capital flows, undermining financial stability. Each paper has a different take on how this effect occurs. In Brunnermeir and Sannikov (2015), firms borrow too much because they do not internalize that an increase in production capacity reduces their selling price and thereby worsens the country's terms of trade. The increased leverage of each firm exposes all firms in the country to further risk as an adverse shock to indebted firms increases their concern about a sudden funding stop and they cut back produciton by fire-selling their capital. In Bengui (2011), credit constraints linking debt to market-determined prices generate an externality which leads private agents to over borrow. Because debt – and the credit constraint – is partially leveraged in income generated in the non-tradable sector, changes in the relative price of non-tradable goods can induce sharp and sudden adjustments in access to foreign financing; and in Korinek (2011), agents take on too much foreign currency debt. Domestic borrowers fail to internalize that the countercyclical payoffs of dollar debt raise not only the volatility of each agent's disposable income, but also make aggregate demand, and by extension exchange rates, more volatile. In all of the papers, macroprudential policies and/or capital controls which limit borrowing can improve welfare.

## Macroprudential Policy in Action

The good news is that macroprudential instruments are already being actively used to address build-ups in systemic risk and excessive levels of debt. Chart 8.5, taken from Reinhardt and Sowerbutts (2015), illustrates the number of macroprudential actions over time taken by advanced economies and emerging markets (EMs). While macroprudential instruments are clearly more used in emerging markets, advanced economies have made more use of these instruments since the global financial crisis.

We encountered several challenges in collecting these data. The multitude of different agencies responsible for various instruments, combined with the fact that there is no international body responsible for collecting information on macroprudential actions, means that collecting information about other countries changes in macroprudential policy is difficult and time consuming. The ESRB has put together a database of notifications that it receives but only covers the EU and Norway; the IMF (Lim et al. (2011)) has undertaken surveys but compliance on these is often poor; Kuttner and Shim (2013) built a database on housing actions from primary sources. We have combined all of these databases, and also looked at primary sources such as financial stability reports from supervisors and central banks, examined presentations at conferences on macroprudential policy and spoke with a number of colleagues from central banks around the world.[3]

The use of macroprudential instruments displays enormous regional diversity. While before the global financial crisis, EMs have accounted for the majority of the actions, the number of actions in AEs increased significantly after the crisis (Figure 8.5). Europe (both West and Central and Eastern Europe) has made largely use of capital instruments, while lending criteria instruments are used more often in Asia. Europe and Oceania have made almost no use of reserve requirements, while reserve requirements have been the most intensively used instrument in South America (Figure 8.6). This reflects the diversity of financial systems,

---

[3] The Bank of England is fortunate enough to have the 'Centre for Central Banking Studies' which conducts seminars and provides expert advice for central banks and regulatory authorities around the world.

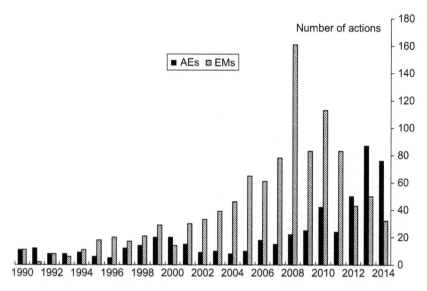

Figure 8.5 Count of macroprudential actions over time.
Source: Reinhardt and Sowerbutts (2015) based on BIS, IMF, central banks' and regulatory agencies' websites and publications and authors' correspondence with authorities. The data were collected on a best-efforts basis and should not be considered as a definitive count

legal powers, credit cycles and sources of systemic risk. However, more work needs to be done on what drives these differences in instrument choice and to enhance our understanding of whether structural features of financial systems may mean that one instrument is more effective than another.

## The Evidence on Effects Domestically

Given the policy relevance, there are a number of academic papers which study the effects of macroprudential policies domestically. Most of these are cross-country panel regressions; generally differing according to the countries and time period studied. Financial imbalances are not studied directly but instead most studies focus on variables which are associated with financial instability. Most of the papers examine the effect on house prices and the quantity of credit, reflecting that there tends to be better data available in this area and that these are indirect indicators of systemic risk. While there are a number of largely unavoidable shortcomings in the analysis, the papers all give broadly

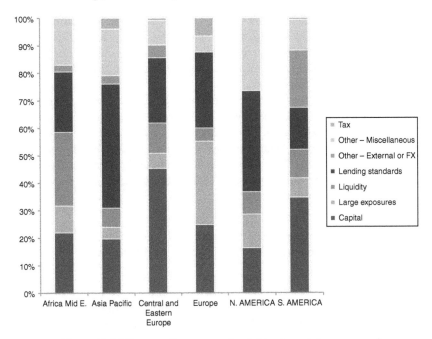

Figure 8.6 The use of macroprudential instruments across regions.
Source: Reinhardt and Sowerbutts (2015) based on BIS, IMF, central banks'
and regulatory agencies' websites and publications and authors' correspondence
with authorities. The data were collected on a best-efforts basis and should not be
considered as a definitive count

similar results: macroprudential measures have an effect – albeit occasionally modest – on the growth in credit and house prices.

Lim et al. (2011) use cross-country panel regressions across ten macroprudential instruments and find that the majority of macroprudential instruments are effective. They find that the pro-cyclicality of credit growth is reduced by 80 per cent after LTV and DTI limits are introduced but limits on FX lending, other capital instruments and restrictions on profit distribution have no significant effect on credit growth. Kuttner and Shim (2012) examine a number of instruments and find that DTI limits are effective in curbing mortgage credit growth in both the short and long-run. Only LTV and exposure limits affect house price growth but the effect of LTVs is modest (yielding about a 4 per cent reduction in house price inflation). Other instruments are jointly significant, partly because they are applied concurrently so separating the effects is difficult. Vandenbussche et al. (2012) (Central and Eastern Europe) show that changes in capital requirements can decrease house price growth; they find that LTV caps, DTI caps, reserve requirements or provisioning rules did not have significant effects and the authors point out that this is likely due to large leakages – for example foreign parent banks' lending directly rather than through regulated subs or due to other ways to avoid such measures.

This last result, that macroprudential measures can be avoided via differing regulation, is at the heart of this chapter on macroprudential policy in a globalised world. Global capital flows can create a role for macroprudential policy measures, but at the same time this very globalisation can undermine their effects. In addition, at the same time macroprudential measures can have effects on other countries as banks adjust their capital positions and lending to comply with the new regulation.

## Cross-Border Spillovers and Leakages of Macroprudential Policy: Theory and Evidence

There are several channels of propagation through which macroprudential policy action can affect neighbouring countries. Some cross-border propagation channels may be particularly relevant in the context of one macroprudential instrument, but negligible for other instruments. There are only a few theoretical studies. Jeanne (2014) provides a simple framework to examine the issue of macroprudential policy in a small open economy. He shows that both domestic macroprudential policies and prudential capital controls generate international spillovers as domestic macroprudential actions in a country lower the global demand for investment and therefore the equilibrium global interest rate. If countries can react with immediate and perfectly applied macroprudential policies then they are able to offset these effects, but if not then there will be negative effects. Bengui and Bianchi (2014) are more explicit on the role of capital flows. They examine how imperfectly applied macroprudential policy can lead to the unregulated sector borrowing more than they would if there was no regulation, due to an implicit insurance provided by regulated agents.

In this section we examine both the leakages and spillovers of macroprudential policy. Spillovers are the effects that a macroprudential policy taken in one country has on the rest of the world. Leakages refer to any effect on the country taking the macroprudential policy action.

### Spillovers

The literature on spillover effects of macroprudential policies is still in its infancy, especially with regard to policies taken by advanced economies.

However, some empirical evidence has begun to emerge on some of the potential spillover channels using lessons from other regulations. Houston, Lin and Ma (2012) use banking flow data aggregated at the country level and survey data on global regulations to argue that banks have transferred funds to markets with fewer regulations. It is not entirely clear that these spillovers reflect regulatory arbitrage given the difficulty of deriving indices measuring the intensity of regulation that are comparable across countries.[4] Nonetheless, it is clear that aggregate cross-border lending from banks seem to respond to regulation applied in other countries. Bremus and Fratscher (2014) examine the effects of changes to regulatory and monetary policy on cross-border bank lending since the global financial crisis. Using the data by Barth et al. (2013), they show that higher capital stringency, supervisory power and independence of supervisors encourage credit outflows from source countries. There is, however, important heterogeneity across countries: if the recipient is a euro area country the results turn and bank lending from source countries declines when there is a tightening in domestic capital regulation or supervision.

Ongena, Popov and Udell (2013) analyse the effect of bank regulation in domestic (i.e. home-country) markets on multinational banks' lending standards in foreign (i.e. host-country) markets using data on lending to firms. They test two alternative hypotheses: whether stricter home country regulation induces banks to develop a more conservative business model which they then export into the foreign markets they are in; or alternatively, they might take risk abroad to make up for the inability to take on risk in their home-country market. Ultimately they find evidence for the latter hypothesis.

To estimate the direct effect on foreign lending of an increase in capital requirements, Aiyar et al. (2014a) uses data on UK banks' minimum capital requirements to study the impact of changes to bank-specific capital requirements on cross-border bank loan supply. They find that a 100 basis point increase in the requirement is associated with a reduction in the growth rate of cross-border credit of between 3 and 5.5 percentage points; although not on a comparable basis this is slightly less than the estimate of the corresponding domestic effect. UK banks tend to favour their most important country relationships, so that the cross-border credit supply response in 'core' countries is significantly less than in others.

---

[4] In their paper Houston et al. (2012) also rely on the index by Barth, Caprio and Levine (2013).

Danisewicz, Reinhardt and Sowerbutts (2017) look explicitly at the cross-border spillovers of macroprudential policy actions via bank lending. Their analysis compares the response of foreign banks' branches versus subsidiaries in the United Kingdom to changes in macroprudential regulations in foreign banks' home countries. By focusing on branches and subsidiaries of the same banking group, the authors are able to control for all the factors affecting parent banks' decisions regarding the lending of their foreign affiliates. Following a tightening of capital regulation in the home country, foreign branches of multinational banks reduce interbank lending growth in the host country by 6 percentage points more relative to subsidiaries of the same banking group.

They suggest that the different behaviour of branches and subsidiaries arises because a branch is an integral part of the parent bank and so parent banks are more easily able to control their branches than their subsidiaries that have their own board of directors.

Other macroprudential policies do not exhibit the same spillover effects. The authors find a tightening in lending standards or reserve requirements at home does not have differential effects on either interbank or non-bank lending to the United Kingdom. This points to an important difference in how macroprudential policies are likely to transmit across borders. Capital regulation ultimately affects the balance sheet of the consolidated bank and affects it in a mechanical way. In contrast, lending standards regulation only affects lending to the country in which it is applied, the potential spillover effects are more behavioural, associated with risk shifting rather changes in the overall quantity of lending. In addition, as Ongena et al. (2013) point out that there are a number of competing alternative hypotheses about the direction of spillovers which could lead to the insignificant result.

Finally, Danisewicz et al. (2017) also find that none of the macroprudential regulations in their sample causes differences by subsidiaries and branches in the provision of lending to non-bank borrowers and conjecture that this is because non-bank lending relationships are more likely to be relationship-based for both subs and branches and therefore more profitable and may not be cut as quickly in response to a change in regulation. In contrast, banks are generally able to substitute funding in the interbank market more easily; this means that any attempt to pass on increased capital costs by an affected branch will be swiftly met by a bank finding an alternative lender, while a subsidiary will be less affected by the increased cost and so their customers are less likely switch to alternative sources of borrowing.

*Leakages*

In a globalised financial system, where regulations differ across countries, the fact that households and firms can borrow from foreign banks or other non-bank lenders can alter the effectiveness of regulations as not all financial entities are subject to the same restrictions as domestically regulated banks. In addition, banks seek to avoid the measures by moving their activities elsewhere.

The debate on the avoidance of macroprudential measures has often focused on more obvious sources of avoidance such as households taking unsecured loans to avoid loan-to-value limits, a behaviour that was prevalent in the United States pre-crisis. But there is another source of uneven regulation: regulators are only able to apply regulation to financial institutions within their regulatory perimeter. As a concrete example, regulators are only able to set capital regulation on the banks which they actually supervise. In practice, this means that they are only able to set capital requirements for domestic-owned banks and foreign subsidiaries but not on foreign branches leading to uneven regulation. This is illustrated in Figure 8.7.

Aiyar et al. (2014b) exploit this in within the unique environment of the United Kingdom. The United Kingdom provides an ideal testing

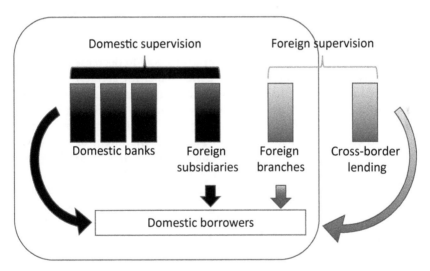

Figure 8.7 A schematic view of the application of macroprudential measures.
Source: ESRB Handbook on Operationalising Macro-Prudential Policy in the Banking Sector

ground for these questions because of the country's policy regime in the 1990s and early 2000s, when the Financial Services Authority (FSA) set time-varying minimum capital requirements ratios' at the level of individual banks. The United Kingdom is host to a large number of branches of foreign-owned banks, which were not subject to FSA regulation, but are regulated by the country authorities of the parent bank. When capital requirements are tightened on FSA-regulated banks, this confers a relative cost advantage on the foreign branches operating in the United Kingdom, which might raise lending in response. The authors find that foreign branches increase lending in response to a regulation-induced decline in lending by competing domestically regulated banks – a competition effect. The average branch increases lending by about 0.3 per cent in response to a decline in lending by its reference group of 1 per cent.

Aiyar et al. (2014c) go further and show within the same UK institutional environment that leakages do not only arise because of their competition effects. In addition, they find that foreign banking groups shifting loans from its UK-regulated subsidiary to their affiliated branch in the face of higher capital requirements is a significantly more important source of leakage.

Although we have called these effects leakages it is not necessarily true that it is an undesirable or even unintended effect. For example, the UK minimum pillar II capital requirements studied by Aiyar et al. (2014a, 2014b, 2014c) were changed by the FSA because of considerations related to operational risks rather than with a goal to decrease borrowing by the private sector; although to give their paper the credit it deserves it does appear that the regulator set the capital requirements in a quasi 'macroprudential' way as witnessed by a strong correlation between average minimum capital requirements and UK GDP growth before the crisis (see figure 4 in their 2014 paper). If the intent of policy was micro rather than macro, redistribution of activity may be ideal or even optimal as the demand for credit is satisfied by reallocating borrowers from the initial institution to other institutions which have more capacity to safely engage in domestic lending. However, if the policy was implemented with macroprudential goals, which often aim to alleviate the domestic credit cycle, credit substation is less desirable and can be interpreted as leakages that undermine the intent of the policy.

These authors' papers focus on leakages arising from *capital* regulation. This partly reflects the UK's unique regulatory environment which focused on capital changes and the fact that the United Kingdom is a major financial centre making it an excellent laboratory to study spillovers and leakages from macroprudential policy. But as illustrated earlier, countries are taking many types of macroprudential actions, not just on capital, and it is important to understand how instruments differ in their external implications. This is a particularly important question at the current conjuncture as macroprudential policymakers have usually been granted legal powers over several different instruments and need to understand which ones might be more effective in the context of open economies with a significant role of foreign banks.

Reinhardt and Sowerbutts (2015) are the first to examine potential leakages for macroprudential policy actions for a range of macroprudential instruments in a large cross-country panel. In particular – using the data we have described in the second section – they distinguish between lending standards actions, capital regulation and also reserve requirements. Due to the long timeframe over which they have collected macroprudential actions they are also able to study the effects of loosening in instruments.

Figure 8.8 shows that there has been a variety of macroprudential policy actions for each of the policies they consider. Measures have been taken both before and after the crisis. And there are both tightening and loosening actions in each category, though it is noteworthy that capital tightening actions were taken more frequently than capital loosening actions.

There are good reasons to believe that different instruments will have different potential for leakages. In contrast to capital regulation where

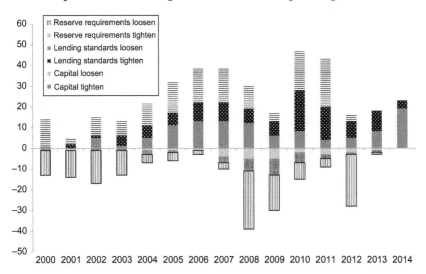

Figure 8.8 Macroprudential policy tightening and loosening over time.
Source: Reinhardt and Sowerbutts (2015)

financial regulators are only able to apply capital regulation to banks which are headquartered in the country or to subsidiaries, product regulation such as loan-to-value (LTV) regulation usually applies to all products sold in a particular country. This means that all financial institutions – domestic and foreign – are subject to the same macropru- dential regulation and there is less potential for avoidance by borrowing from a foreign institution. The effect of reserve requirements is more nuanced. Replacing liquidity is costly and they hypothesis that foreign banks are able to replace it from abroad or their parents more easily leading to a competitive advantage. This is not a disparity in regulation but arises from having a heterogeneous banking system where some banks have more options to raise liquidity than others.

Using BIS data on local and external borrowing by the domestic non- bank private sector from foreign banks they examine whether non-banks adjusts their borrowing from foreign banks after a macroprudential action is taken, controlling for a number of other factors which could explain the demand for loans.

Figure 8.9, taken from Reinhardt and Sowerbutts (2015), illustrates their results, which are in line with the hypotheses outlined previously. A tightening in lending standards does not result in domestic non- banks borrowing more from foreign banks – which is consistent with the view that lending standards regulation applies to all products and is therefore hard to avoid. In contrast, it appears that households and firms borrow more from abroad after a tightening in capital require- ments or reserve requirements. The results are weaker when consider- ing the *loosening* of capital requirements. This is perhaps not unexpected as capital regulations are likely to be loosened at times when they are no longer binding.

These results suggest that the ability of agents to borrow from abroad and avoid the measures should be taken into consideration by policy- makers when they choose which instruments should be deployed against particular sources of systemic risk.

### The International Banking Research Network: Spillovers and Leakages of Regulation

A unique project is currently underway by the International Banking Research Network to examine both the spillovers and leakages of macro- prudential policy. The IBRN was founded in 2012 to analyse issues pertinent to internationally active banks. The network brings together researchers from more than twenty-five central banks and international institutions, with most teams having access to confidential bank-level

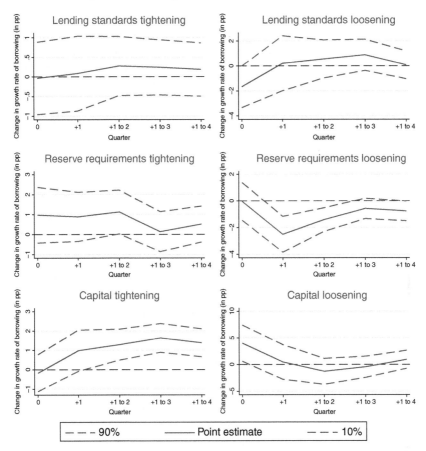

Figure 8.9 The impact of regulations on borrowing of domestic non-banks from foreign banks.
Source: Reinhardt and Sowerbutts (2015)

data on domestic and cross-border banking activities.[5] The researchers participating in the study focus on either of two questions:

1. **'Outward' transmission** of macroprudential policies
   - How does destination country regulation affect the international lending of banks?
   - How does the (weighted) exposure of banks to regulation abroad affect their international lending?

---

[5] More information on the IBRN can be found here: https://www.newyorkfed.org/ibrn.

2. **'Inward' transmission** of macroprudential policies
  – A: Do domestically owned banks change their domestic lending when they are exposed to countries change regulation?
  – B: Do foreign owned affiliates change their domestic lending
  when their home countries change regulation?

Importantly, because the researchers in the network are able to use
confidential regulatory data, they are able to examine how banks' balance
sheet characteristics affect how spillovers or leakages occur. And because
each country uses the same empirical specification they are able to
perform a meta-analysis on the results.

The project is new and the papers are not yet published. But the
preliminary meta-analysis (Buch and Goldberg, 2017) shows that interbank exposure limits, loan-to-value ratios, and reserve requirements are
the prudential instruments that most frequently spill over across borders
and affect bank lending. These spillovers are most likely to occur via the
affiliates of foreign banks hosted in a country (when country A takes an
action its affiliates cut back or expand lending in country B), although
some evidence exists of inward transmission through home-country
global banks (when country A takes an action, country B's banks – which
do some lending in A – change their lending to B).

Banks' balance sheets also matter: spillovers of interbank exposure
limits through foreign bank affiliates are affected by banks' illiquid asset
shares, deposit shares, and internal capital market positions with their
parent banks.

The structure of the banking system also plays a role for how spillovers
manifest themselves. Capital requirements are more likely to spillover
into lending in countries with higher levels of foreign bank participation,
and when there are fewer banking entities in that particular category of
lending.

## What Does This Mean for Policy?

As the analysis of the previous section shows, a world of globalised capital
flows poses two important considerations for macroprudential policy:
coordination and reciprocity. Coordination implies an authority taking
into account the impact of their policies on other economies, potentially
sharing information and even jointly maximising welfare. In contrast,
reciprocity is an arrangement whereby the authority in one jurisdiction
applies the same measure set by an authority in another jurisdiction to
the lending of institutions supervised by it to the former institutions – in
other words reciprocity is helping to make macroprudential policies in

other jurisdictions more effective. While reciprocity is potentially welfare improving even for the country that applies it, it does not imply any joint maximisation of welfare.

**Spillovers** are where there is the greatest need for coordination. They generally arise from behavioural adjustment and by changes in lending across countries and financial sectors. These do not necessarily result from regulatory arbitrage.

Implementing macroprudential policy has a cost, both politically and in terms of regulatory resources, so there may be free-riding if a country implements a policy that has a positive outward spillover on another. Both of these issues raise the question of whether and how macroprudential policy should be *coordinated*.

In contrast **'leakages'** is the area where reciprocity plays the biggest role. Reciprocity arragements have three key potential benefits. Reciprocity by foreign regulators has the positive effect of making domestic macroprudential policies more effective. Reciprocity also ensures that domestic regulations are applied with a similar strength by other countries and should hence limit the scope for regulatory arbitrage. Finally, extending reciprocity may also avoid domestic banks expanding their lending into frothy economies (the ones tightening their regulations) and exposing themselves to excessive risks.

Complicating this discussion and policy response is that the question can, in practice, not be split into reciprocation versus coordination, as these effects arise simultaneously on application of the same instrument.

### The Case for Coordination?

The existence of evidence of sizable spillovers does not by itself warrant intensified international policy coordination. Spillovers would need to also have a significant negative impact on other countries. Whether spillovers are negative or positive will depend, among other things, on the credit cycle prevailing in the economy that receives the spillover. Table 8.1 presents two scenarios for spillovers to country B following a tightening of country A's macroprudential policies.

In the case of **synchronised credit cycles** – top left (bottom right) quadrant – a tightening (loosening) of domestic macropru results in a positive spillover because it reduces (increases) external lending and acts to dampen (increase) credit cycles abroad as well as at home. There would be no need for policy coordination per se, but there would be a need for domestic authorities to take into account the positive inward spillovers from macropru policy changes in other countries when setting their own policy. In fact, not taking into account this positive externality

Table 8.1 *The effect of macroprudential countries taken by one country on another depends on credit conditions in the other country*

|  | Credit gap in country B | |
| --- | --- | --- |
| Country A Action | Positive | Negative |
| **Tightening of macroprudential policies *(likely positive credit gap in A)*** | Positive spillover on B (reduces cross border lending) | Negative spillover on B (reduces cross border lending) |
| **Loosening of macroprudential policies *(likely negative credit gap in A)*** | Negative spillover on B (increases cross border lending) | Positive spillover on B (increases cross border lending) |

would result in both countries setting a too tight level of macroprudential policies when acting unilaterally to dampen a domestic credit boom. Greater information exchange among supervisors on macropru policy intentions may form an important lower layer of cooperation and help to set macroprudential policies at the optimal level. There may also be a role here for the IMF in helping to assess the cross border impact of changes in national macropru policies.

When **credit cycles are asymmetric** – bottom left (to right) quadrant – the opposite holds: if the authorities in country A tighten macropru to dampen domestic credit cycles, negative spillover could result due to a reduction in lending to countries already facing a slowdown in domestic credit growth. Banks in country B may not have the capacity to expand their domestic lending to make up for reduced cross-border credit. So here there may be a case, in principle, for actual policy coordination rather just information sharing. In the context of current low global growth, emerging market economies (EMEs) complain that a tightening in regulator policy in AE banking systems has reduced lending to their economies.

The country facing the slow-down in domestic credit could ask the country tightening its macroprudential policies to exempt assets held by its banks in the recipient country from the policy tightening. Whether such bilateral agreements have a chance of success will depend among other things on whether the two countries see the process as a repeated game suggesting that cooperation today may be answered by cooperation tomorrow.

This suggests one important condition for successful coordination: if countries are on a level playing field in terms of their banks lending to each other's economy, the benefits of cooperation may be large and

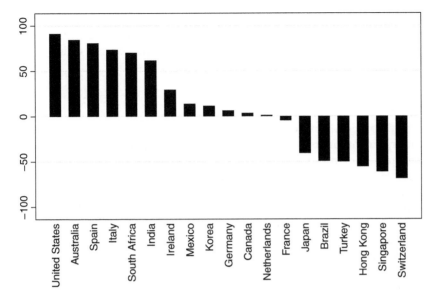

Figure 8.10 Correlation of credit gaps to GDP between the United Kingdom and other countries (2000Q1–2013Q3, %).
Source: BIS, WEO, Bank Calculations

two-sided. Of course, if bilateral exposures are one-sided, the benefits of coordination will apply mostly to only one of the partners. Ostry and Ghosh (2013) highlight that there is less policy coordination in practice because of asymmetries in country size: spillovers often originate from large countries, but small countries are usually not involved in international negotiations (e.g. G20). However, given the likely future rise of capital flows originating from EMEs, the roles of lenders and borrowers may change over time even between AEs and EMEs.

To illustrate, for the case of the United Kingdom there are important differences in the degree of credit cycle correlation with major countries. Figure 8.10 shows the correlation of credit gaps (relative to GDP) between the United Kingdom and other countries between 2000Q1 and 2013Q3. Credit cycles are most strongly synchronised between the United Kingdom and the United States suggesting that there are likely to be positive spillover effects of macroprudential policies between the United States and the United Kingdom. The correlation of credit cycles is also large with other countries that in the past have recorded large current account deficits. Conversely, correlations tend to be either negative (Hong Kong, Switzerland) or close to zero (Germany, the Netherlands) with structural current account surplus countries, suggesting the potential for negative spillovers of macroprudential policies and a greater need for coordination.[6] More work is needed to what determines the degree of credit cycle correations and examine the extent to which these correlations change over time.

### The Case for Reciprocation?

The theoretical work of Ostry, Ghosh and Korinek (2012) strengthens the argument for applying the principle of reciprocity to macroprudential policies. They make the case for global coordination between recipient and source countries. Their paper focuses on capital flow management CFMs used for macroprudential purposes, but their model can, in principle, be extended to domestically oriented macroprudential policies. A key aspect is that there is cost of implementing prudential measures related to administration and compliance as well as economic distortions. The case for coordination between source and recipient countries in Ostry, Ghosh and Korinek (2012) rests on the shape of these costs: if they rise more than a ratio of one-for-one with the level of the CFM tax it would be globally more efficient to share the cost between borrowing and lending countries. In this case, the total global cost would be lower than if the borrowing country acted on its own.

The big question here is that although the global cost of implementing the policy may be lower, what does the foreign authority gain *itself* from such policy coordination other than a feel good factor of significantly helping the domestic authority?

To the extent that there is convexity in the cost of unilateral macroprudential measures, then at the global level it would be more efficient to share the costs between authorities. Take the situation where policy effectiveness is hindered by leakages (as illustrated earlier in the chapter). If the domestic authorities acts unilaterally it will need to tighten macropru further on domestic banks. But the joint cost of policy implementation would be lower if the foreign authorities simultaneously tighten regulation on lending of their banks cross border. In the context of the reciprocity principle agreed for the Countercyclical Capital Buffer (CCyB) in Basel III, the country tightening policy would ask the foreign authority to reciprocate capital requirements on its bank lending cross border and locally via foreign branches.

[6] Following the procedure recommended by the BIS, credit gaps are calculated using a HP filter with a smoothing parameter of 400000 (See BIS Quarterly Review, June 2013 for details). We use a two-sided filter. Following Baxter and King (1993), the first and last three quarters are dropped to alleviate the endpoint problem found for HP filters. The sample includes only countries with at least 10 years of quarterly data.

In practice, it will be difficult for countries to share any of the outlined short-term global gains from the lower joint costs of implementing macroprudential policy (i.e. it will be hard to find a mechanism for the recipient to partly repay the source country for the latter's help in limiting spillovers).

However, it may not be necessary as it may be in the interest of the foreign country to reciprocate/cooperate. If financial supervisors in the two countries share the same objectives, have similar administrative capacities to implement prudential regulations, and there are information asymmetries (implying that the domestic supervisor can judge better the domestic financial stability risks) there is a strong case for the foreign country supervisor to restrict foreign lending by its banks in order to ensure that its banks also price risk appropriately. Otherwise, to the extent that their institutions have a competitive advantage, they could be incentivised to increase their exposure to the relevant macroprudential risks, thereby putting their domestic financial stability at risk.

There is another dimension to the authorities incentive to reciprocate: assuring that the foreign authorities macroprudential measures are successful and achieve their end result in adressing systemic risk. As outlined in the opening section of this chapter, financial systems are highly globalised and the potential scope for contagion is high. The Global Financial Crisis illustrated this starkly as problems in a localised sector of the US market spread rapidly throughout the globe.

This is an issue of particular importance in the United Kingdom because the United Kingdom is one of the central nodes in the world interbank network (Figure 8.11).

*Monetary Policy Coordination versus Macroprudential Policy Coordination*

We have so far focused only on macroprudential policy coordination. But before concluding, it is useful to learn from the older debate on monetary policy coordination. Specifically, are there are any key conceptual differences between the need or benefits of coordination on macroprudential policies compared to monetary policy coordination? As discussed, given the novelty of macroprudential policies in many countries, work on the international coordination of macroprudential policies is only just emerging; even more so for work on comparing macroprudential policy coordination with coordination in other fields. The comparison here can hence only be tentative, potentially stimulating further work down the road.

Monetary policy coordination has been discussed recently in the face of monetary policy divergence between major economic regions and the

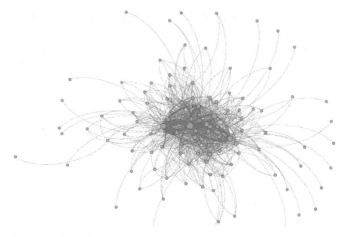

Figure 8.11 The international interbank network.
Note: This chart shows cross-border interbank claims of BIS reporting countries
on locational basis as of 2013 Q2. We inferred the interbank claims of non-BIS-
reporting countries through mirror statistics where available. The size of the edges
indicates the size of the bilateral cross-border claims. The size of the node indicates
network degree (a measure of interconnectedness). The positions of the nodes of
the diagram are based on the node's network centrality. Due to reasons of data
confidentiality we cannot indicate which node belongs to which banking system.
Source: BIS and Bank calculations

potential role in US monetary policy in driving global capital flows (e.g.
Rey 2013, Bruno and Shin, 2013).

We think there may be four interesting differences between monetary
and macroprudential policy coordination that speak for a higher need or
higher potential success of coordinating macropru policies over monetary policies.

First, the discussed policy leakages that require international cooperation on reciprocity arrangements may be more relevant for macroprudential policy than for monetary policy. The fact that one important
potential source of leakage – foreign branches not regulated by home
authorities – are *resident in the domestic economy* suggests that such leakages may be more immediate than comparable leakages of monetary
policies. That holds even if a given macrorprudential policy instruments
is comprehensive in targeting all domestic lending. Leakages by both
foreign and domestic sources may be larger in case macrorpu becomes
more targeted. For example, Dell'Erba and Reinhardt (2015) findings
suggest that financial sector FDI may have been used to evade bond
inflow controls in EMEs. Monetary Policy on the other hand gets, one
could think, into all the cracks as recently put by Fed Governor Stein

(2013). But while this is likely true with regard to domestic channels of leakages, Cetorelli and Goldberg (2012) make the point that global operations of banks insulate them from changes in monetary policy, potentially weakening the bank lending channel of monetary policy. The channel for this result is simple: if the home central bank raises interest rates, global banks may raise more funding from jurisdictions where rates are relatively lower and channel the funding back to the home market. More research is needed to explore the relative strenght of monetary and macroprudential policy leakages.

Second, the fact that macroprudential policies can be targeted at specific types of lending allows for the possibility for domestic policy makers to cooperate with other jurisdictions *without* deviating from optimal macroprudential policy at home. This may be harder for monetary policy given that it is a blunter tool. To illustrate, if one country (A) is in a credit-cycle downswing it can ask partner countries (say B) which are potentially in a tightening-cycle to exempt exposures specifically to A from such tightening or directly loosen regulations on exposures to A. Regulators in country B would be able to cooperate without adjusting their optimal policy on domestic exposures. This is of course just an illustration of the reciprocity regime agreed for the CCB.

Third, in the sphere of macroprudential policies cooperation by *all* major players – especially financial centers – seems crucial because of the mobility of international capital flows, raising the need for more comprehensive global cooperation. To illustrate using the example of the CCB: if all countries in the world but one would reciprocate a rise in the CCB in country A, banks may channel their lending to country A via subsidiaries[7] in the non-cooperating country and avoid the increased capital charges on lending to country A with important implications for the effectiveness of macroprudential regulation in country A. This channel is potentially less relevant for monetary policy for two reasons. First, in the same example, funding would need to be *raised* in the non-cooperating country and then lend onwards to the country that raised its interest rate. In the CCB example earlier, it is enough to merely *channel* funding through subsidiaries. Second, it will be costly for another country to deviate from optimal interest rates to open such a channel of policy leakages, whereas the costs of deviating from optimal macroprudential policies may be lower if it is mainly foreign-owned banks that expose themselves to excessive risks by avoiding recirpocity arrangements.

---

[7] Branches would be captured by the reciprocity agreement.

*Coordination and Reciprocation: The State of Play and*
*Next Steps*

There is good news in the policy space: reciprocity of the counter-cyclical capital buffer is a cornerstone of Basel III, and EU law requires that the United Kingdom and other EEA countries to begin reciprocation of CCB rates from 2016. In the United Kingdom the Financial Policy Committee reciprocated the Norwegian and Swedish counter-cyclical buffer ahead of 2016. On top of this, 'given the benefits to global financial stability of a coordinated approach across national boundaries, the Committee noted the desirability of other jurisdictions taking a similar approach to reciprocation of macroprudential decisions.'[8]

However, these existing rules do not proscribe rules for all potential macroprudential instruments. The research we discussed here suggests, however, that there are likely to be also leakages with regard to other capital and liquidity-like policies suggesting that there may be benefits from extending the principle of reciprocity further. In the United Kingdom, the Financial Policy Committee (FPC) has announced that it recognises that 'in most cases reciprocation would enhance the resilience of the UK financial system'[9] and also that it would consider reciprocity for capital requirements other than the counter-cyclical capital buffer.

At the European level assessing the cross-border impact of macro-prudential policies and coordinating Member States' actions is at the heart of the mandate of the European Systemic Risk Board (ESRB). Capital rules (CRD IV/CRR) which have been in force since 1 January 2014 already foresee some coordination procedures involving the ESRB for specific instruments. In January 2016 the ESRB adopted a framework for voluntary cross-border reciprocity to 'safeguard the effectiveness and consistency of macroprudential policy across borders within the EU'.[10]

At the international level, the FSB has made important progress on driving forward the regulatory reform agenda. Over time, it is conceivable that the FSB or another global institution becomes a global forum for discussing spillovers and fostering macroprudential coordination between authorities at an global level.

---

[8] https://www.bankofengland.co.uk/-/media/boe/files/record/2014/financial-policy-committee-meeting-september-2014
[9] See the link in note 11.
[10] https://www.esrb.europa.eu/pub/pdf/recommendations/2015/ESRB_2015_2.en.pdf

## References

Aiyar, S., C. Calomiris, J. Hooley, Y. Korniyenko and T. Wieladek (2014a). 'The international transmission of bank capital requirements: Evidence from the UK', *Journal of Financial Economics*, vol 113, 368–382.

Aiyar, S., C. Calomiris and T. Wieladek (2014b). 'Does macroprudential regulation leak? Evidence from a UK policy experiment', *Journal of Money, Credit and Banking*, vol 46, 181–214.

(2014c). 'Identifying Channels of Credit Substitution When Bank Capital Requirements Are Varied', *Bank of England Working Papers*, no. 485.

Barth, J. R., G. Caprio and R. Levine (2013). 'Bank regulation and supervision in 180 countries from 1999 to 2011', *Journal of Financial Economic Policy*, vol 5, no 2, 111–219.

Bengui, J. and J. Bianchi (2014). Capital flow management when capital controls leak. Mimeo.

Bianchi, J. (2011) 'Overborrowing and systemic externalities in the business cycle', *American Economic Review*, vol 101, no 7, 3400–3426.

Bremus, F. and M. Fratzscher (2014). 'Drivers of Structural Change in Cross-Border Banking Since the Global Financial Crisis', *DIW Discussion Paper*, no 1411.

Brunnermeier, M and Y. Sannikov (2015). 'International Credit Flows and Pecuniary Externalities', *CEPR Discussion Papers*, no 10339.

Bruno, V. and H. S. Shin (2013). 'Capital flows and the risk-taking channel of monetary policy', *NBER Working Papers*, no. 18942.

Buch C. and L. Goldberg (2017). 'Cross-border prudential policy spillovers: How much? How important? Evidence from the International Banking Research Network', *International Journal of Central Banking*, vol 13, no 2, 505–508.

Bush, O., S. Knott and C. Peacock (2014). 'Why is the UK banking system so big and is that a problem?', *BoE Quarterly Bulletin*, no 4.

Cerutti, E. C. S. and L. Laeven (2015). 'The use and effectiveness of macroprudential policies: New evidence', *IMF Working Papers*, no 15/61.

Cetorelli, N. and L. Goldberg (2012). 'Banking globalization and monetary transmission', *Journal of Finance*, vol 67, no 5.

CEPR 2014 (2014). 'Macroprudentialism' Vox eBook.

Danisewicz, P., D. Reinhardt and R. Sowerbutts (2017). 'On a tight leash: Does bank organisational structure matter for macroprudential spillovers?', *Journal of International Economics*, vol 109, 174–194.

Dell'Erba, S. and D. Reinhardt (2015). 'FDI, debt and capital controls', *Journal of International Money and Finance*, no 58, 29–50.

Hoggarth, G., J. Hooley and Y. Korniyenko (2013). 'Which way do foreign branches sway? Evidence from the recent UK domestic credit cycle' *Bank of England FS Paper*, no 22.

Houston, J., C. Lin and Y. Ma (2012). 'Regulatory arbitrage and international bank flows', *Journal of Finance*, vol 67, no 5.

Jeanne, O. (2014). 'Macroprudential policies in a global perspective,' *NBER Working Papers*, no 19967.

Korinek, A. (2011). *Excessive Dollar Borrowing in Emerging Markets: Balance Sheet Effects and Macroeconomic Externalities*. Baltimore: University of Maryland.

Kuttner, K. N. and I. Shim (2013). 'Can Non-Interest Rate Policies Stabilize Housing Markets? Evidence from a Panel of 57 Economies', *NBER Working Papers*, no 19723.

Lane, P. R. and G. M. Milesi-Ferretti (2007). 'The external wealth of nations mark II: Revised and extended estimates of foreign assets and liabilities, 1970–2004', *Journal of International Economics*, vol 73, 223–250.

Lim, C., F. Columba, A. Costa, P. Kongsamut, A. Otani, M. Saiyid, T. Wezel and X. Wu (2011). 'Macroprudential Policy: What instruments and how to use them?', *IMF Working Paper*, no. 11/238.

Ongena, S., A. Popov and G. F. Udell (2013). 'When the cat's away the mice will play: Does regulation at home affect bank risk-taking abroad?', *Journal of Financial Economics*, vol 108, no 3, 727–750.

Ostry, J., R. Ghosh and A. Korinek (2012). 'Multilateral Aspects of Managing the Capital Account', *IMF Staff Discussion Note*, no 12/10.

Ostry, J. and R. Ghosh (2013) 'Obstacles to International Policy Coordination and How to Overcome Them,' IMF Staff Discussion Note No 13/11.

Peek, J., and E. Rosengren (1997) 'The international transmission of financial shocks: The case of Japan', *American Economic Review*, vol 87, 495–505.

(2000). 'Collateral damage: Effects of the Japanese bank crisis on the United States', *American Economic Review*, vol 90, 30–45.

Reinhardt, D. and R. Sowerbutts (2015). 'Regulatory arbitrage in action: Evidence from banking flows and macroprudential policy', *Bank of England Staff Working Paper*, no. 546.

Rey, H. (2013). 'Dilemma not trilemma: The global financial cycle and monetary policy independence'. Paper presented at the Jackson Hole Symposium, August 2013.

Stein, J. (2013) 'Overheating in credit markets: Origins, measurement, and policy responses', Speech at the 'Restoring Household Financial Stability after the Great Recession: Why Household Balance Sheets Matter' research symposium sponsored by the Federal Reserve Bank of St. Louis, St. Louis, Missouri.

Vandenbussche, J., V. Ursula and D. Enrica (2012). 'Macroprudential policies and housing price', *IMF Working Papers*, no 12/303.

# 9 Systemic Risk of European Banks
## Regulators and Markets[*]

*Maarten R.C. van Oordt[†] and Chen Zhou[‡]*

Regulatory rules may have different impacts on risk-taking by individual banks and on banks' systemic risk levels. That is why implementing prudential rules and policies requires careful consideration of their impact on bank risk and systemic risk. This chapter assesses whether market-based measures of systemic risk and recent regulatory indicators provide similar rankings on the systemic importance of large European banks. We find evidence that regulatory indicators of systemic importance are positively related to systemic risk. In particular, banks with higher scores on regulatory indicators have a stronger link to the system in the event of financial stress, rather than having a higher level of bank risk.

## Introduction

There is a general consensus that prudential regulation before the recent financial crisis focused mainly on the soundness of individual financial institutions. In other words, prudential regulation was primarily based on the microprudential objective of limiting the level of bank risk. This might be one of the reasons why the recent financial crisis was not prevented. By contrast, the macroprudential objective of regulation is maintaining the stability of the financial system as a whole or, in other words, limiting systemic risk.

The ultimate concern of policy makers in the context of systemic risk is the macroeconomic cost of financial instability (i.e. the macroeconomic consequences of a serious disruption of the financial system); see Borio (2003). Evidence of such costs is documented by Peek and Rosengren

[*] The authors thank Willem L. H. Evers, the editors and participants in the Conference of the Centre for Finance, Credit and Macroeconomics on '*Effective Macroprudential Instruments*' (Nottingham, 2014) for useful comments and suggestions. This chapter draws on Van Oordt and Zhou (2014). Views expressed do not necessarily reflect positions of the Bank of Canada or De Nederlandsche Bank.
[†] Email: mvanoordt@bankofcanada.ca    [‡] Email: C.Zhou@dnb.nl, zhou@ese.eur.nl

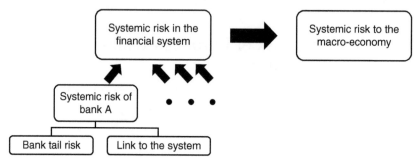

Figure 9.1  Systemic risk: A multilayer concept
Note: The figure presents a diagram of the portfolio view on systemic risk explained in Borio (2003) and the decomposition of the systemic risk of financial institutions in Van Oordt and Zhou (2014).

(2000), Boyd et al. (2005) and Dell'Ariccia et al. (2008). The systemic risk to the macro-economy depends on the level of systemic risk in the financial system, which, in turn, depends on the systemic risk of individual financial institutions; see Figure 9.1. Gaining a full understanding of each of these layers of systemic risk is not without its challenges. That is why most studies focus on one single aspect of systemic risk.

Instead of measuring the ultimate macroeconomic cost of financial instability, a growing literature examines the level and determinants of systemic risk in the financial system, or – in other words – the likelihood of a collapse of the financial system and the potential magnitude of such a collapse. Examples are the studies on financial stress indicators and early warning indicators, which focus on evaluating the variation in systemic risk over time. Those papers are sometimes referred to as studies on systemic risk in the time dimension; see, for example, De Bandt et al. (2010) and Galati and Moessner (2013).

Rather than studying the time dimension, this chapter focuses on the cross-sectional dimension – that is, the distribution of systemic risk across financial institutions. While there are many definitions of systemic risk, there is a general consensus that the health of some institutions is more essential to the stability of the financial system than that of others. Broadly speaking, the term "systemic risk" consists of two elements: "systemic" and "risk." Systemic risk thus not only depends on the risks taken by individual banks, but also on how these risks relate to other institutions in the system. "Common exposures" and "interlinkages" are also of paramount importance for systemic risk; see, for example, Borio (2003, 2014). This suggests that, conceptually, the systemic risk of a bank may be broken down into two subcomponents: the downside tail risk of the bank and its link to the rest of the system in the event of financial stress; see Figure 9.1.

The distinction between bank risk and systemic risk steers the ongoing debate about the micro- and macroprudential objectives of regulation. By focusing on bank risk, the microprudential objective of regulation considers one side of the "systemic risk coin" only. There is no guarantee that policies aimed at achieving the microprudential objective of regulation will simultaneously deal with the macroprudential objective, or vice versa. This depends on how policies with an impact on bank "risk" are related to the "systemic" component of "systemic risk."

One of the recently introduced policies in the context of macroprudential regulation is to identify global systemically important banks (G-SIBs) and to require them to fund themselves with more equity capital as an additional loss-absorbing buffer. Identification of the G-SIBs and the level of the additional capital buffer depend on the scores of banks in terms of systemic importance according to regulators; see BCBS (2013a, 2014a). Regulators calculate the scores on the basis of information provided by the individual banks. Parallel to the regulatory approach, academic literature provides several measures of systemic risk on the cross-sectional dimension using market-based information. These market-based measures can also be used to rank financial institutions in terms of systemic risk.

This chapter assesses whether market-based measures of systemic risk and recent regulatory indicators provide similar rankings of systemically important banks. After a brief review of both approaches, we compare their rankings for a group of large European banks. We document evidence that regulatory scores used for the identification of G-SIBs have a positive relation to market-based measures of systemic risk. The positive relation to systemic risk is mainly because banks with higher regulatory scores on systemic importance have a much stronger link to the system in the event of financial stress, rather than having a higher level of bank risk. These results support the regulators' choice of indicators to identify systemic important institutions.

### Regulatory Approach to Systemic Importance

Regulators worldwide haven taken several steps to enhance the stability of the global financial system. One of these steps is to require higher levels of Common Equity Tier 1 (CET1) funding for internationally active, systemically important banks (G-SIBs). The additional buffer requirement will be phased in between 2016 and 2019. The proposed additional buffer ranges from 1 percent to 3.5 percent of risk-weighted assets (RWA), but it may be raised further if institutions become more systemically important. The additional buffer requirement for an individual bank depends on its regulatory score for systemic importance.

The methodology for determining the systemic importance score of individual banks has been developed by the Basel Committee on Banking Supervision (BCBS). The method has an indicator-based approach and relies on measuring the extent to which banks are involved in certain activities. Large banks have to publish amounts for twelve G-SIB indicators grouped into five categories; see IMF/BIS/FSB (2009) and BCBS (2013a, 2014a).[1] The European Banking Authority (EBA) collects these data for a number of large banks in the European Economic Area (EEA) and publishes them on its website; see EBA (2014). Our data set is based on the EBA data but also includes data on three large banks not included in the dataset published by the EBA.[2] Overall, our study considers the G-SIB indicators for twenty-five large listed banks in the EEA.

Table 9.1 presents the summary statistics of the G-SIB indicators for the twenty-five publicly listed large European banks included in our data set. The standard deviations indicate a considerable level of dispersion in the reported amounts across banks. Moreover, each of the indicators exhibits positive skewness, which suggests that the sample for each indicator includes, to a certain extent, several exceptionally high values.

The category "Size" captures the notion that the importance of a bank is positively related to the volume of services provided. This view is supported by the positive relation between bank size and systemic risk documented in, for example, Brunnermeier et al. (2012), López-Espinosa et al. (2012), Huang et al. (2012), Vallascas and Keasey (2012) and Girardi and Ergün (2013). With size defined as total exposures, it also captures off-balance sheet items, rather than focusing on balance sheet exposures only.

The category "Interconnectedness" captures the view that linkages among financial institutions may increase contagion risk; see, for example, Allen and Gale (2000) and Freixas et al. (2000). The first two indicators, intra-financial system assets and liabilities, cover direct linkages to other financial institutions, including those resulting from deposits, credit lines and several other transactions; see BCBS (2014b).

[1] The regulatory approach is still undergoing reviews and revisions; see e.g. BCBS (2015) for some recent changes.
[2] Given our intention to compare the regulatory approach with the market-based approach, we exclude six banks without a stock market listing from our data set, while adding three large EEA banks (with total exposures of more than EUR 200 billion) not included in the EBA dataset: Commerzbank, Danske Bank and Deutsche Bank. Their G-SIB indicator amounts were obtained from their websites.

Table 9.1 *Summary statistics of G-SIB indicators of large European banks (EUR billion).*

| Category | Indicator | Mean | Sd | Skewness |
|---|---|---|---|---|
| Size | Total exposures | 1,379 | 654 | 0.9 |
| Interconnectedness | Intra-financial system assets | 102 | 98 | 1.3 |
| | Intra-financial system liabilities | 129 | 113 | 1.4 |
| | Securities outstanding | 276 | 82 | 0.3 |
| Substitutability | Payments activity | 11,527 | 33,130 | 3.4 |
| | Assets under custody | 874 | 1,357 | 1.8 |
| | Underwriting activity | 27 | 96 | 1.8 |
| Complexity | OTC derivatives (RHS) | 3,815 | 16,136 | 1.6 |
| | Trading and AfS securities | 27 | 59 | 1.5 |
| | Level 3 assets | 1 | 9 | 2.3 |
| Cross-jurisdictional | Cross-jurisdictional claims | 733 | 296 | 1.0 |
| | Cross-jurisdictional liabilities | 652 | 273 | 1.7 |

Note: Summary statistics of G-SIB indicators of 25 publicly traded large banks in the European Economic Area in EUR billion at the end of 2013. See Table 9.2 for the list of banks.
Source: EBA (2014) and banks' websites

The indicator "Securities outstanding" represents the amount of securities issued by a bank, regardless of whether they are held by other financial institutions.

The potential harm caused by the collapse of a bank is incorporated in the category "Substitutability" by measuring the size of critical functions provided to the economy. This is a category with three indicators, namely the amount of outgoing cash payments excluding those made through retail payment systems, the value of assets under custody held on behalf of clients, and the value of underwritten equity and debt instruments.

The category "Complexity" focuses on a bank's complexity and opacity, which are associated with potential fire sales or substantial haircuts in the event of severe market stress; see, for example, Brunnermeier (2009), Diamond and Rajan (2011) and Flannery et al. (2013). The first indicator is the notional amount of over-the-counter derivatives either cleared bilaterally or through a central counterparty. The second indicator is the amount of held-for-trading or available-for-sale securities that do not qualify as sufficiently high-quality liquid assets.[3] The third indicator is the amount of Level 3 assets – that is, the amount of assets

---

[3] More specifically, high-quality liquid assets that qualify as Level 1 assets for liquidity coverage ratio (LCR) purposes are excluded. Assets that qualify as Level 2 assets receive a lower weight; for more details, see BCBS (2013b).

held at fair value that are difficult to value in the sense that the measurement is based on a pricing model using parameters that are not observable in the market.

The last category "Cross-jurisdictional activities" captures both the difficulties associated with the resolution of international financial institutions and the transmission of shocks across the globe through internationally active banks; see, for example, Goodhart and Schoenmaker (2009) and Cetorelli and Goldberg (2011).

In order to express the systemic importance of each institution in a single score, regulators have to aggregate the twelve indicator values shown in Table 9.1. To normalize the reported amounts across different indicators, the score of a bank for an indicator is expressed in basis points of the total amount reported by all large banks. A bank's category score is obtained by averaging that bank's indicator scores within the category.[4] Finally, a bank's systemic importance score is the simple average of that bank's five category scores. In the first column of Table 9.2 we calculate the regulatory systemic importance scores of European banks. Banks are allocated to a G-SIB bucket based on these scores, with the buckets determining the additional capital buffer requirement. Allocation to bucket 1 implies an additional CET1 loss absorbency requirement of 1 percent of RWA; a bank in bucket 4 faces an additional requirement of 2.5 percent of RWA.

## Market-Based Approaches to Systemic Risk

This section discusses market-based approaches to measuring systemic risk. There are both pros and cons of market-based approaches to estimating the systemic risk of financial institutions. The main advantages of using market data are their public nature and the low cost of data collection. Moreover, information based on market data is often available at a higher frequency and on a more timely basis than accounting-based measures, because of the higher frequency and the forward-looking nature of asset prices.

However, market-based measures could result in underestimation of systemic risk if prices incorporate potential responses of governments and regulators to a potential crisis. For example, bond prices and CDS spreads are directly affected by bailout expectations; see, for example, Flannery and Sorescu (1996) and Demirgüç-Kunt and Huizinga (2013). Market prices may also misrepresent actual risk levels given that they may

---

[4] An exception is the score for the category "Substitutability," which is capped at 500 basis points; see BCBS (2014a, subsection 3.3).

Table 9.2 *Regulatory and market-based indicators of systemic risk of large European banks.*

| Bank (country code) | Regulatory approach: | | Market-based approach: | | |
|---|---|---|---|---|---|
| | Score | Bucket | Bank risk | Link to system | Systemic risk |
| Banco Monte dei Paschi (IT) | 22 | 0 | 1.60 | 0.61 | 0.98 |
| Banco Santander (ES) | 196 | 1 | 1.18 | 0.90 | 1.07 |
| Barclays (UK) | 384 | 3 | 1.85 | 0.83 | 1.54 |
| BBVA (ES) | 92 | 0 | 1.25 | 0.88 | 1.11 |
| BNP Paribas (FR) | 407 | 3 | 1.51 | 0.88 | 1.33 |
| Caixabank (ES) | 26 | 0 | 0.95 | 0.61 | 0.58 |
| Commerzbank (DE) | 121 | 0 | 1.78 | 0.76 | 1.35 |
| Credit Agricole (FR) | 218 | 1 | 1.68 | 0.82 | 1.38 |
| Danske Bank (DK) | 76 | 0 | 1.24 | 0.75 | 0.93 |
| Deutsche Bank (DE) | 417 | 3 | 1.36 | 0.80 | 1.10 |
| DNB ASA (NO) | 60 | 0 | 1.45 | 0.77 | 1.12 |
| Erste Group Bank (AT) | 33 | 0 | 1.62 | 0.74 | 1.20 |
| HSBC (UK) | 477 | 4 | 0.90 | 0.84 | 0.76 |
| ING Bank (NL) | 144 | 1 | 1.90 | 0.88 | 1.67 |
| Intesa Sanpaolo (IT) | 80 | 0 | 1.66 | 0.84 | 1.40 |
| KBC Group (BE) | 36 | 0 | 1.96 | 0.69 | 1.34 |
| Lloyds Banking Group (UK) | 98 | 0 | 1.84 | 0.73 | 1.35 |
| Nordea Bank (SW) | 121 | 0 | 1.31 | 0.84 | 1.10 |
| Royal Bank of Scotland (UK) | 238 | 2 | 1.75 | 0.80 | 1.40 |
| SEB (SW) | 58 | 0 | 1.49 | 0.81 | 1.21 |
| Society Generale (FR) | 225 | 1 | 1.72 | 0.84 | 1.45 |
| Standard Chartered (UK) | 133 | 1 | 1.11 | 0.76 | 0.84 |
| Svenska Handelsbanken (SW) | 45 | 0 | 1.18 | 0.76 | 0.89 |
| Swedbank (SW) | 32 | 0 | 1.63 | 0.81 | 1.32 |
| Unicredit (IT) | 148 | 1 | 1.86 | 0.80 | 1.48 |

Note: This table presents regulatory scores on systemic importance and market-based systemic risk measures for 25 publicly traded large banks in the European Economic Area at the end of 2013. The regulatory scores and buckets are obtained by applying the methodology described by BCBS (2014a) on the data released by EBA (2014) and individual banks' websites. The market-based measures are estimates based on daily stock market returns over the period 2009–2013 by applying the methodology of Van Oordt and Zhou (2014). Source: authors' calculations

be prone to panics, runs, illiquidity and fire sales. Moreover, regulators may have confidential information on the financial system that is not available to market participants. Nevertheless, regardless of whether market prices are in line with the information available to regulators, they may still provide information about the perceptions of market participants on the systemic risk of financial institutions. This information is valuable because it may reveal the willingness of investors and other agents in the economy to extend finance or roll-over existing bank debt once a large shock hits the financial system.

A difficulty with market-based measures is the identification of the origin of comovement in market prices. For example, joint failures of multiple banks may be caused by losses at one bank which are contagiously spread through the interbank market, or may be the consequence of losses on a common exposure. The distinction between the two is important for certain policy decisions. In the event of contagion through the interbank market, bailing out the bank suffering the initial loss would directly help the other banks survive. However, in case of a common exposure, bailing out any bank is unlikely to support the other institutions. It is difficult to distinguish between the two with the use of market information only. Nevertheless, even if market information only shows whether a bank is likely to face difficulties together with the rest of the system without revealing the cause, this information is still valuable because the bank's failure would place a larger burden on the economy during a banking crisis. Therefore, such information would still be useful for macroprudential regulation.

In recent years, many scholars have developed methods to measure the systemic risk of financial institutions based on market prices. Examples are the Volatility Contribution (VC) of Lehar (2005), the Conditional Value-at-Risk (CoVaR) of Adrian and Brunnermeier (2016), the Marginal Expected Shortfall (MES) of Acharya et al. (2009, 2012) and the Distressed Insurance Premium (DIP) of Huang et al. (2009, 2012). VC measures the risk contribution of a bank to the global regulator's portfolio, CoVaR is the level of risk in the financial system conditional on financial distress at a particular bank, or vice versa; MES is the expected loss of a bank's stock price conditional on a large shock to the financial system; and DIP measures the insurance premium required to cover the expected losses of an institution as a consequence of distress in the banking system. All these systemic risk measures help to differentiate financial institutions in the cross-sectional dimension based on market data.

The purpose of this chapter is to assess whether the regulatory approach and the market-based approach result in similar ranking orders of banks. The regulatory approach to measuring the systemic importance of financial institutions explicitly sets out to isolate systemic importance from the level of bank risk.

The Committee is of the view that global systemic importance should be measured in terms of the impact that a bank's failure can have on the global financial system and wider economy, rather than the risk that a failure could occur. (BCBS, 2013a, p. 5)

Therefore, when comparing rankings based on regulatory systemic importance scores with rankings based on market-based approaches, the relation between the two might be distorted by the differences in the level of bank risk. To achieve our goal, we will rely on a market-based approach for measuring systemic risk that can abstract from the level of bank risk.

Van Oordt and Zhou (2014) introduce a methodology to estimate a market-based systemic risk measure that can be broken down into two subcomponents reflecting the level of bank risk ("bank tail risk") and the strength of the link of the bank to the system in the event of financial stress ("link to the system"). This breakdown is consistent with the conceptual framework in Figure 9.1. The "link to the system"-component measures the strength of the link between the bank and the system in the event of system-wide distress, without containing information on the risk level of the underlying bank. The fact that it abstracts from bank tail risk suggests that it might be closely related to the regulatory indicators of systemic importance.

The systemic risk of a bank is measured as the sensitivity of the bank's stock returns to extremely large adverse shocks in the financial system. Figure 9.2 provides an illustration by showing the scatter between the daily returns of ING Group and a European banking index (excluding ING Group). It uses euro-denominated stock market returns and market capitalizations of twenty-five large European banks for the period 2009–2013, collected from Datastream. The observations to the left of the dashed vertical line are regarded as observations corresponding to extremely adverse shocks in the banking system.[5] The systemic risk of ING Group is measured as the slope of a fitted line among the large losses in the banking system indicated by solid circles (both grey and black).

The sensitivity to large shocks in the banking system is closely related to the MES measure proposed by Acharya et al. (2009). As MES stands for the expected loss of a financial institution conditional on a large loss in the system, the MES is estimated as the sample average of the observations indicated by the solid circles (both gray and black). The MES not only depends on the slope of the fitted line among the large losses in the banking system, but also on the magnitude of the losses in the banking system. The close relation between the two is supported by the scatter plot between the MES of European banks and their sensitivity to large

---

[5] More precisely, this chapter sets the threshold at such a level that the $k = 30$ worst returns of the European banking index out of $n = 1{,}304$ observations are regarded as extremely adverse shocks, which corresponds to $k/n \approx 2.3\%$ of the observations. The results remain qualitatively unchanged when using $k = 20$ or $k = 40$ instead.

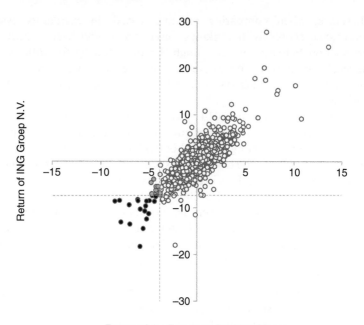

Return of the European Banking Sector

Figure 9.2  Scatter of daily returns, 2009–2013.
Note: The filled dots mark the 30 days during which the European banking
sector index sustained the largest losses.
Source: Datastream

shocks in the banking system; see Figure 9.3. The R-squared of the trend
line between the two is 0.84, which is in line with the theoretical result
that the sensitivity to large shocks in the banking system describes all
cross-sectional dispersion in the MES across institutions; see Van Oordt
and Zhou (2014).

Formally, we measure the sensitivity of bank $i$'s stock returns, $R_{i,t}$, to
large shocks in the financial system as the coefficient $\beta_i^T$ in the following
linear tail model

$$R_{i,t} = \beta_i^T R_{S^{-i},t} + \varepsilon_{i,t} \text{ for } R_{S^{-i},t} < -VaR_{S^{-i}}(\bar{p}), \tag{1}$$

where $R_{S^{-i},t}$ is the return of the European banking index (excluding
bank $i$), where $VaR_{S^{-i}}(\bar{p})$ is the Value-at-Risk of the system for some
small probability $\bar{p}$, and where $\varepsilon_{i,t}$ are shocks that are assumed to be
independent of $R_{S^{-i},t}$. The estimation of $\beta_i^T$ does not rely on an ordinary
least square regression conditional on extreme observations. Such an
estimation strategy would have a relatively large estimation error due to
the small number of observations and the heavy tails of stock returns; see,

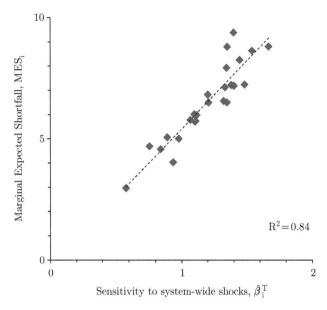

Figure 9.3 Scatter of two market-based approaches to systemic risk, 2009–2013.

Note: The figure presents a scatter between estimates of the sensitivity to systemic shocks and Marginal Expected Shortfall for 25 large European banks. Estimates are based on the 30 days with the largest market losses. For technical details on the estimation procedure, see the Appendix in this chapter; Table 9.2 for the list of banks.

Source: Datastream and authors' calculations

for example, Mikosch and De Vries (2013). Instead, Van Oordt and Zhou (2014) apply a methodology based on Extreme Value Theory (EVT), of which the technical details can be found in the Appendix. We apply this method, which gives the estimator of the systemic risk measure in (1) as

$$\widehat{\beta}_i^T = SL_i \times IR_i, \qquad (2)$$

where $SL_i$ measures the strength of the link between the bank and the system in the event of financial stress, and where $IR_i$ measures the tail risk of a bank. Hence, the systemic risk measure $\beta_i^T$ in (1) can be broken down into two subcomponents: the level of bank risk and the link to the system.

The intuition of the methodology to measure each subcomponent is described as follows. The subcomponent bank tail risk, $IR_i$, is the ratio between the Value-at-Risk of the bank and that of the banking system. The Value-at-Risk of the system is estimated by the threshold value of the vertical dashed line that indicates large losses to the banking index in Figure 9.2. We draw a similar dashed horizontal line, indicating the threshold below which we have the same number of extremely large losses for ING Group. The threshold value of this dashed line is an estimate of the Value-at-Risk of ING Group. The ratio between the two Value-at-Risks is a normalized measure of the downside tail risk of ING Group. The column "bank risk" in Table 9.2 presents this ratio for all banks in our sample.

The strength of the link between the bank and the system in the event of financial stress, $SL_i$, relies on the concept tail dependence. See Hartmann et al. (2007) and De Jonghe (2010) for two early empirical studies on the level of tail dependence in the context of banking. This subcomponent is estimated as follows. The observations to the left of the vertical dashed line in Figure 9.2 correspond to large adverse shocks in the banking system. Some of the large shocks in the system occurred at the same time as the extreme losses for ING Group. These observations are indicated by the black solid circles. For the other large losses in the system, the link between ING Group and the banking system was not strong enough to coincide with an extreme loss for ING Group. The fraction of the co-extreme events (black solid circles) among all large shocks in the system (gray and black solid circles) is an estimator of the tail dependence between ING Group and the banking system. The $SL_i$ is a strictly increasing function of the tail dependence and takes a value between zero and one. The column "link to system" in Table 9.2 reports the level of $SL_i$ for each bank.[6] The systemic risk measure $\widehat{\beta}_i^T$, which is reported in the column "systemic risk," and can be obtained as the product of the values in the columns "bank risk" and "link to system."

The estimates in Table 9.2 show that neither a high level of bank risk nor a strong link to the system in the event of financial stress are a sufficient condition to have a high level of systemic risk. After abstracting from bank risk, Banco Santander's link to the financial system is strongest with a value of 0.90. However, because of a low risk level, this bank's systemic risk is still limited (1.07). Similarly, KBC Group has the highest level of bank risk with a value of 1.96, but it is not among the institutions with the highest sensitivity to large shocks in the financial system. This is because of a weaker link to the system. ING Group has

[6] Like the level of tail dependence, the $SL_i$ is bounded between zero and one. See the Appendix for more details. The average value is 0.79 and suggests a relatively strong link between large banks and the system in financial stress. This is consistent with the finding of Mink and De Haan (2014) that a substantial part of the changes in market values of G-SIBs can be explained by G-SIBs as a group.

the highest sensitivity to large shocks in the financial system because it ranks relatively high on both subcomponents of systemic risk.

### Regulators and Markets

Our aim is to assess whether the regulatory scores of systemic importance and the market-based systemic risk measure lead to similar rankings of systemically important banks. Therefore, we explore the empirical relation between the market-based measures of systemic risk and the regulatory scores of systemic importance and its categories. Because of the low number of observations, estimating a cross-sectional regression including the scores on each of the five G-SIB categories as explanatory variables is not feasible. Instead, we calculate Spearman rank correlations between the estimated market-based systemic risk measure and the banks' scores on each of the five G-SIB categories.[7] We further consider rank correlations between regulatory scores and the two subcomponents of systemic risk. Given the purpose of the regulatory approach to abstract from bank risk, we expect primarily a strong correlation between the scores for the G-SIB categories of systemic importance and the "link to the system"-component, because it abstracts from the "bank risk"-component in systemic risk.

Table 9.3 presents the results. The bank scores for each of the five G-SIB categories correlated positively with the market-based measure of systemic risk, with correlation coefficients ranging from 0.25 to 0.35. Nevertheless, due to the small sample size, these coefficients cannot be regarded as statistically significant. However, after decomposing the systemic risk measure into the two subcomponents, the scores for all five G-SIB categories exhibit statistically significant positive correlations with the "link to the system"-component, ranging from 0.47 to 0.71. Each of these coefficients is statistically significant at the 5 percent level. This is in line with our expectation that the "link to the system"-component is stronger related to the regulatory approach to systemic importance as the regulatory approach aims to abstract from the level of bank risk. In contrast, we do not detect statistically significant relations between the five G-SIB categories and the level of the bank tail risk component in our sample. The results weakly support the intention of the G-SIB categories to capture the level of banks' systemic importance without having a strong relation to bank risk. Moreover, the "link to the system"-component is

---

[7] We also conducted correlation analysis using the Pearson correlation coefficients between the market-based risk measures and the log-level of the scores on the regulatory categories and indicators. This leaves the results qualitatively unchanged.

Table 9.3 *Rank correlations between G-SIB categories and market-based measures*

| Category | Bank risk | Link to system | Systemic risk |
|---|---|---|---|
| Size | 0.02 | 0.59 | 0.27 |
| Interconnectedness | 0.02 | 0.60 | 0.26 |
| Substitutability | 0.03 | 0.56 | 0.25 |
| Complexity | 0.16 | 0.47 | 0.35 |
| Cross-Jurisdictional Activity | −0.03 | 0.71 | 0.26 |
| Total Score | 0.04 | 0.65 | 0.30 |
| G-SIB Bucket (Pearson correlation) | −0.11 | 0.41 | 0.07 |

Note: The table presents rank correlations between the scores of 25 large European banks for regulatory G-SIB categories and the market-based measures on risk and systemic risk in Table 9.2. Rejection of the null hypothesis of zero rank correlation (two-sided) at the 10%, 5% and 1% significance level is indicated by absolute values above 0.34, 0.40 and 0.51, respectively.

also positively correlated to the G-SIB bucket allocation, with a Pearson correlation coefficient of 0.41, which is statistically significant at the 5 percent significance level.[8] In summary, the estimated systemic risk measures based on market data provide some support for the use of the G-SIB categories to measure banks' systemic importance.

To gain further insights into the relation between the regulatory approach to systemic importance and systemic risk, we consider a parallel analysis for the twelve G-SIB indicators that are used to construct the scores for the five categories in Table 9.4. Similar to the results for G-SIB category scores, the correlations between the indicators and systemic risk are all positive (insignificant), ranging from 0.02 to 0.33. The correlations with the "link to the system"-component are all positive and statistically significant, with the only exception of the indicator "Level 3 assets" which has a statistically insignificant correlation coefficient of 0.26. For the other indicators, the rank correlations range from 0.47 to 0.71. The correlations with the level of bank tail risk remain insignificant, with Level 3 assets having the highest positive correlation. In summary, there are no qualitative changes in the results if we analyze G-SIB indicator scores rather than G-SIB category scores.

Although the indicator Level 3 assets is less correlated to the "link to the system"-component than the other G-SIB indicators, this is no reason to doubt its validity as an indicator for systemic importance.

---

[8] Since the G-SIB Bucket is a categorical data item with a limited number of categories, a Spearman correlation is not feasible.

Table 9.4 *Rank correlations between G-SIB indicators and market-based measures*

| Category | Indicator | Bank risk | Link to system | Systemic risk |
|---|---|---|---|---|
| Size | Total exposures | 0.02 | 0.59 | 0.27 |
| Interconnectedness | Intra-financial system assets | 0.10 | 0.51 | 0.30 |
| | Intra-financial system liabilities | 0.12 | 0.56 | 0.33 |
| | Securities outstanding | −0.13 | 0.67 | 0.15 |
| Substitutability | Payments activity | 0.10 | 0.47 | 0.28 |
| | Assets under custody | −0.22 | 0.59 | 0.02 |
| | Underwriting activity | −0.11 | 0.49 | 0.11 |
| Complexity | OTC derivatives (RHS) | 0.07 | 0.51 | 0.27 |
| | Trading and AfS securities | −0.04 | 0.60 | 0.21 |
| | Level 3 assets | 0.22 | 0.26 | 0.31 |
| Cross-Jurisdictional | Cross-jurisdictional claims | −0.10 | 0.70 | 0.20 |
| | Cross-jurisdictional liabilities | −0.06 | 0.71 | 0.23 |

Note: The table presents rank correlations between the scores of 25 large European banks for regulatory G-SIB indicators and market-based measures on their level of risk and systemic risk in Table 9.2. Rejection of the null hypothesis of zero rank correlation (two-sided) at the 10%, 5% and 1% significance level is indicated by absolute values above 0.34, 0.40 and 0.51, respectively.

Because of the positive relation between Level 3 assets and bank risk, the indicator seems to be relatively strongly correlated to systemic risk before abstracting from bank risk (although insignificant). Level 3 assets may be considered as relatively opaque and relatively illiquid, which may be more vulnerable to fire sales than other assets. Market participants may regard banks with a higher exposure to these assets as more risky rather than considering those banks more strongly linked to the rest of the banking system. This may explain why Level 3 assets do not have a strong relation to the "link to the system"-component, but are still associated with a higher level of systemic risk.

### Concluding Remarks

Not all operations of banks that have an impact on the level of risk are similarly related to systemic risk. A single policy measure may have opposing effects on individual risk and systemic risk. That is why policy measures emanating from the microprudential objective of regulation – focusing on the risk of individual banks – may differ in scope and direction from policy measures that emanate from the macroprudential objective of regulation, and focus on systemic risk. Therefore, implementing prudential policies requires careful consideration of their impacts on bank risk and systemic risk.

Regulators worldwide have developed an approach to identify and categorize G-SIBs for higher loss absorbency requirements. This chapter contributes to the policy discussion by examining whether the regulatory approach to systemic importance is consistent with the perceptions of market participants. Our study provides some evidence supporting the regulators' choice of systemic importance indicators. In particular, we evaluate the relation between G-SIB categories and indicators, on the one hand, and market-based (systemic) risk measures on the other, for a sample of large banks in the EEA. The results support all G-SIB categories and most G-SIB indicators used to measure banks' systemic importance.

# Appendix

This appendix presents technical details on how the market-based measure of systemic risk and its two subcomponents are estimated. Because of the small number of banks in our sample, we follow López-Espinosa et al. (2012) and construct for each bank $i$ an index of the European banking system $S^{-i}$ based on the 24 other banks. Let $R_{i,t}$ denote the stock return of bank $i$ on day $t$. We construct the return of $S^{-i}$ as

$$R_{S^{-i},t} = \frac{\sum_{j \neq i} e_{j,t-1} R_{j,t}}{\sum_{j \neq i} e_{j,t-1}}, \tag{3}$$

where $e_{j,t-1}$ is the market capitalization of bank $j$ at the end of the previous trading day, and where $R_{j,t}$ is the return of bank $j$ on day $t$.

Following Van Oordt and Zhou (2014), we measure the systemic risk of a bank by evaluating its sensitivity to large shocks in the European banking system. The coefficient $\beta_i^T$ is estimated based on the EVT approach proposed by Van Oordt and Zhou (forthcoming). More specifically, let $R_{i,t}$ and $R_{S^{-i},t}$ follow heavy-tailed distributions with tail indices $\zeta_i$ and $\zeta_{S^{-i}}$, respectively.[9] Under the weak conditions $\zeta_{S^{-i}} < 2\zeta_i$ and $\beta_i^T \geq 0$, $\beta_i^T$ can be estimated by

$$\widehat{\beta}_i^T := \hat{\tau}_i(k/n)^{1/\zeta_{S^{-i}}} \frac{\widehat{VaR}_i(k/n)}{\widehat{VaR}_{S^{-i}}(k/n)}, \tag{4}$$

where the tail index $\zeta_{S^{-i}}$ is estimated by the estimator proposed in Hill (1975); $\widehat{VaR}_i(k/n)$ and $\widehat{VaR}_{S^{-i}}(k/n)$ are estimated by the $(k+1)th$ worst return on the bank's stock and the European banking index; and $\hat{\tau}_i(k/n)$ is the non-parametric estimator of tail dependence between $R_{i,t}$ and $R_{S^{-i},t}$ established in multivariate EVT, see Embrechts et al. (2000), as

---

[9] Formally, the distribution of $R_{i,t}$ is heavy-tailed if $\Pr(R_{i,t} < -u) = u^{-\zeta_i} l_i(u)$ with $\lim_{u \to \infty} \frac{l_i(tu)}{l_i(u)} = 1$ for all $t > 1$. To guarantee the consistency of $\widehat{\beta}_i^T$ in (4), theoretically, $k$ is a sequence depending on $n$ such that $k := k(n) \to \infty$ and $k(n)/n \to 0$ as $n \to +\infty$.

$$\hat{\tau}_i(k/n) = \frac{1}{k} \sum_{t:R_{S^{-i},t} < -\widehat{VaR}_{S^{-i}}(k/n)} 1\left( R_{i,t} < -\widehat{VaR}_i(k/n) \right). \qquad (5)$$

The estimator of $\beta_i^T$ can be decomposed into two subcomponents reflecting measures of the strength of the link of bank $i$ to the system in the event of financial stress and the level of bank tail risk, respectively. With the subcomponent measuring the link to the system defined as $SL_i = \hat{\tau}_i(k/n)^{1/\xi_{S^{-i}}}$, and with the subcomponent measuring bank $i$'s risk level as $IR_i = \widehat{VaR}_i(k/n)/\widehat{VaR}_{S^{-i}}(k/n)$, the estimator of $\beta_i^T$ in (4) can be rewritten as Eq. (2).

Following Acharya et al. (2009), we estimate the $MES_i$ in Figure 9.2 as

$$\widehat{MES}_i(k/n) = -\frac{1}{k} \sum_{t:R_{S^{-i},t} < -\widehat{VaR}_{S^{-i}}(k/n)} R_{i,t}. \qquad (6)$$

### References

V. V. Acharya, L. Pedersen, T. Philippon and M. Richardson (2009). "Regulating systemic risk." In V. V. Acharya and M. Richardson (Eds.), *Restoring Financial Stability: How to Repair a Failed System*, New York: John Wiley & Sons, 283–304.

V. V. Acharya, R. Engle and M. Richardson (2012). "Capital shortfall: A new approach to ranking and regulating systemic risks," *American Economic Review: Papers & Proceedings*, vol 102, no 3, 59–64.

T. Adrian and M. K. Brunnermeier (2016). "CoVaR," *American Economic Review*, vol 106, no 7, 1705–1741.

F. Allen and D. Gale (2000). "Financial contagion," *Journal of Political Economy*, vol 108, no 1, 1–33.

BCBS (2013a). "Global systemically important banks: Updated assessment methodology and the higher loss absorbency requirement." *Technical Document*.

(2013b). "Basel III: The Liquidity Coverage Ratio and liquidity risk monitoring tools," *Technical Document*.

(2014a). "The G-SIB assessment methodology: Score calculation," *Technical Document*, no19.

(2014b). "Instructions for the end-2013 data collection exercise of the macroprudential supervision group," Technical Document.

(2015). "Instructions for the end-2014 G-SIB assessment exercise," Technical Document.

C. Borio (2003). "Towards a macroprudential framework for financial supervision and regulation?," *CESifo Economic Studies*, vol 128, no 9, 181–215.

(2014). "The international monetary and financial system: Its Achilles heel and what to do about it," *BIS Working Papers*.

J. H. Boyd, S. Kwak and B. Smith (2005). "The real output losses associated with modern banking crises," *Journal of Money, Credit, and Banking*, vol 37, no 6, 977–999.

M. K. Brunnermeier (2009). "Deciphering the liquidity and credit crunch 2007–2008," *Journal of Economic Perspectives*, vol 23, no 1, 77–100.

M. K. Brunnermeier, G. Dong and D. Palia (2012). "Banks' non-interest income and systemic risk," *Working Paper*.

N. Cetorelli and L. S. Goldberg (2011). "Global banks and international shock transmission: Evidence from the crisis," *IMF Economic Review*, vol 59, no 1, 41–76.

O. De Bandt, P. Hartmann and J. L. Peydró (2010). "Systemic risk in banking: An update." In A. N. Berger, P. Molyneux and J. O. S. Wilson (Eds.), *The Oxford Handbook of Banking*, Oxford: Oxford University Press, 633–672.

O. De Jonghe (2010). "Back to the basics in banking? A micro-analysis of banking system stability," *Journal of Financial Intermediation*, vol 19, no 3, 387–417.

G. Dell'Ariccia, E. Detragiache and R. Rajan (2008). "The real effect of banking crises," *Journal of Financial Intermediation*, vol 17, no 1, 89–112.

A. Demirgüç-Kunt and H. Huizinga (2013). "Are banks too big to fail or too big to save? International evidence from equity prices and CDS spreads," *Journal of Banking & Finance*, vol 37, no 3, 875–894.

D. W. Diamond and R. G. Rajan (2011). "Fear of fire sales, illiquidity seeking, and credit freezes," *Quarterly Journal of Economics*, vol 126, no 2, 557–591.

EBA (2014). "EBA publishes indicators from Global Systemically Important Institutions (GSIIs)." http://www.eba.europa.eu/-/eba-publishes-indicators-from-global-systemically-important-institutions-g-siis. [Online; release date September 29, 2014].

P. Embrechts, L. de Haan and X. Huang (2000). "Modelling multivariate extremes." In *Extremes and Integrated Risk Management*. Risk Waters Group, 59–67.

M. J. Flannery and S. M. Sorescu (1996). "Evidence of bank market discipline in subordinated debenture yields: 1983–1991," *Journal of Finance*, vol 51, no 4, 1347–1377.

M. J. Flannery, S. H. Kwan and M. Nimalendran (2013). "The 2007–2009 financial crisis and bank opaqueness," *Journal of Financial Intermediation*, vol 22, no 1, 55–84.

X. Freixas, B. M. Parigi and J. C. Rochet (2000). "Systemic risk, interbank relations, and liquidity provision by the central bank," *Journal of Money, Credit and Banking*, vol 32, no 3, 611–638.

E. B. G. Galati and R. Moessner (2013). "Macroprudential policy: A literature review," *Journal of Economic Surveys*, vol 27, no 5, 846–878.

G. Girardi and A. T. Ergün (2013). "Systemic risk measurement: Multivariate GARCH estimation of CoVaR," *Journal of Banking & Finance*, vol 37, no 8, 3169–3180.

C. Goodhart and D. Schoenmaker (2009). "Fiscal burden sharing in cross-border banking crises," *International Journal of Central Banking*, vol 5, no 1, 141–165.

P. Hartmann, S. Straetmans and C. G. de Vries (2007). "Banking system stability: A cross-Atlantic perspective." In M. Carey and R. M. Stulz (Eds.), *The Risks of Financial Institutions*. Chicago: University of Chicago Press, 133–192.

B. M. Hill (1975). "A simple general approach to inference about the tail of a distribution," *Annals of Statistics*, vol 3, no 5, 1163–1174.

X. Huang, H. Zhou and H. Zhu (2009). "A framework for assessing the systemic risk of major financial institutions," *Journal of Banking & Finance*, vol 33, no 11, 2036–2049.

(2012). "Systemic risk contributions," *Journal of Financial Services Research*, vol 42, no 1–2, 55–83.

IMF/BIS/FSB (2009). "Guidance to assess the systemic importance of financial institutions, markets and instruments: Initial considerations," *Report to G20 Finance Ministers and Governors*.

A. Lehar (2005). "Measuring systemic risk: A risk management approach," *Journal of Banking & Finance*, vol 29, no 10, 2577–2603.

G. López-Espinosa, A. Moreno, A. Rubia and L. Valderrama (2012). "Short-term wholesale funding and systemic risk: A global CoVaR approach," *Journal of Banking & Finance*, vol 36, no 12, 3150–3162.

T. Mikosch and C. G. De Vries (2013). "Heavy tails of OLS," *Journal of Econometrics*, vol 172, no 2, 205–221.

M. Mink and J. De Haan (2014). "Spillovers from systemic bank defaults," *CESifo Working Paper*, no 4792.

J. Peek and E. S. Rosengren (2000). "Collateral damage: Effects of the Japanese bank crisis on real activity in the United States," *American Economic Review*, vol 90, no 1, 30–45.

F. Vallascas and K. Keasey (2012). "Bank resilience to systemic shocks and the stability of banking systems: Small is beautiful," *Journal of International Money and Finance*, vol 31, no 6, 1745–1776.

M. R. C. Van Oordt and C. Zhou (2014). "Systemic risk and bank business models," *DNB Working Paper*, no 442.

M. R. C. Van Oordt and C. Zhou (forthcoming). "Estimating systematic risk under extremely adverse market conditions," *Journal of Financial Econometrics*.

# 10    Macroprudential Tools of Systemic Risk Analysis

*Marcin Łupiński*[*]

This chapter is aimed at presenting tools of systemic risk analysis used as a part of stress testing framework and their application to address systemic risk questions facing macroprudential policy decision makers with special attentions to problems present in the Polish banking sector. In the first part of the paper alternative definitions of the systemic risk are described. Then alternative tools of systemic risk measurement and analysis are presented. The reference network model is integrated with stress testing framework to empirically evaluate impact of the systemic risk on the Polish banking sector. Gained results of the research show that, in general, banks operating in Poland are immune to endogenous and exogenous sources of systemic risk and this type of risk is not a source of instability for the domestic banking sector. However some shocks emerging (inter alia) from the structure of the Polish banks' capital ownership and characteristics of the mortgage credit portfolio should be carefully monitored in the future.

## Introduction

Successive waves of the financial crisis that have shaken the global financial system since 2007 turned central bankers', supervisors' and academics' attention to systemic risk. A painful lesson of consequences of extreme risks transmission between financial institutions operating often in remote geographical and sector jurisdictions have become a prerequisite for the formulation of the policy governing over whole financial sectors and systems. Leading central banks, supervisors and international organizations have worked out definitions of systemic

[*] Faculty of Economics and Management, Lazarski University (marcin.lupinski@lazarski.pl)
National Bank of Poland (marcin.lupinski@nbp.pl)

risk, proposed general frameworks of the macroprudential policy and credit, liquidity and capital-related instruments for implementation. Analogously to the monetary policy frameworks, macroprudential policy needs specialised analytical tools and data repositories to monitor and anticipate potential threats to the stability of financial systems. Although steps have been made to close statistical data gaps and develop systemic risk models, there still is definitely room for improvement, especially in the case of the emerging market economies.

The main goal of this article is to present analytical tools that are applied to the systemic risk analysis for countries with banking sectors characterised with limited statistical data availability. That is pretty common among post-transformation emerging market economies with strongly developing financial institutions and markets. The research described in this paper is part of the mainstream of the academic surveys and central banks' and supervisors' initiatives aimed at analysing mechanisms responsible for the outbreak and amplifications of the recent financial with the impact of interconnected (Globally) Systemically Important Financial Institutions (GSIFIs). Three main drivers of the systemic risk transmission are considered: (1) the complexity of the cross-border relations between financial institutions (being a function of the number and strength of existing connections); (2) the lack of individual approach to risk management (similar approaches and models used by whole population of financial entities); and (3) ongoing introduction of financial innovations leading to construction of complex financial engineering instruments with almost unpredictable profiles of payment and risk.

From the perspective of emerging-market macroprudential policy decision makers it is difficult to overestimate the usefulness of dedicated analytical tools, arming them with precious information about roles of particular systemically important (foreign) institutions in generating and transmitting of the extreme risk shocks affecting local financial system. Equipped with reliable and up-to-date knowledge about vulnerabilities of particular institutions and the transmission channels decision makers can prepare strategies and actions to preserve domestic financial stability. Results of the surveys conducted with these tools can optimise precautionary bailout actions within the crisis management framework.

The author presents in this paper a set of analytical frameworks used for systemic risk assessment and chooses network model to provide research findings that can then be applied to the Polish banking sector's entities and its connection with foreign systemically important institutions. The network model is used to empirically analyse the impact of systemic risk on the Polish banking sector that is strongly linked with the international banking system, but simultaneously shows its own characteristics, different in many respects to its Western Europe and US counterparts.

The paper proceeds as follows. The next section briefly reviews the literature on the main sources and econometric models of systemic risk. The following section presents the key definitions of systemic risk that emerged in the literature during the past two decades. The fourth section discusses alternative approaches to systemic risk quantification and provides detailed description of the network model used as the reference framework in the empirical part of the survey. The fifth section is devoted to the short description of the data used for the Polish banking sector systemic risk analysis. The penultimate section describes gained results and investigates their consequences for the Polish banking sector stability. The final section concludes with some macroprudential policy implications.

## Literature Review

First papers describing theoretical and practical concepts of systemic risk modelling started to appear at the turn of the 1980s and 1990s. Authors of these papers usually disagreed about the sources of analysed risk. At that time three main competing approaches emerged:

1. Impact of banks' runs and mutual contagions of banks with limited liquidity;
2. Consequences of crises in the banking sector implied by negative shocks to the real economy;
3. Observed amplifications of financial risks on the global financial markets.

The examples of the research conducted with compliance to the first approach can be found in Chen (1999), Sheldon and Maurer (1998), Allen and Gale (2000), Freixas, Parig and Rochet (2000), Wells (2002) and Upper and Worms (2004). The majority of these surveys presented application of the models using data reflecting the structure and power of connections among financial institutions.

From the macroprudential policy point of view it is important to take a closer look at the literature describing relations between fluctuations of real economy and financial system crises. In this context it is worthy to reference articles of Gorton (1988) and Lindgren, Garcia and Saal (1996) with theoretical concepts of ties between the business cycle and fluctuations of bank's credit. A similar approach was presented in the papers of Bordo, Mizrach and Schwarz (1995), Kodres and Pritsker (1999) and Kyle and Xiong (2000).

During the last financial crisis, substantial magnitudes of financial institutions' losses were caused by failures of their systemically important counterparts, which created incentives to further explore systemic risk origins. It seems this goal was the main objective of Gai and Kapadia (2010) and Drehmann and Tarashev (2011). In the same stream were written papers by Borio and Lowe (2004), Borio and Drehmann (2009), who used early warning indicators approach to identify potential sources of financial systems instability. The situation observed during the past six years was also a stimulus to introduce empirical simplified models of systemic risk measurement and evaluation. Among the most popular ones were: Adrian and Brunnermeier's CoVaR (2011), Chan-Lau's Co-Risk (2009) and Acharya, Pedersen, Philippon and Richardson's (2010) Systemic Expected Shortfall models. All mentioned models will be described in a separate section of this paper, being a reasonable alternative to the proposed network approach.

The author's main interest is a network framework of systemic risk analysis, described for the first time in the paper of Eisenberg and Noe (2001). This approach takes directly into account two of three aforementioned key sources of systemic risk: impact of banks' runs and mutual contagions of banks with limited liquidity and amplifications of financial risks on the global financial markets (e.g. second round effects). It allows policy makers analysing institutions' insolvencies using data from a common payment system used to settle finalized contracts. Solution of the model is reached by an iterative procedure applying a fixed point theorem with a clearing payments vector reflecting risk of insolvency of particular financial institutions taking into account transmission of Systemically Important Financial Institutions (SIFI) risk.

As mentioned before, this approach will be used as a cornerstone of the empirical systemic risk evaluation exercise described in this paper. Examples of their applications can be found in Eboli (2004), and after outbreak of the last financial crisis in the work of Allen and Babus (2009), Hale (2011) and Minoiu and Ryes (2011).

## Systemic Risk's Definitions

One of the first systemic risk definitions was enclosed in the Annual Report of Bank for International Settlements (BIS, 1994). According to this source systemic risk materializes when lack of ability to fulfil outstanding liabilities by one of the institutions belonging to financial system results in insolvency of other institutions connected with contracts with the previous one, what finally can lead to a chain reactions (domino effect) causing whole financial system instability.

Mishkin (1997) tried to define systemic risk as a special case of market ineffectiveness. According to his proposal systemic risk stems from the probability of sudden, unexpected distortions of the flow of the information on financial markets, which limits the possibility of using them as a floor for traditional intermediary between savers and entrepreneurs with investing opportunities.

Observations made during the last financial crisis allowed Haldane (2009) to characterize the most important features of systemic risk. His general conclusions were based on analogy of the situation on the global financial markets after Lehman bankruptcy to a pandemic of Severe Acute Respiratory Syndrome (SARS) that broke out in 2002. According to Haldane both phenomena were caused by sudden 'external' incidents affecting at the beginning one entity then panic in other entities, where the first has relationships with others, which finally results in the malfunction of the whole system. In such a circumstances, common irregular activity of the connected entities caused damage (losses in the case of financial system) disproportionate to the initial scale of the shock starting the chain reaction. Hence systemic risk can be perceived as a problem of reaction of the complex, adaptive network of entities to the primal exogenous shock. The complexity of the network is a derivative of multiplicity and diversity of formal and informal financial system entities' mutual relations. Adaptation of the network can be defined as mutual interactions of the entities that try to continue taking their decisions after the initial shock occurred with the same optimisation procedures of the previously chosen criterions. However, in the case of irregular circumstances these decisions are in fact based on incomplete or misleading information, which deforms their consequences for the whole financial system. Haldane's systemic risk definition was creatively connected with network models to analyse relations within banking sector, used as a reference model of this paper.

More recently the IMF, the FSB and the BIS (2011) define systemic risk as 'disruption to the flow of financial services that is 1) caused by an impairment of all or parts of the financial system and 2) has the potential to have serious negative consequences for the real economy'.

Regardless of the source of the definition it can be easily noticed that there is a substantial gap between the theoretical approach to systemic risk and practical guidelines on how this type of risk should be measured and analysed. In the next part of the paper we focus on the empirical approach to systemic risk analysis trying to maintain its consistency with systemic risk definitions of BIS and Haldane emphasising its network nature.

### Alternative Systemic Risk Models

Generally three main approaches to systemic risk modelling can be distinguished as: (1) construction of early warning indicators; (2) computation of quintile risk measures considering relations between financial entities (group of quintile risk models); and (3) network analytical structures allowing directly quantify strengths of connections between financial institutions. At the beginning we present methods from the quintile risk measures approach that can easily be integrated with the stress-testing framework.

#### CoVaR Model

The CoVaR model was first proposed by Adrian and Brunnermeier (2011) as an augmentation of the well-known value-at-risk (VaR) approach to compute the impact of the systemically important institutions' risk (entities, which are too big to fail or too interconnected to fail) on each other, on connected less-significant financial institutions operating in a financial sector and on a sector itself. The level of risk of a bank (indexed with $j$) or of a whole sector (index omitted) considered at period $t$ is computed as conditional value-at-risk (CoVaR) dependent on the risk generated by systemically important institution (indexed with $i$)

$$\Pr\left(AR_t^j \leq CoVaR_t^{j|i,k} | AR_t^i = VaR_t^{i,k}\right) = k \qquad (1)$$

where $AR_t^j$ represents return on assets of the institution indexed with $j$, $AR_t^i$ describes the return on assets of the institution $i$ and $k$ is a quintile of returns of institution $j$'s distribution (usually $k = 1\%$ or $k = 5\%$). $VaR_t^i$ is the return on assets for the value-at-risk computed for the $k$ quintile.

The force of the risk propagation from the institution $i$ to institution $j$ is calculated as the difference between conditional value-at-risk of the first institution, when returns on institution $j$ assets are equal to VaR at the level of confidence $(1-k)$ and conditional value-at-risk of the bank $j$ generated for VaR. This equals the median:

$$\Delta CoVaR_t^{j|i,k} = CoVaR_t^{j|i,k} - CoVaR_t^{j|i,50\%} \qquad (2)$$

The easy integration of CoVaR methods with a stress testing framework follows from the fact that the $\Delta CoVaR_t^{j|i,k}$ distribution is dependent on the vector of factors $(RF_t)$ that represents observed financial and economic situations. From a technical point of view, this distribution is computed with a quintile regression applied to the equation of returns of the institution $i$ assets at period $t$:

$$AR_t^i = a^i + b^i RF_{t-1} + \varepsilon_t^i \tag{3}$$

($a^i$ and $b^i$ are parameters vectors) with analogous equation describing return on the institution $j$ assets at period $t$:

$$AR_t^j = a^{j|i} + b^{j|i} AR_{t-1}^j + c^{j|i} RF_{t-1} + \varepsilon_t^{j|i} \tag{4}$$

where $c^{j|i}$ is a vector of parameters.

Quintile regression is applied to the Equation (2) separately for the selected level of confidence and for the median.

According to the paper of Adrian and Brunnermeier the considered risk factors ($RF_t$) embrace:

1. Volatility indicator of the selected stock exchange index (VIX);
2. Spread of the 3M repo rate and rate of the government bonds at 3M residual maturity;
3. 3M money bills' rate of return one week change;
4. 10Y government bonds spread over 10 3M WIBOR rate one week change;
5. Credit spread one week change, returns on corporate bonds and 10Y government bonds;
6. Selected stock exchange index one week change;
7. Index of the one year dynamics of the real-estate enterprises returns (developers, building industry);

### Co-Risk Model

In the Chan-Lau's (2009) Co-Risk model dependencies among individual risk exposures of an institutions' group are quantified with help of relations among prices of their credit default swaps (CDS). The distributions of relations' strength are estimated with quintile regression. Practical application of Co-Risk models to systemic risk evaluation is described *inter alia* in the International Monetary Fund's report (IMF, 2009).

According to the Co-Risk model for particular $k$ quintiles of the risk distribution, prices of the selected (indexed $j$) financial institution's CDS (or alternatively for a banking sector, in this case index is omitted) at period $t$ are connected with analogous instrument of the systemically important financial institution using linear expression:

$$\text{CDS}_t^{j,k} = a^{i,k} + b_i^{i,k} \, \text{CDS}_t^{i,k} + c^{i,k} \, RF_{t-1} \tag{5}$$

where $RF_{t-1}$ is vector of risk factors generated with macroeconomic and financial environment and $a^{i,k}$, $b^{i,k}$ and $c^{i,k}$ are vectors of parameters.

Risk factors considered in the Co-Risk models are usually the same as in the case of CoVaR structures: local stock exchange VIX, spread of government 10Y bonds and money market 3M rate, etc.). The Co-Risk model is estimated with prices (spreads) of 5Y CDS of the financial institutions considered in the survey.

Parameters of the Equation (5) estimated with quintile regression applied to $(1-k)$ tail percentile are used to compute final measure of mutual systemic risk:

$$CoRisk_t^{j,i,q} = \left( \frac{\hat{a}^{i,95\%} + \hat{b}_i^{i,95\%} \, CDS_t^{i,95\%} + \hat{c}^{i,95\%} \, RF_{t-1}}{CDS_t^{j,95\%}} - 1 \right) 100\%$$

(6)

where $CDS_t^{j,95\%}$ ($CDS_t^{i,95\%}$ respectively) is the selected 95 percentile of the empirical distribution of the $j$ ($i$ respectively) CDS's price at period $t$.

### Systemic Expected Shortfall Model

The third most popular method of systemic risk measurement and evaluation is the Systemic Expected Shortfall (SES) model. This approach is based on a model that allows analysing characteristics of the expected loss distribution's tail. Authors of this method (Acharya, Pedersen, Philippon and Richardson, 2010) proposed their structure of systemic risk measurement compatible with observations of real banks' losses materialized in the American banking sector after 2007. These losses were measured by amount of money spent by the US Treasury to bail-out insolvent banks and the cumulated loss of the banks that were seriously affected by the last financial crisis but did not go bankrupt. Acharya et al. assumed that recorded bail-outs and losses are good empirical approximations of the SES of the whole US banking sector. The total amount of mentioned SES depends linearly on two variables characterizing United States Systemically Important Financial Institutions (indexed with $i$), the marginal expected shortfall, (MES) and leverage level, (L):

$$SES_t^i = a + b \, MES_t^i + cL_t^i + \varepsilon_t^i$$

(7)

In this equation, $SES_t^i$ is estimated as the total value of real loss of the whole banking sector on its capital or the amount of capital needed to bail-out the insolvent banks. Marginal expected shortfall for institution indexed $i$ at period t is defined as average return on shares during 5 per cent of the days with recorded the worst returns in the history. It is also acceptable to compute marginal expected shortfall with help of systemically important institutions CDS spreads.

Coefficients of the Equation (7) are estimated with help of linear regression, separately for each index $t$. After substituting mentioned parameters' estimators to the equation systemic risk (SR) of the institution $i$ at period $t$ generated for the whole banking sector is computed:

$$SR_t^i = \frac{\hat{b}}{\hat{b} + \hat{c}} MES_t^i + \frac{\hat{c}}{\hat{b} + \hat{c}} L_t^i \tag{8}$$

The three discussed systemic risk models obviously are not the complete universe of the analytical structures that can be easily introduced to stress-testing framework. It is also worthy to mention the Distressed Insurance Premium (DIP) model of Huang, Zhou and Zhu (2009) or Contingent Claims Analysis (CCA) model of Gray and Jobst, (2010). However presented CoVaR, Co-Risk and SES are the three most popular models, with many references in the empirical literature and central banks' and supervisors' reports.

### Banking Sector Network Model

The network model of systemic risk proposed initially by Eisenberg and Noe (2001) is usually applied as a complementary analytical structure to credit, financial and liquidity risk assessment models used in macroprudential analysis. Its main advantage is the possibility of directly modelling the relation between banking sector entities quantifying both debt instruments (secured and unsecured short term loans) and structure of the capital channels. Taking into these characteristics the network model is used as the reference framework in the empirical part of the paper.

One of the key assumptions of the presented network model is that each of analysed financial entities owes at period $t = 0$ certain portfolio of liabilities characterized with conditions of contracts signed with counterparties. When a convolution of negative shocks in financial and the macroeconomic environment occurs, it is possible that one or more entities will not pay back their liabilities. Following this scenario, these institutions can pay only part of their due payments, which can initialize a chain reaction, with a cascade of connected financial institutions' insolvencies. Taking into account multistage effects of the systemic risk propagation, complexity of bilateral banking sector entities' relations and the idiosyncratic character of the systemic risk influence on selected institutions, it seems that the network approach is one of the most appropriate ways of risk modelling. It is a bottom-up framework that allows us to identify sources and unique reactions of particular institutions on their counterparts' problems.

234    Marcin Łupiński

The Eisenberg and Noe (2001) model assumes that the banking sector consists of $N$ entities (network nodes) connected with each other with bilateral liabilities settled within a clearing system. Each entity's balance sheet (indexed with subscript $i$) consists of:

- Liabilities
  - Aggregated equity capital $\sum_{j=1}^{N} CS^{i,j} EV_t^j$, where $CS^{i,j}$ ($CS^{i,j} \geq 0$) is a fraction of shares (ranged $[0,1]$) of the bank $j$ belonging to the bank $i$ and $EV_t^j$ is equity capital of the bank $j$;
  - External liabilities with net due value $EV_t^j$;
  - Interbank liabilities owed to the institution $j$ with net due value $L_t^{i,j}$ ($L_t^{i,j} \geq 0$);
- Assets:
  - External assets replenished with net income $EI_t^i$;
  - Interbank assets replenished with net receivables from the institution $k$ $L_t^{k,i}$ ($L_t^{k,i} \geq 0$);

The following Schema (Figure 10.1) presents balance sheet and cash flows of the institution $i$.

The stream of supposed (contractual) payments of the bank $i$ at period $t$ is given by

$$P_t^i = \sum_{j=1}^{N} L_t^{i,j} + EL_t^i \tag{9}$$

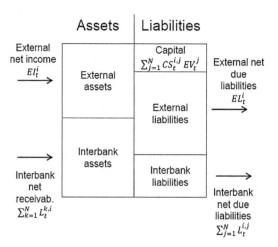

Figure 10.1 Balance sheet/cash flows of the institution $i$.
Source: The author's drawing

If the bank $i$ net exogenous income and receivables from other entities are not enough to cover its net due liabilities to other entities from the sector and outside, it pays it proportionally:

$$\Pi_t^{i,j} = \begin{cases} \dfrac{L_t^{i,j}}{P_t^i} \; if \; P_t^i > 0 \\ 0 \; \text{in the other case} \end{cases} \tag{10}$$

Actual payments of the bank i at period t can be finally formulated as:

$$AP_t^i = \begin{cases} P_t^i \; if \; P_t^i \le \sum_{k=1}^{N} L_t^{k,i} + EI_t^i \\ \sum_{k=1}^{N} L_t^{k,i} + EI_t^i \; \text{in the other case} \end{cases} \tag{11}$$

Taking into account presented assumptions, the model is fully described with the set of matrices/vectors $\{CS_t, EV_t, L_t, EI_t, EL_t\}$, where:

- $CS_t$ is a matrix of analysed banks' capital shares;
- $EV_t$ is a vector of banks' equity capital;
- $L_t$ is a matrix that gathers mutual net due liabilities of the banking sector entities;
- $EI_t$ is a vector of banks' external income;
- $EL_t$ is finally a vector of banks' external net due liabilities.

For the initial period of time ($t = 0$) elements of the mentioned matrices' set are calculated (or approximated) with help of prudential statistics. Mentioned matrices and vectors are used to derive the supposed due payments vector ($P_t$), the proportional payments matrix ($\Pi_t$) and the actual payments vector ($AP_t$).

The solution of the model is based on the fixed point theorem. Initially for the above set of matrices a map of projection is constructed:

$$M\left(EI_t^i, \Pi_t, CS_t, EV_t^i, AP_t\right) = \left[EI_t^i + \Pi_t' AP_t - AP_t + CS_t EV_t^i\right] \vee \vec{0} \tag{12}$$

where $\vec{0}$ is a vector of nulls (sized $Nx1$). For a given vector of real payments $AP_t$ exists only one fixed point $M$, corresponding to a vector of values of the share capital of particular banks $\overline{(EV(AP_t)}$ computed as:

$$\overline{EV_t(AP_t)} = \left[EI_t^i + \Pi_t' AP_t - AP_t + CS_t \overline{EV_t(AP_t)}\right] \vee \vec{0} \tag{13}$$

The selected fixed point corresponds to a vector of real payments $\overline{AP_t}$, called also clearing payment vector. It is defined conditionally as:

$$\overline{AP^i_t} = \begin{cases} 0 \text{ if } EI^i_t + \sum_{j=1}^{N}\left(\Pi^{i,j}_t\overline{AP^j_t} + CS^{i,j}_t\overline{EV^i_t\left(\overline{AP^j_t}\right)}\right) \leq 0 \\ EI^i_t + \sum_{j=1}^{N}\left(\Pi^{i,j}_t\overline{AP^j_t} + CS^{i,j}_t\overline{EV^i_t\left(\overline{AP^j_t}\right)}\right) \text{ if } 0 < EI^i_t + \sum_{j=1}^{N}\left(\Pi^{i,j}_t\overline{AP^j_t} + CS^{i,j}_t\overline{EV^i_t\left(\overline{AP^j_t}\right)}\right) \leq P^i_t \\ P^i_t \text{ if } P^i_t < EI^i_t + \sum_{j=1}^{N}\left(\Pi^{i,j}_t\overline{AP^j_t} + CS^{i,j}_t\overline{EV^i_t\left(\overline{AP^j_t}\right)}\right) \end{cases}$$

$$(14)$$

In their work, Eisenberg and Noe prove the existence and uniqueness of the clearing payment vector. Beside that they proposed a series of augmentations allowing better representation of analysed financial entities' behaviour. Their extension takes into account idiosyncratic costs of the bankruptcy ($BC^i_t > 0$). This type of costs is of the highest priority when paid from operational income of particular financial institution. Its introduction to the model causes redefinition of the clearing payments vector:

$$\overline{AP^i_t} = \begin{cases} P^i_t \text{ if } P^i_t < EI^i_t + \sum_{j=1}^{N}\left(\Pi^{i,j}_t\overline{AP^j_t} + CS^{i,j}_t\overline{EVX^i_t\left(\overline{AP^j_t}\right)}\right) \\ \max\left(0, EI^i_t - BC^i_t + \sum_{j=1}^{N}\left(\Pi^{i,j}_t\overline{AP^j_t} + CS^{i,j}_t\overline{EVX^i_t\left(\overline{AP^j_t}\right)}\right)\right) \text{ in the o.c.} \end{cases}$$

$$(15)$$

where $EVX\left(\overline{AP^j_t}\right)$ is modified vector of values of share capital belonging to institution indexed $i$ computed according to the following expression:

$$\overline{EVX^i_t\left(\overline{AP^j_t}\right)} = \begin{cases} EI^i_t - \overline{AP^i_t} + \sum_{j=1}^{N}\left(\Pi^{i,j}_t\overline{AP^j_t} + CS^{i,j}_t\overline{EVX^i_t\left(\overline{AP^j_t}\right)}\right) \text{ if } \overline{AP^j_t} = P^i_t \\ 0 \text{ in the other case} \end{cases}$$

$$(16)$$

Their second augmentation of the model assumes that liabilities of the particular financial institution can be characterized with different seniorities. Liabilities of the bank are classified with $SC$ classes $\left(S^i_t = (1,2,\ldots,SC^i)\right)$. Maximum number of seniority classes is given with $\overline{SC} = \max_i\left(SC^i\right)$.

Introduction of liabilities' seniorities causes the need of reconstruction of almost all equations of the model. The value of liabilities with seniority $s$ possessed with bank $i$ at period $t$ equals:

$$P_t^{i,s} = \sum_{j=1}^{N} L_t^{i,j,s} + D_t^{i,s} \tag{17}$$

where $P_t^{\cdot,s} = \left(P_t^{1,s}, P_t^{2,s}, \ldots, P_t^{N,s}\right)'$. Elements of the proportional payments matrix $\Pi_t^s$ are characterized with the expression:

$$\Pi_t^{i,j,s} = \begin{cases} \dfrac{L_t^{i,j,s}}{P_t^i} \ if \ P_t^{i,s} > 0 \\ 0 \ \ in \ the \ other \ case \end{cases} \tag{18}$$

The real payment of the bank $i$ corresponding to certain class of seniority $(S_t^i)$ at period $t$ equals to $AP_t^{i,s}$. For vector gathering these payments $AP_t^{\cdot,s} = \left(AP_t^{1,s}, AP_t^{2,s}, \ldots, AP_t^{N,s}\right)$ the augmented projection map is of the form:

$$M\left(EI_t^i, \Pi_t^s, CS_t, EV_t^i, AP_t^{\cdot,s}\right) = \left[ EI_t^i + \sum_{s=1}^{\overline{SC}} \Pi_t' AP_t^{\cdot,s} - \sum_{s=1}^{\overline{SC}} AP_t^{\cdot,s} + CS_t EV_t^i \right] \vee \vec{0} \tag{19}$$

Moreover, vector of the clearing payments $S \in \{1, 2, \ldots \overline{SC}\}$ is redefined as:

$$\overline{AP_t^{i,S}} = \min\left( \max\left( EI_t^i + \sum_{j=1}^{N} \sum_{s=1}^{\overline{SC}} \Pi_t^{i,j'} \overline{AP_t^{j,s}} - \sum_{s=1}^{\overline{SC}} P_t^{i,s} \right. \right.$$
$$\left. \left. + \sum_{j=1}^{N} \sum_{s=1}^{\overline{SC}} \overline{CS_t^{i,j} EV_t^j \left(\overline{AP_t^{j,s}}\right)}, 0 \right), P_t^{i,S} \right) \tag{20}$$

Vector of the clearing payments can be computed as the fixed point $M1(AP_t) = M1\left(AP_t^{1,1}\right), M1\left(AP_t^{1,2}\right), \ldots, M1\left(AP_t^{1,\overline{SC}}\right), \ldots, M1\left(AP_t^{N,1}\right),$
$\ldots, M1\left(AP_t^{N,\overline{SC}}\right)$) of the alternative map M1:

$$\overline{M1\left(AP_t^{i,S}\right)} = \min\left( \max\left( EI_t^i + \sum_{j=1}^{N} \sum_{s=1}^{SC} \Pi_t^{i,j'} \overline{AP_t^{j,s}} - \sum_{s=1}^{\overline{SC}} P_t^{i,s} \right. \right.$$
$$\left. \left. + \sum_{j=1}^{N} \sum_{s=1}^{\overline{SC}} \overline{CS_t^{i,j} EV_t^j \left(\overline{AP_t^{j,s}}\right)}, 0 \right), P_t^{i,S} \right) \tag{21}$$

that is a monotonically increasing function of $AP_t$ in the whole considered domain. Hence it can be easily deduced that maximum and minimum clearing vector exists. Finally the clearing vector is computed as:

$$\overline{AP_t^{i,S}} = \left\{ \left[ \overline{EVV_t(P_t)} + \sum_{s=S}^{\overline{SC}} p_t^{i,s} \right] \vee 0 \right\} \wedge p_S^i \tag{22}$$

with a helper function $\overline{EVV_t(P_t)}$ defined as follows:

$$\overline{EVV_t(P_t)} = EI_t + \sum_{s=1}^{\overline{SC}} \Pi_t^s AP_t^s - \sum_{s=1}^{\overline{SC}} P_t^s + \overline{CS_t(EVV_t(AP_t))} \vee \vec{0} .$$

$$\tag{23}$$

The actual model solution is found with an iterative Fictitious Default Algorithm (FDA). In each step of this algorithm (corresponding to period $t$) the clearing vector is computed and insolvent banks are identified. Insolvent banks found at period $t$ can cause insolvencies of their counterparts in the subsequent iterations. Output of this procedure, ranked (with respect to time) sequence of clearing vectors, is interpreted as realization of unobserved process of $N$ banking sector's institutions' insolvencies.

The FDA starts with computation of initial net due liabilities of initial group of the banks and the clearing vector what allows to identify set of insolvent banks. Then iterative part begins. For each step (period $t$):

• Net due liabilities of surveyed banks (taking into account solvency of other institutions) are computed. If all banks' liabilities are covered with current income/capital cushion, the algorithm is stopped;
• If some insolvent institutions are identified, the clearing vector is computed and all connected institutions that lost their solvency due to lack of payments from counterparties are identified. If the propagation of first-order defaults doesn't imply bankruptcies of the banks, the algorithm is stopped. If it does, the next iteration is started.

The FDA stops when:

• there are no defaults in the certain step,
• all N banks have defaulted.

The index of iteration in which particular bank was found insolvent is interpreted as the measure of vulnerability of this institution to systemic risk. Institutions that were found bankrupt in the first round can be perceived as fundamentally/exogenously insolvent. In the next step, entities which are fundamentally solvent but vulnerable to Systemically Important Financial Institutions' insolvencies are identified. Analogously the third round reveals banks that are vulnerable to systemically important banks and their (less significant) counterparties. Taking into account characteristics of FDA it can be perceived as classification algorithm that classifies each bank belonging to the banking sector into (maximum) $N$ classes of systemic risk. The value of unpaid liabilities of the insolvent banks is often used as a measure systemic risk impact on the analysed banking sector.

## Data Used for Systemic Risk Stress Testing

Modelling systemic risk is one of the latest risk types included into stress testing framework and macroprudential analysis. Hence, especially emerging markets economies' central banks and supervisors cannot use ready-to-use reference input datasets. The situation is different from the one characterising credit or market risk modelling, where subsequent Basel Recommendations and local regulations went hand-in-hand with statistical activity of the institutions. Data gaps in the area of systemic risk analysis were identified mainly after the outbreak of the last financial crisis. In the response to this situation national and international regulators (BCBS, EBA) and central banks (inter alia, European Central Bank) started many initiatives aimed at the development of macroprudential statistics. Very good discussion of issues concerning systemic risk data gaps can be found in Lucas (2011) and report of FSB and IMF (2011).

## Empirical Analysis of the Polish Banking Sector Systemic Risk

For this survey, Polish prudential statistics of National Bank of Poland was used. Liabilities and receivables of the forty Polish biggest banks (according to total assets criterion) constituting approximately 95 per cent of Polish banking sector total assets registered on the interbank market were taken from EU Large Exposures (ELE) database (registered with more or equal to 10 per cent of institution capital criterion) and Domestic Large Exposures (DLE) database (registered with more or equal to 120.000 EUR criterion). Records from both mentioned sources allowed identification of both counterparties of the transaction and expositions of the local banks to their abroad counterparts (mainly parent banks). FINREP and COREP databases were complementary data sources used mainly to provide balance sheet/off-balance sheet and capital requirements/capital structure data respectively. The time coverage of the data spanned from 2008 to 2012. The two subsequent years (2011–2012) were selected for analysis, three previous years were applied for model calibration.

Analysis of the Polish banking sector's systemic risk was part of the stress testing exercise used by the author to evaluate its stability in the macro context. The computations were conducted in two phases:

1. For three selected stress test scenarios of the credit, market, funding and liquidity risk reactions of exogenous income/liquidity buffers to generated shocks were computed (reactions have taken into account losses from all three mentioned sources of risk);
2. The iterative procedure of Factious Default Algorithm were then used to identify the number of insolvent financial institutions and their uncovered losses that, as was mentioned before, were considered as systemic risk measures. The algorithm was stopped when no insolvencies were discovered.

Figure 10.2 presents system of relations between Polish commercial banks based on the matrix of liabilities/receivables computed from National Bank of Poland's prudential data for 2010. As it can be noticed, almost 75 per cent from forty analysed banks (marked with black) can be perceived as strongly connected with the rest of the domestic financial institutions. However it is worth emphasising that in Poland the power of relations between banks is not as strong as in the economies with far more developed financial systems. Banks operating in Poland are also much less likely to use unsecured interbank loans than their Western European counterparts. Polish commercial bankers have a far more

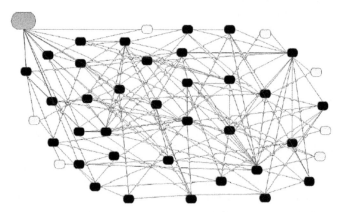

Figure 10.2 Mutual expositions of forty Polish biggest banks due to (secured and unsecured) loans and deposits on the interbank market in 2010 (banks with strong relations with other entities marked with black, foreign /aggregated/ banking sector marked with grey).
Source: The author's drawing based on NBP's prudential statistics

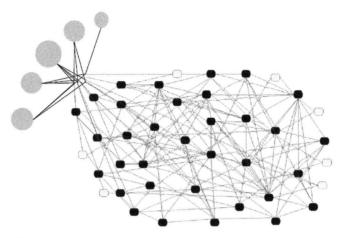

Figure 10.3 Impact of the five biggest non-resident banks on the forty biggest Polish banks in 2010.
Source: The author's drawing based on NBP's prudential statistics

traditional approach to business and balanced ratio of Polish banking sector assets to GDP.

The relations of the banks operating in Poland with non-resident banks (Figure 10.3) are consequence of the structure of ownership of the local banking sector's entities and observed in 2006–2008 rapidly growing credit action with mortgage loans denominated mainly in foreign currencies. During the first phase of the last financial crisis (2007–2010) non-resident banks were sources of liquidity for their dependent banks operating in Poland. This time the hypothetical bankruptcies of some parent banks could only indirectly contribute to systemic risk in Polish banking sector. The situation changed in the second half of 2011 when, owing to turbulences tackling parent banks in their local jurisdictions and planned introduction of the Basel III recommendations (that tightened requirements on own capital and rules of leverage and liquidity management), these banks had to redefine relations with dependent banks operating in Poland. In such circumstances the main activities of parent banks were focused on sustaining stability of core business in their domestic jurisdictions and fulfilling new regulations introduced by local and international supervisors. The potential willingness of some group of the parent banks to 'drain-out' their dependent banks (e.g. with treasury transactions or transfer prices allowing to circumvent limitations in direct capital transfer abroad) was limited with smooth supervision of local financial supervisory office.

## Results of the Stress Testing of the Polish Banking Sector to Systemic Risk

Stress tests of Polish banking sector to systemic risk were conducted in two phases. In the first phase, the systemic risk caused by hypothetical insolvencies within the sector itself was surveyed. In the second phase the impact of the foreign parent bank on the Polish dependent banks was analysed.

The first phase of the systemic risk stress testing exercise was divided into three scenarios: according to the first one, only the influence of macroeconomic and financial scenarios (transmitted with credit and market risk channel) was analysed. The second phase was devoted to funding and liquidity scenarios. Within the final phase, the combination of the four sources of shocks was considered. Three different levels of shocks impact were also considered: baseline, moderate and severe. The results were presented in the Table 10.1, and in two subsequent charts.

In the first scenario, accompanied by moderate shocks, all entities of the Polish banking sector were immune to generated shocks regardless of their source and strength. The same result was gained when moderate funding and liquidity shocks. The third scenario, with the application of the four sources of shocks with moderate power, caused insolvency of three banks (all lost their solvency in the first round). All failed banks were not systemically important institutions, as their combined balance sheet sum was less than 2 per cent of the whole surveyed group.

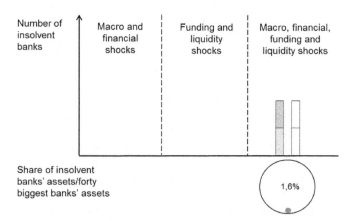

Figure 10.4 Results of the Polish banking sector stress testing exercise – moderate shocks scenarios.
Source: The author's drawing based on own computations

Table 10.1 *Results of the stress testing of Polish banking sector systemic risk. (Base year = 2010, scenarios generated for 2011–2012)*

| 1st scenario: Macroeconomic and financial shocks only | | | |
|---|---|---|---|
| Type of the scenario | Baseline shocks | Moderate shocks | Severe shocks |
| Number of insolvent banks | 0 | | |

| 2nd scenario: Funding and liquidity shocks only | | | |
|---|---|---|---|
| Type of shocks | Baseline shocks | Moderate shocks | Severe shocks |
| Number of insolvent banks | 0 | 0 | 4 (1st round) + 2 (2nd round) |
| Share (in %) of insolvent banks balance sheets sum in the balance sheets sum of the surveyed entities | – | – | 4.3% |

| 3rd scenario: Macroeconomic, financial and funding shocks combined with liquidity shocks | | | |
|---|---|---|---|
| Type of the macroeconomic/financial shocks | Baseline shocks | Moderate shocks | Severe shocks |
| Type of the funding/liquidity shocks | Baseline shocks | Moderate shocks | Severe shocks |
| Number of insolvent banks | 0 | 3 (1st round) | 5 (1st round) + 3 (2nd round) |
| Share (in %) of insolvent banks balance sheets sum in the balance sheet sum of the surveyed entities | – | 1.6% | 7.6% |

Source: The author's own computations

Funding and liquidity extreme shocks caused insolvency of three less significant banks with combined balance sheet share of 4.3 per cent of the analysed banks' balance sheet sum. The convolution of severe macroeconomic, financial, funding and liquidity shocks caused in the first round insolvencies of five banks. In this case, two additional banks were also found bankrupt in the second round. Even in this case the combined balance sheet sum of insolvent banks has not exceeded 8 per cent of the sector balance sheet. It is worthy to notice, that regardless of the output, the identified insolvent banks were not part of the top ten of the Polish banks with the biggest balance sheets (Figure 10.5).

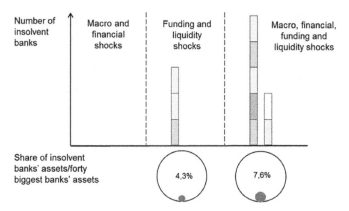

Figure 10.5  Results of the Polish banking sector stress testing exercise –
severe shocks scenarios.
Source: The author's drawing based on own computations

Summing up results of the first part of the systemic risk stress testing
exercise it can be noticed that the traditional business model, chosen by
the majority of the banks operating in the Polish banking sector (balanced financing of the credit action with deposits coming mainly from
individuals) and general excess of liquidity the Polish banking sector,
prevented it from serious impact of the systemic risk. Although systemic
risk materializes in the case of extreme macroeconomic, financial,
funding and liquidity risks, but still it does not affect the Systemically
Important Institutions.

In the second part of systemic risk, stress testing survey the impact of
the foreign banking sector on the local banks was analysed. It was
assumed that five non-resident banks (mainly parent banks) have lost
their solvency. Reduction of the possibility of the Polish dependent
banks' current activity financing and loss of value of part of their assets
haven't caused any bankruptcy in the Polish banking sector. It is important to emphasize however, that the analysis was performed with the data
available at the end of 2010, where some problems of the major European foreign banks were not revealed or not so important as one year
later. Therefore it is advisable to monitor regularly the financial condition of the Polish banks' parent institutions and the power of their mutual
connections to have an early view on risks building outside local banking
sector.

Concluding both parts of the stress testing exercise, it can be stated
that taking into account current stage of development of the Polish
banking sector and most popular business strategies applied by its

institutions systemic risk poses limited threat for the sector stability and doesn't affects substantially financial conditions of its systemically important institutions.

## Conclusions

This article was aimed at presenting tools of systemic risk analysis integrated within stress testing framework. It then turns to their application to evaluate macro-stability of the Polish banking sector. In the first part of the paper alternative definitions of the systemic risk were described. It was noticed that perspectives of systemic risk perception have changed substantially after the outbreak of the last financial crisis and materialization of the consequences of the Lehman Brothers fall. It is nowadays often emphasised that banks are operating in connected vessels system of financial markets where shocks are immediately transmitted across jurisdictions with help of unsecured loans and complex profile derivative instruments.

The proposed tools of systemic risk analysis, especially the reference network model, are complementary to credit, market and liquidity risk analytical structures combined within stress testing frameworks. The results gained from applying stress testing approach to the Polish banking sector show that the traditional model of running business by the vast majority of the banks operating in Poland, makes the local banking sector generally immune to endogenous and exogenous sources of systemic risk. Relative low liabilities of Polish banks resulting from (secured and unsecured) interbank loans, balanced structure of assets (with extremely small value of structured instruments like ABS, MBS, etc.), adequate level of leverage of the majority of institutions and general excessed liquidity of the Polish banking sector are strong pillars of the Polish banking sector stability.

This situation is consistent with the results of the quantitative stress testing exercises, according to which even in the case of severe macroeconomic, financial, funding and liquidity shocks' combination, one-fifth of the forty analysed banks will be affected by systemic risk. None of these banks is a |Systemically Important Financial Institution from the group of the top ten banks with largest balance sheets. Additionally, the eventual domino effect will have limited influence on the banks operating in Poland, depending on the scenario, causing two or three banks insolvencies in the second round of the systemic risk impact simulation. However the author would like to emphasise the importance of the structure of ownership capital of the part of national banks. Although the stress testing of the exogenous risk confirmed lack of statistically important influence on the domestic institutions of the five parent banks' insolvencies, but still due to the structure of capital ownership of some domestic banks and structure of some banks credit portfolios foreign banks' bankruptcies can affect financial conditions of dependent banks operating in Poland.

## References

Acharya, V., L. Pedersen, T. Philippon and M. Richardson (2010). 'Measuring systemic risk', *New York University Working Paper*.

Adrian, T. and M. Brunnermeier (2011). 'CoVaR', *NBER Working Paper*, no. 17454.

Allen, F. and A. Babus (2009). 'Networks in finance'. In Kleindorfer P., Wind Y. and Gunther R. (Eds.) *The Network Challenge: Strategy, Profit, and Risk in an Interlinked World*, Upper Saddle River, NJ: Pearson Prentice Hall.

Allen, F. and D. Gale (2000). 'Financial contagion', *Journal of Political Economy* vol 108, no 1, 1–33.

BIS 1994. *Yearly Report*. Basel

Bordo, M. D., B. Mizrach, A. J. Schwartz (1995). 'Real versus pseudo-international systemic risk: Lessons from history', *NBER Working Paper*, no 5371.

Borio, C. and M. Drehmann (2009). 'Towards and operational framework for financial stability: "Fuzzy" measurement and its consequence', *BIS Working Paper*, no 284.

Borio, C. and P. Lowe (2004). 'Securing sustainable price stability: Should credit come back from the wilderness?', *BIS Working Paper*, no 157.

Chan-Lau, J. (2009). 'Co-risk measures to assess systemic financial linkages', *IMF Working Paper*.

Chen, Y. (1999). 'Banking panics: The role of the first-come, first-served rule and information externalities', *Journal of Political Economy*, vol 107, no 5, 946–968.

Drehmann, M. and N. Tarashev (2011). 'Measuring the systemic importance of interconnected banks', *BIS Working Papers*, no 342.

Eboli, M. (2004). *Systemic Risk in Financial Networks: A Graph Theoretic Approach*, Mimeo, Universita di Chieti, Pescara.

Eisenberg, L. and T. Noe (2001). 'Systemic risk in financial systems', *Management Science*, vol 47, no 2, 236–249.

Freixas, X., B. Parigi, J. C. Rochet (2000). 'Systemic risk, interbank relations and liquidity provision by the central bank', *Journal of Money, Credit, and Banking*, vol 3, no 3/2, 611–640.

FSB and IMF (2011). 'The financial crisis and information gaps: Implementation', Progress Report.

Gai, P. and S. Kapadia (2010). 'Contagion in financial networks', *Bank of England Working Paper*, no 383.

Gray, D. and A. Jobst (2010). 'Systemic CCA: A model approach to systemic risk', *IMF Working Paper*.

Gorton, G. 1988. 'Banking panics and business cycles', *Oxford Economic Papers*, no 40.

Haldane, A. G. 2009. *Rethinking the Financial Network*, public speech

Hale, G. 2011. 'Bank relationships, business cycles, and financial crises', *Federal Reserve Bank of San Francisco Working Paper*, no 2011–14.

Huang, X., H. Zhou, H. Zhu (2009). 'A framework for assessing the systemic risk of major financial institutions', *University of Oklahoma Working Paper*.

IMF (2009). 'Responding to the financial crisis and measuring systemic risks', *Global Financial Stability Report*.

   (2011). 'Towards operationalizing macroprudential policy—When to act?', *Global Financial Stability Report*.

Kodres, L. E. and M. Pritsker (1999). 'Rational expectations model of financial contagion', *Joint IMF and Federal Reserve Board Report*.

Kyle, A. S. and W. Xiong (2000). 'Contagion as a wealth effect', *CFSC Paper presented on June 2000 at Rethinking Risk Management Conference in Frankfurt am Main*.

Lindgren C. J., G. Garcia, M. I. Saal (1996). 'Bank soundness and macroeconomic policy', *IMF Report*.

Lucas, D. (2011). 'Evaluating the government as a source of systemic risk', *Proceedings to Conference on Systemic Risk and Data Issues, University of Maryland*.

Minoiu, C. and J. Ryes (2011). A network analysis of global banking: 1978–2010, *IMF Working Paper*

Mishkin F. S. (1997). 'The causes and propagation of financial instability: Lessons for policy makers, Maintaining financial stability in a global economy', *Federal Reserve Bank of Kansas City*.

Sheldon, G. and M. Maurer (1998). 'Interbank lending and systemic risk: An empirical analysis of Switzerland', *Swiss Journal of Economics and Statistics*, vol 134, 685–704.

Upper C. and A. Worms (2004). 'Estimating bilateral exposures in the German interbank market: is there a danger of contagion?', *European Economic Review*, vol 48, 827–849.

Wells, S. (2002). 'UK Interbank Exposures: Systemic Risk Implications', *Bank of England Financial Stability Review*, no 13, 175–181. Available at https://www.bankofengland.co.uk/-/media/boe/files/financial-stability-report/2002/december-2002.pdf

# 11    When Is Macroprudential Policy Effective?

*Chris McDonald**

Previous studies have shown that limits on loan-to-value (LTV) and debt-to-income (DTI) ratios can stabilize the housing market, and that tightening these limits tends to be more effective than loosening them. This paper examines whether the relative effectiveness of tightening versus loosening macroprudential measures depends on where in the housing cycle they are implemented. I find that tightening measures have greater effects when credit is expanding quickly and when house prices are high relative to income. Loosening measures seem to have smaller effects than tightening, but the difference is negligible in downturns. Loosening being found to have small effects is consistent with where it occurs in the cycle.

## Introduction

Loan-to-value (LTV) and debt-to-income (DTI) limits have become increasingly popular tools for responding to house price volatility since the global financial crisis. Nonetheless, our understanding of the effects of these policies is uncertain. One aspect not well understood is how their effectiveness varies over the cycle. It is also not clear if the effects of tightening and loosening are symmetric. This paper seeks to address these issues by considering the effects of policy changes at different parts of the housing cycle. Then, controlling for this, I evaluate if the effects of tightening and loosening are symmetric or not.

* I would like to thank my colleagues at the BIS Hong Kong office, especially Frank Packer, Ilhyock Shim and James Yetman, for their helpful comments. I am also thankful to Paul Mizen and others at the University of Nottingham's Centre for Finance, Credit and Macroeconomics (CFCM) and the Money, Macro and Finance Research Group (MMF) conference in Nottingham in November 2014 for their comments. Steven Kong deserves a special mention for assisting me with collecting data. This essay was mostly completed while on Secondment at the Bank for International Settlements Representative Office for Asia and the Pacific in Hong Kong during 2014. Since then I have returned to the Reserve Bank of New Zealand. Email: chris.mcdonald@rbnz.govt.nz.

There are at least two interrelated reasons for using macroprudential policies: (i) to create a buffer (or safety net) so that banks do not suffer overly heavy losses during downturns; and (ii) to restrict the build-up of financial imbalances and thereby reduce the risk of a large correction in house prices. Here I examine the relationship between changes in LTV and DTI limits and the build-up of financial imbalances. There is a growing group of economies that use macroprudential policies to target imbalances in their housing markets in this way. This analysis relies on the experience of these economies: many of which are from Asia, though the results are likely to be relevant to other economies as well.

The literature on the effectiveness of macroprudential policies at taming real estate cycles has grown quickly since the 2008 financial crisis. For a wider discussion on the effectiveness of macroprudential policies, the background papers by the Committee on the Global Financial System (2012) and the International Monetary Fund (2013) provide a good overview. The consensus is that these measures can contain housing credit growth and house price acceleration during the upswing. Kuttner and Shim (2013) estimate the effects of a range of policy changes on housing credit growth and house price inflation across fifty-seven economies. They find that tightening DTI limits reduces housing credit by 4 to 7 percent, while tightening LTV limits reduces housing credit by around 1 percent. Crowe et al. (2011) also find evidence that LTV limits prevent the build-up of financial imbalances. They find that the maximum allowable LTV ratio between 2000 and 2007 was positively correlated with the rise in house prices across twenty-one economies.

Previous papers on the cyclical impacts of macroprudential policy look at the entire lifespan of policy, and not just around changes. Classaens et al. (2013) use bank-level data from 2800 banks across forty-eight countries to consider if macroprudential policies can help reduce growth in bank vulnerabilities. They find that several macroprudential policies (including LTV and DTI limits) reduce growth in bank leverage, assets and noncore-to-core liabilities during boom times, and that their effectiveness strengthens with the cycle. During downturns, the effects of LTV and DTI limits differ: LTV limits continue to reduce growth in bank assets and noncore-to-core liabilities, making the downturn worse, whereas DTI limits increase growth in these measures.[1] Research by the International Monetary Fund (2012) that uses country level data to

---

[1] The authors suggest that LTV limits may have perverse effects during credit contractions because, as borrowers' net worth and income decline, strict LTV limits make it even harder for lenders to extend loans, possibly leading to further declines in house prices, and setting off a perverse cycle of even tighter LTV ratios.

examine the effectiveness of macroprudential policy finds that LTV and DTI limits lower quarterly credit growth by between 0.6 and 1.0 percent in emerging market economies. They find little evidence that the effects are any different during recessions or credit busts.

While the persistent (or long-run) effects of LTV and DTI limits are important, the shorter-term impact of changes to them may also be important for policymakers – for instance, to respond appropriately to current financial conditions. Loosening LTV or DTI limits may not simply reverse their long-run effects. Relaxing lending requirements may not lead to an expansion of credit if demand is weak. It would be useful to know if loosening measures are capable of stimulating mortgage lending, even in downturns, for example. Kuttner and Shim (2013) and Igan and Kang (2011) consider the effects of tightening and loosening LTV and DTI limits separately. Both papers find that loosening these policies does little to boost the housing market, whereas tightening them can reduce housing credit growth and house price inflation. The effects of tightening, and lack of effects of loosening, can be seen by looking at mean real housing credit growth and mean real house price inflation before and after such changes – see Figure 11.1. When LTV and DTI limits have been tightened, quarterly credit growth has on average fallen by around 1.5 percent and quarterly house price inflation by around 3 percent. Loosening on the other hand seems to have had little or no effect on either housing credit or house prices.

One of the aims of this paper is to determine if loosening measures are ineffective because they are often implemented during downturns. In particular, I examine whether tightening and loosening measures have

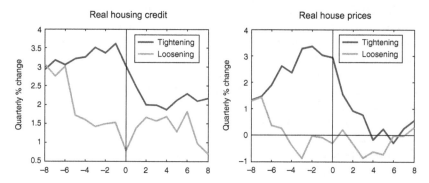

Figure 11.1  Housing credit growth and house price inflation before and after policy changes

Note: This shows the mean quarterly growth of real housing credit and real house prices X-quarters before and after policy changes.

the same effect once you control for where in the cycle changes are made. The effects of changing LTV and DTI limits are estimated using the model outlined by Kuttner and Shim (2013) on data for seventeen economies. This group of economies includes the most active users of macroprudential policy and, as a result, includes most of the changes to LTV and DTI limits that have occurred over the past two decades. The effects of policy changes are estimated on real housing credit growth and real housing price inflation. These estimates rely on a counterfactual: what would have happened without the policy change? This counter-factual is constructed using real interest rates, income growth and assuming persistence in credit growth (or house price inflation). I estimate the effects of policy changes over the succeeding year, like Kuttner and Shim (2013), but I also compare before and after policy changes as an alternative measure. Accounting for what happens before policy changes seems to better account for endogeneity. For example, if surprisingly weak credit growth leads to a policy loosening it can seem as if the loosening contribute to the weakness, even though it was driven by something else. While allowing for persistence in the dependent variable partly accounts for this, any persistence in the residuals is not accounted for.

Another contribution of this paper is that I allow the effects of changes to LTV and DTI limits to vary across the cycle. I account for this by interacting the effects of policy changes with various cyclical measures, such as the house-price-to-income ratio. House-price-to-income ratios are common measures of housing affordability and are often used by regulators to measure financial imbalances. Intuitively, LTV and DTI limits should bind most when house prices are expensive relative to income. Higher house prices imply down payments take longer to accumulate, so fewer people can afford the deposit required to meet the LTV limit. Higher house prices also make the size of loans bigger so that DTI limits are more likely to be binding. Policy changes can also affect housing demand by changing expectations of future house prices, as shown by Igan and Kang (2011). Expectations might be more vulnerable to a negative shock when house prices are high. Other cyclical measures that I examine include annual housing credit growth and annual house price inflation. These measures may correlate with the effectiveness of LTV or DTI policies if, for example, lending standards are more stretched during booms.

The results suggest that tightening LTV and DTI limits tend to have bigger effects during booms. Several measures of the housing cycle correlate with the effects of changing LTV and DTI limits; annual housing credit growth and house-price-to-income ratios are some examples. Loosening LTV and DTI limits seems to stimulate lending by less than tightening constrains it. The difference between the effects of tightening and loosening is small in downturns, however. This is consistent with loosening being found to have small effects because of where it occurs in the cycle.

### Data

The starting point for this empirical analysis was collecting data for each economy. The data is categorized into two parts: LTV and DTI limits and other macro data.

#### LTV and DTI limits

The changes to LTV and DTI limits used in this analysis are from Shim et al. (2013).[2] The full dataset covers sixty economies from 1990 to mid-2012. I have updated it to the end of 2013 for the seventeen economies used in this analysis. This includes eleven economies from Asia-Pacific: Australia, China, Chinese Taipei, Hong Kong, Japan, Korea, Malaysia, New Zealand, Philippines, Singapore and Thailand. Six other active users of macroprudential policies are also included: Iceland, Denmark, Canada, Sweden, Latvia and Norway. In the dataset, LTV limits have been tightened fifty-four times and loosened twenty-one times, and DTI limits have been tightened twenty times and loosened five times. Policy has been tightened three times as often as it has been loosened.

To estimate the effects of policy changes, I construct time series for LTV and DTI tightening and loosening measures for each country. Following the approach of Kuttner and Shim (2013), the time series are given values of 1 when policy is tightened (or loosened) and zero at other times. Four time series are constructed: a tightening and a loosening series for each of LTV and DTI policies. LTV policies include any changes to loan requirements relative to the value of the house on which the loan is issued. Loan prohibitions, such as loans to foreigners or for third homes, are thought of as zero LTV limits and therefore – when they are implemented – the LTV tightening series is given a value of 1, and when they are removed the LTV loosening series is given a value of 1. DTI requirements are those that limit the size, or the servicing cost, of a loan relative to the borrower's income. Not all tightening measures and loosening measures are equivalent. For example, LTV limits may only apply to second homes or in certain regions. Their effects may be quite different, reducing the statistical significance of key parameters in the

---

[2] This macroprudential policy database is available on the BIS website.

regressions. However, the approach offers the advantage that it is simple and easily replicable.[3]

### Other Macro Data

The effects of changes to LTV and DTI limits are estimated on real housing credit growth and real house price inflation. Housing credit data is sourced from CEIC, official statistics agencies, and central banks. House price indices are mainly sourced from CEIC and the BIS property price database. The control variables in the regression also come from a variety of sources. The short-term interest rates (which are mainly money market rates) and CPI data come from the International Financial Statistics (IFS) database produced by the International Monetary Fund. Household disposable income is proxied by real gross national income per capita from the World Bank (interpolated from annual to quarterly frequency).

Several cyclical measures are considered as possible indicators of the effectiveness of LTV and DTI policy changes: including, for example, annual housing credit growth and annual house price inflation. House-price-to-income ratios, both in absolute terms and relative to each economy's mean, are also considered.[4] House-price-to-income ratios are constructed in the following way. House prices are, where possible, in terms of median price per unit and are not necessarily the same as the house price indices used as the dependent variable. Measures based on housing transactions, such as the median house price, are more representative of what buyers are willing to pay and, therefore, may be more appropriate for considering the effects of LTV and DTI policies. For most Asian economies, the house price measures are for the capital city (or for a selection of major cities). These measures are more widely available and a large portion of housing credit goes to borrowers in cities anyway. Gross household income, from household surveys undertaken by national statistics agencies, is the measure of income.[5]

---

[3] By looking at the effects in the year after LTV and DTI changes, and not over their lifetime, the results focus on the ability of these policies to lean against the build-up of financial imbalances, rather than how they buffer the financial system in a downturn. There are some similarities between this and the use of monetary policy to lean against the business cycle.

[4] When house-price-to-income ratios are relative to average they mainly capture cyclical movements within each economy, whereas in absolute terms they also capture differences between economies.

[5] Where available, median house price and income measures are used and, if not, the mean is used. An alternative method would be to use official house prices indices and scale them to match the level of house prices.

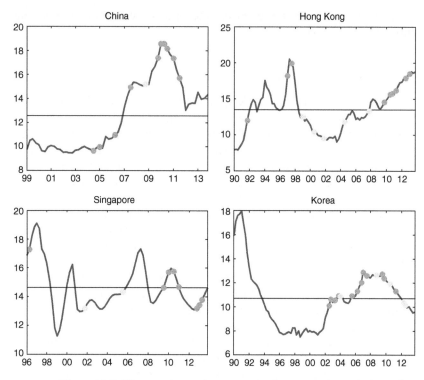

Figure 11.2 House-price-to-income ratios in economies actively setting LTV and DTI limits
Note: Each dark-gray dot shows a tightening of LTV or DTI limits; each light-gray dot shows a loosening. House price measures are transaction based, either median or mean price per unit. Income measures are estimates of nominal household income.

House-price-to-income ratios for the four most active economies, in terms of LTV and DTI policy changes, are shown in Figure 11.2. Red dots represent when LTV or DTI limits were tightened and light-blue dots show when LTV or DTI limits were loosened. The horizontal black line shows the average house-price-to-income ratio for the post-1990 sample. House-price-to-income ratios are currently high in many economies. The current ratio in Hong Kong SAR is the highest, at nearly twenty times the median income. The house-price-to-income ratio in China is also very high (at around 14) but is down from its peak of 18 in 2010.[6] The Asian financial crisis had a notable impact on these measures

---

[6] This house-price-to-income measure is the average for Beijing, Shanghai and Shenzhen.

in Hong Kong and Singapore. House prices in Korea had already fallen by this stage, the result of a large correction in the early 1990s. House-price-to-income ratios in many developed economies are currently high relative to average: Australia, New Zealand, Sweden, Norway and Canada are some examples – see Figure A1 in the Appendix.

Hong Kong SAR is probably the best example of an economy in which macroprudential policy has been set in line with the house-price-to-income ratio. In the 1990s, rising house prices relative to incomes were met by tighter LTV limits. After the Asian financial crisis, these limits were eased on several occasions up until the 2008 financial crisis. Only since 2009, when house prices have once again become relatively expensive, has policy been tightened. Across the sample of seventeen economies, house-price-to-income ratios have typically been above average when policy has been tightened and around average when policy has been loosened – see Table A1 in the Appendix. Regulators look at many measures of financial imbalances though, so some policy changes appear to be at odds with the house-price-to-income ratio. For example, both Korea and China loosened lending requirements during the 2008 crisis, even though they had high house-price-to-income ratios at the time. Singapore has recently tightened policy even though house prices remain low relative to income.

### Empirical Specifications

This section outlines how the effects of changes to LTV and DTI limits are estimated over the cycle. The effects are estimated in a panel regression using data from 1990Q1 to 2014Q1, although for many economies the data starts later. The model is from Kuttner and Shim (2013). The dependent variables are real housing credit growth and real house price inflation.[7] The control variables, which account for other factors that influence the housing market, include real interest rates, real disposable income growth and the lagged dependent variable. Housing credit, house prices, and income are in terms of annualized quarterly percent changes. The following equation outlines the baseline regression for housing credit:

$$\Delta Credit_{j,t} = A_j + B(controls)_{j,t-i} + C(policy\ changes)_{j,t-i} + residual_{j,t}$$

$$(1)$$

---

[7] The range of housing credit data available for each country is in the appendix.

Economies are represented by subscript $j$, $t$ represents time, and $i$ represents lags on the control and policy variables.[8] Country-fixed effects allow for cross-country differences in average credit growth. The parameters in the model are estimated using generalized method of moments (GMM) as introduced by Arellano and Bover (1995) and Blundell and Bond (1998). The standard errors are robust.

Policy changes are lagged so that the correlation between credit growth and policy changes ($C$) is more likely to capture the effect of policy on credit and not policy responding to credit growth. If regulators set policy based on information not included in the model, and this information is relevant for future credit growth, the effects of policy changes could be underestimated. For example, if regulators expect the housing market to weaken (as in the early stages of the global financial crisis) and loosened policy accordingly, it may look like the loosening contributed to the downturn. Including the lagged dependent variable in the regression helps control for past unexplained influences of credit growth.

Kuttner and Shim (2013) came up a way to summarize the impacts of policy changes on credit, referred to as the four-quarter effect. This captures the effects of policy changes on the level of housing credit (or house prices) over the succeeding four quarters, accounting for the persistence in credit growth. This is defined as:

$$4Q \; effect = \frac{1}{4} \left[ \gamma_{t+1} \left( 1 + \rho + \rho^2 + \rho^3 \right) + \gamma_{t+2} \left( 1 + \rho + \rho^2 \right) \right.$$
$$\left. + \gamma_{t+3} (1 + \rho) + \gamma_{t+4} \right] \qquad (2)$$

where $\rho$ is the coefficient on the lagged dependent variable and $\gamma_i$ is the coefficient on the policy variable lagged $i$ quarters.[9] A positive sign for the four-quarter effect implies a policy change increases the level of credit, whereas a negative sign implies a policy change reduces it.

I also estimate the difference between the four-quarter effects in years before and after policy changes as an alternative measure of their effects. Policy is usually tightened (or loosened) when credit has been surprisingly strong (weak). Figure 11.3 demonstrates this for tightening measures. It shows estimates for dummy variables placed eight quarters before tightening measures through to eight quarters after tightening measures. The estimated dummies are positive prior to tightening suggesting that

---

[8] One and two quarter lags of interest rates and income growth are included. Only the first lag of the dependent variable is included.
[9] The delta method is used to calculate the standard errors.

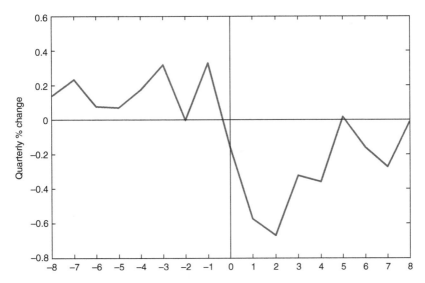

Figure 11.3 Dummy variable estimates before and after tightening measures
Note: The regression includes the policy variable advanced up to 8 quarters, contemporaneously, and lagged up to 8 quarters.

credit growth is usually stronger than implied by the model. If lending requirements stayed the same, some of the preceding strength may be expected to continue and the effect of tightening may be larger than implied by Kuttner and Shim's four-quarter effect. The difference between the four-quarter effects in the years before and after policy changes – referred to as the Before/After difference – assumes prior surprises will have continued and gives an upper bound for the effects of policy changes. The four-quarter effect from Kuttner and Shim (2013) provides the lower bound.

I use two approaches to estimate the effects of policy changes over the cycle. First, I split policy changes into two groups for each cyclical indicator (a top half and a bottom half). The effects for the two groups are estimated using the following equation:

$$\Delta Credit_{j,t} = A_j + B(controls)_{j,t-i} + C(policy\ changes\ above\ X)_{j,t-i}$$
$$+ D(policy\ changes\ below\ X)_{j,t-i} + residual_{j,t} \qquad (3)$$

The second way that policy changes are allowed to have different effects over the cycle is by interacting the policy change variable with the various cyclical measures, such as:

$$\Delta Credit_{j,t} = A_j + B(controls)_{j,t-i} + C(policy\ changes)_{j,t-i}$$
$$+ D(policy\ changes \times cycle)_{j,t-i} + residual_{j,t} \qquad (4)$$

$C$ is the effect of policy changes when the cyclical indicator is at zero, and D is how this effect changes with the cycle. The statistical significance of the interaction term determines if policy changes have different effects across the cycle. An assumption of this approach is that the effects of policy changes increase or decrease monotonically. Of these two approaches, splitting policy changes into two groups is simple and easy to understand, whereas including an interaction term is likely to be less sensitive to the small sample size.[10]

## Results

The baseline regression shows the parameter estimates on the control variables. These control variables determine the underlying counterfactual from which the impacts of policy changes are calculated. The results from two regressions are shown in Table 11.1: one on housing credit growth and the other on house price inflation. Housing credit growth and house price inflation both display persistence. Higher interest rates tend to reduce housing credit growth and house price inflation, while higher income growth increases them. The parameters are re-estimated in each regression in the remainder of the paper and, although they are not shown, their values are generally similar to those presented here.

The baseline regression also shows the average effects of LTV and DTI policy changes – as in Kuttner and Shim (2013). For each type of policy change, both the four-quarter effect and the Before/After difference in four-quarter effects are displayed. The results suggest that tightening LTV limits has a bigger effect, reducing housing credit by 4 to 6 percent and reducing house prices by 5–9 percent. Tightening DTI limits seems to reduce housing credit by 2–3 percent and, while the point estimates are negative, they have an insignificant effect on house prices. These effects are different from Kuttner and Shim (2013); they find that tightening DTI limits has bigger effects than tightening LTV limits. The effects of loosening LTV and DTI limits on both housing credit and house prices are not significantly positive.

---

[10] One and two quarter lags of the cyclical indicators are added as additional control variables if they are not already included. Cyclical indicators are lagged one-quarter when they are interacted with policy changes or used to split the sample. This accounts for policy changes affecting the cyclical indicators immediately. For example, if tightening policy lowered annual credit growth immediately it might appear that bigger effects occur when annual credit growth is initially lower.

Table 11.1 *Baseline regression*

| Variables | Real housing credit growth | Real house price inflation |
|---|---|---|
| Real housing Credit growth {−1} | 0.66*** (0.07) | |
| Real house price inflation {−1} | | 0.46*** (0.13) |
| Real interest rate {−1} | −0.33*** (0.06) | −0.39*** (0.09) |
| Real interest rate {−2} | −0.01 (0.10) | 0.10* (0.08) |
| Real GNI per capita growth {−1} | 0.36** (0.17) | 0.96*** (0.32) |
| Real GNI per capita growth {−2} | −0.14 (0.16) | −0.51* (0.28) |
| | | |
| Tightening measures | | |
| LTV 4-quarter effect (after) | −3.88*** (1.23) | −4.67*** (1.17) |
| Before/After difference | −6.32*** (1.83) | −9.80*** (1.95) |
| DTI 4-quarter effect (after) | −3.50** (1.25) | −0.10 (2.85) |
| Before/After difference | −2.03 (1.93) | −3.70 (5.41) |
| | | |
| Loosening measures | | |
| LTV 4-quarter effect (after) | 0.59 (2.20) | −3.93 (2.80) |
| Before/After difference | −0.92 (1.87) | −2.38 (3.01) |
| DTI 4-quarter effect (after) | −5.25*** (1.84) | −3.08 (1.95) |
| Before/After difference | −1.76 (2.02) | −3.63 (3.68) |
| | | |
| Observations | 1309 | 1450 |

Note: Robust standard errors are in parenthesis. Standard errors for the four-quarter effects and the Before/After differences are constructed using the delta method. Lag length is shown in curly brackets. */**/*** represents statistical significance at the 10/5/1 percent levels. The effects of policy changes are jointly estimated (i.e. each column is a single regression).

Throughout the following analysis, LTV and DTI limits are grouped together in order to maximize the sample size, though as a robustness check their effects are separately estimated. Either grouped together or kept separate, the individual effects of changes to LTV or DTI limits at different times and in different countries will vary – some will be larger, others smaller, and the magnitude may depend on many factors. Therefore, in the next section I consider if the timing of a policy change (i.e. where in the housing cycle the change occurs) is a determinant of its effectiveness.

## Do the Effects of LTV/DTI Changes Depend on the Cycle?

In this section, I examine the effects of tightening measures and consider whether they are different depending on where they occur in the cycle.

The comparison of tightening and loosening measures is left to the next section. These results show the combined effects of tightening LTV and DTI limits on real housing credit; their individual effects are considered in a later section.

The first approach to examine if policy changes have different effects across the cycle is to split policy changes into two groups based on the preceding state of the cycle. For example, the threshold house-price-to-income ratio that splits the tightening observations into two similarly sized groups is 1.12 times each economy's average. Tightening measures above this threshold reduce the level of housing credit by between 3.4 and 5.5 percent over the following year. Tightening measures below this threshold reduce housing credit by 3–4 percent. This difference is small, but if we look at some of the other cyclical measures in Table 11.2 the effects can be significantly different.

The first thing to note is that for most of the cyclical indicators the top half have bigger effects than the bottom half. The differences are bigger and more significant when looking at the Before/After difference, but they are in the same direction for the four-quarter effects as well. The cyclical measures that seem to correlate with different effects are annual housing credit growth, annual house price inflation, the housing credit gap and annual GNI growth. Based on prior annual credit growth, the top half of tightening measures reduce the level of credit by 4 to 8 percent while the bottom half reduce it by around 3 percent. This suggests that when credit grows quickly it tends to be affected more by tightening measures.

Figure 11.4 illustrates this slightly differently. It shows mean housing credit growth before and after tightening measures and splits tightening measures into the top half and bottom half based on the preceding annual credit growth. By construction, the top half have stronger credit growth before tightening than the bottom half. The black line shows that, on average, tightening measures are preceded by around 3.5 percent quarterly credit growth and followed by around 2 percent quarterly credit growth. The decline is biggest for tightening measures with the highest rates of preceding annual credit growth, with mean quarterly credit growth falling from nearly 5 percent to around 2.5 percent. Conversely, when preceding credit growth was lower, the mean growth rate started between 1 and 2 percent and barely fell at all.[11] Even with this simple

---

[11] Credit growth seems to increase in the quarter immediately before tightening when credit growth is initially strong – perhaps reflecting buyers rushing in to get loans – something not seen when credit growth is initially slower.

Table 11.2 *Effects of tightening measures on real housing credit over the cycle*

| Cyclical variables | 4-qtr effect (after) | | | Before/After difference | | |
|---|---|---|---|---|---|---|
| | Bottom half | Top half | Difference | Bottom half | Top half | Difference |
| *Housing* | | | | | | |
| HP-to-income relative to mean | −3.04*** (1.04) | −3.41*** (0.66) | −0.37 (1.26) | −4.06*** (1.16) | −5.49*** (1.56) | −1.43 (2.03) |
| Absolute HP-to-income ratio | −2.16* (1.23) | −4.15*** (0.55) | −1.99 (1.29) | −3.10** (1.54) | −6.30*** (1.51) | −3.20 (2.52) |
| Annual housing credit growth | −3.65*** (0.62) | −3.97*** (1.39) | −0.32 (1.45) | −2.79*** (0.61) | −8.04*** (1.55) | −5.25*** (1.53) |
| Annual house price inflation | −2.68** (1.10) | −2.80*** (0.60) | −0.12 (1.28) | −1.93** (0.80) | −6.33*** (1.41) | −4.40*** (1.34) |
| Housing credit gap | −2.56*** (0.94) | −2.80*** (0.95) | −0.24 (1.38) | −0.79 (1.39) | −6.49*** (1.39) | −5.70*** (1.86) |
| *Other* | | | | | | |
| Annual CPI inflation | −3.32*** (0.82) | −4.06*** (0.99) | −0.74 (1.05) | −6.06*** (1.88) | −4.65*** (1.01) | 1.40 (1.94) |
| Annual GNI growth | −2.87*** (1.01) | −4.84*** (0.72) | −1.97* (1.13) | −3.39*** (0.77) | −7.22*** (1.29) | −3.83*** (1.19) |
| GNI gap | −3.61*** (0.93) | −3.91*** (1.01) | −0.30 (0.89) | −3.50*** (0.79) | −6.52*** (1.86) | −3.01* (1.60) |
| Real interest rate | −4.43*** (1.05) | −2.99*** (1.07) | 1.45 (1.50) | −6.59*** (1.56) | −3.06*** (1.28) | 3.53* (2.09) |

Note: Standard errors in parenthesis. */**/*** represents statistical significance at the 10/5/1 percent levels. The gap measures are in terms of percent deviations from HP-filtered trends, where lambda is set to 1600. The cyclical variables are added as controls to the regression if they are not there already.

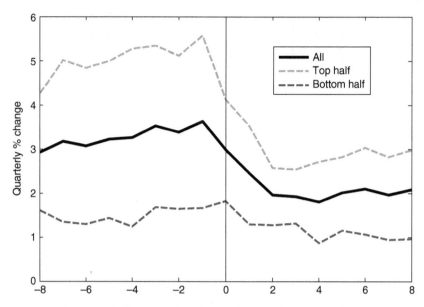

Figure 11.4 Mean real housing credit growth before and after policy tightening

Note: Top half is when annual housing credit growth was above 10.8 percent at t-1.

approach, the effects of tightening seem to be bigger when preceding credit growth is stronger.

Another approach is where the effects of tightening measures are interacted with various cyclical indicators. This can also tell us if tightening measures have bigger or smaller effects depending on the preceding state of the cycle. Table 11.3 displays the results for both the interactions with the four-quarter effects and with the Before/After difference. A negative sign on an interaction term implies the effects are bigger during booms.

Almost all of the interaction terms are negative implying tightening measures are more effective during expansionary phases. Additionally, the interaction terms between the Before/After difference and the absolute house-price-to-income ratio, annual housing credit growth, annual house price inflation, the housing credit gap and annual GNI growth are significantly negative. The four-quarter effect from tightening when the absolute house-price-to-income ratio is 10 is 1.5 percentage points larger than when the ratio is 5. Similarly, the Before/After difference is 2.5 percentage points bigger when the house-price-to-income ratio is

Table 11.3 *Interactions between tightening effects on credit and cyclical measures*

| Cyclical variables | Interaction with 4-qtr effect | Interaction with Before/After difference |
|---|---|---|
| *Housing* | | |
| HP-to-income relative to mean | −1.72 (3.81) | −9.59 (6.95) |
| Absolute HP-to-income ratio | −0.31** (0.14) | −0.49* (0.27) |
| Annual housing credit growth | −0.03 (0.03) | −0.37*** (0.05) |
| Annual house price inflation | −0.05 (0.06) | −0.34*** (0.06) |
| Housing credit gap | −0.02 (0.12) | −0.95*** (0.18) |
| | | |
| *Other* | | |
| Annual CPI inflation | −0.51 (0.43) | −0.57 (0.83) |
| Annual GNI growth | −0.30* (0.17) | −0.56*** (0.19) |
| GNI gap | −0.11 (0.30) | −0.72* (0.36) |
| Real interest rate | 0.34 (0.41) | 0.53 (0.51) |

Note: Standard errors in parenthesis. */**/*** represents statistical significance at the 10/5/1 percent levels. The gap measures are in terms of percent deviations from HP-filtered trends, where lambda is set to 1600.

10 compared to 5. At high absolute house-price-to-income ratios tightening measures reduce credit by roughly 4–6 percent. At low absolute house-price-to-income ratios the effects of tightening are more like 2 percent. This suggests the effects of LTV and DTI limits in places like Singapore, Hong Kong and China may be larger than they are in most developed countries which have lower house-price-to-income ratios.

Figure 11.5 illustrate the different effects of tightening measures across the cycle – both in terms of the absolute house-price-to-income ratio and in terms of the preceding rate of annual housing credit growth. The effects of tightening are larger at higher house-price-to-income ratios and when preceding credit growth is faster, though there is some inconsistency with the different approaches for credit growth. The Before/After difference assumes that the strength prior to tightening would have continued, whereas the four-quarter effect ignores it. If tightening had not occurred then some, but perhaps not all, of this strength would have continued.[12] The likely effect of tightening is, therefore, somewhere between the four-quarter effect and the Before/After difference. This also

---

[12] The own lag captures the persistence of credit growth but not any persistence in the underlying residuals.

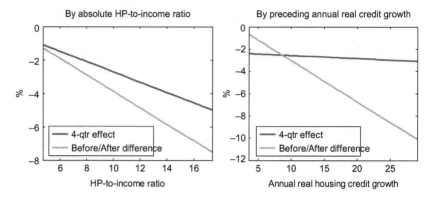

Figure 11.5 Effects of tightening measures on real housing credit over the cycle

Note: The range of the x-axis is set to include the middle 80 percent of tightening measures.

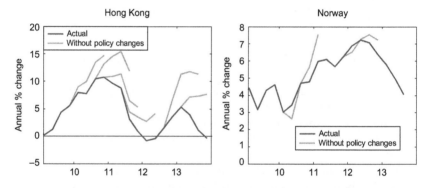

Figure 11.6 Effects of tightening on real housing credit in Hong Kong and Norway

Note: The lines show implied credit growth if tightening had not occurred. The effects are estimated for only 1 year after each tightening measure. Tightening measures include changes to both LTV and DTI limits.

suggests that tightening may have bigger effects when credit growth is initially stronger – consistent with what we saw in Figure 11.4.

To address the economic significance of these results, I calculate what credit growth would have been if Hong Kong SAR and Norway had not tightened LTV and DTI lending requirements since 2008 (Figure 11.6). I allow the effects of tightening measures to depend on the preceding house-price-to-income ratio using the interaction approach. The blue line shows observed housing credit growth and the red lines show what would have happened in the years following policy changes if tightening measures had not occurred. These plots are based on the estimated four-quarter effect in years following policy tightening, not the Before/After difference. When the house-price-to-income ratio is high, as it has been in Hong Kong, changing LTV and DTI limits has substantial effects on housing credit according to the model estimates. Policies implemented in 2012Q3 and 2013Q1 each lowered credit growth by more than 5 percent in the year following their implementation. As a result, credit growth was nearly zero at the end of 2013. The effects in Norway are quite different. Tightening measures taken there did little to reduce credit growth because they occurred at low house-price-to-income ratios. This suggests the effects of tightening lending standards can be large and variable.

### Are Tightening and Loosening Measures Symmetric?

The baseline regression showed that the effects of loosening LTV and DTI limits were insignificant – not an uncommon finding. As mentioned in the Introduction, both Kuttner and Shim (2013) and Igan and Kang (2011) also find that loosening has insignificant effects. I examine in this section whether the effects of tightening and loosening measures are different because of where they occur in the cycle. The previous section showed that the effects of tightening during weaker parts of the cycle were smaller than during booms. We also know that loosening measures tend to occur more often during downturns; maybe this is why loosening measures have been found to have little effect.

Figure 11.7 shows mean quarterly credit growth before and after loosening measures, separating them by prior annual credit growth. The top half includes the thirteen loosening measures preceded by annual credit growth above 7 percent and the bottom half are the thirteen measures preceded by credit growth below 7 percent. By construction, the top half have higher quarterly credit before loosening than the bottom half (2.5 percent compared to 0.5 percent). In contrast to tightening, there is no clear change in credit growth after loosening. Credit growth tends to be stronger after loosening when it was stronger before loosening and weaker after loosening when it was weaker before.[13] Table 11.4 displays the estimated effects of loosening measures more

---

[13] One thing that might suggest loosening has a stimulatory effect is that average credit growth declines in the quarter that loosening occurs, particularly when credit growth had previously been strong (Figure 11.7). This decline is not accounted for in Table 11.4, as it only looks at before and after loosening.

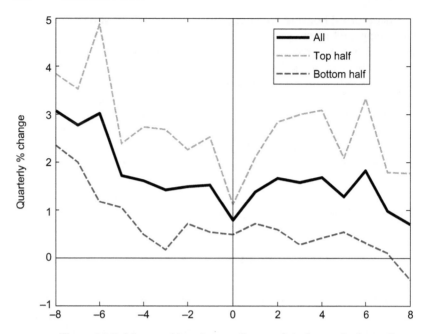

Figure 11.7  Mean real housing credit growth before and after policy loosening

Note: "Top half" includes the 13 loosening measures when annual credit growth was above 7 percent in the quarter just before tightening (t-1). The "bottom half" are those preceded by annual credit growth below 7 percent.

formally. To compare their effects at different parts of the cycle I split them by the absolute house-price-to-income ratio, annual credit growth and annual GNI growth.

Table 11.4 highlights a flaw in the four-quarter effect measure and helps to demonstrate why I have included the Before/After difference as an alternative. The four-quarter effects for the top half and bottom half of loosening measures by prior annual credit growth are very different. The four-quarter effect is significantly negative when credit growth was previously weak, whereas it is significantly positive when credit growth was previously strong. This reflects what is shown in Figure 11.7, that weak credit growth prior to loosening is matched by weak credit growth after loosening. The four-quarter effect, therefore, suggests that when credit is weak loosening makes the downturn worse. This is almost certainly not the actual impact of loosening lending standards. By subtracting the four-quarter effect prior to loosening, the Before/After difference may be a better measure of the effect of loosening policy. The Before/After

Table 11.4 *Effects of loosening measures on real housing credit by cyclical measures*

| | 4-qtr effect (after) | | | Before/after difference | | |
|---|---|---|---|---|---|---|
| Cyclical variables | Bottom half | Top half | Difference | Bottom half | Top half | Difference |
| Absolute HP-to-income ratio | 2.00 (2.31) | −0.15 (2.65) | −2.15 (3.77) | −0.06 (2.05) | 1.38 (3.14) | 1.44 (3.87) |
| Annual housing credit growth | −3.09*** (0.86) | 5.12** (2.57) | 8.21*** (2.84) | 1.75 (1.17) | 1.90 (3.48) | 0.15 (3.45) |
| Annual GNI growth | 2.04 (2.34) | −0.60 (2.41) | −2.65 (2.34) | 2.78 (2.52) | 0.81 (2.71) | −1.97 (3.50) |

Note: Standard errors in parenthesis. */**/*** represents statistical significance at the 10/5/1 percent levels.

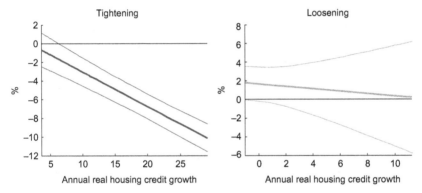

Figure 11.8 Tightening and loosening effects by prior annual real housing credit growth
Note: Effects are calculated between the 10th and 90th percentiles of annual credit growth from quarters when policy was tightened or loosened. The dashed lines show the 90 percent confidence intervals, where standard errors are calculated using the delta method. The effects are based on the Before/After difference, i.e. the four-quarter effect in the year after minus the four-quarter effect in the year before.

differences are almost all positive, though not significantly so, and are similar at different parts of the cycle. This measure suggests that loosening increases the level of housing credit by 0–3 percent. These effects are difficult to disentangle though and not that consistent.

With tightening and loosening measures, one way to compare like with like is to estimate their effect at equivalent parts of the cycle. Figure 11.8

shows the estimated effects of loosening compared with those of tightening, given various rates of preceding credit growth (by interacting annual credit growth with policy changes). These effects are based on the difference between the four-quarter effects in years before and after policy changes (the Before/After difference). When preceding annual credit growth is low, say below 10 percent, the point estimates suggest loosening raises the level of credit by 1–2 percent, while tightening has a negative effect of about the same size. There are few loosening measures available with strong credit growth so it is difficult to get a read of their effects. So are tightening and loosening measures symmetric? It seems that at least some of the difference between the estimated effects of tightening and loosening could be because of where they occur in the cycle. Loosening occurs during downturns when, in general, changes to lending standards have relatively small effects.

## Robustness

I test if the results are sensitive to two variations of the model: (i) replacing housing credit with house price inflation as the dependent variable and (ii) estimating the effects of LTV and DTI changes separately.

### House Prices

The effects of policy changes on house prices lead to similar conclusions to those found using housing credit. Figure 11.9 shows that mean house price inflation before and after policy changes, with changes split based

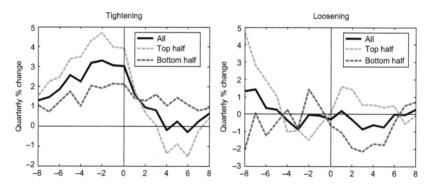

Figure 11.9 Mean house price inflation before and after policy changes by prior credit growth

Note: The top and bottom halves are split based on the preceding rate of annual credit growth.

Table 11.5 *Effects of policy changes on real house prices*

|  | 4-qtr effect (after) | | Before/after difference | |
| --- | --- | --- | --- | --- |
| Cyclical variables | Bottom half | Top half | Bottom half | Top half |
| Tightening | | | | |
| Absolute HP-to- | −1.99* | −2.67** | −6.92*** | −8.31*** |
| income ratio | (1.10) | (1.27) | (2.40) | (2.50) |
| Annual housing credit | −1.61** | −5.77*** | −4.02** | −12.23*** |
| growth | (0.70) | (1.92) | (1.96) | (2.31) |
| Loosening | | | | |
| Absolute HP-to- | −6.51 | 0.56 | −3.51 | 1.96 |
| income ratio | (4.52) | (1.73) | (3.95) | (2.66) |
| Annual housing credit | −5.23** | 1.29 | −6.54 | 9.84** |
| growth | (2.35) | (2.24) | (4.03) | (3.80) |

Notes: Standard errors in parenthesis. */**/*** represents statistical significance at the 10/5/1 percent levels.

by preceding annual credit growth. House price inflation tends to be around 3 percent before tightening and around zero before loosening. Quarterly house price inflation tends to fall following tightening measures and the decline is largest for those measures preceded by high credit growth – similar to the effects on credit. Loosening measures cause little change in mean house price inflation, in line with loosening having little or no effect on house prices. When splitting loosening measures by prior credit growth the effects appear to diverge.

Table 11.5 shows the estimated effects of policy changes on house prices, with policy changes split by house-price-to-income ratios and annual housing credit growth. Tightening measures have significant negative effects on house prices and these effects are larger at higher house-price-to-income ratios and when prior annual credit growth is stronger. The differences are largest given differences in preceding annual credit growth. Tightening reduces house prices by 6–12 percent when credit growth is strong and by 2–4 percent when credit growth is weak. The effects of loosening measures on house prices are varied but mostly insignificant. There are few loosening observations available and the standard errors are large.

### Individual Effects of LTV and DTI Limits

The individual effects of changing LTV and DTI limits on credit growth are summarized in Table 11.6. Tightening LTV and DTI limits have

Table 11.6 *Individual effects of policy changes on real housing credit*

| | 4-qtr effect (after) | | Before/after difference | |
|---|---|---|---|---|
| | Bottom half | Top half | Bottom half | Top half |
| **Tightening LTV** | | | | |
| Absolute HP-to-income ratio | −2.41 | −4.73*** | −4.83** | −8.08*** |
| | (1.80) | (0.76) | (2.21) | (2.04) |
| Annual housing credit growth | −5.28*** | −4.11** | −4.80*** | −9.09*** |
| | (0.79) | (1.79) | (1.25) | (2.13) |
| **Tightening DTI** | | | | |
| Absolute HP-to-income ratio | −2.52*** | −6.92*** | −0.29 | −8.58*** |
| | (0.83) | (0.62) | (1.45) | (1.37) |
| Annual housing credit growth | −6.61*** | −5.97*** | −4.54*** | −7.10*** |
| | (1.63) | (1.47) | (1.00) | (2.36) |
| **Loosening LTV** | | | | |
| Absolute HP-to-income ratio | 2.68 | 1.60 | 0.95 | 0.31 |
| | (2.92) | (3.13) | (2.34) | (4.93) |
| Annual housing credit growth | −3.58*** | 5.67** | 2.13 | 0.28 |
| | (1.35) | (2.63) | (1.51) | (3.73) |

Note: Standard errors in parenthesis. */**/*** represents statistical significance at the 10/5/1 percent levels. Loosening DTI limits are not split into two groups because there are only five observations available – the results for these five are available in Table 1.

similar effects. At higher house-price-to-income ratios and stronger prior credit growth the effects are greater, especially when looking at the Before/After difference. During upturns tightening LTV limits seem to reduce the level of credit by 4–9 percent, whereas during downturns they reduce credit by around 2–5 percent. Tightening DTI limits also seems to have bigger effects given higher house prices and faster credit growth: 6–8 percent during upturns compared to 0–6 percent during downturns.

LTV loosening measures raise the level of credit by 0–2 percent, according to the Before/After difference, suggesting loosening may have small positive effects. The effects of loosening, though, do not seem to be different at stronger or weaker parts of the cycle. The effects of loosening LTV limits seem, if anything, low compared to the tightening measures, even compared to tightening measures in downturns (i.e. the bottom half). The standard errors are large though, so their effects are quite uncertain.

### Conclusion

By looking at 100 policy adjustments across seventeen economies, I find that changes to LTV and DTI limits tend to have bigger effects when credit is expanding quickly and when house prices are relatively expensive. Tightening measures (such as lowering the maximum LTV ratio) during upturns lower the level of housing credit over the following year by 4–8 percent and the level of house prices by 6–12 percent. Conversely, during downturns they reduce housing credit by 2–3 percent and house prices by 2–4 percent. This is consistent with the finding of Classeans et al. (2013): that the persistent (or long-run) effects of LTV and DTI limits increase with the intensity of the cycle.

Several measures of the housing cycle correlate with the effects of changes to LTV and DTI limits. Stronger credit growth before tightening is associated with bigger effects. While there might be several reasons for this, one explanation is that lending is available to more marginal borrowers during booms. High house-price-to-income ratios are also correlated with bigger tightening effects. Limits on LTV and DTI ratios appear to become more constraining when houses are expensive. This may be an important element for explaining cross-country differences in the effectiveness of macroprudential policies, given that house-price-to-income ratios can differ substantially.

Tightening LTV and DTI limits appears to be more effective than loosening them, as found in past research. In downturns (i.e. when credit growth is weak and house prices are relatively cheap) tightening reduces the level of housing credit by around 2–3 percent and loosening raises it by 0–3 percent. Given the bounds of uncertainty, these are not that different – consistent with loosening having small effects because it usually occurs during downturns.

### References

Arellano, M and O. Bover (1995). "Another look at the instrumental-variable estimation of error-components models," *Journal of Econometrics*, vol 68, 29–52.

Blundell, R. and S. Bond (1998). "Initial conditions and moment restrictions in dynamic panel data models," *Journal or Econometrics*, vol 87, 115–143.

CGFS (2012). "Operationalising the selection and application of macroprudential instruments," *CGFS Papers*, vol 48, December.

Claessens, S., S. Ghosh and R. Mihet (2013). "Macro-prudential policies to mitigate financial system vulnerabilities," *Journal of International Money and Finance*, vol 39, 153–185.

Crowe, C., G. Dell'Ariccia, D. Igan and P. Rabanal (2011). "How to deal with real estate booms: Lessons from country experiences," *IMF Working Paper* 11/91.

Igan, D. and H. Kang (2011). "Do Loan-to-Value and Debt-to-Income Limits Work? Evidence from Korea," *IMF Working Paper* 11/297.

IMF (2012). "The interaction of monetary and macroprudential policies – background paper," December 27.

    (2013). "Key aspects of macroprudential policy – background paper," June 10.

Kuttner, K. and I. Shim (2013). "Can non-interest rate policies stabilise housing markets? Evidence from a panel of 57 economies," *BIS Working Paper*, no 433.

Shim, I., B. Bogdanova, J. Shek and A. Subelyte (2013). "Database for policy actions on housing markets," *BIS Quarterly Review*, September.

# Appendix

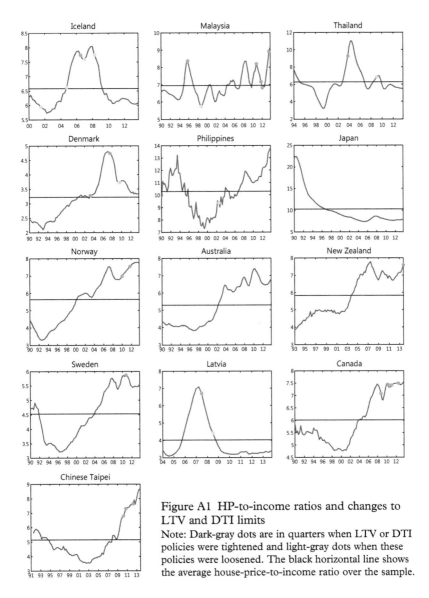

Figure A1 HP-to-income ratios and changes to LTV and DTI limits

Note: Dark-gray dots are in quarters when LTV or DTI policies were tightened and light-gray dots when these policies were loosened. The black horizontal line shows the average house-price-to-income ratio over the sample.

273

Table A1 *Summary statistics: Policy changes relative to HP-to-income ratios*

| Policy change | | Observations | Median | 10th percentile | 90th percentile |
|---|---|---|---|---|---|
| Tightening | LTV | 54 | 1.18 | 0.90 | 1.43 |
| | DTI | 20 | 1.16 | 0.91 | 1.35 |
| Loosening | LTV | 21 | 0.98 | 0.80 | 1.18 |
| | DTI | 5 | 1.04 | 0.95 | 1.18 |

Note: This table shows the median, 10th percentile and 90th percentile for the house-price-to-income ratio (relative to mean in each country) from quarters when LTV and DTI limits were changed.

Table A2 *Summary statistics of regression variables*

| Variable | Obs | Mean | SD | Max | Min |
|---|---|---|---|---|---|
| Real housing Credit growth | 1425 | 9.0 | 11.8 | 77.4 | −26.1 |
| Real house price inflation | 1469 | 2.4 | 13.5 | 72.5 | 77.8 |
| Real short-term interest rate | 1866 | 2.5 | 6.1 | 76.7 | −70.5 |
| Real GNI per capita growth | 1898 | 2.8 | 4.8 | 23.8 | −44.7 |
| HP-to-income ratio (relative to average) | 1525 | 1.0 | 0.2 | 2.2 | 0.5 |

Notes: Growth rates are annualized quarter-on-quarter changes. The real interest rate is deflated using the annualized quarterly percent change in the CPI.

Table A3 *Range of real housing credit growth data by country*

| Country | Start | End | Country | Start | End |
|---|---|---|---|---|---|
| Australia | 1990Q1 | 2013Q4 | Thailand | 1992Q1 | 2014Q1 |
| China | 2001Q2 | 2013Q4 | Chinese Taipei | 1992Q1 | 2014Q1 |
| Hong Kong | 1990Q1 | 2013Q4 | Iceland | 1992Q1 | 2014Q1 |
| Japan | 1990Q1 | 2013Q4 | Denmark | 2000Q4 | 2013Q3 |
| Korea | 1996Q1 | 2013Q4 | Canada | 1990Q1 | 2014Q1 |
| Malaysia | 1997Q1 | 2014Q1 | Sweden | 2002Q1 | 2014Q1 |
| New Zealand | 1991Q2 | 2014Q1 | Latvia | 2003Q4 | 2013Q4 |
| Philippines | 1997Q2 | 2013Q4 | Norway | 1990Q1 | 2013Q3 |
| Singapore | 1990Q1 | 2013Q4 | | | |

Note: Housing credit data comes from a variety of places: CEIC, national statistics offices, and central banks. I have tried to use mortgage credit data but in a couple of economies, like Norway, I have had to use total household credit. Nominal series have been deflated using the consumer price index.

# 12 Macroprudential Policy
## Practice Ahead of Theory and a Clear Remit

*Richard Barwell**

*The scientific approach to economic policy requires clear objectives and a reliable model of the system. Macroprudential policymakers have neither, and that greatly complicates the conduct of policy. The rush to define the instrument set of macroprudential policy is premature and potentially counterproductive. There is a natural sequencing which should be respected: first, identify market failures and write down a model; second, pin down the objectives of the regime; and then, third allocate effective instruments to policy institutions. Six recommendations are made to help deal with the problem of 'learning whilst doing' in the conduct of macroprudential policy: how to achieve the goals of public policy as our understanding of the system we are trying to stabilise evolves.*

## Introduction

In his 2009 Mansion House speech, Governor Mervyn King sounded a note of caution about the speed with which the new macroprudential regime was taking shape in the aftermath of the financial crash (King, 2009):

The resulting 'macro-prudential' toolkit will contain a number of instruments to reduce risk, both across the system and over time. It must not be put together in a hurry. And I share the concerns of many of you that we are a long way from identifying precise regulatory interventions that would improve the functioning of markets.

King's warning appears to have gone unheeded with potentially serious consequences. The title of this paper is in homage to another of the former Governor's speeches – entitled *Monetary Policy: Practice Ahead of Theory* – in which he discussed the conduct of monetary policy given an

* The views expressed in this paper are my own and are not necessarily those of BNP Paribas Asset Management. I am very grateful to David Aikman, Nicola Anderson, Marnoch Aston, Oliver Burrows, Jagjit Chadha, Andrew Mason, Jack McKeown, Paul Mizen and Philip Turner for helpful comments and discussions about the issues in this paper over the course of several years.

incomplete and constantly evolving understanding of the economy and concluded the following (King, 2005): 'Thirty years ago the theory of monetary policy was ahead of its practice, at least in the United Kingdom. Now I hope that the practice has given the theorists something to think about.'

Practice is running far ahead of theory in the macroprudential arena. Perhaps of greater concern is the absence of a formal remit, defining precisely the objectives of the regime. At this early stage in the gestation of macroprudential policy, discussion of – and certainly reaching conclusions about – the instrument set is therefore premature and potentially worrisome. It is premature because it makes little sense to decide which tools policymakers should use until we have a clear idea of the precise market failures that policymakers are trying to address or the objectives that they are trying to achieve. It is potentially worrisome because once a decision has been taken on instruments it is likely to influence how policymakers behave, as the *Law of the Instrument* reminds us (Maslow, 1966): 'I suppose it is tempting, if the only tool you have is a hammer, to treat everything as if it were a nail.'

The basic message of this paper is that the rush to identify macroprudential instruments and then to start using them in earnest is mistaken. The building blocks of the scientific approach to economic policy – the preferences and constraints which guide policy decisions – need to be articulated first. Lest there be any confusion, this message should not be misunderstood as an argument that there is no need for a macroprudential perspective in the policy regime, or more generally that the regulatory reforms of recent years are 'over the top'. The frequency and severity of systemic financial crises are surely too high for the social planner's comfort (Haldane, 2010). The question is *what* should be done, not *whether* something should be done, and in particular, how to manage the problem of 'learning whilst doing': taking decisions whilst still learning about the system you are trying to stabilise.

The rest of this paper is structured as follows. I begin with a brief illustration of the scientific approach to economic policy in the next section. The two sections that follow review how the macroprudential regime measures up against that template, discussing the uncertainty around the objectives of macroprudential policy and the essential features of a fit-for-policy-purpose model of the macro-financial system respectively. The fifth section focuses on the theme of the conference – effective macroprudential instruments – and argues that too much of the debate in policy circles is concentrated on an unnecessarily narrow set of instruments. The penultimate section offers six constructive suggestions on how the 'learning whilst doing' problem should be handled. The final section concludes.

### The Scientific Approach to Economic Policy

There is a long-standing debate among macroeconomists about whether the conduct of monetary policy qualifies as an art or a science (Clarida, Galí and Gertler, 1999; Walsh, 2001; Blanchard, 2006; Mankiw, 2006). However, the terminology here is somewhat confusing: when macroeconomists speak of monetary policy as an art they mean that policymakers must use judgement to compensate for the known limitations of the science; to qualify as a science, the theory must consistently provide the 'right' answer to policy problems. This is a high hurdle indeed: policymakers habitually emphasise the importance of judgement in the conduct of monetary policy, and as White (2013) observes: 'beliefs pertaining to every aspect of monetary policy have also changed markedly and repeatedly'. However, it is important to keep in mind that the artists setting policy are applying judgement *within a rigorous scientific framework*.

The scientific approach to the conduct of policy is based on two familiar building blocks: a clear description of the social planner's preferences and the constraints under which the policymaker operates. Given this information the policymaker can calculate the optimal setting of the policy instrument at any moment in time, to achieve the highest possible level of welfare given the structure of the economic system she is trying to influence.

In the case of monetary policy, we speak of a loss function and a macroeconomic model informing the conduct of policy. That model may be imperfect and the description of the loss function may be incomplete and policymakers may disagree over the fine detail of both, but there is a broad consensus over the big picture. The debate around the appropriate model of the economy is familiar, so we shall focus here on the other key ingredient of the scientific approach to monetary policy (the loss function) to fix ideas.

The loss function of monetary policy describes the implied welfare loss in different states of nature as the macroeconomic variables of interest deviate around their optimal or target levels. When it comes to the functional form of the loss function one particular specification reigns supreme: the quadratic. This functional form has become so ingrained in macroeconomic thinking that as Alan Blinder (1997) once observed: 'Most academic economists begin and end their formal thinking about the goals of monetary policy by positing a periodic loss function that weights the squared deviations of unemployment and inflation from their target values.'

The choice of the unemployment gap as a measure of the real imbalance in the economy is controversial – others might prefer a more comprehensive measure of the output gap – but the assumption of a symmetric and greater than proportional welfare loss as inflation and output (unemployment) deviate in either direction from their 'natural' levels is not. In theory the loss function should correspond to the preferences of the social planner and the utility of the population, and that in turn will reflect the structure of the economy in which they exist. In other words, the loss function should be model (friction) specific: the variables that feature and their relative importance should depend on the structure of the model (Walsh, 2005). Fortunately, it can be shown that under certain conditions, the conventional quadratic loss function is appropriately equivalent to the expected utility of the representative agent. (Woodford, 2003).

Although the high-level preferences of policymakers are well understood, there is still uncertainty about the precise loss function that guides decisions in practice – for example, the relative importance of the output gap and inflation deviations in the loss function. By revealed preference central bankers implicitly concede this point through their choice of communication strategy (Barwell and Chadha, 2014). 'Delphic' communication about how policy will respond to future events would be redundant if agents understood the loss function (Campbell, Evans, Fisher and Justiniano, 2012) and potentially even counter-productive (the only news in the communication would be about how the policymaker's assessment of the economic outlook had changed).[1] There is a solution to this residual source of uncertainty: avoid the 'ambiguity and obfuscation' about the preferences which invite 'misunderstandings of the precise objectives' and publish an explicit loss function (Svensson, 2002). The case for doing so is stronger the greater the scope for, and the costs of, those misunderstandings.

Without a basic understanding of that loss function it is hard to see how central bankers could set monetary policy. Consider the policy response to a cost shock which drives the variables that central bankers care about (output and inflation) in opposite directions: without a loss

---

[1] Indeed, the Bank of England argued that one of the key virtues of its forward guidance framework was to provide greater clarity about the MPC's view of the appropriate trade-off between the horizon over which inflation is returned to the target and the speed with which growth and employment recover (Bank of England, 2013).

function to evaluate outcomes how would a policymaker know whether to loosen or tighten monetary policy?

Monetary policy has not reached a state of nirvana. There is no perfect macroeconomic model of the economy and no precise explicit loss function that accompanies it, so central bankers are forced to apply judgement when they take decisions. With the benefit of hindsight it is clear that those judgements and the models which informed them were less than perfect; mistakes were made. Nonetheless, those decisions were still made within a scientific approach in which the objectives of policy and the structure are understood. It was not always this way – the scientific approach has evolved over the course of several decades – and nobody is hankering for the halcyon days of the past. Returning to the theme of this paper – the state of play in the macroprudential arena – it is worth noting Alan Blinder's (1997) comments about how the absence of a clear mandate stymied the conduct of US monetary policy in days gone: 'During my time on the committee, I viewed the lack of consensus on the ultimate targets for unemployment and inflation as a severe handicap to rational policymaking. How can you know what to do if you do not even know where you want to go?'

## The Uncertain Objectives of Macroprudential Policy

In theory, the model comes first and the loss function follows from that, but at the risk of putting the cart before the horse, I start with a discussion of the preferences of macroprudential policymakers and then turn to a discussion of constraints in the next section of this paper. I begin with a theoretical discussion of the possible objectives of macroprudential policy before turning to discuss how the remit has evolved in practice.

### *The Macroprudential Loss Function in Theory*

The crisis has prompted a flurry of reforms designed to make financial institutions more resilient and easier to resolve when those institutions fail. There is a broad agreement within the policy community that something else is required to deliver financial stability: macroprudential policy. Macroprudential policy is the 'missing link' in the world of macro-policy, designed to respond to the build-up in systemic risk that falls off the radar screen of those responsible for monetary policy and microprudential supervision. The macroprudential policy agenda is usually thought to have two dimensions according to the source of the threat to financial stability (IMF, 2011): a time-series element in which policy responds to the ebb and flow of the 'financial cycle' and a cross-sectional element in which policy responds to changes in the structure of the financial system.[2] In each case, the objective is either to build additional resilience in response to the increased threat, or to change behaviour to discourage the activities which threaten resilience. Of course, the ultimate objective of the macroprudential regime should be to raise social welfare; increasing the resilience of financial institutions or the system as a whole is a means to an end, not an end in itself. The social planner cares about financial stability because disruptions in the supply of core financial services impact on the real economy.

*In theory*, there are a number of ways to translate the macroprudential agenda – to safeguard the resilience of the system in order to protect the supply of core financial services – into an operational remit, depending on how you define terms and how you choose to safeguard the provision of core services.

There is what could be described as the macro-**prudential** remit which is written in terms of safeguarding the resilience of the institutions and markets which provide these services, in order that they are capable of performing their function. Here we can differentiate between a narrow remit, which focuses on the banking sector, and a broad remit, which covers the wider financial system, recognising the role that the non-bank financial sector plays both in the provision of core services to the real economy and as a source and amplifier of stress in a crisis.

Alternatively, there is what could be called the **macro**-prudential remit, which encompasses both safeguarding the resilience of key institutions and an explicit reference to outcomes in the markets of interest. There are a number of possible justifications for extending the remit in this way: outcomes in these markets are what the social planner ultimately cares about; the financial cycle can lead to distress at the micro-level; financial imbalances in the real economy can pose a latent threat to resilience of the financial system. The remit can be written in terms of stabilising the terms on which core financial services are supplied to the

---

[2] This separation into a cross-sectional and time series component feels a touch contrived (Barwell, 2013). It would be something of a(nother) divine coincidence if the incidence and extent of the behavioural and contractual inter-linkages between financial institutions that contribute to the cross-sectional dimension did not have a cyclical component, or if the ebb and flow of leverage, maturity mismatch, risk aversion that contribute to the time-series dimension were everywhere and always common to all financial institutions and markets. In practice, these components of systemic risk have a cross-sectional and time-series dimension and an attempt to structure the policy framework around an implausible orthogonality assumption could prove counterproductive: cyclical variation in inter-linkages within the system or changes in key behaviours within certain institutions or markets could go unnoticed.

real economy; or even to stabilise the flow of credit, the stock of debt or even the level of key asset prices (such as residential property).

Hopefully, it should be clear that these remits are not observationally equivalent. In simple terms the difference between the two remits is that under the latter (**macro**-prudential) the policymaker would care about outcomes in retail credit markets even if she was convinced that there was no *direct* threat to the resilience of the financial system; in the former (macro-**prudential** she would not). It should also be clear these regimes would require different institutional and intellectual capabilities, and different instrument sets too.

Deciding the remit of macroprudential policy is only the beginning, in just the same way that stating that the remit of monetary policy is to achieve price stability is insufficient. The remit needs to be fleshed out; the arguments, targets and functional form of an operational loss function must be articulated. In other words, someone needs to supply concrete answers to the following questions:

- Which set of institutions and markets are systemically important?
- What is the set of core services which the financial sector provides?
- What is the optimal level of resilience of institutions and the system?
- What is the optimal level of provision of core financial services?
- Is too little resilience and too little provision (relative to their respective targets) more costly than too much resilience and provision, and if so, how much more?
- What is the relative importance of these different objectives?

One further complication in the calibration of the macroprudential loss function needs to be addressed. It is typically assumed that monetary policy can do very little to help or hinder the social planner's pursuit of equity and efficiency, over and above delivering price stability (Cœuré, 2012). In particular, we do not believe that there is a long-run trade-off between price stability and the sustainable rate of growth of output or the distribution of income within society. We cannot make the same assumptions in the macroprudential sphere. There might be a long-run trade-off between the resilience of the financial sector and the terms on which it provides core services, and therefore indirectly the sustainable rate of growth of output. Equally, there might be a long-run trade-off between the resilience of the financial sector and the incidence of credit constraints in the real economy, and therefore the capacity of low-income households to smooth consumption in the face of an uneven and uncertain income profile (Zeldes, 1989). To be clear, enhancing resilience may support the social planner's pursuit of greater efficiency and equality up to a point – financial crises appear to damage the supply side and hurt the poor – but at some stage, a trade-off likely emerges. These equity and efficiency concerns must be reflected in the calibration of the loss function.

To repeat the message from earlier, without a basic understanding of the loss function it is hard to see how macroprudential policymakers will be able to make decisions on an objective basis. Knowledge that society pays a heavy price for financial instability is not sufficient to make good decisions in the macroprudential arena any more than knowledge that hyperinflations are costly was sufficient to allow previous generations of central banks to set monetary policy effectively. It matters a great deal whether your 'resilience target' is to reduce the frequency of a systemic crisis to once a century or once a millennium. It matters a great deal whether your 'credit provision target' is to simply avoid a 'credit crunch' (a sudden stop in the provision of core services) or to smooth out all cyclical variation in the terms on which those services are provided. If there is no objective yardstick to evaluate outcomes then policymakers cannot be sure that they will satisfy the Hippocratic Oath of economic policy (first do no harm), let alone take decisions in the ball-park of optimality. Indeed, without a well specified loss function, the revealed preferences of policymakers may fail the transitivity test.

There is another argument for providing much greater clarity over the remit of macroprudential policy, and that is to make policymakers accountable for their decisions. If politicians, market participants and general public do not know what macroprudential policy is for, then it is hard to see how there can be any scrutiny of the decisions that are taken. Because property prices are the most visible signal of the financial cycle to the masses there may be an expectation that the primary goal of macroprudential policy is to bring stability to the property market. It is far from clear that policymakers share that view: for example, they may be perfectly content to see property prices increase rapidly if banks fund a significant proportion of their mortgage portfolios through equity and indicators of stress such as loan to value and debt servicing to income ratios do not rise too far. That misunderstanding about the role of macroprudential policy would not be a healthy state of affairs.

### The Remit of Macroprudential Policy in Practice

Macroprudential policy is slowly taking shape. Policy institutions have been given high-level objectives but formal targets for system resilience – let alone an approximate loss function – remain elusive.

There is a broad consensus on the need for a systemic perspective on the regulation of the financial system to complement microprudential supervision and regulation – as first articulated by a former General Manager of the BIS (Crockett, 2000):

The macro-prudential objective can be defined as limiting the costs to the economy from financial distress, including those that arise from any moral hazard induced by the policies pursued. One could think of this objective as limiting the likelihood of the failure, and corresponding costs, of significant portions of the financial system. This is often loosely referred to as limiting 'systemic risk'. In contrast, the micro-prudential objective can be seen as limiting the likelihood of failure of individual institutions. Again, loosely put, this means limiting 'idiosyncratic risk'.

However, there are important differences of interpretation about the ambitions of the regime among academics and policymakers. For example, in the introduction to a collection of papers on macroprudential policy Schoenmaker (2014) notes: 'Some analysts would be modest and aim just to increase the resilience of the financial system against financial shocks ... Others would go further, preferring countercyclical policies to constrain financial booms, which are largely related to housing and property market.'

In terms of policy institutions, the International Monetary Fund has warned against asking too much of macroprudential policy (IMF, 2013):

Macroprudential policy should be used to contain systemic risk, including systemic vulnerabilities from pro-cyclical feedback between credit growth and asset prices and from interconnectedness within the system, but that it should not be overburdened with other objectives.

Consistent with that, the Federal Reserve has espoused a narrow vision of the macroprudential remit, focused on developments within the financial sector (Tarullo, 2015):

I would like to suggest some specific macroprudential objectives that I regard as both realistic and important to incorporate into a near- to medium-term policy agenda: first, continuing the task of ensuring that very large, complex financial institutions do not threaten financial stability; second, developing policies to deal with leverage risks and susceptibility to runs in financial markets that are not fully contained within the universe of prudentially regulated firms; and third, dealing with the vulnerabilities associated with the growing importance of central counterparties.

In contrast, the European Central Bank has embraced a more radical and ambitious remit for the macroprudential regime (Constâncio, 2014a)

I will argue that macro-prudential policy should be ambitious in trying to smooth the cycle and, if so, it has to be prepared to be bold and intrusive... The aim of macro-prudential policy should definitely be about tempering the cycle, rather than merely enhancing the resilience of the financial sector ahead of crises ...

Admittedly, fully controlling the financial cycle is an unattainable objective, but it would not be worth setting up the macro-prudential policy area if it were to refrain from attempting to fulfil the ambitious goal of influencing the credit cycle.

These various visions of the role of macroprudential policy translate into concrete differences of view on whether, why and how policymakers should respond to events, with the response to 'bubbles' in asset prices being a case in point. The Chair of the Board of Governors of the Federal Reserve seems unconvinced of the merits of a bubble-bursting strategy (Yellen, 2014):

> I think efforts to build resilience in the financial system are critical to minimizing the chance of financial instability and the potential damage from it. This focus on resilience differs from much of the public discussion, which often concerns whether some particular asset class is experiencing a 'bubble' and whether policymakers should attempt to pop the bubble. Because a resilient financial system can withstand unexpected developments, identification of bubbles is less critical.

Don Kohn, formerly of the Federal Reserve but now an external member of the Bank of England's Financial Policy Committee (FPC) reaches a similar conclusion (Kohn, 2013):

> In deploying our tools, the objective of the FPC, as the macroprudential authority, would not necessarily be to micro-manage housing or other asset and credit cycles. Instead it primarily would be about stopping these cycles from being amplified by financial markets and generating costly fallout for the wider economy. Financial cycles, imbalances and asset bubbles will persist.

However, the Vice President of the ECB argues that it would be a mistake not to intervene proactively to burst bubbles (Constâncio, 2014a):

> It seems unacceptable from a welfare perspective that, for instance, we would passively watch the development of a bubble in housing and other asset prices, comforted by the idea that the banking sector is prepared to weather the storm and that the central bank would deal with the painful aftermath.

### Elastic Remits, Unconstrained Discretion and Mission Creep

The conventional approach to the conduct of monetary policy is 'constrained discretion' (Bernanke and Mishkin, 1997). Policymakers are not required to slavishly follow a rule, but a clear and transparent policy framework constrains their room for manoeuvre – they are required to demonstrate that their actions are consistent with delivering price stability. It is routinely claimed that macroprudential policy will follow the same approach of constrained discretion (BoE, 2009; IMF, 2013; Knot, 2014). However, it is hard to see where the constraints come from, when the remit of policy is so vague (and in particular when there is no target), when there is no way of measuring the success or failure of the regime in real-time or rules of thumb about how policymakers should respond (there is not equivalent of the monthly release of consumer prices and no Taylor principle guiding the adjustment of interest rates) and there is little understanding of how policy decisions influence the system.

In practice, the choice is between a regime based on flawed rules or unconstrained discretion, which is no choice at all; after all, central bankers feel that the rules are not fit for purpose in the monetary policy arena where the state of knowledge is far higher. One obvious concern about unconstrained discretion in the macroprudential arena is inertia: without the discipline provided by a clear remit, policymakers will not feel sufficient pressure to respond to evidence of mounting financial imbalances. There is also the possibility of mission creep: of policy-makers acting beyond what was intended by the politicians who drafted the remit. In the rest of this section I review a topical example which at the very least raises interesting questions about the scope for mission creep in the United Kingdom.

In the United Kingdom, the remit of the Bank of England's Financial Policy Committee (FPC) is defined in terms of a primary objective:

Contributing to the achievement by the Bank of the Financial Stability Objective – where the FPC's responsibility relates primarily to the identification of, monitoring of, and taking of action to remove or reduce systemic risks with a view to protecting and enhancing the resilience of the UK financial system...

and subject to that, a secondary objective of 'supporting the economic policy of Her Majesty's Government, including its objectives for growth and employment'.

The remit is conventional both in its emphasis and the absence of specifics: the Bank's Financial Stability Objective – to protect and enhance the resilience of the UK financial system – is suitably opaque. The one point where there is clarity is around the potential trade-off between resilience and economic growth: the Committee is given a clear instruction to tread carefully – it is neither required nor authorised 'to exercise its functions in a way that would in its opinion be likely to have a significant adverse effect on the capacity of the financial sector to contrib-ute to the growth of the UK economy in the medium or long term'.

It is interesting to note that the Committee has been willing to inter-pret its remit in a flexible fashion. In particular, in June 2014 the FPC decided to take action to limit the share of very high loan-to-income ratio mortgages in the flow of new lending, for reasons that were certainly not *exclusively* to do with increasing the resilience of the financial system and arguably not predominantly to do with those financial stability concerns.

There is a straightforward financial stability justification for the type of intervention that the FPC announced: to avoid a build-up of fragile mortgage debt on banks' balance sheets, which might ultimately be the source of large losses. However, it is interesting to note that the Committee was far from convinced that mortgage lending posed a direct threat to the resilience of the UK banks through this channel (BoE, 2014):

Looking at previous episodes of housing market distress, some members felt that there had been limited evidence of UK banks sustaining severe, direct losses from mortgage lending. Others put more weight on evidence from overseas, where losses for banks had been more marked.

Instead, the Committee focused predominantly on an *indirect* threat to financial stability via aggregate demand. That is the Committee was concerned about the risk that highly indebted households might significantly cutting back on spending in response to bad news in the future, exacerbating the slowdown in activity at the aggregate level, which might then feed-back into a threat to financial stability. Tighter macroprudential policy in a boom therefore reduces the need for looser monetary policy in a bust. Indeed, the intervention looks a lot like an attempt to narrow the spread of risks round the central case outlook for the UK economy that is determined by monetary policy (BoE, 2014):

The Committee also discussed how this package of macroprudential measures could be considered to interact with monetary policy. They were intended to act as a complement to monetary policy by insuring against risks arising in specific sectors and therefore seeking to make the central projection in the MPC's forecast more likely.

In conclusion, the Committee's intervention speaks to an intermediate objective of *economic stability* in the remit, as the Bank's Chief Economist made clear in the press conference in which the measures were unveiled (Dale, 2014):

There's much micro evidence and macroeconomic evidence that highly indebted households, in response to shocks - be it income shocks or interest rates shocks - respond disproportionately in terms of cutting back that spending, generating economic instability and hence financial instability.

The point is not that the Committee's intervention was misguided; rather that the justification – to respond to latent threats to economic stability, which might then pose an ultimate risk to financial stability – relied upon a generous interpretation of the formal remit of the FPC. On this interpretation, the Committee has a policy interest in *any* factor which could contribute to future volatility, and thereby financial stability: certainly this interpretation accommodates almost any intervention designed to smooth the credit cycle on the grounds of reducing economic instability.

## A Fit-for-Policy-Purpose Model

A reliable general equilibrium model of the system is a pre-requisite for the *optimal* conduct of economic policy. Without a fit-for-purpose model policymakers will struggle to understand and explain the system that they are trying to influence or predict the impact of their decisions. I now turn to discuss progress towards building a macroprudential policy model. I begin with a brief aside on the academic benchmarks on the relationship between models and the conduct of policy.

### An Aside: Optimal and Robust Policy

The academic literature provides two benchmarks for the link between models and the decisions that policymakers take: optimal policy and robust policy. We shall briefly introduce both concepts.

Optimal policy is about maximising social welfare given the constraints imposed by the structure of the economy (Ramsey, 1927). In simple monetary policy models (where the only distortion is sticky prices), the name of the game is *simply* adjusting the nominal interest rate to mimic the real interest rate that would emerge in the flex-price economy – that is, to lean against the inefficiency created by those sticky prices. But as soon as we are working with multiple market failures (departures from that benchmark economy) the conduct of optimal policy becomes more complicated. Central banks should judiciously set policy to lean against the manifold inefficiencies created by those multiple distortions. For example, the inclusion of matching friction in the workhorse warrants the inclusion of an additional unemployment gap term in the loss function which then modifies the optimal policy response to shocks; simply mimicking the flex-price outcome is sub-optimal in this more complicated (realistic) world (Ravenna and Walsh, 2011).

Optimal policy is a model-specific concept: it describes a strategy which minimises the welfare loss in the context of a particular description of the economy. If the model is wrong, which all models are, then the policy prescription is not necessarily optimal. If the policymaker wants to have any confidence that a given policy decision will deliver a reasonable outcome in the real world then she will want to know that it performs well across a suite of models which collectively reflect our uncertainty about the behaviour of the system. That is the essence of robust policy: given known model mis-specification, policymakers search for decisions or rules that perform well across a range of models (McCallum, 1998; Hansen and Sargent, 2007).

### *Irreducible Set of Macroprudential Frictions and Features*

There is no doubt that the profession has made huge strides in explaining various features of the financial cycle. A macroprudential research agenda has blossomed in academia and policy institutions.[3] However, there is a difference between a model which describes a particular friction or market failure and a general equilibrium model which is suitable for policy analysis. A model which is fit-for-purpose for macroprudential policy analysis must contain the irreducible set of frictions and features which collectively explain the key features of the financial cycle (in just the same way that a monetary policy model must contain the right blend of real and nominal rigidities to match business cycle dynamics) and embed the transmission mechanism of policy instruments to enable rigorous policy analysis. Working with a model which has only a partial treatment of the causes and consequences of financial stability is ill advised, in just the same way that central bankers discovered that it was a mistake to work with macro models which did not cover financial markets. The sheer scale of the challenge of building a reliable general equilibrium model that is fit for purpose for macroprudential policy analysis is formidable.

In part, the problem is one of complexity. In order to capture the key features of the financial cycle these models will need to simultaneously relax many of the simplifying assumptions in the literature. We need models with heterogeneously bounded rational agents, who can exhibit rule of thumb behaviour given simplistic forecasts of the payoffs from different decisions, who are confronted by an environment of asymmetric information and incomplete contracts, who are able to default on debt, and so on. Any notion that this research agenda is simply about including a financial friction or a financial intermediary in an otherwise standard workhorse model should be positively discouraged. Incorporating a bank into the workhorse model may provide new insights on the conduct of monetary policy (Gerali, Neri, Sessa and Signoretti, 2010), but because the banks that typically populate those models bear no more than a

---

[3] See, for example, the output of the European Central Bank's Macroprudential Research Network (MaRs).

passing resemblance to their real world counterparts, it is not clear that we will learn the right lessons from this approach when it comes to questions of financial stability.

The problem is also one of scale, scope and geography. A simple macroeconomic model which has a stylised market for labour and output may be fit for purpose in the monetary policy domain. For example, it is not obvious that we lose any great insight by aggregating together all the prices of the individual items in the consumption basket into one representative index, or the expenditure of tens of millions of households into the consumption of the one representative household sector. However, the default assumption of no great harm done through aggregation clearly does not apply in the macroprudential domain. For example, we cannot aggregate together all the banks into one representative agent, because that implicitly assumes that the strong will absorb the losses of the weak, and would render any discussion of stress in the interbank market moot. An enormous number of securities and markets, of balance sheet entries and balance sheets in the financial sector and beyond have to be tracked if the transmission of systemic risk is to be reflected in the model. Of course, the financial system is highly interconnected across national boundaries, and the banks themselves have substantial overseas exposures, and that suggests that models designed for policy analysis would have to reflect developments overseas and *in some detail*.[4]

Finally, there is the problem of the multiplicity of policy instruments and policy makers. Changes in the stance of micro- and macroprudential regulation (and for that matter, monetary policy too) at home *and abroad* will impact on the resilience of the banks. So too will the circumstances and terms on which emergency liquidity insurance is provided to banks and non-bank systemically important financial institutions in a crisis, although we will argue later that the lender of last resort function should be considered part of the macroprudential toolkit. Plausible reaction functions for those policymakers need to be specified, as do the beliefs of private sector agents about how those policy settings will evolve in the future, and it is far from clear that the default assumption of model consistent expectations in the monetary policy literature is appropriate here.[5]

---

[4] To take one topic example, in recent years it mattered a great deal to markets and policymakers alike whether a particular bank's exposures to other banks, sovereigns and companies in the rest of Europe were predominantly located in the core or the periphery of the Eurozone.

[5] Even sophisticated financial institutions may struggle to forecast the future stance of regulatory policy given the lack of any formal objective or past history to guide expectations; households and companies in the real economy may be blissfully unaware of the existence of macroprudential policy.

When it comes to robust macroprudential policy, it is surely uncontroversial to argue that our uncertainty in the macroprudential sphere is an order of magnitude greater than in the monetary domain. Robust macroprudential policy would require a much larger suite of (as yet unwritten) models than is required in the conduct of monetary policy. That is problematic because the penalty attached to using the wrong model is surely far higher too in the macroprudential domain, given the social costs of systemic crises. Another Blinder aphorism suggests that when presented with the results of many potentially mis-specified models, little is lost by discarding the unusual and the extreme in the conduct of monetary policy (Blinder, 1999):

> My usual procedure was to simulate a policy on as many of these models as possible, throw out the outlier(s), and average the rest to get a point estimate of a dynamic multiplier path. This can be viewed as a rough—make that very rough—approximation of optimal information processing. As they say: Good enough for government work.

The opposite may well apply in the conduct of macroprudential policy: throw out the middle-of-the-road simulations and focus on the outliers, and in particular, the worst case scenario (Onatski, 2000). In other words, not only will policymakers want to inspect the output of many models, they will also want to be able to focus on the eccentric and the unusual and make sure policy works well in that worst case scenario.

As noted earlier, a key source of uncertainty in the macroprudential policy debate is the nature of the trade-off between the intermediate objectives of financial stability (a resilient financial system) and the ultimate objectives of the social planner. We do not know if there is a long-run trade-off between the resilience of the financial system and the provision of core financial services, and if there is what the slope of that trade-off is. This trade-off is usually expressed in terms of the provision of bank credit to specific groups (low income households and small businesses) but one can imagine other trade-offs. We have highlighted elsewhere the potential trade-off between the resilience of financial institutions and inequality via the incidence of credit constraints. Market participants might point to a potential trade-off between the resilience of institutions which act as market makers in wholesale markets and their capacity to warehouse risk and therefore dampen sharp swings in asset prices (which could in theory have welfare implications). Policymakers will be keen to learn if their decisions – indeed the entire regime – are robust to assumptions about the deep parameters of the model which determine the existence and slopes of those trade-offs.

*Uncertainty over the Transmission Mechanism*

One key source of uncertainty centres on the transmission mechanism of policy itself. In the monetary domain we have the benefit of a large body of evidence (drawn from several decades and many countries) on the impact of a single policy instrument, which we can use to train our models, and refine our estimates of the interest rate multiplier. In contrast in the macroprudential domain we have little to no evidence on the impact of multiple macroprudential instruments. Former Deputy Governor Charles Bean graphically illustrated the scale of the macroprudential policy problem, relative to the state of knowledge in the monetary sphere (Bean, 2012):

The application of these so-called macroprudential policies is still very much at the developmental stage. When the Bank gained operational responsibility for monetary policy in 1997, there was a long history of practical experience, together with a vast theoretical and empirical literature for us to draw on. That didn't make setting monetary policy easy, but it certainly helped. By comparison, we are still in the Stone Age in respect of deploying macroprudential policies. There is lots of scope for academia to help us out here, on both the theoretical and empirical fronts.

It is true that policymakers have started intervening and that in turn creates evidence which can be used to refine our understanding of the transmission mechanism of these instruments. However, this learning process has been complicated by the multi-faceted and far-reaching reforms in the microprudential arena and the background noise of changes in the state of the economy and financial markets; so much is changing that it is hard to pin down the impact of one particular intervention. Nor is it clear that evidence from macroprudential interventions in the emerging economies can shed too much light on the problem, given the different setting (size and scope of the financial system) and different policy mix (stance of monetary policy). In short, the impact of a tweak in any one macroprudential instrument on the policymaker's objectives is likely to be highly uncertain relative to the uncertainty around the impact of a change in official interest rates.

To illustrate the scale of the uncertainty around the transmission mechanism of macroprudential policy we focus here on the uncertainty around what is assumed by many to be a key instrument in the macroprudential toolkit: macroprudential capital surcharges that sit on top of the regulatory floor, which can be adjusted either across the board in response to the state of the financial cycle, or linked to a specific exposure (often referred to as varying the risk-weight on that exposure).

In part this uncertainty reflects the familiar debate around whether the Modigliani Miller (MM) propositions are a reasonable approximation to reality. There are those who believe that the impact of mandated changes in the capital structure of the bank on the average cost of funding a bank's balance sheet has been grossly exaggerated (see, for example, Admati, DeMarzo, Hellwig and Pfleiderer, 2013). In an MM world, the capital structure of a bank is irrelevant: the cost of funding is determined by the other side of the balance sheet. Although these MM advocates concede that various distortions complicate the story and explain a private preference for debt over equity, they claim that the basic insight holds: the cost of equity is endogenous with respect to the capital structure, so if banks (are forced to) issue more equity then that equity becomes safer, and therefore cheaper.[6] From this perspective, forcing banks to become less leveraged will make them safer, but will not impact on the cost of the services banks provide. By the same token you cannot have your MM cake and eat it too: if raising capital requirements has no impact on the banks' cost of funding then it is hard to believe that this intervention will have a material impact on their behaviour, so one should not expect asset-specific surcharges to discourage banks from engaging in a particular activity. Those who believe in the macroprudential agenda will be instinctively sceptical about the MM propositions, because they describe what happens in a theoretical benchmark of perfect capital markets. The irrelevance of higher capital requirements relies on investors understanding that the change in the capital structure of the bank has made bank equity a safer investment and re-pricing the asset accordingly. Real-world investors may be sceptical that bank equity will offer less volatile returns. They may fear that the mandated reduction in leverage will lead to an endogenous and unobservable increase in the risk appetite of the bank – an example of risk homeostasis (see Wilde, 1998; Barwell, 2013 for its application to macroprudential policy).

Even if we can reach agreement over the extent to which the MM propositions are a reliable approximation to reality that does not resolve all the uncertainty around how banks will respond to a change in the macroprudential capital surcharge, both because it is unclear whether those surcharges will bind and how the banks will respond if they do.

Banks may plan on permanently operating above the regulatory floor for one of a couple of reasons. First, banks may incur significant costs if

---

[6] Those distortions include: the favourable tax treatment of debt interest payments; the costs of bankruptcy; asymmetric information about the quality of the bank's portfolio; the presence of deposit guarantees; and the value that households and companies attach to demand deposits.

they fall below the regulatory floor, depending on the severity of the financial penalties or restrictions on behaviour that regulators are likely to impose on banks in those circumstances (e.g. restricting dividend payments), how long banks expect to be in that situation, and how expensive it will be to make large and rapid adjustments to their balance sheets in response to a change in the macroprudential stance. Second, at certain points in the financial cycle banks may be penalised by the market for operating too close to the regulatory floor or too far below their peers; at other points, the converse may be true. These so-called market requirements may create a time-varying floor above the regulatory requirements.

Furthermore, the notion that banks may be evaluated relative to their peers opens up the possibility of strategic complementarity – that is, where one bank responds to a policy intervention it may create pressure on others to follow suit (Bulow, Geanakoplos and Klemperer, 1985) resulting in a synchronised, disproportionate and even discontinuous response to a given policy intervention via these market requirements. It is even possible to imagine a scenario where capital ratios could *fall* in an upswing despite the fact that policymakers are raising the counter-cyclical surcharge (in response to that upswing) because the market requirement to operate above the regulatory floor falls. Changes in the regulatory regime which do not bite will only have traction to the extent that banks seek to maintain a constant safety margin above the regulatory floor and there is no offsetting shift in the market requirements.

Moreover, even if policy bites – that is, even when banks are prompted to adjust their behaviour in response to a change in the stance of policy – there are a number of ways in which they can respond in order to comply with higher regulatory (or market) requirements. Those responses cover a wide range: rights issues and sales of whole business units; deleveraging portfolios of liquid assets; reducing the riskiness (average risk weight) of their portfolios; reining in the creation of new assets (including loans); cutting dividend payments, cutting costs or charging higher spreads. These responses will rebuild capital ratios over different time horizons and by varying degrees. Unfortunately, the macroprudential policymaker is unlikely to be indifferent over the choices that banks make – and in particular whether deleveraging takes place at home or abroad – but may have relatively little power to influence that choice.

## Instrument Set – Self-Imposed Constraints

The selection of policy instruments tends to revolve around questions of effectiveness, predictability and efficiency: effective in the sense that a good instrument has a sizeable and speedy impact on the variables of interest; predictable in the sense that a good instrument has a stable and relatively tightly defined transmission mechanism; and efficient in the sense that the use of a good instrument does not involve significant undesirable side effects (social costs). The rush to select macroprudential instruments which satisfy these three conditions is premature: until you know what your objective is and the market failures you are trying to correct, it is very hard to assess the effectiveness, predictability and efficiency of a particular instrument. Moreover, the debate around the macroprudential toolkit appears to have been artificially constrained in some quarters to an unnecessarily narrow set of instruments, and that could have unfortunate consequences for the future evolution of the macroprudential regime. As the saying goes, once you have a hammer, every problem looks like a nail.

### Piggybacks and Approximations to Pigou

The default assumption when it comes to the selection of macroprudential instruments has been to piggy-back on top of a microprudential regime and the default assumption when discussing those instruments is that the microprudential regime is inert. The first assumption may be reasonable, the second is not.[7]

In theory, a macroprudential capital or liquidity regime can be designed in the form of surcharges which sit on top of the respective microprudential baseline, establishing a new higher standard for capital or liquid assets which regulated institutions are *expected* to meet, although the restrictions imposed on banks which do not meet this standard should not be so penal that they establish a new higher floor. This approach has the advantage that it builds on a framework that is widely understood, and therefore could make for a more transparent regime where market participants more clearly understood *what* the macroprudential policymaker has done, and it is therefore easier for them to form views over what they might do in the future. In practice, there is limited scope for national authorities to explore this option within the European single market. Instead, the UK

---

[7] The microprudential authority has tools at her disposal which can be varied through the cycle in response, and remit of microprudential regulation has been written to allow authorities like the PRA to use those tools to pursue macroprudential aims. For example, the microprudential authority can and will adjust Pillar 2 capital buffers based on an assessment of the risks that may emerge over a longer time horizon to a particular institution based on its particular balance sheet and behaviour. An exchange between Andy Haldane and Andrew Bailey in the Bank of England's November 2012 FSR press conference illustrates this point perfectly.

FPC has the power of direction (with respect to the microprudential authority) over sectoral capital requirements (SCRs), and has responsibility for setting the countercyclical capital buffer (CCB).

Macroprudential interventions are often motivated on Pigovian grounds (Jeanne and Korinek, 2010; Markose, 2013) – that is, as a means to address externalities that lead to sub-optimal outcomes (elevated risk of a systemic crisis) – whether that be a 'cross-sectional' intervention to force systemically important financial institutions (SIFIs) to internalise the spillover costs on the rest of the system in the event of their default, or 'time-series' interventions to address certain behaviours which leave the system more vulnerable in an upswing. These interventions have to consistently shift the cost-benefit analysis of private individuals and institutions in a predictable fashion if they are to be worthy of the name of Pigovian taxes. It is far from clear that capital surcharges pass that test (given the discussion about the Modigliani Miller propositions discussed earlier). We can be more confident that macroprudential liquidity surcharges will have an impact on the bottom line, because they reduce the liquidity premia spread that banks can earn across their balance sheets by forcing banks to hold a higher proportion of highly liquid (low return) assets. Nonetheless, if the purpose is to tax social bads, it is not clear why the policy community is not discussing the use of actual taxes, rather than quasi-taxes.

### Prohibition – From Structural Reform to LTI/V Caps

There is an alternative to 'taxing' bad behaviours: prohibition – that is, outlawing certain activities either outright or beyond some specified limit. The *Pigou versus Prohibition* debate has a long tradition in economics. Essentially, the difference between them is that the tax (or subsidy) might correct costs (or benefits) by a known amount, but it does not guarantee a given outcome (such as a given level of production of pollutants in the case of environmental regulation). In contrast, a quantity restriction guarantees an outcome but it cannot guarantee an efficient outcome (an intersection of marginal cost and benefit).[8]

---

[8] In the context of the debate about regulating environmental pollution, Weitzman's (1974) argued that the choice between these two options should be driven by the relative sensitivity to a change in production of the private cost (to the polluter) of abating pollution and the marginal benefit (to the consumer) of increased production (of marketable output and pollution). If the costs of abatement are more sensitive (if the curve is steeper), then price-based interventions are optimal, because the private costs of the wrong quantity restriction are likely to be high; in contrast, if the abatement cost curve is pretty flat, then quantity-based interventions are preferable.

When it comes to the regulation of the financial sector, the prohibition debate is usually framed in terms of the merits of structural reforms to improve the resilience of the financial network (Haldane, 2010), such as imposing a Glass-Steagall type structural separation between retail and investment banking. The prohibition solution certainly has its attractions. Imagine for the sake of argument that one could design a set of simple arbitrage-proof rules which could effectively limit the size, leverage and activities of the regulated sector. It is not unreasonable to believe that these rules would give policymakers greater confidence that the probability and severity of future crisis had been materially reduced. The problem with this approach should be clear: the macro-financial implications of these simple rules and their ultimate impact on social welfare are hard to predict and *if* the loss function of macroprudential policy includes equity and efficiency arguments, as well as stability, then the rules *may* perform badly. Once again, it would seem wise to reach a preliminary conclusion on the structure of the system and the objectives of the policy regime before taking decisions on this scale, which would codify the policy stance for potentially a decade or more.

In practice, macroprudential prohibition is more likely to arise when policymakers ponder interventions in the mortgage market. The FPC's cap on the proportion of very high LTI mortgages in the flow of new lending is illustrative of a broader trend. Borrower-based prohibitions which cap loan to value (LTV), loan to income (LTI) or debt servicing to income (DSTI) may be more effective at containing bubbles in the housing market than capital surcharges targeted at mortgage lending (Hartmann (2015)). These caps may limit the build-up of high risk loans on bank balance sheets, however, these borrower-based measures do not necessarily build resilience (loss absorbing capacity) against those loans, and supervisory vigilance is required to prevent borrowers evading the cap (e.g. by borrowing money from other sources).

### The Central Bank Balance Sheet

Generations of macroeconomists have thought of the central bank's balance sheet as a critical tool of financial stability policy in a crisis. The central bank balance sheet is a *legitimate* tool of macroprudential policy (see the discussion in Goodhart, 2011 and Turner, Chapter 1 in this volume), and it has been used to novel effect in this crisis to achieve macroprudential aims, although the operations are rarely described in these terms by those implementing the policy. It is curious that the institutions which have been established to conduct macroprudential policy have not been given a voice in how this key instrument – the central bank balance sheet – has been used in a crisis, let alone operational independence in its use (Barwell, 2013).

Take lender of last resort (LOLR) operations. The central bank community argues that only solvent but illiquid and systemically important financial institutions are supported through LOLR operations. That necessary condition sounds like a macroprudential justification in all but name: by definition a market failure must have occurred if funding markets have closed on a solvent bank, and the failure of that bank must be considered to pose a threat to the resilience of the wider financial system and/or the provision of core financial services.

More broadly, any unconventional use of the balance sheet to provide liquidity insurance to the banking system in a crisis – whether a change in the collateral framework (haircut policy) the spread over the policy rate at which liquidity insurance is extended to the system, the maturity of the loan (like the European Central Bank's vLTROs), or facilities which are only activated in an emergency (like the Bank of England's Contingent Term Repo Facility) – is arguably macroprudential in nature. The same goes for the innovative use of the liquidity insurance facilities to encourage lending: the Bank of England's FLS and the European Central Bank's TLTRO. The conflation of concerns about the funding position of the banks and the provision of core financial services suggests that the FLS and the TLTRO are classical macroprudential operations in all but name.

Beyond the liquidity insurance facilities for banks, central banks have been innovative in the use of their balance sheets in the crisis to support the flow of non-bank finance to the real economy by applying the logic of LOLR to the capital markets. The Bank of England acted as a market maker of last resort (MMLR), back-stopping liquidity in core wholesale markets to ensure that companies in the real economy could continue to tap the commercial paper and corporate bond markets for funding. The first two ECB covered bond purchase programmes were launched for broadly similar reasons.

Finally, there is what could be described as the risk taker of last resort (RTLR) operation (Barwell, 2013): the use of the balance sheet to purchase risk assets to quell panic and arrest a collapse in risk appetite that might otherwise have macroeconomic consequences. Purchases of stocks during the 1987 stock market crash would have qualified as a RTLR operation. Arguably the European Central Bank's purchase of peripheral sovereign bonds – the Securities Market Programme – was a RTLR operation.

*Endnote: The Mismatch between Objectives and Instruments*

The toolkit described earlier is *very* bank-centric and in all but the most modest interpretations of the macroprudential remit that is problematic. If policymakers wish to safeguard the resilience of the wider financial system then either the regulatory perimeter will have to be redrawn to include systemically important non-bank institutions and markets and/or the macroprudential authority will have to be equipped with tools which bite beyond the banking sector. The capacity to influence the haircuts that apply in repo transactions or the margin requirements of central counterparties are obvious examples. Likewise, if policymakers wish to influence outcomes in retail credit markets or even the stock of debt in the non-financial real economy then they may require tools which impact on the demand side of the market, rather than relying on a mixture of capital surcharges and LTV/LTI/DSTI caps. To be fair, those policymakers who believe in this more ambitious agenda have been quite vocal on this point (Constâncio, 2014a, 2015), but the toolkit debate needs to catch up with the aspiration.

## Recommendations

The message of this paper is that policymakers are not taking a scientific approach to the conduct of macroprudential policy. So what then should be done? To repeat the message from the Introduction: doing nothing is not an option. Six tentative conclusions spring to mind.

First, *learn to walk before you try to run*: the ambitions and objectives of the macroprudential regime should evolve at the same pace as our understanding of the macro-financial system. The authorities should set modest goals at the outset and revisit the objectives in due course.

Second, *work out roughly where you want to go*: the objectives of macroprudential policy need to be articulated to anchor the policy debate, inform the choice of instruments and to enable accountability. This means providing *preliminary approximate* answers to the questions posed earlier in this paper: about the desired resilience of the scheme; the extent to which the resilience motive extends beyond the banking sector into financial markets; and the appetite for stabilising outcomes in retail and wholesale markets.

Third, *pick your battles wisely*: given the limited state of knowledge, macroprudential policymakers should focus on major issues where there is a genuine threat to system resilience or the provision of core services, the cost benefit analysis is compelling, and the risks of doing more harm than good are low.

Fourth, *we are all macroprudentialists now*: if macroprudential interventions are likely to be modest for the time being then the wider policy community needs to be prepared to play a more active role in the pursuit of the counter-cyclical macroprudential agenda. In particular, central banks might have to use the one tool that 'gets in all of the cracks' (Stein, 2013) in response to mounting evidence of financial stability.

Fifth, *toughen up the microprudential regime*: if we do not know enough to execute a nimble counter-cyclical macroprudential regime (to be tough when necessary and loose otherwise) we may need to revisit the calibration of the microprudential regime. In other words, we may need to increase the size of the capital conservation and counter-cyclical buffers and the surcharge for systemically important institutions in the Basel III regime and the TLAC buffer required to make resolution credible, so that financial institutions are in better shape and the authorities are better prepared to deal with another crisis before the embryonic macroprudential regime takes shape.

Sixth, *education, education, education*: if the fundamental problem is that we do not know enough about the macro-financial system to adopt a scientific approach to macroprudential policy then the solution is surely to devote significant resources to learning more about the system – to ascend the macroprudential learning curve as fast as possible, to bring forward the point at which macroprudential policy can play its intended role.

### Conclusions

This paper has argued that the scientific approach to economic policy is not being applied: the objectives of policy have not been clearly articulated beyond a high-level mission statement and a reliable general equilibrium model of the system that is fit-for-policy purpose is absent. To use ECB Vice President Vítor Constâncio's expression, the macroprudential field experiments have begun in earnest so it is high time the analytical foundations were developed (Constâncio, 2014b):

Many policies in history have been developed through trial and error. It is rare that a perfect theory or academic paradigm is established before at the time when a new policy needs to be used for the first time. But it is important that once the policy community has realised that a new policy is indispensable and starts 'field experiments', the analytical foundations are developed in parallel.

## References

Admati, A., P. DeMarzo, M. Hellwig and P. Pfleiderer (2013). 'Fallacies, irrelevant facts and myths in the discussion of capital regulation', *Stanford University Graduate School of Business Research Paper*, no 13–7.

Bank of England (2009). 'The role of macroprudential policy', *Discussion Paper*, November.

(2013). 'Monetary policy trade-offs and forward guidance'.

(2014). 'Record of the June 17 and 25 meetings of the Financial Policy Committee'.

Barwell, R. (2013). *Macroprudential Policy: Taming the Wild Gyrations of Credit Flows, Debt Stocks and Asset Prices*, Palgrave, New York.

Barwell, R. and J. Chadha (2014). 'Publish or be damned – or why central banks need to say more about the path of their policy rates', *VoxEU*, 31 August.

Bean, C. (2012). 'Central banking in boom and slump', *JSG Lecture*, 31 October.

Bernanke, B. and F. Mishkin (1997). 'Inflation Targeting: A New Framework for Monetary Policy?', *Journal of Economic Perspectives*, vol 11, 97–116.

Blanchard, O. (2006). 'Monetary policy: science or art?', *Paper presented for an ECB Colloquium held in honour of Otmar Issing*.

Blinder, A. (1997). 'What central bankers could learn from academics and vice versa', *Journal of Economic Perspectives*, vol 11, no 2, 3–19.

(1999). *Central Banking in Theory and Practice*, MIT Press, Cambridge, MA.

Bulow, J., J. Geanakoplos and P. Klemperer (1985). 'Multimarket Oligopoly: Strategic Substitutes and Complements', *Journal of Political Economy*, vol 93, no 3, 488–511.

Campbell, J., C. Evans, J. Fisher and A. Justiniano (2012). 'Macroeconomic effects of Federal Reserve forward guidance', *Federal Reserve Bank of Chicago Working Paper*, no 2012–03.

Clarida, R, J. Galí and M. Gertler (1999). 'The science of monetary policy: A New Keynesian perspective', *Journal of Economic Literature*, vol 37, 1661–1707.

Cœuré, B. (2012). 'What can monetary policy do about inequality?', Speech, 17 October.

Constâncio, V. (2014a). 'Making macroprudential policy work', Speech, 10 June.

(2014b). 'The ECB and macro-prudential policy: From research to implementation', Speech, 23 June.

(2015). 'Strengthening macroprudential policy in Europe', Speech, 3 July.

Crockett, A. (2000). 'Marrying the micro- and macro-prudential dimensions of financial stability', Speech, 20–21 September.

Gerali, A., S. Neri, L. Sessa and F. Signoretti (2010). 'Credit and banking in a DSGE model of the euro area', *Journal of Money, Credit and Banking*, vol 42, no s1, 107–141.

Goodhart, C. (2011). 'The macro-prudential authority: Powers, scope and Accountability', *Financial Markets Group Special Paper*, no 203.

Haldane, A. (2010). 'The $100 billion question', Speech, 30 March.

Hansen, L. and T. Sargent (2007). *Robustness*. Princeton University Press, Princeton, NJ.

Hartmann, P. (2015). 'Real estate markets and macroprudential policy in Europe', *ECB Working Paper*, no 1796.

IMF (2011). 'Macroprudential policy: An organizing framework', Staff background paper.

(2013). 'IMF executive board discusses key aspects of macroprudential policy', Press release 13/342.

Jeanne, O. and A Korinek (2010). 'Managing credit booms and busts: A Pigouvian taxation approach', *NBER Working Paper*, no 16377.

King, M. (2005). 'Monetary policy: Practice ahead of theory', Mais lecture, 17 May.

(2009). 'Mansion House speech', Speech at the Lord Mayor's Banquet for Bankers and Merchants of the City of London, 17 June.

Kohn, D. (2013). 'The interactions of macroprudential and monetary policies: A view from the Bank of England's Financial Policy Committee', Speech, 6 November.

Knot, K. (2014). 'Macroprudential policies: Implementation and interactions', *Banque de France Financial Stability Review*, vol 18, 25–32.

Mankiw, N. (2006). 'The macroeconomist as scientist and engineer', *Journal of Economic Perspectives*, vol 20, no 4, 29–46.

Markose, S. (2013). 'Systemic risk analytics: A data-driven multi-agent financial network (MAFN) approach', *Journal of Banking Regulation*, vol 14, 285–305.

Maslow, A. (1966). *The Psychology of Science: A Reconnaissance*, Kaplan, New York.

McCallum, B. (1998). 'Robustness properties of a rule for monetary policy', *Carnegie-Rochester Conference Series on Public Policy*, vol 29, 173–203.

Onatski, A. (2000). 'Minimax analysis of monetary policy under model uncertainty', *Econometric Society World Congress 2000 Contributed Paper*, no 1818.

Ramsey, F. (1927). 'A contribution to the theory of taxation', *Economic Journal*, vol 37, 47–61.

Ravenna, F. and C. Walsh (2011). 'Welfare-based optimal monetary policy with unemployment and sticky prices', *American Economic Journal: Macroeconomics*, vol 3, 130–162.

Schoenmaker, D. (2014). 'Introduction'. In D. Schoenmaker (Ed.) *Macroprudentialism*, CEPR.

Stein, J. (2013). 'Overheating in credit markets: origins, measurements and policy responses', Speech, 7 February.

Svensson, L. (2002). 'Monetary policy and real stabilization', Proceedings of the Economic Policy Symposium at Jackson Hole hosted by the Federal Reserve Bank of Kansas City, 261–312.

Tarullo, D. (2015). 'Advancing macroprudential policy objectives', Speech, 30 January.

Walsh, C. (2001). 'The science (and art) of monetary policy', *FRBSF Economic Letter*, no 2001–13.

(2005). 'Endogenous objectives and the evaluation of targeting rules for monetary policy', *Journal of Monetary Economics*, vol 52, no 5, 889–911.

Weitzmann, M. (1974). 'Prices vs. quantities', *Review of Economic Studies*, vol 41, no 4, 477–491.

White, W. (2013). 'Is monetary policy a science? The interaction of theory and practice over the last 50 years'. In M. Balling and E. Gnan (Eds.), *50 Years of Money and Finance – Lessons and Challenges*, SUERF.

Wilde, G. (1998). 'Risk homeostasis theory: An overview', *Injury Prevention*, vol 4, no2, 89–91.

Woodford, M. (2003). *Interest and Prices*, Princeton University Press, Princeton, NJ.

Yellen, J. (2014). 'Monetary policy and financial stability', Speech, July 2.

Zeldes, S. (1989). 'Consumption and liquidity constraints', *Quarterly Journal of Economics*, vol 97, no 2, 305–346.

# Index

For EU product safety concerns, contact us at Calle de José Abascal, 56–1°, 28003 Madrid, Spain or eugpsr@cambridge.org.

www.ingramcontent.com/pod-product-compliance
Ingram Content Group UK Ltd.
Pitfield, Milton Keynes, MK11 3LW, UK
UKHW012157180425
457623UK00018B/248